TEXTBOOK ON

EEC LAW

TEXTBOOK ON

EEC LAW

Third Edition

Josephine Steiner, BA, LLB

First published in Great Britain 1988 by Blackstone Press Limited,
9–15 Aldine Street, London W12 8AW. Telephone: 081-740 1173

© Josephine Steiner, 1988
First edition, 1988
Second edition, 1990
Reprinted, 1991 twice
Third edition, 1992

ISBN: 1 85431 224 3

British Library Cataloguing in Publication Data
A CIP cataloguing record for this book is available from the British Library

Typeset by Style Photosetting Limited, Mayfield, East Sussex
Printed by Ashford Colour Press, Gosport, Hampshire

CONTENTS

approach — Other barriers to freedom — Activities connected with the
exercise of official authority — Freedom to provide services and the exercise of
industrial property rights — Freedom to receive services — Education:
vocational training — Scholarships and grants — Scope of equality principle
— Harmonisation of company law — Further reading

Public policy, public security, public health — Personal conduct — Procedural
rights — Further reading

Personal scope — Principles — Material scope — Social assistance —
Operation of the system — Applicable law: *lex laboris* — Principle of
apportionment — Payment of benefits to persons resident outside the
competent State: special provisions — A practical exercise — Further reading

Introduction — Equal pay for equal work: Article 119 — Equal pay — Equal
work — Discrimination — Objective justification — Equal pay for work of
equal value (Directive 75/117) — Principle of equal treatment for men and
women (Directive 76/207) — Derogation from the equal treatment principle
(Article 2(2), (3) and (4)) — Pregnancy — Direct effects of Directive 76/207 —
Principle of equal treatment in matters of social security (Directive 79/7)
— Principle of equal treatment in occupational pension schemes (Directive
86/378) — Equal treatment in self-employment (Directive 86/613) — Remedies — Further reading

Introduction — The procedure — Jurisdiction of the Court of Justice —
Limitations on the Court's jurisdiction — Jurisdiction of national courts —
Discretionary or 'permissive' jurisdiction — When will a decision be necessary? — *Acte clair* — Exercise of discretion — Mandatory jurisdiction (Article
177(3)) — Effect of a ruling — Interim measures — Conclusions — Further
reading

PREFACE

If the two years between the launching of this book in 1988 and its second edition in 1990 saw important changes in the European Community, developments since 1990 have been even more significant. The Community has been subject to powerful pressures, internal and external, both to strengthen and deepen ties between existing member States and to widen membership. At home there has been steady progress towards the completion of the internal market. Two intergovernmental conferences in 1991 led to the signing of a new Treaty at Maastricht, the Treaty on European Union, committing the Community to economic and monetary, and a greater degree of political, union. At the same time the Community has joined forces with a number of EFTA States to form the European Economic Area, and many other States from Western and Eastern Europe are seeking some form of Community membership.

The purpose of this third edition is not however to chart these developments, except in outline, but to continue to build on previous editions. There is still a need for a single textbook, of manageable size, covering the major areas of EEC law — constitutional, institutional and administrative as well as substantive — to cater for the growing body of students (and not only lawyers) from around the world who wish to study EEC law, and for practitioners who realise that they can no longer afford to ignore it. The completion of the internal market in December 1992 simply reinforces that need.

A book of this type cannot of necessity provide an in-depth account of the EEC institutions, nor can it cover all areas of substantive law. Much EEC law, for example in the field of company or commercial or environmental law, or the law relating to employment or consumer protection, is increasingly, and perhaps more appropriately, incorporated into the general textbooks on these subjects. Some topics, such as agriculture, are too large and specialised for inclusion. Others, such as transport, are still in the process of development. Thus, the book continues to concentrate on the more highly developed areas of EEC law, what one might describe as fundamental community law, the law relating to the free movement of goods, persons and services, competition law and sex discrimination, and on the remedies available for breaches of community law. In this way it is hoped to provide sufficient insight into the principles of EEC law and the processes of the European Courts to enable the reader to pursue studies, resolve problems and enforce rights, in areas of law not covered by the book, as and when the need arises. The full range of EEC law, including developments proposed in the Treaty of European Union, is indicated in Chapter one. The principal sources of EEC law and a selection of textbooks on specialised topics are listed at the end of the book. Each chapter provides a list of further reading.

My thanks go to all those who helped in the preparation of this book. First to the secretaries for their perennial willingness and good sense, and particularly to Shirley Peacock who processed most of the book; secondly to colleagues Clare Campbell, John Tilltoson and the late Vaughan Bevan for their interest and advice; and finally to my family, Martin, Katie, Ben and Helen, for their unflinching support, and for providing a welcome distraction from the the demands of academic research.

Following ratification of the Treaty on European Union by the member States the European Economic Community was to be renamed the European Community, and all references to the EEC were to be amended to EC accordingly. However, since some doubts exist as to whether such ratification will occur (at the time of writing Denmark has voted in a referendum against ratification) it was decided to retain the term EEC for matters relating specifically to what is now the European Economic Community, leaving the reader to make the appropriate adjustment of title in the event of the Treaty's ratification.

Jo Steiner

ABBREVIATIONS

Bull. EC	Bulletin of the European Communities
CAP	common agricultural policy
CCT	common customs tariff
CDE	Cahiers de Droit Européen
CET	common external tariff
CMLR	Common Market Law Reports
CML Rev	Common Market Law Review
COREPER	Committee of Permanent Representatives
D/G	Directorate-General
EAGGF	European Agriculture Guidance and Guarantee Fund
EC	European Community/Communities
ECB	European Central Bank
EEA	European Economic Area
EEC Bull	Bulletin of the European Communities
ECHR	European Convention for the Protection of Human Rights and Fundamental Freedoms 1950
ECJ	European Court of Justice
ECR	European Court Reports (official reports of the judgments of the European Court, English version)
ECSC	European Coal and Steel Community
EEC	European Economic Community
EFTA	European Free Trade Association
EL Rev	European Law Review
ESCB	European System of Central Banks
Euratom	European Atomic Energy Community
GATT	General Agreement on Tariffs and Trade
ICLQ	International and Comparative Law Quarterly
JO	Journal Officiel (French version of OJ)
LIEI	Legal Issues of European Integration
LQR	Law Quarterly Review
MCA	Monetary Compensatory Amount
MLR	Modern Law Review
OJ	Official Journal (of the European Communities)

PL	Public Law
RPM	relevant product market
SEA	Single European Act
TEU	Treaty on European Union
YEL	Yearbook of European Law

Unless otherwise stated, cases cited were decided by the ECJ and Articles cited are Articles of the EEC Treaty.

TABLE OF CASES

Court of Justice of the European Communities

Cases have been arranged in chronological order by case number and year. See page xxix for alphabetical list of European Communities Court of Justice cases.

Table of cases

Court of Justice of the European Communities

Cases have been arranged in alphabetical order. See page xv for chronological list of European Communities Court of Justice cases.

Belgian Courts

French Courts

German Courts

United States Courts

TABLE OF COMMISSION DECISIONS

TABLE OF UK STATUTES

TABLE OF EUROPEAN
COMMUNITY TREATIES

TABLE OF EUROPEAN COMMUNITY SECONDARY LEGISLATION

PART ONE

Sources, nature and effect of EEC law

ONE

Historical background to the EEC, the EEC Treaty, the institutions of the Community, Acts of the institutions

The European Economic Community (EEC) came into existence following the signing of the Treaty of Rome in 1957 by the six original member States, France, Germany, Italy, Belgium, the Netherlands and Luxembourg. A second Rome Treaty signed by the same six States created Euratom (the European Atomic Energy Community) on the same day. These treaties, but particularly the EEC Treaty, represented the culmination of a movement towards international cooperation which had been growing throughout the 20th century, and which was given particular impetus in Europe following the devastation inflicted by the Second World War.

The institutional model for the EEC had already been provided by the European Coal and Steel Community (ECSC) set up in 1951 with the Treaty of Paris by the same six States. However, the scope of the EEC was altogether wider. The ECSC was concerned only with creating a single market in coal and steel; the EEC was designed to create an economic community. Although its aims were primarily economic, to create a single 'common' market in Europe, they were not exclusively so. The founder members of the EEC were fired by ideals as well as economic practicalities. As stated in the preamble to the EEC Treaty, its signatories were 'Determined to lay the foundations of an ever closer union among the peoples of Europe', 'Resolved by thus pooling their resources to preserve and strengthen peace and liberty'.

These words were not pious platitudes; they represented the spirit and purpose underlying the treaty, and, in interpreting the treaty and legislation enacted thereunder, the Court of Justice, the court of the EEC, has never lost sight of these aims.

Although the institutional framework of the EEC, as of Euratom, was modelled on that of the ECSC, the three communities at the outset held only two institutions in common, the Assembly (or Parliament) and the Court. It was not until the Merger Treaty 1965 that the other two main institutions merged. The High Authority, the executive body of the ECSC, merged with the EEC and Euratom Commission to form the new Commission, and the Council of Ministers of the ECSC with that of the EEC and Euratom to become a single Council. Henceforth the three communities continued to function as separate entities, but with shared institutions.

The United Kingdom, together with Denmark and the Republic of Ireland, finally joined the communities in 1973 with the Treaty of Accession under a Conservative government led by Edward Heath. Incorporation of the treaties into UK law was achieved by the European Communities Act 1972. (Norway joined at the same time but subsequently withdrew following a referendum which came out against membership.)

There were many reasons for our remaining outside the Community for so long. We were reluctant to loosen our existing ties with the Commonwealth, which membership of the EEC would clearly entail; we wished to retain our (perceived) 'special relationship' with the USA; and as an island nation which had not been subject to enemy occupation during the First and Second World Wars we no doubt lacked the sense of urgency which inspired our Continental neighbours. Suspicious that membership of the EEC would involve an unacceptable loss of sovereignty, we preferred the looser ties of the European Free Trade Association (EFTA) which we entered on its creation in 1959. When we did seek to join the EEC, persuaded by its clear economic success, our entry was blocked for some years, largely due to the efforts of the French President, General de Gaulle. Even after accession in 1973 public opinion in the UK was divided; it was only following a referendum in favour of membership conducted in 1975 under the government of the Labour Party that our membership was fully and finally confirmed.

In 1979 Greece, and in 1986 Spain and Portugal, signed acts of accession to join the Communities, bringing the total membership to 12.

An important development in 1986 was the signing by the 12 member States of the Single European Act. A White Paper issued by the Commission in 1985 had revealed that despite the Community's long existence, many barriers still existed to the achievement of the single internal market. If the Community were to achieve the full economic benefits of the single market and meet the challenge of world competition further progress must be made. The result was a new treaty, the Single European Act. The principal purpose of this Act was to eliminate the remaining barriers to the single internal market within the deadline of 31 December 1992, to be achieved by a massive programme of harmonisation (see chapters 5, 8, 19). In addition the Act extended the sphere of community competence and introduced a number of procedural changes designed to accelerate the community decision-making process. The Act, incorporated in the UK by the European Communities (Amendment) Act 1986, has undoubtedly injected a new dynamism into community affairs. In February 1992, 218 of the 282 proposals forming the complete programme for the completion of the internal market had been adopted.

The late 1980s saw a growing movement within the Community towards closer European Union. In December 1989, two intergovernmental conferences were convened pursuant to cooperation procedures introduced by the Single European Act to consider the questions of (a) economic and monetary and (b) political union. The conferences, which lasted for a year, resulted in the signing, at Maastricht, in December 1991, of a Treaty on European Union (TEU). Like the Single European Act the Maastricht Treaty enlarged the scope of Community competence and strengthened the decision-making process, particularly increasing Parliament's powers. It pledged member States to, *inter alia*, full economic and monetary union, including the creation of a single currency, by 1 January 1999 at the latest (with an 'opt-out' provision for Britain and Denmark), and to the development of a common foreign and security policy with a view to the eventual creation of a common defence policy. An expressed 'federal' goal was dropped from the final draft of the TEU, in favour of a more palatable pledge to an 'ever closer union'; but, if the aims of the Maastricht Treaty are achieved, the Community will have taken a historic step towards a federal system. However, the power to adopt legislation remains with the representatives of the member States, albeit shared increasingly with the European Parliament; and the Treaty expressly affirms the principle of 'subsidiarity', whereby the Community is required to take action 'only if and insofar as the objectives of the proposed action cannot be achieved sufficiently by the member States and can therefore, by reason of the scale or effects of the proposed action, be better achieved by the Community' (EEC Treaty, Article 3b, see also preamble). This important principle will no doubt be tested in future years.

The Treaty is due to come into effect on 1 January 1993. It will not take effect until ratified by all the member States. Doubts have been expressed about whether such ratification will occur. In referenda conducted in Ireland and Denmark Ireland voted in favour of ratification, Denmark voted against. In a number of States enthusiasm seems to be waning. This book must proceed on the assumption that the Treaty will eventually be ratified. From that date, assuming it is after 1 January 1993, the name European Economic Community (EEC) is to be changed to 'European Community' (EC), reflecting its wider purposes.

The Community has from its inception been described as 'unique in international law', the first truly supranational organisation'. If these statements are true wherein is it 'unique'? Other international organisations such as the UN or GATT have similar features; they possess their own institutions, which exert some power and influence over their member States; depending on these States' constitutional laws the obligations contained in international agreements may be enforced by individuals before their national courts.

Although to use the word 'unique' is perhaps to overstate the case, there is no doubt that the differences between the EEC and other international institutions were, even from the Community's earliest days, substantial. Several features may be singled out as significant. First, the EEC Treaty is wider in its scope than most other international treaties. Secondly, the EEC is unusual in the extent to which its members have endowed it with autonomous institutions and ceded power to these institutions over all matters within the scope of the Treaty. This is particularly true in the case of the Court of Justice (the European Court), which, in carrying out its task of interpretation and application of the Treaty (Article 164), has exerted a significant influence on the development of the law. Thirdly, also unusual in international law is the extent to which the law emanating from the Treaty, whether in the form of Treaty law or secondary legislation, penetrates the domestic legal systems of member States, and creates rights and obligations for individuals enforceable within their national courts. This was provided for to some degree by the Treaty; it has been greatly assisted by the vigorous jurisprudence of the Court.

As will become apparent in the course of this book, those who feared a loss of national sovereignty as a result of membership were right to do so. As the scope of Community competence increases, following the SEA, and now the TEU, so will that loss. On the other hand, advocates of the EEC would argue that the losses are more than offset by the gains; not least the creation of a trading block to rival any to the East or West of Europe (the EEC is now responsible for over one third of all world trade in imports and exports), with the potential that affords to influence world affairs, and a period of unprecedented peace in Europe.

The prospect of a free internal market within the EEC and ever-closer union between its members, together with a fear of a 'fortress', protectionist Europe, has led to a growing demand from European States outside the EEC either to seek special trading agreements with, or to join, the Community. October 1991 saw the creation of the European Economic Area (EEA) comprising the EEC and the seven EFTA States. Under the EEA agreement these States will be subject to Community rules relating to the internal market and competition, but will not be represented in the Community institutions. The agreement provided for the setting up of a special EEA Court, the existence and jurisdiction of which was challenged by the Court of Justice (Opinion 1/91, matter awaiting resolution). Turkey has now formally applied for, and Austria, Sweden, Finland, Switzerland, Cyprus and Malta are currently seeking, full membership of the EEC. Following their liberation from Communist rule in 1989, East Germany, reunited in October 1990 with West Germany, has been absorbed into the Community, albeit subject to special transitional arrangements, and Poland, Czechoslovakia and Hungary have entered into trading agreements with the EEC with a view to eventual membership. These developments, together with pressure for increased trade with and aid for the newly liberated European States of the former USSR with their growing economic, social and political problems, will clearly influence the course of the community, and its priorities, in the 1990s. It remains to be seen whether there will in the future be a deepening of Community ties, as envisaged at Maastricht, or a widening of membership. Doubts have been expressed whether both goals can be achieved. It has been suggested that the Community might move towards a multi-tiered system of graded and gradual membership. The creation of the EEA and Maastricht, with its opting-out provisions, already represent a move in this direction.

Scope of EEC Treaty

Although primarily an economic treaty, concerned with creating a single market in Europe, the original EEC Treaty extended far beyond the traditional free-trading agreement such as we find in GATT and EFTA, to cover a wide range of matters only peripherally economic, and expressly included a number of purely social goals. The Single European Act (SEA) further extended the scope of Community competence into new areas which had hitherto been dealt with only on a piecemeal basis. It also provided a formal framework for political cooperation by member States which was absent from the original Treaty. This led at Maastricht to a further and significant extension of Community goals.

The EEC Treaty is essentially a 'framework' treaty (*traité cadre*); that is, it sets out as broad general principles the aims to be achieved, leaving its institutions, in the form of the Commission and the Council, often in consultation with Parliament, to fill the gaps by means of secondary legislation.

The general aims of the Treaty are set out in Article 2:

The Community shall have as its task, by establishing a common market and progressively approximating the economic policies of member States, to promote throughout the Community a harmonious development of economic activities, a continuous and balanced expansion, an increase in stability, an accelerated raising of the standard of living and closer relations between the States belonging to it.

The activities of the Community are spelt out in Article 3. These include:

(a) the elimination, as between member States, of customs duties and of quantitative restrictions on the import and export of goods, and of all other measures having equivalent effect;

(b) the establishment of a common customs tariff and of a common commercial policy towards third countries;

(c) the abolition, as between member States, of obstacles to freedom of movement for persons, services and capital;

(d) the adoption of a common policy in the sphere of agriculture;

(e) the adoption of a common policy in the sphere of transport;

(f) the institution of a system ensuring that competition in the common market is not distorted;

(g) the application of procedures by which the economic policies of member States can be coordinated and disequilibria in their balances of payments remedied;

(h) the approximation of the laws of member States to the extent required for the proper functioning of the common market;

(i) the creation of a European Social Fund in order to improve employment opportunities for workers and to contribute to the raising of their standard of living;

(j) the establishment of a European Investment Bank to facilitate the economic expansion of the Community by opening up fresh resources;

(k) the association of the overseas countries and territories in order to increase trade and to promote jointly economic and social development.

The principles of Article 3 are fleshed out in further more specific provisions of the Treaty. In addition and as a supplement to the activities listed in Article 3, the Treaty lays down a principle of non-discrimination on the grounds of nationality (Article 7) and provides for action in the field of social policy (Articles 117–128), requiring member States to promote improved working conditions and improved living standards for workers (Article 117) and to observe a principle of equal pay for equal work for men and women (Article 119). There is provision also for the harmonisation of indirect taxation (Articles 95–99).

To these extended objectives the Single European Act 1986 added the further goals of economic and monetary cooperation, health and safety of workers, research and technological development, environmental and consumer protection, and cooperation in the field of foreign policy. These latter activities had been subject to some Community regulation, but lacked a specific basis in the EEC Treaty. The SEA thus reflected and reinforced existing practice.

The Treaty on European Union (1991) has now re-emphasised these goals and substituted for cooperation *common* foreign and security *policies*, adding the ultimate goal of a common currency and full economic and monetary union. Article 2 of the EEC Treaty is to be amended so that it reads as follows:

> The Community shall have as its task, by establishing a common market and an economic and monetary union and by implementing the common policies or activities referred to in Articles 3 and 3a, to promote throughout the Community a harmonious and balanced development of economic activities, sustainable and non-inflationary growth respecting the environment, a high degree of convergence of economic performance, a high level of employment and of social protection, the raising of the standard of living and quality of life, and economic and social cohesion and solidarity among member States.

Article 3 has been reworded and expanded to include the adoption of policies in the social sphere (new Article 3(i)), and in the sphere of the environment (new 3(k)) and developmental cooperation (Article 3(q)); a 'contribution' to a high level of health protection (Article 3(o)), consumer protection (Article 3(s)), education and training of quality and the flowering of the cultures of the member States (Article 3(p)); 'measures' in the spheres of energy, civil protection and tourism (Article 3(t)), the strengthening of economic and social cohesion (new Article 3(j)), and encouragement for the establishment and development of trans-European networks (Article 3(n)). A new Article 3a(2) sets out in general terms the aims of economic and monetary union (for details see Article G 25 TEU). Title V (Articles J and J.1 to J.11) of the TEU provides for a common foreign security and defence policy, and Title VI (Articles K and K.1 to K.9) provides for cooperation in the field of justice and home affairs. A 'social chapter', based on the Community's Social Charter of 1989, which was included in the original draft of the TEU, failed to obtain the approval of the UK and was added as a protocol, binding only on the remaining 11 signatory States. This Agreement on Social Policy sets out as its objectives: 'the promotion of employment, improved living and working conditions, proper social protection, dialogue between management and labour, the development of human resources with a view to lasting high employment and the combating of exclusion' (Article 1). Member States are required to take into account 'the need to maintain the competitiveness of the Community economy' (Article 1). Disputes over the borderline between social measures permissible under the EEC Treaty, binding on all member States, and those appropriate to the Agreement on Social Policy, appear inevitable.

In order to enable the Community to carry out its policies towards third countries the EEC Treaty provides that 'The Community shall have legal personality' (Article 210), and Article 228 empowers the Commission to negotiate, and the Council, 'after consulting the Assembly where required by this Treaty' to conclude, 'agreements between the Community and one or more States or an international organisation'.

Many such agreements have been concluded in the field of trade and aid (e.g., the Lomé and Yaoundé Conventions with African, Caribbean and Pacific countries, and, more recently, agreements with newly liberated states of Eastern Europe).

Such is, or, when and if the TEU comes into effect, will be, the framework. The three main institutions of the Community – the Commission, the Council and the European Parliament – are empowered to legislate (subject to review by the European Court) on any of the matters within this framework. Many of the Treaty provisions, for example, the articles relating to free movement of goods and workers (Articles 12, 30 and 48) contain obligations which are sufficiently precise to be applicable as they stand. Others provide for, and often require, further measures of implementation before they can take full legal effect. Even where the institutions are not specifically empowered to act, Article 235 provides:

If action by the Community should prove necessary to attain, in the course of the operation of the common market, one of the objectives of the Community and this Treaty has not provided the necessary powers, the Council shall, acting unanimously on a proposal from the Commission and after consulting the Assembly, take the appropriate measures.

This blanket power had been used as a basis for legislation on matters of regional or social policy (e.g., equal treatment for men and women) which fell within the broad aims of the Community as expressed in the preamble, but which were not spelt out specifically in the EEC Treaty. Many, but not all, of these have now been included as a result of the SEA.

The degree to which this framework has been filled in will form the subject-matter of later chapters of this book. Suffice it to say that all the main areas of activity outlined above, apart from commitments entered into for the first time at Maastricht, in both the internal and external field, have been subject to some measures of implementation. In some cases, such as agriculture and competition policy, implementation has been extensive. In others, such as the free movement of capital, transport, and freedom to provide services, progress was, initially, slow. As a result of the Single European Act there has been substantial progress in these areas during the last few years, as well as in the 'new' areas of health and safety and environmental and consumer protection.

From the foregoing outline two matters will be clear:

(a)   The framework provided by the Treaty, both originally and as now amended by the SEA, is extremely broad, embracing many areas of economic and social activity which had hitherto been within the sole competence of member States. Maastricht has reinforced and widened the Community's commitment in these areas and added further specific economic and political goals.

(b)   Within that framework there is almost unlimited (though not uncontrolled) scope for legislation by the Community institutions.

Since, under Article 5 of the EEC Treaty, member States are required to 'take all appropriate measures, whether general or particular, to ensure fulfilment of the obligations arising out of this Treaty or resulting from action taken by the institution of the Community' and 'shall abstain from any measure which could jeopardise the attainment of the objectives of this Treaty' perhaps it is not surprising that Lord Denning MR was moved to say, in *H. P. Bulmer Ltd* v *J. Bollinger SA* [1974] Ch 401: ' . . . the Treaty is like an incoming tide. It flows into the estuaries and up the rivers. It cannot be held back'.

The institutions of the EEC

The principal institutions set up by the EEC Treaty (Article 4) are:

(a)   the Assembly or Parliament,
(b)   the Council,
(c)   the Commission, and
(d)   the Court of Justice.

In addition, Article 4 provided for the setting up of an Economic and Social Committee and a Court of Auditors, and the Merger Treaty (Article 4) for the creation of a Committee of Permanent Representatives of the member States (COREPER). As a result of the Single European Act a new Court of First Instance was set up in October 1988 (Decision 88/591 (1989) OJ No. C 215, p. 1). Under the TEU the Court of Auditors has now been added to the institutions listed in Article 4, a European Investment Bank has been created (Article 4b), and provision made for the creation of a Committee of the Regions and the setting up of a European System of Central Banks (ESCB) and a European Central Bank (ECB) (new Article 4a).

Parliament (Articles 137-44 as amended)

As created by the Treaty of Rome in 1957, the European Parliament, called in that Treaty the Assembly (but now required by the SEA to be called the Parliament), was not a democratic body, although the Treaty provided for the eventual introduction of direct elections. It consisted of representatives of member States who were required to be members of a national parliament. The introduction of direct elections which occurred in 1979 has now resulted in increased democracy (although no uniform voting procedure has yet been agreed) and increased concentration and expertise, since members are responsible to their electorate, and, as anyone is now eligible to stand, many are no longer subject to the rigorous demands of the 'dual mandate' at home and in Europe. It has also, not unexpectedly, resulted in demands for increased powers.

As befitted a non-elected body the original Parliament had few powers. Its functions were advisory and supervisory. It was not intended as a legislative body. This is still the case, although since direct elections Parliament has played an increasingly important consultative role in the legislative process and has been given the final say over certain aspects of the budget. The Maastricht Treaty has further and substantially increased its powers.

In its advisory role, Parliament was required by the Treaty to be consulted by the Council of Ministers where legislation is proposed in a number of specific (and important) areas, e.g., Articles 54, 63, 87 and 235, but cf. Article 49 (workers). In these areas the Council must seek, and is obliged to consider, Parliament's opinion, although there is no obligation to follow it. This is an essential procedural requirement. In *Roquette Frères SA* v *Council* (case 138/79) and *Maizena GmbH* v *Council* (case 139/79) a Regulation of the Council was annulled because, although Parliament's opinion had been sought, the Regulation had been passed by the Council before that opinion had been obtained. It has, however, been suggested that the Council is not required to wait interminably; Parliament is not entitled to delay for tactical purposes; it must act within a reasonable time. In *Roquette* the Council had failed to indicate to Parliament that the matter was of some urgency.

The requirement for consultation and cooperation by Parliament, and consequently Parliament's influence, was strengthened by the introduction of conciliation procedures in 1977 (Joint Declaration of the European Parliament, the Council and the Commission, OJ No. C 89, 22.4.75, p. 1) and new cooperation procedures introduced by the SEA. Under the latter provisions Parliament was given a second opportunity to consider draft legislation. If, following a second look, Parliament continues to object to the proposal the Council may still adopt it, but it must do so within three months and it must act unanimously. Where Parliament proposes amendments, the proposal may be sent back to the Commission for examination. Where the Commission rejects Parliament's amendments, the Council may still adopt them, provided it does so unanimously. Thus Parliament may act as a brake on the Council by requiring unanimity where it might otherwise act by qualified majority. The SEA also greatly extended the range of matters on which Parliament must be consulted, with the result that the majority of measures relating to the internal market now require such consultation. The Act also gave Parliament the power of (final) assent in respect of the admission of new members and the conclusion of association agreements with non-member countries.

As well as a right to be *consulted*, and to participate in *conciliation* and *cooperation* procedures, the TEU 1991 introduced for Parliament a right of *co-decision* with the Council in certain defined areas. Under this procedure, laid down in (new) Article 189b of the EEC Treaty, the Council must first adopt a common position, after obtaining an opinion from Parliament. Parliament may then either confirm or reject that common position, or propose amendments to it (by absolute majority of its component members). The Council may then approve these amendments by qualified majority. Where the Commission has delivered a negative opinion on the proposed amendments the Council must approve the amended act unanimously. Thus far the procedure resembles the cooperation procedure. However, if the Council does not approve the amended act the matter must be referred to a Conciliation committee, composed of equal members of the Council and Parliament. The Commission is required to take part in the Committee's proceedings with a view to reconciling the positions of the Council and Parliament. If a joint text is approved the Council and Parliament may together adopt it. If not, and if they cannot agree a common position, Parliament may reject the text by an absolute majority of its component members. Strict time-limits are imposed at every stage of the proceedings.

Thus the European Parliament will, when these provisions come into effect, have a significant power of veto in matters subject to the new procedures. This co-decision procedure will apply in a number of areas previously governed by the less onerous cooperation procedures (e.g., Articles 49, 54(2), 56(2), 100A (internal market)) and in some new spheres of activity (e.g., culture, health, consumer protection). In other areas, the consultation or cooperation procedures (the latter now laid down in (new) Article 189c) will continue to apply. In cases of doubt it will be necessary to consult the Treaty to ascertain which procedure is applicable.

There have been cases in which the correctness of the legal basis and thus the procedures for the adoption of a particular measure have been challenged (e.g., *Commission* v *Council (Re Erasmus)* (case 242/87)). Given that the procedural requirements, and the nature of the vote required, will differ according to the chosen basis, this is not surprising, since the choice of legal base will determine the distribution of power between and within the institutions concerned. Such challenges can only increase when the new procedures come into effect.

In its supervisory role, Parliament exercises direct political control over the Commission. Commissioners must reply orally or in writing to its questions. The Commission must publish a general report which is discussed in Parliament in open session. Parliament meets members of the Commission in committees, and in practice, though this is not required by law, members of Parliament are consulted by the Commission at the pre-legislative stage. Parliament also has the power to dismiss the Commission, by passing a vote of censure (Article 144) although it has no say in the reappointment of Commissioners. Such a motion has been tabled, but never carried.

The Council is not subject to the control of Parliament, but is subject to extensive supervision. Parliament reports on the activities of the Council three times a year, and the President of the Council must present an address to Parliament at the beginning of every year. This is followed by a general debate. The incoming President also presents a survey of the previous six months' presidency, and the chairman of the conference of foreign ministers reports to Parliament once a year on the progress of European political cooperation (Bull. EEC 10-1979, 129). Unlike proceedings in the Council and the Commission, proceedings in Parliament are published in the *Official Journal*.

Although the Treaty does not give Parliament *locus standi* to challenge acts of the Council or the Commission, Parliament was held to be allowed to intervene in such cases before the European Court in *Roquette Frères SA* v *Council* (case 138/79). Moreover, since it has *locus standi* to bring an action against these institutions for failure to act (under Article 175, see chapter 28), and succeeded in doing so in *European Parliament* v *Council* (case 13/83) it was thought that it must have *locus standi* to bring a complementary action for annulment of acts of the Council and the Commission under Article 173 (see chapter 27). The Court of Justice has now decided that it does not have a general power to challenge such acts (*Parliament* v *Council (Comitology)* (case 302/87)) but that it may bring an action under Article 173 in order to protect its own prerogative powers (*Parliament* v *Council (Chernobyl)* (case C 70/88); see chapter 27).

In order further to broaden Parliament's role it was given power under the TEU to set up a temporary committee of inquiry to investigate alleged contraventions or maladministration in the implementation of Community law (except where the alleged facts are being examined before a court or subject to legal proceedings) (Article G41) and has been required to appoint an Ombudsman to receive and enquire into complaints of maladministration in the activities of the EEC institutions or bodies (with the exception of the Court of Justice and the Court of First Instance acting in their judicial capacity) (new Article 138e). In addition, any natural or legal person residing or having its registered office in a member State is to be given the right to address a petition to the European Parliament on a matter which comes within the Community's fields of activity, and which affects him, her or it directly (new Article 138d). Parliament was also given a new power of initiative. Under (new) Article 138b it may, acting by a majority of its members, request the Commission to submit any appropriate proposals on matters on which it considers that a Community act is required for the purpose of implementing the Treaty.

Parliament at present consists of 518 members, with the 'big four', France, Germany, Great Britain and Italy each having 81 representatives, Spain 60, the Netherlands 25, Belgium, Greece and Portugal 24, Denmark 16, Ireland 15 and Luxembourg 6. They meet principally in Strasbourg (formerly they met alternatively in Luxembourg and Strasbourg). Members, who are drawn from 75 political parties, sit in 11 broad multinational political groupings, the largest being the Socialist group (181 members); they are required to vote 'on an individual and personal basis' and 'They shall not be bound by any instructions and shall not receive a binding mandate' (Act Concerning Direct Elections, Article 4(1)). They are elected for five years.

The new powers given to the European Parliament at Maastricht will, if the TEU is ratified, go some way to redress the institutional balance in the Community, in which national interests as represented by the Council of Ministers have predominated, and to remedy the much-criticised 'democratic deficit' in the decision-making process. It is hoped that these changes will stimulate interest, and increase participation, in the elections to the European Parliament, particularly in the UK, where both have been regrettably wanting.

Council (Articles 145-54)

The Council consists of representatives of the member States, each State delegating to it one of its members (Article 147). Although it is a political body, its task is 'to ensure that the objectives set out in this Treaty are attained' (Article 145). To this end it 'shall . . . ensure coordination of the general economic policies of the member States; [and] have power to take decisions'.

Since the Council has the final power of decision on most secondary legislation some control by the member States is thus assured. However, in most cases it can only act on the basis of a proposal from the Commission, and in an increasing number of circumstances it must consult Parliament and the Economic and Social Committee. Under the procedures introduced by the SEA, if it wishes to override Parliament's opposition to a measure it must do so by unanimous vote. Similarly it may amend the Commission's proposals provided it does so unanimously (Article 149). When the TEU comes into effect it will share some decision-making with Parliament.

The Council is not a fixed body. Although it is limited to one voting delegate from each State, membership may fluctuate depending on the topic under discussion. For example, where matters of agriculture are at stake, the Ministers of Agriculture will normally participate; if the matters relate to general economic policy the Chancellors may be present; where high-level policy matters are to be discussed, the Council may consist of Heads of State. When meeting as Heads of State the body is termed the European Council. Its status was given formal recognition by the Single European Act, under which it was required to meet at least twice a year.

Since the Council has the final say in assenting to legislative measures, at least until the co-decision system operates, its methods of voting are crucial. The Treaty (Article 148 as amended) provides that voting may be by a simple majority (which is rare), by qualified majority, or unanimity. Voting by qualified majority is a system of weighted voting, in which the big four States carry 10 votes each, Spain 8, Belgium, Greece, the Netherlands and Portugal 5, Denmark and Ireland 3 and Luxembourg 2 (total 76). The required minimum vote for a qualified majority is 54. Thus two big or up to six small States may be outvoted. Clearly from the Community standpoint it makes for more rapid and effective decision-making than a system of unanimity.

Originally a number of the more sensitive areas of the Treaty were required to be implemented only by unanimous vote (e.g., Article 100 on the approximation of laws). However, it was intended that once the period of adjustment to membership, known as the transitional period, provided by the Treaty had expired, States would be required to move towards voting by qualified majority. This did not happen. A crisis in the Council in 1962 resulted, at the insistence of the French, in the Luxembourg Accords (1966). Under the Accords, where vital national interests are at stake, States may insist on a unanimous vote. The Accords noted 'a divergence of views on what should be done in the event of a failure to reach agreement'.

The Luxembourg Accords did not have the force of law, but they were followed in practice, with the result that in many cases the Council sought unanimity where the Treaty would not have required it. In only one case, in 1982, was a measure passed by the Council by qualified majority vote against the wishes of the UK government, in a situation in which it was suggested that the UK was abusing its veto by attempting to force the Council's hand in a matter unrelated to the measure under discussion. The veto was invoked successfully by Germany in 1985.

Perhaps the most significant innovation of the SEA was to increase the number of areas in which voting was to be by qualified majority. The majority of legislation required to complete the internal market will now be enacted by qualified majority. Only fiscal measures, measures relating to the free movement of persons and to the rights and interests of employed persons (Article 100A(2)) and measures relating to professional training and standards (Article 57(2)) now require a unanimous vote. Since the more 'sensitive' areas remain subject to unanimous approval, States have so far been prepared to accede to a qualified majority vote in the areas in which it has been required, although in some cases they have challenged the appropriateness of the legal basis of a measure demanding such a vote. But, 'as a last resort, the Luxembourg compromise remains in place untouched and unaffected by the SEA' (the Foreign Secretary, HC Parl. Deb. vol. 96, col. 320, 23 April 1986).

The provision for political cooperation by member States through the Council, particularly in the field of foreign policy, introduced by the SEA (Article 30), whereby Heads of State meet on a regular basis as the 'European Council' to discuss matters both in and outside the formal framework of the Treaty, produced an impetus for increased activity in this area and led in 1991 to the intergovernmental conferences which resulted in the Maastricht Treaty.

Since the Council is not a permanent body, meeting only a few days a month, and its members have full-time responsibilities at home, either as ministers or civil servants (civil servants have no power to vote), much of its work has been taken over by the Committee of Permanent Representatives (COREPER). COREPER is a permanent and full-time body, also consisting of representatives of member States, whose main task is to scrutinise and sift proposals coming from the Commission prior to a final decision being made by the Council. COREPER is assisted in turn by a number of working groups, similarly represented, operating at different levels and in specialised areas. This sifting process, from working group to COREPER to Council, enables the more straightforward issues to be decided at the appropriate level, leaving the Council to focus on the more difficult or controversial decisions. The final power of decision however always remains with the Council.

Commission (Articles 155-63 as amended)

The Commission has been described as the 'guardian of the Treaties'. The present Commission consists of 17 members (two from each of the big four and Spain, and one from each of the other States), chosen on the grounds of their general competence and 'whose independence is beyond doubt' (Merger Treaty, Article 10). Appointed by 'common accord of the governments of the member States' (Merger Treaty, Article 11), they must, in the performance of their duties, 'neither seek nor take instructions from any government or from any other body' (Merger Treaty, Article 10).

The Commission is headed by a President appointed from among the Commissioners 'by common accord of the Member States' for a renewable term of two years (Merger Treaty, Article 4). It is divided into 20 directorates-general, each one responsible for certain aspects of Community policy (e.g., D/G IV competition policy), and headed by a director-general. Commissioners are given responsibility for particular directorates (a 'portfolio'). Portfolios vary considerably in size and prestige.

The functions of the Commission are threefold. First, it acts as initiator or 'motor' of Community action. All important decisions made by the Council must be made on the basis of proposals from the Commission (subject to the Council's power to 'request the Commission to undertake any studies which the Council considers desirable for the attainment of the common objectives, and to submit to it any appropriate proposals' (EEC Treaty, Article 152)). Using the EEC Treaty as its brief, the Commission may formulate proposals on any matter provided for under the Treaty, either where the power is specifically granted or under the more general power provided by Article 235. Clearly as long as a policy of unanimous voting was pursued by the Council the Commission's power of initiative was limited to what was politically acceptable; measures must of necessity be diluted for common consumption. The increase in qualified majority voting as introduced by the SEA has provided a welcome boost to the Commission's power of initiative.

Secondly, the Commission acts as the Community watchdog. Member States are obliged under Article 5 to: 'take all appropriate measures . . . to ensure fulfilment of the obligations arising out of this Treaty or resulting from action taken by the institutions of the Community. . . . They shall abstain from any measure which could jeopardise the attainment of the objectives of this Treaty.' It is the Commission's task to seek out and bring to an end any infringements of EEC law by member States, if necessary by proceedings under Article 169 (see chapter 25) before the European Court. (See also similar provisions for the enforcement of the law relating to State aids, Article 93.) The Commission has a complete discretion in this matter (see *Alfons Lütticke GmbH* v *Commission* (case 48/65) noted in chapter 25). The Commission is also entrusted with administering and enforcing EEC competition policy and has the power to impose sanctions in the form of fines and penalties on individuals in breach of EEC competition law (see chapter 15).

In order to carry out its role as watchdog it has extensive investigative powers (see e.g., Article 213 and Regulation 17/62, Article 14), and member States and individuals (e.g., under Regulation 17/62) may be required to furnish any information required pursuant to these powers.

Thirdly, the Commission functions as the executive of the Community. Once a policy decision has been taken by the Council, the detailed implementation of that policy, often requiring further legislation, falls to the Commission.

The Commission has in addition have 'its own power of decision' (EEC Treaty, Article 155). Competition policy is enforced solely by the Commission. Similarly Regulations enacted, for example, in the field of agriculture to implement Community rules may provide for decisions of an executive nature to be taken by the Commission alone.

Finally, in pursuit of the Community's external policies, the Commission is required to act as negotiator, leaving agreements to be 'concluded by the Council, after consulting the Assembly where required by this Treaty' (Article 228).

Budgetary procedures

These are laid down by Article 203 as amended by the Budgetary Treaty 1975.

As might be expected, the Commission is responsible for drawing up a preliminary draft budget. The Commission thus sets the parameters, and fixes the 'maximum rate of increase' for 'non-compulsory items' of expenditure, which neither the Council nor the Parliament is free to exceed. The preliminary draft is forwarded to the Council, which establishes the draft budget and forwards it to Parliament. At this stage Parliament may approve the budget within 45 days, in which case it stands adopted. Alternatively Parliament may suggest 'modifications' or 'amendments'. 'Modifications' may be proposed to items of 'compulsory' expenditure — expenditure already accounted for by Community rules, principally the amount (around 70%) allocated to the common agricultural policy. 'Amendments' refer to non-compulsory expenditure, principally concerned with regional or social policy. In this case the draft is returned to the Council, Parliament's 'modifications' may then be rejected by the Council acting by a qualified majority. Its 'amendments' too may be subject to 'modification' by the Council within a 15-day time-limit. However, on return to Parliament that body may reject the Council's 'modifications' within a 15-day time-limit, acting by a majority of its members and three fifths of the votes cast. Parliament may then adopt the budget.

Thus Parliament is responsible for adopting the budget and has the final say over 'non-compulsory' expenditure. It does too have one further weapon. If it is not satisfied with the budget overall it may reject it (Article 203(8)) and in 1979 and 1984 it did not hesitate to do so.

Court of Justice (Articles 164-8)

The task of the European Court is to 'ensure that in the interpretation and application of this Treaty the law is observed' (Article 164). It is the supreme authority on all matters of Community law, and in this capacity may be required to decide matters of constitutional law (see e.g., chapter 3), administrative law (see chapters 27-9), social law (chapters 17-22) and economic law (chapters 5-16) in matters brought directly before it or on application from national courts. In its practices and procedures it draws on Continental models; in developing the substantive law it draws on principles and traditions from all the member States.

Since the EEC Treaty is a framework treaty the Court has been extremely influential in 'filling the gaps', and in doing so has created law in bold, and, to those accustomed to English methods of interpretation, often surprising ways.

As Lord Diplock pointed out in *R* v *Henn* [1981] AC 850:

The European Court, in contrast to English courts, applies teleological rather than historical methods to the interpretation of the Treaties and other Community legislation. It seeks to give effect to what it conceives to be the spirit rather than the letter of the Treaties; sometimes, indeed, to an English judge, it may seem to the exclusion of the letter. It views the Communities as living and expanding organisms and the interpretation of the provisions of the Treaties as changing to match their growth.

The Court has on occasion been criticised for its activism. Others have argued that such boldness was necessary to carry the Community forward at a time, during the seventies and early eighties, when progress was blocked by political inertia. Whether in response to criticism, or as a result of the increased dynamism of the other institutions following the Single European Act, more recent judgments of the Court show signs of a new conservatism, although in certain areas, for example, sex discrimination, it continues to surprise, (see e.g., *Barber* v *Guardian Royal Exchange Assurance Group* (case C 262/88); see chapter 22).

The Court consists of 13 judges, one from each member State and a President of the Court, assisted by six advocates-general. They must be 'chosen from persons whose independence is beyond doubt' (Article 167). An advocate-general's function is to assist the Court by presenting his 'sub-missions' — a detailed analysis of all the relevant issues of fact and law together with his recommendations to the court. Although his recommendations are not always followed, where they are they are useful as a means of ascertaining the reasoning behind the Court's decision. The judgment itself, which is a single collegiate decision, is, to English eyes, terse, cryptic, with little indication of the reasoning on which it is based. Even where the advocate-general's recommen-dations are not followed they may still be invoked as persuasive authority in a subsequent case. Although the European Court seeks to achieve consistency in its judgments, its precedents are not binding in the English sense; it always remains free to depart from previous decisions in the light of new facts.

In order to meet the increasing workload of the Court, the SEA provided for the setting up of a new Court of First Instance (CFI). Approval for this court was obtained in October 1988 ((1989) OJ No.C 215/1). The court commenced proceedings on 1 September 1989. Its jurisdiction is confined to disputes between the community and its servants ('staff cases'), cases involving EEC competition law (excluding Article 177 references), and applications for judicial review and damages in respect of certain matters under the European Coal and Steel Community. There is a right of appeal on matters of law from this court to the Court of Justice.

Court of Auditors

The Court of Auditors was established in 1975 under the Budgetary Powers Treaty (OJ No. L 359, 31.12.1977, p. 1). Its function is to exercise control and supervision over the implementation of the budget. Its creation represents an important step forward in the accountability of the institutions, particularly the Commission. Its annual report is published in the *Official Journal*. As a sign of its importance it was added to the list of Community institutions in Article 4 of the EEC Treaty by the Treaty on European Union.

These five major institutions – Parliament, Council, Commission, Court of Justice and Court of Auditors – are required to act 'within the limits of the powers conferred' upon them by the EEC Treaty (Article 4).

Any illegal act or failure to act on the part of the first three is subject to proceedings before the Court under Article 173 or Article 175 (see chapters 27 and 28). There is no possibility of challenge to decisions of the Court of Justice.

Economic and Social Committee (Articles 193-8)

The Economic and Social Committee plays a consultative role in the Community decision-making process. Its members are appointed by the Council in their personal capacity, and represent a variety of sectional interests such as farmers, workers, trade unionists, or merely members of the general public. Where consultation is provided for by the Treaty this is an essential procedural requirement: such consultation must also be referred to in any resulting legislation. The Committee may also be consulted by the Council and the Commission whenever they consider it appropriate. In addition it is entitled to advise the Community institutions on its own initiative on all questions affecting Community law (summit declaration 1972, Bull. EEC 10-72, 23).

Committee of the Regions

This new Committee was established by the TEU in order to represent regional interests, and to act, like the Economic and Social Committee, in an advisory capacity in specified circumstances, as provided by the EEC Treaty (e.g., Article 126(4) education; 128(5) culture; 130d and 130e regional development).

Legislative acts

The legislative powers of the Community institutions are laid down in Article 189:

In order to carry out their task the Council and the Commission shall, in accordance with the provisions of this Treaty, make regulations, issue directives, take decisions, make recommendations or deliver opinions.

Article 189 is to be amended by the TEU to take into account Parliament's power of co-decision.

These measures, described as 'acts', are defined as follows:

A regulation shall have general application. It shall be binding in its entirety and directly applicable in all member States.

A directive shall be binding, as to the result to be achieved, upon each member State to which it is addressed, but sh all leave to the national authorities the choice of form and methods.

A decision shall be binding in its entirety upon those to whom it is addressed.

Recommendations and opinions shall have no binding force.

Thus there is a division between binding and non-binding acts. Only the first three are binding.

The principle feature of a *Regulation* is its general application. A Regulation is a normative rather than an individual act, designed to apply to situations in the abstract. Since it is 'binding in its entirety and directly applicable in all member States' it does not require further implementation in order to take effect. Thus it may give rise to rights and obligations for States and individuals as it stands. Indeed, it has been held *(Leonesio* v *Ministero dell' Agricoltura e delle Foreste* (case 93/71)) that the rights bestowed by a Regulation cannot be subjected, at the national level, to implementing provisions diverging from those laid down by the Regulation itself.

A *Directive* is binding 'as to the result to be achieved, upon each member State to which it is addressed', but allows States a discretion as to the form and method of implementation. Thus it is a measure intended to be addressed to, and binding on *States,* either individually or collectively, but apparently requiring implementation by States before it can be fully effective in law.

A *Decision* is an individual act designed to be addressed to a specified person or persons. As a 'binding' act it has the force of law and does not therefore require implementation in order to take effect. Decisions may be addressed to States or individuals.

Regulations, Directives and Decisions are subject to certain procedural safeguards — they must 'state the reasons on which they are based and shall refer to any proposals or opinions which were required to be obtained pursuant to this Treaty' (Article 190).

These are essential procedural requirements. Any act which does not comply with these requirements will be subject to annulment (see chapter 27 on Article 173, chapter 24 on Article 177).

Recommendations and *Opinions,* since they have no binding force, are ineffective in law, although clearly of persuasive authority (see *Grimaldi* (case C 322/88) noted in chapter 2).

With regard to publication, Article 191 provides:

Regulations shall be published in the *Official Journal* of the Community. They shall enter into force on the date specified in them or, in the absence thereof, on the 20th day following their publication.

Directives and decisions shall be notified to those to whom they are addressed and shall take effect upon such notification.

Thus only Regulations require publication in the *Official Journal;* in fact Directives are also published in the OJ, as are many Decisions.

The line between these acts is not as clear-cut as Art. 189 would suggest. It was held in *Confédération Nationale des Producteurs de Fruits et Légumes* v *Council* (cases 16 & 17/62) that the true nature of an act is determined not by its form but by its content and object. Thus the label attached to the measure is not decisive, and in the case of *International Fruit Co. NV* v *Commission* (No. 1) (cases 41-4/70) what was termed a Regulation was found to comprise a 'bundle of decisions'. Measures have been found to be hybrid; to contain some parts in the nature of a Regulation, and other parts in the nature of Decisions (see Advocate-General Warner's submissions in *NTN Toyo Bearing Co. Ltd* v *Council* (case 113/77)). In ascertaining the true nature of the act, the essential distinction seems to be between a Regulation, which is normative, applicable not to a limited identifiable number of designees but rather to categories of persons envisaged both in the abstract and as a whole, and a Decision, which concerns designated persons individually *(Confédération Nationale des Prod- ucteurs de Fruits et Légumes* v *Council)*. The nature of a Directive has not been called into question, but considerable controversy has arisen over its effects. These will be discussed in chapter 2.

Sources of EEC law

The sources of EEC law comprise the following:

(a)   The EEC Treaty and Protocols, as amended by the succeeding Treaties: Merger Treaty 1965; Acts of Accession 1972 (UK, Ireland, Denmark), 1979 (Greece), 1985 (Spain, Portugal); Budgetary Treaties 1970, 1975; Single European Act 1986, Treaty on European Union 1991 (when ratified).

(b)   EEC secondary legislation in the form of Regulations, Directives and Decisions. Recommendations and Opinions are of persuasive force only.

(c)   Such international agreements as are entered into by Community institutions on behalf of the Community pursuant to their powers under the EEC Treaty. These agreements may result from accession by the Community to existing agreements, such as GATT, or from new agreements such as the Lomé Convention 1979. Conventions entered into by *member States,* on the other hand, even though entered into pursuant to EEC Treaty, Article 220, cannot be considered as forming part of Community law.

(d) Judicial legislation. This comprises the entire jurisprudence of the European Courts, embracing not only decisions, but general principles and even expressions of opinion, provided they concern matters of *Community law.* The importance and the extent of the Court of Justice's contribution to the corpus of EEC law will become apparent in the course of this book.

As a matter of international law the law arising from all these sources is binding on member States which are obliged under EEC Treaty, Article 5, to 'take all appropriate measures, whether general or particular, to ensure fulfilment' of all these obligations. Special provision was made for certain provisions of the EEC Treaty to apply to countries linked to member States by particular association agreements (Article 227 and Annex IV).

Since we in the UK are dualist in our approach to international law, that is, we do not regard international law as part of our own legal system unless it is incorporated by an Act of Parliament, EEC law did not become binding on us as a matter of *internal* law until incorporated by the European Communities Act 1972.

Further reading

Campbell, A., 'The S.E.A. and the Implications' (1986) 35 ICLQ 932.

Capelletti, M., *The Judicial Process in Comparative Perspective* (Oxford: Clarendon Press, 1989).

Dué, O., 'The Court of First Instance' (1988) 8 YEL 1.

Edwards, D., 'The Impact of the Single Market' (1987) 24 CML Rev 19.

Hartley, T., 'Federalism, Courts and Legal Systems: the emerging constitutions of the European Community' (1986) 34 Am J Comp L 229.

Koopmans, T., 'The Role of Law in the Next Stage of European Integration' (1986) 35 ICLQ 925.

Lang, J. Temple, 'Community Constitutional Law: Article 5 EEC Treaty' (1990) 27 CML Rev 645.

Mackenzie Stuart, Lord, 'Problems of the European Community; some Transatlantic Parallels' (1987) 36 ICLQ 183.

Mancini, G. F. 'The Making of a Constitution for Europe' (1989) 26 CML Rev 594.

Nicoll 'The Luxembourg Compromise' (1984) 23 JCMS 35.

Pescatore, P., 'Some Critical Remarks on the Single European Act' (1987) 24 CML Rev 9.

Rasmussen, H., 'Between Self-Restraint and Activism; a Judicial Policy for the European Court' 13 EL Rev 28.

Rasmussen, H., 'On Law and Policy-making in the European Communities' (1986) Nijhoff Publications.

Slynn, G., 'The Court of Justice of the European Communities' (1984) 33 ICLQ 409.
Wilke, M. and Wallace, H., 'Subsidiarity: Approaches to Power sharing in the EEC' (Royal Institute of International Affairs Discussion Paper No. 27) (1990).

TWO

Principles of direct applicability and direct effects

As was noted in chapter 1, the European Community Treaties were incorporated into UK law by the European Communities Act 1972. With the passing of this Act all Community law became, in the language of international law, directly applicable, that is, applicable as part of our own internal system. Henceforth, 'Any rights or obligations created by the Treaty are to be given legal effect in England without more ado' (per Lord Denning MR in *H. P. Bulmer Ltd* v *J. Bollinger SA* [1974] Ch 401). As directly applicable law, EEC law thus became capable of forming the basis of rights and obligations enforceable by individuals before their national courts.

Provisions of international law which are found to be capable of application by national courts *at the suit of individuals* are also termed 'directly applicable'. This ambiguity (the same ambiguity is found in the alternative expression 'self-executing') has given rise to much uncertainty in the context of EEC law. For this reason it was suggested by Winter that the term 'directly effective' be used to convey this secondary meaning. Although this term has generally found favour amongst British academic writers the Court of Justice as well as our own courts tend to use the two concepts of direct applicability and direct effects interchangeably. However, for purposes of clarity it is proposed to use the term 'directly effective' or 'capable of direct effects' in this secondary meaning, to denote those provisions of EEC law which give rise to rights or obligations which individuals may enforce before their national courts.

Not all provisions of directly applicable international law are capable of direct effects. Some provisions are regarded as binding on, and enforceable by States alone; others are too vague to form the basis of rights or obligations for individuals; others are too incomplete and require further measures of implementation before they can be fully effective in law. Whether a particular provision is directly effective is a matter of construction, depending on its language and purpose as well as the terms on which the Treaty has been incorporated into domestic law. Although most States apply similar criteria of clarity and completeness, specific rules and attitudes inevitably differ, and since the application of the criteria often conceals an underlying policy decision, the results are by no means uniform from State to State.

The question of the direct effects of Community law is of paramount concern to EEC lawyers. If a provision of EEC law is directly effective, domestic courts must not only apply it, but, following the principle of primacy of EEC law (this principle will be discussed in full in chapter 3), must do so in priority over any conflicting provisions of national law. Since the scope of the EEC Treaty is wide, the more generous the approach to the question of direct effects, the greater the potential for conflict.

Which provisions of EEC law will then be capable of direct effect? The European Communities Act, s. 2(1), provides that:

All such rights, powers, liabilities, obligations and restrictions from time to time created or arising by or under the Treaties, and all such remedies and procedures from time to time provided for by or under the Treaties, as in accordance with the Treaties are without further enactment to be given legal effect or used in the United Kingdom shall be recognised and available in law, and be enforced, allowed and followed accordingly; and the expression 'enforceable Community right' and similar expressions shall be read as referring to one to which this subsection applies.

This section thus provides for the direct application of Community law but offers no guidance as to which provisions of EEC law are to be directly effective.

The EEC Treaty merely provides in Article 189 that Regulations (but only Regulations) are 'directly applicable'.

Since, as has been suggested, direct applicability is a necessary pre-condition for direct effects this would seem to imply that only Regulations are capable of direct effects.

This has not proved to be the case. In a series of landmark decisions, the Court of Justice, principally in its jurisdiction under Article 177 to give preliminary rulings on matters of interpretation of EEC law on reference from national courts, has extended the principle of direct effects to Treaty articles, Directives, Decisions, and even to provisions of international agreements to which the EEC is a party.

Treaty Articles

The question of the direct effect of a Treaty Article was first raised in *Van Gend en Loos* v *Nederlandse Administratie der Belastingen* (case 26/62). The Dutch administrative tribunal, in a reference under art. 177, asked the Court of Justice:

Whether Article 12 of the EEC Treaty has an internal effect . . . in other words, whether the nationals of member States may, on the basis of the Article in question, enforce rights which the judge should protect?

Article 12 prohibits States from:

... introducing between themselves any new customs duties on imports or exports or any charges having equivalent effect.

It was argued on behalf of the defendant customs authorities that the obligation in Article 12 was addressed to States and was intended to govern rights and obligations between States. Such obligations were not normally enforceable at the suit of individuals. Moreover the Treaty had expressly provided enforcement procedures under Articles 169 and 170 (see chapter 25) at the suit of the Commission or member States. Advocate-General Roemer suggested that Article 12 was too complex to be enforced by national courts; if such courts were to enforce Article 12 directly there would be no uniformity of application.

Despite these persuasive arguments the Court of Justice held that Article 12 was directly effective. The Court held:

... this Treaty is more than an agreement creating only mutual obligations between the contracting parties . . . Community law . . . not only imposes obligations on individuals but also confers on them legal rights.

These rights would arise:

... not only when an explicit grant is made by the Treaty, but also through obligations imposed, in a clearly defined manner, by the Treaty on individuals as well as on member States and the Community institutions. . . .
    The text of Article 12 sets out a clear and unconditional prohibition, which is not a duty to act but a duty not to act. This duty is imposed without any power in the States to subordinate its application to a positive act of internal law. The prohibition is perfectly suited by its nature to produce direct effects in the legal relations between the member States and their citizens.

And further:

The vigilance of individuals interested in protecting their rights creates an effective control additional to that entrusted by Articles 169 to 170 to the diligence of the Commission and the member States.

Apart from its desire to enable individuals to invoke the protection of EEC law the court clearly saw the principle of direct effects as a valuable means of ensuring that EEC law was enforced uniformly in all member States even when States had not themselves complied with their obligations.

It was originally thought that, as the Court suggested in *Van Gend*, only prohibitions such as Article 12 would qualify for direct effects; this was found in *Alfons Lütticke GmbH* v *Hauptzollamt Saarlouis* (case 57/65) not to be so. The Article under consideration in this case was Article 95(1) and (3); Article 95(1) contains a prohibition on States introducing discriminatory taxation; Article 95(3) contains a positive obligation that:

Member States shall, not later than at the beginning of the second stage, repeal or amend any provisions existing when this Treaty enters into force which conflict with the preceding rules.

The Court of Justice found Article 95(1) was directly effective; Article 95(3), which was subject to compliance within a specified time-limit, would, the Court implied, become directly effective once that time-limit had expired.

The Court has subsequently found a large number of Treaty provisions to be directly effective. All the basic principles relating to free movement of goods and persons, competition law, discrimination on the grounds of sex and nationality may now be invoked by individuals before their national courts. In deciding whether a particular provision is directly effective certain criteria are applied; the provision must be sufficiently clear and precise; it must be unconditional, and leave no room for the exercise of discretion in implementation by member States or Community institutions. The criteria are, however, applied generously, with the result that many provisions which are not particularly clear or precise, especially with regard to their scope and application, have been found to produce direct effects. Even where they are conditional and subject to further implementation they have been held to be directly effective once the date for implementation is past. The Court reasons that whilst there may be discretion as to the means of implementation, there is no discretion as to ends.

In *Van Gend* the principle of direct effects operated to confer rights on Van Gend exercisable against the Dutch customs authorities. Thus the obligation fell on an organ of the State, to whom Article 12 was addressed. (This is known as a 'vertical' direct effect, reflecting the relationship between individual and State.) But Treaty obligations, even when addressed to States, may fall on individuals too. May they be invoked by individuals against individuals? (This is known as a 'horizontal effect', reflecting the relationship between individual and individual.)

Van Gend implies so, and this was confirmed in *Defrenne* v *Sabena* (No. 2) (case 43/75). Ms Defrenne was an air hostess employed by Sabena, a Belgian airline company. She brought an action against Sabena based on Article 119 of the EEC Treaty. Article 119 provides that:

Each member State shall during the first stage ensure and subsequently maintain the application of the principle that men and women should receive equal pay for equal work.

Ms Defrenne claimed, *inter alia*, that in paying their male stewards more than their air hostesses, when they performed identical tasks, Sabena was in breach of Article 119. The gist of the questions referred to the Court of Justice was whether, and in what context, art. 119 was directly effective. Sabena argued that the Treaty articles so far found directly effective, such as Article 12, concerned the relationship between the State and its subjects, whereas Article 119 was primarily concerned with relationships between individuals. It was thus not suited to produce direct effects. The Court, following Advocate-General Trabucci, disagreed, holding that:

> ... the prohibition on discrimination between men and women applies not only to the action of public authorities, but also extends to all agreements which are intended to regulate paid labour collectively, as well as to contracts between individuals.

This same principle was applied in *Walrave and Koch* v *Association Union Cycliste Internationale* (case 36/74) to Article 7 of the EEC Treaty which provides that:

> Within the scope of application of this Treaty, and without prejudice to any special provisions contained therein, any discrimination on grounds of nationality shall be prohibited.

The plaintiffs, Walrave and Koch, sought to invoke art. 7 in order to challenge the rules of the defendant association which they claimed were discriminatory.

The Court of Justice held that the prohibition of any discrimination on grounds of nationality

> ... does not only apply to the action of public authorities but extends likewise to rules of any other nature aimed at regulating in a collective manner gainful employment and the provision of services.

To limit the prohibition in question to acts of a public authority would risk creating inequality in their application.

As will become evident in the chapters of this book devoted to the substantive law of the Community many Treaty provisions have now been successfully invoked vertically and horizontally. The fact of their being addressed to, and imposing obligations on, States has been no bar to their horizontal effect.

Regulations

A Regulation is described in Article 189 as of 'general application. . . binding in its entirety and directly applicable in all member States'. It is clearly intended to take immediate effect without the need for further implementation.

Regulations are thus by their very nature apt to produce direct effects. However, even for Regulations direct effects are not automatic. There may be cases where a provision in a Regulation is conditional, or insufficiently precise, or requires further implementation before it can take full legal effect. But since a Regulation is of 'general application', where the criteria for direct effects are satisfied, it may be invoked vertically or horizontally.

Directives

A Directive is (Article 189):

> ... binding, as to the result to be achieved, upon each member State to which it is addressed, but shall leave to the national authorities the choice of form and methods.

Because Directives are not described as 'directly applicable' it was originally thought that they could not produce direct effects. Moreover the obligation in a Directive is addressed to States, and gives the State some discretion as to the form and method of implementation; its effect thus appeared to be conditional on the implementation by the State. This was not the conclusion reached by the Court of Justice, which found, in *Grad* v *Finanzamt Traunstein* (case 9/70) that a Directive could be directly effective. The plaintiff in *Grad* was a haulage company seeking to challenge a tax levied by the German authorities which the plaintiff claimed was in breach of an EEC Directive and Decision. The Directive required States to amend their VAT systems to comply with a common EEC system. The Decision required states to apply this new VAT system to, *inter alia*, freight transport from the date of the Directive's entry into force. The German government argued that only Regulations were directly applicable. Directives and Decisions took effect internally only via national implementing measures. As evidence they pointed out that only Regulations were required to be published in the *Official Journal*. The Court of Justice disagreed. The fact that only Regulations were described as directly applicable did not mean that other binding acts were incapable of such effects:

> It would be incompatible with the binding effect attributed to Decisions by Article 189 to exclude in principle the possibility that persons affected may invoke the obligation imposed by a Decision. . . . the effectiveness of such a measure would be weakened if the nationals of that State could not invoke it in the courts and the national courts could not take it into consideration as part of Community law.

Although expressed in terms of a Decision, it was implied in the judgment that the same principle applied in the case of Directives.

So both Directives and Decisions may be directly effective. Whether they will in fact be so will depend on whether they satisfy the criteria for direct effects — they must be sufficiently clear and precise, unconditional, leaving no room for discretion in implementation. These conditions were satisfied in *Grad*. Although the Directive was not unconditional in that it required action to be taken by the State, and gave a time-limit for implementation, once the time-limit expired the obligation became absolute. At this stage there was no discretion left.

The reasoning in *Grad* has been repeated on many occasions to justify the direct effect of Directives once the time-limit for implementation has expired.

A Directive cannot, however, be directly effective before that time-limit has expired. It was tried unsuccessfully in the case of *Pubblico Ministero* v *Ratti* (case 148/78). Mr. Ratti, a solvent manufacturer, sought to invoke two EEC harmonisation Directives on the labelling of dangerous preparations in order to defend a criminal charge based on his own labelling practices. These practices, he claimed, were not illegal according to the Directive. The Court of Justice held that since the time-limit for the implementation of one of the Directives had not expired it was not directly effective. He could, however, rely on the other Directive for which the implementation date had passed.

Even when a State has implemented a Directive it may still be directly effective. The Court of Justice held this to be the case in *Verbond van Nederlandse Ondernemingen (VNO)* v *Inspecteur der Invoerrechten en Accijnzen* (case 51/76), thereby allowing the Federation of Dutch Manufacturers to invoke the Second VAT Directive despite implementation of the provision by the Dutch authorities. The grounds for the decision were that the useful effect of the Directive would be weakened if individuals could not invoke it before national courts. By allowing individuals to invoke the Directive the Community can ensure that national authorities have kept within the limits of their discretion. Arguably this principle could apply to enable an individual to invoke a 'parent' Directive even before the expiry of the time-limit, where domestic measures have been introduced for the purpose of complying with the Directive (see *Officier van Justitie* v *Kolpinghuis Nijmegen* (case 80/86), Article 177 proceedings).

Certain Directives, such as Directive 64/221 and Directive 68/360 (see chapters 20, 18) which do not require extensive legislative implementation, have been found to be directly effective almost in their entirety. Directive 64/221 was invoked for the first time by Ms Van Duyn in *Van Duyn* v *Home Office* (case 41/74) in order to challenge the Home Office's refusal to allow her to enter to take up work with the Church of Scientology. Since the criteria were found to be satisfied she was entitled to invoke Article 3 of the Directive. The Court went further and suggested that even if the provision in question was not clear the matter could be referred to the Court of Justice for interpretation under Article 177.

Not all national courts have been prepared to concede that Directives can be directly effective. The Conseil d'Etat, the supreme French administrative court, in *Minister of the Interior* v *Cohn-Bendit* [1980] 1 CMLR 543, refused to follow *Van Duyn* v *Home Office* and allow the plaintiff to invoke Directive 64/221. The English Court of Appeal in *O'Brien* v *Sim-Chem Ltd* [1980] ICR 429 found the Equal Pay Directive (75/117) not to be directly effective on the grounds that it had purportedly been implemented in the Equal Pay Act 1970 (as amended 1975). *VNO* was apparently not cited before the court. The German federal tax court, the Bundesfinanzhof in *Re VAT Directives* [1982] 1 CMLR 527 took the same view on the direct effects of the Sixth EEC VAT Directive, despite the fact that the time-limit for implementation had expired and existing German law appeared to run counter to the Directive. The courts' reasoning in all these cases ran on similar lines. Article 189 expressly distinguishes Regulations and Directives; only Regulations are described as 'directly applicable'; Directives are intended to take effect within the national order via national implementing measures.

On a strict interpretation of Article 189 this is no doubt correct. On the other hand the reasoning advanced by the Court of Justice is compelling. The obligation in a Directive is 'binding "on member states" as to the result to be achieved'; Directives are in fact published; their useful effect would be weakened if States were free to ignore their obligations. Enforcement of EEC law would be less effective if it were left to direct action by the Commission or member States under Article 169 or Article 170. Moreover States are obliged under Article 5 to 'take all appropriate measures . . . to ensure fulfilment of the obligations arising out of this Treaty or resulting from action taken by the institutions of the Community'.

If they have failed in these obligations why should they not be answerable to individual litigants?

The reasoning of the Court of Justice is persuasive where an individual seeks to invoke a Directive vertically, against the State, on whom the obligation to achieve the desired results has been imposed. In cases such as *VNO, Van Duyn,* and *Ratti,* the plaintiff sought to invoke a Directive against a public body, an arm of the State. Yet as with Treaty Articles, there are a number of Directives, impinging on labour or company law for example, which a plaintiff may wish to invoke against a private person. Is the court's reasoning in favour of direct effects adequate as a basis for the enforcement of Directives horizontally, against individuals?

The arguments for and against horizontal effects are finely balanced. Against horizontal effects is the fact of uncertainty: Directives are not required, as are Regulations (by Article 191), to be published. More compelling, the obligation in a Directive is addressed to the State. The rationale for allowing individuals to invoke it against a public person, expressed by the Court of Justice in the case of *Becker* v *Finanzarnt Münster-Innenstadt* (case 8/81) (applicant held entitled to invoke the Sixth VAT Directive against the German tax authorities), was that in an action against the State, based on a Directive, a State cannot plead its own failure to implement the Directive. This reasoning is clearly inapplicable in the case of an action against a private person. In favour of horizontal effects is the fact that Directives are in fact published; that Treaty provisions addressed to, and imposing obligations on, member States have been held to be horizontally effective; that it would be anomalous, and offend against the principles of equality, if an individual's rights to invoke a Directive were to depend on the status, public or private, of the party against whom he wished to invoke it; that the useful effect of Community law would be weakened if individuals were not free to invoke the protection of Community law against *all* parties.

Although a number of references were made in which the issue of the horizontal effects of Directives was raised, the Court of Justice for many years avoided the question, either by declaring that the claimant's action lay outside the scope of the Directive, as in *Burton* v *British Railways Board* (case 19/81) (Equal Treatment Directive 76/207) or by falling back on a directly effective Treaty provision, as in *Worringham* v *Lloyds Bank Ltd* (case 69/80) in which

Article 119 was applied instead of Directive 75/117, the Equal Pay Directive.

The nettle was finally grasped in *Marshall* v *Southampton & South West Hampshire Area Health Authority (Teaching)* (case 152/84). Here Mrs Marshall was seeking to challenge the health authority's compulsory retirement age of 65 for men and 60 for women as discriminatory, in breach of the Equal Treatment Directive 76/207. The difference in age was permissible under the Sex Discrimination Act 1975, which expressly excludes 'provisions relating to death or retirement' from its ambit. The Court of Appeal referred two questions to the Court of Justice:

(a)   Whether a different retirement age for men and women was in breach of Directive 76/207?

(b)   If so, whether Directive 76/207 could be relied on by Mrs Marshall in the circumstances of the case?

The relevant circumstances were that the area health authority, though a 'public' body, was acting in its capacity as employer.

The question of vertical and horizontal effects was fully argued. The Court, following a strong submission from Advocate-General Slynn, held that the compulsory different retirement age was in breach of Directive 76/207 and could be invoked against a public body such as the health authority. Moreover:

... where a person involved in legal proceedings is able to rely on a Directive as against the State he may do so regardless of the capacity in which the latter is acting, whether employer or public authority.

On the other hand, since a Directive is, according to Article 189, binding only on 'each member State to which it is addressed':

It follows that a Directive may not of itself impose obligations on an individual and that a provision of a Directive may not be relied upon as such against such a person.

If this distinction was arbitrary and unfair:

Such a distinction may easily be avoided if the member State concerned has correctly implemented the Directive in national law.

So, with *Marshall* v *Southampton & South West Hampshire Area Health Authority (Teaching)* the issue of the horizontal effect of Directives was finally laid to rest. By denying their horizontal effect on the basis of Article 189 the court strengthened the case for their vertical effect. The decision has undoubtedly served to gain acceptance for the principle of vertical direct effects (see, e.g., *R* v *London Boroughs Transport Committee ex parte Freight Transport Association Ltd* [1990] 3 CMLR 495). But problems remain.

First, the concept of a 'public' body, or an 'agency of the State', against whom a Directive may be invoked, is unclear. The area health authority in *Marshall* was deemed a 'public' body, as was the Royal Ulster Constabulary in *Johnston* v *RUC* (case 222/84), Article 177 proceedings. But what of the status of publicly-owned or publicly-run enterprises such as British Rail or British Coal? Or semi-public bodies? Are universities 'public' bodies?

Some of these issues were clarified in *Foster* v *British Gas plc* (case C 188/89). In a claim against the British Gas Corporation in respect of different retirement ages for men and women, based on Equal Treatment Directive 76/207, the Court of Appeal had held that British Gas, a statutory corporation carrying out statutory duties under the Gas Act 1972 at the relevant time, was not a public body against which the Directive could be enforced. On appeal the House of Lords sought clarification on this issue from the Court of Justice. That court refused to accept British Gas's argument that there was a distinction between a nationalised undertaking and a State agency and ruled (at para. 18) that a Directive might be relied on against organisations or bodies which were 'subject to the authority or control of the State or had special powers beyond those which result from the normal relations between individuals'. Applying this principle to the specific facts of *Foster* v *British Gas plc* it ruled that a Directive might be invoked against 'a body, whatever its legal form, which has been made responsible, pursuant to a measure adopted by the State, for providing a public service under the control of the State and has for that purpose special powers beyond those which result from the normal rules applicable in relations between individuals' (para. 20). On this interpretation a nationalised undertaking such as British Rail would be a 'public' body against which a Directive might be enforced,, as the House of Lords subsequently decided in *Foster* v *British Gas plc* [1991] 2 AC 306. Indeed, the principle expressed at para. 18 seems wide enough to embrace any nationalised undertaking, and even bodies such as universities with a more tenuous public element, but which are subject to *some* State authority or control. However, in *Doughty* v *Rolls-Royce plc* [1992] IRLR 126, the Court of Appeal, applying the *Foster* test, found that Rolls-Royce, a nationalised undertaking at the relevant time, although 'under the control of the State', had not been 'made responsible pursuant to a measure adopted by the State for providing a public service'. The public services which it provided, for example, in the defence of the realm, were provided to the *State* and not to the *public* for the purposes of benefit to the State: nor did the company possess or exercise any special powers of the type enjoyed by British Gas.

Such fine distinctions are not convincing: nor are they consistent with the purpose of the Court of Justice, namely to ensure the effective protection of individuals' rights under Directives by giving the concept of a 'public' body the widest possible scope. However, no matter how generously the concept of a 'public' body is defined, as long as the public/private distinction exists there can be no uniformity in the application of Directives as between one State and another. Nor will it remove the anomaly as between individuals. Where a State has failed to fulfil its obligations in regard to Directives, whether by non-implementation or inadequate implementation, an individual will, it appears, be powerless to invoke a Directive in the context of a 'private' claim.

The *Von Colson* principle: indirect effects

One way out of this dilemma was suggested in a pair of cases decided shortly before *Marshall*, *Von Colson v Land Nordrhein-Westfalen* (case 14/83) and *Harz v Deutsche Tradex GmbH* (case 79/83).

Both cases were based on Article 6 of the Equal Treatment Directive 76/207. Article 6 provides that:

Member States shall introduce into their national legal systems such measures as are necessary to enable all persons who consider themselves wronged by failure to apply to them the principle of equal treatment . . . to pursue their claims by judicial process after possible recourse to other competent authorities.

The plaintiffs had applied for jobs with their respective defendants. Both had been rejected. It was found by the German court that the rejection had been based on their sex, but it was justifiable. Under German law they were entitled to compensation only in the form of travelling expenses. This they claimed did not meet the requirements of Article 6. Miss Von Colson was claiming against the prison service; Miss Harz against Deutsche Tradax GmbH, a private company. So the vertical/horizontal, public/private anomaly was openly raised and argued in Article 177 proceedings before the Court of Justice.

The Court's solution was ingenious. Instead of focusing on the vertical or horizontal effects of the Directive it turned to Article 5 of the EEC Treaty. Article 5 requires States to 'take all appropriate measures' to ensure fulfilment of their Community obligations.

This obligation, the Court said, applies to *all* the authorities of member States, including the courts. It thus falls on the courts of member States to interpret national law in such a way as to ensure that the objectives of the Directive are achieved. It was for the German courts to interpret German law in such a way as to ensure an effective remedy as required by Article 6 of the Directive. The result of this approach is that although Community law is not applied directly — it is not 'directly effective' — it may still be aplied indirectly as domestic law by means of interpretation.

The success of the *Von Colson* principle of indirect effect depends on the extent to which national courts perceive themselves as having a discretion, under their own constitutional rules, to interpret domestic law to comply with Community law. Courts in the UK are constrained by the terms of the European Communities Act. It was thought by some commentators that s. 2(1) of this Act, which provides for the direct application of Community law within the UK, only applied to directly effective Community law. If such were the case it would leave little room for the application of the *Von Colson* principle. This was the view taken by the House of Lords in *Duke v GEC Reliance Ltd* [1988] 1 All ER 626 (HL). However, special facts obtained in that case. The House of Lords was being asked to construe section 6(4) of the Sex Discrimination Act 1975 to comply with EEC Equal Treatment Directive

76/207, as interpreted in *Marshall*. The Sex Discrimination Act had been amended to comply with the Court's ruling in *Marshall*, but it had not been made retrospective. The plaintiff's claim for damages, based on unequal treatment (different retirement ages for men and women), was in respect of the period prior to the amendment of the Sex Discrimination Act. The House of Lords clearly felt that it would be most unfair to penalise the defendant, a 'private' party, by interpreting the section against its literal meaning in order to comply with the 'oblique language' of the Directive, *a fortiori* when Parliament had clearly chosen *not* to amend the Act retrospectively.

A similarly constituted House of Lords took a different view in *Litster* v *Forth Dry Dock & Engineering Co. Ltd* [1990] 1 AC 546. Here, in a 'private' claim against an employer based on EEC Directive 77/187 (safeguarding employees' rights in the event of transfer of undertakings), the House was prepared to interpret a domestic Regulation contrary to its prima facie meaning in order to comply with the Directive as interpreted by the Court of Justice in the case of *Bork* (case 101/87). The reason for its so doing was that the domestic Regulation in question had been introduced *for the purpose of* complying with the Directive.

The House of Lords' approach in *Litster* clearly represents an advance on *Duke v GEC Reliance Ltd*. But it does not ensure that the *Von Colson* principle will be applied to give Directives an indirect effect where, either deliberately or inadvertently, legislation has not been introduced for the purpose of complying with a Directive; nor where the question of whether legislation which has been introduced, either before or after the EEC Directive, was intended to comply with community law, is unclear.

In *Finnegan* v *Clowney Youth Training Programme Ltd* [1990] 2 AC 407, in a claim under the Sex Discrimination (Northern Ireland) Order 1976 (SI 1976/1042), on facts very similar to those of *Duke v GEC Reliance Ltd*, concerning different retirement ages for men and women, the House of Lords refused to interpret art. 8(4) of the order to comply with Directive 76/207, as interpreted in *Marshall, even though the order had been made after the Court of Justice's decision in Marshall*. Their lordships' reason for so doing was that the provision in question, an exclusion from the non-discrimination principle for provision 'in relation to death or retirement' was enacted in terms identical to the parallel provision (s. 6(4)) of the Sex Discrimination Act 1975 which had been considered in *Duke v GEC Reliance Ltd*, and 'must have been intended to' have the same meaning as in that Act.

These cases should now be read in the light of the Court of Justice's decision in *Marleasing SA* v *La Comercial Internacional de Alimentación SA* (case C 106/89). In this case, which was referred to the Court of Justice by the Court of First Instance, Oviedo, the plaintiff company, was seeking a declaration that the contracts setting up the defendant companies were void on the grounds of 'lack of cause', the contracts being a sham transaction carried out in order to defraud their creditors. This was a valid basis for nullity under Spanish law. The defendants argued that this question was now governed by EEC Directive 68/151. The purpose of Directive 68/151 was to protect the members of a company and third parties from, *inter alia*, the adverse effects of the doctrine of nullity. Article 11 of the Directive provides an exhaustive list of situations in which nullity may be invoked. It does not include 'lack of cause'. The Directive should have been in force in Spain from the date of accession in 1986, but it had not been implemented. The Spanish judge sought a ruling from the Court of Justice on whether, in these circumstances, Article 11 of the Directive was directly effective.

The Court of Justice reiterated the view it expressed in *Marshall* that a Directive cannot of itself 'impose obligations on private parties'. It reaffirmed its position in *Von Colson* that national courts must as far as possible interpret national law in the light of the wording and purpose of the Directive in order to achieve the result pursued by the Directive. And it added that this obligation applied *whether the national provisions in question were adopted before or after the Directive.*

Given that in *Marleasing* no legislation had been passed, either before or after the issuing of the Directive, to comply with the Directive, and given the Court of Justice's suggestion that the Spanish court must nonetheless strive to interpret domestic law to comply with the Directive, it seems that, according to the European Court, it is not necessary to the application of the *Von Colson* principle that the relevant national measure should have been introduced for the purpose of complying with the Directive, nor even that a national measure should have been specifically introduced at all.

It may be argued that in extending the principle of indirect effect in this way the Court of Justice is attempting to give horizontal effect to Directives by the back door, and impose obligations, addressed to member States, on private parties, which are prima facie contrary to domestic law. As the House of Lords remarked in *Duke* v *GEC Reliance Ltd* (see also *Finnegan* v *Clowney Youth Training Programme Ltd*), this could be 'most unfair'. (For a similar view see *Webb* v *EMO Air Cargo (UK) Ltd* [1992] 2 All ER 43, English CA.)

However in the case of *Kolpinghuis Nijmegen* (case 80/86) the Court of Justice had suggested a limitation to the *Von Colson* principle which might meet this objection. Here, in the context of criminal proceedings against Kolpinghuis for breach of EEC Directive 80/777 on water purity, which at the relevant time had not been implemented by the Dutch authorities, the Court of Justice held that national courts' obligation to interpret domestic law to comply with EEC law was 'limited by the general principles of law which form part of community law [see chapter 4] and in particular the principles of legal certainty and non-retroactivity'. Thus, where an interpretation of domestic law would run counter to the legitimate expectations of individuals, the *Von Colson* principle will not apply. The decision in *Duke* v *GEC Reliance Ltd* could be justified on this basis; that of *Finnegan* v *Clowney Youth Training Programme Ltd*, concerning, as it did, an order made after *Marshall*, and capable of interpretation in compliance with *Marshall*, could not. Where domestic legislation has been introduced in order to comply with a Community Directive, it is surely legitimate to expect that domestic law will be interpreted in conformity with Community law, even if, as in *Litster*, this might require a 'creative' approach to interpretation. Where legislation has not been introduced with a view to compliance domestic law should still be interpreted in the light of the aims of the Directive as long as the domestic provision is reasonably capable of the meaning contended for. But here an interpretation 'contra legem' is not permissible (for further discussion see chapter 3).

An interesting corollary to the principle of direct effects, with important practical consequences, was introduced by the Court of Justice in Emmott v Minister for Social Welfare (case C 208/90). The case concerned the time-limits for initiating proceedings based on directly effective Directives. As a normal rule EEC law does not itself prescribe limitation periods in respect of actions based on EEC law: national limitation rules continue to apply, subject to the proviso that they be non-discriminatory and appropriate to ensure the effective protection of individuals' directly effective Community rights. However, in Emmott the Court of Justice held that since individual litigants seeking to rely on Directives are in a state of uncertainty until a Directive has been properly transposed into national law, time will not begin to run until such transposition has occurred. This will apply *even where the Court of Justice has declared that a member State has not fulfilled its obligations*. Thus whilst the right of action vests as soon as the claimant becomes entitled to invoke the Directive, national limitation periods will not begin to run until the Directive has been fully and correctly implemented. The decision is ingenious, and designed to spur recalcitrant States into prompt and full implementation of their obligations under Directives. If, prior to Emmott, nothing was lost by postponing implementation, during which time individuals might not be aware of their directly effective rights, or tardy in enforcing them, following Emmott, there is nothing to be gained by delay.

Francovich: a radical alternative

The need for individuals to invoke the principles of both direct and indirect effects, particularly in the context of Directives, may diminish following the Court's ruling in Francovich v Italian State (cases C 6 & 9/90). Here a group of employees were seeking compensation against the Italian State for its failure to implement a Directive (80/987) designed to guarantee the payment of arrears of wages to employees in the event of their employer's insolvency. The time-limit for the implementation of the Directive had expired and the Court of Justice had ruled, in Article 169 proceedings, that Italy was in breach of its Community obligations in failing to implement the Directive (Commission v Italy (case 22/87)). In response to questions submitted by the Preture di Vicenza and Bassano del Grappa the Court of Justice held that the Directive was not in itself sufficiently clear and precise as regards the identity of the institutions responsible for payment to be directly effective against the State. On the other hand Italy's obligation to implement the Directive, arising from Article 5 of the EEC Treaty, required the State to compensate individuals for damage suffered as a result of its failure to implement the Directive if certain conditions were satisfied. That is, where:

(a)   the Directive involved rights conferred on individuals,

(b)   the content of those rights could be identified on the basis of the provisions of the Directive, and

(c)   there was a causal link between the State's failure and the damage suffered by the persons affected.

Thus, where these criteria are fulfilled, individuals seeking compensation as a result of activities and practices which are inconsistent with EEC Directives may proceed directly against the State. There will be no need to rely on the principle of direct effects. Responsibility for the non-implementation of the Directive will be placed not on the employer, 'public' or 'private', but squarely on the shoulders of the State. As the Court pointed out in *Francovich*, this is inherent in the scheme of the Treaty.

The reasoning in *Francovich* is compelling; its implications for member States have yet to be clarified. In cases of non-implementation, as in *Francovich* itself, the State's failure is clear; *a fortiori* when established by the Court under Article 169. But in cases of faulty or inadequate implementation it is not. The State's 'failure' may only become apparent following an interpretation of the Directive by the Court (see, e.g., the sex discrimination cases such as *Marshall* and *Barber* in chapter 22). Here the case for imposing liability in damages on the State is less convincing. These questions, and the whole issue of when, and on what basis, damages may be claimed against the State will raise serious problems for the courts of member States (see further chapters 22 and 23).

Decisions

A decision is 'binding in its entirety upon those to whom it is addressed' (Article 189).

Decisions may be addressed to member States, singly or collectively, or individuals. Although, like Directives, they are not described as 'directly applicable', they may, as was established in *Grad* v *Finanzamt Traustein* (case 9/70), be directly effective provided the criteria for direct effects are satisfied. The direct application of Decisions does not pose the same theoretical problems as Directives, since they will only be invoked against the addressee of the Decision. If the obligation has been addressed to him and is 'binding in its entirety', there seems no reason why it should not be invoked against him.

Recommendations and opinions

Since recommendations and opinions have no binding force and are not 'enforceable Community rights' within s. 2(1) of the European Communities Act 1972 it would appear that they cannot be invoked by individuals, directly or indirectly, before national courts. However, in *Grimaldi* v *Fonds des Maladies Professionnelles* (case C 322/88), in the context of a claim by a migrant worker for benefit in respect of occupational diseases, in which he sought to invoke a Commission recommendation concerning the conditions for granting such benefit, the Court of Justice held that national courts were 'bound to take Community recommendations into consideration in deciding disputes submitted to them, in particular where they clarify the interpretation of national provisions adopted in order to implement them or where they are designed to supplement binding EEC measures'. Such a view is open to question. It may be argued that recommendations, as non-binding measures, can at the most only be taken into account in order to resolve ambiguities in domestic law.

International agreements to which the EEC is a party

There are three types of international agreements capable of being invoked in the context of EEC law. First, agreements concluded by the Community institutions falling within the treaty-making jurisdiction of the EEC; secondly, 'hybrid' agreements, in which the subject-matter lies partly within the jurisdiction of member States and partly within that of the EEC; and thirdly, agreements concluded prior to the EEC Treaty, such as GATT, which the EEC has assumed as being within its jurisdiction, by way of succession. There is no indication in the EEC Treaty that such agreements may be directly effective.

The Court of Justice's case law on the direct effect of these agreements has not been wholly consistent. It purports to apply similar principles to those which it applies in matters of 'internal' law. A provision of an association agreement will be directly effective when 'having regard to its wording and the purpose and nature of the agreement itself, the provision contains a clear and precise obligation which is not subject, in its implementation or effects, to the adoption of any subsequent measure'. Applying these principles in some cases, such as *International Fruit Co. NV v Produktschap voor Groenten en Fruit* (No. 3) (cases 21 & 22/72), the Court, in response to an enquiry as to the direct effects of Article XI of GATT, held, following an examination of the agreement as a whole, that the Article was not directly effective. In others, such as *Bresciani* (case 87/75) and *Kupferberg* (case 104/81), Article 2(1) of the Yaoundé Convention and Article 21 of the EEC-Portugal trade agreement were examined respectively on their individual merits and found to be directly effective. The different result is hard to explain, particularly since the provisions in all three cases were almost identical in wording to EEC Treaty Articles already found directly effective. The suggested reason (see Hartley (1983) 8 EL Rev 383) for this inconsistency is the conflict between the Court of Justice's desire to provide an effective means of enforcement of international agreements against member States and the lack of a solid legal basis on which to do so.

Thus in the case of international agreements it appears that the criteria for direct effects will be applied more strictly, no doubt in order to prevent abuse. However, where the agreement or legislation issued under the agreement confers clear rights on individuals the Court of Justice has not hesitated to find direct effects (e.g., *Sevince* (case C 192/89) judgment of 20 September 1990; *Bahia Kziber* (case C 18/90) judgment of 31 January 1991).

Where provisions of international agreements are found directly effective an individual in a dualist State such as the UK will, paradoxically, be in a stronger position than he would normally be *vis-à-vis* international law, which is not as a rule incorporated into domestic law.

Conclusions

A uniform interpretation of the concept of direct effects and its application, as has been supplied by the Court of Justice, is desirable. Had the matter been left to member States alone the internal application of EEC law would have been spasmodic and piecemeal. But there is no doubt that the Court of Justice, in its jurisdiction under Article 177 to give preliminary rulings, has extended the concept well beyond its apparent scope as envisaged by the EEC treaty. It has done so in the interests of the uniform application and enforcement of EEC law in all member States.

Perhaps sensing that it had gone far enough, the Court of Justice in *Marshall* (case 152/84) imposed a clear limitation on the direct effects of Directives. In view of the inequality of position of an individual seeking to invoke a Directive against a private party it is likely that the Court of Justice will interpret the concept of a 'public' authority in the widest sense. In an action based on a Directive against a 'private' party domestic courts should, following *Von Colson* (case 14/83) and *Harz* (case 79/83), interpret domestic law to conform with the Directive, provided that this is consistent with the intentions of Parliament and does not infringe the legitimate expectations of individuals. Where it is not possible to apply the *Von Colson* principle, enforcement should be left to direct action by the Commission under Article 169.

The criteria applied by the Court of Justice for assessing the question of direct effects appear straightforward. In reality they are applied loosely, and any provision which is justiciable has, until recently, been found to be directly effective, no matter what difficulties may be faced by national courts in its application to the facts. As Advocate-General Roemer pointed out in *Van Gend* (case 26/62), this could result in less, not more uniformity. The uncertainty with regard to international agreements is particularly acute.

There are signs that the Court of Justice, having, with a few exceptions, won acceptance from member States of the principle of direct effects, is now prepared to impose some limits in its extension. *Marshall* is an example. In *Hurd* v *Jones* (case 44/84) the Court held that a tax, levied by the UK authorities on the headmaster of a European school in England, was contrary to Article 5 of the EEC Treaty but that Article 5 could not in such a context be enforced at the suit of individuals. In *Bulk Oil (Zug) AG* v *Sun International Ltd* (case 174/84) the Court found that certain Articles from a number of Council Decisions, requiring States to give prompt and adequate notice of any proposed change in their trading rules *vis-à-vis* third countries, concerned only the institutional relationship between member States and the Community and other member States. They did not create individual rights which national courts must protect. (See also *Enichem Base* (case 380/87).)

These cases indicate that the Court of Justice may have taken heed of the problems posed to national courts by the direct application of Community law and may, in the future, apply the criteria for direct effects with more rigour, and some thought to possible difficulties and divergencies in application amongst the member States. For individuals suffering damage as a result of non or faulty implementation of directives, *Francovich* may now supply an alternative remedy against the State.

Further Reading

Bebr, G., 'Agreements concluded by the Community and their possible direct effects; from International Fruit Company to Kupferberg' (1983) 20 CML Rev 35.

Curtin, D., 'The Province of Government; Delimiting the Direct Effect of Directives' (1990) 15 EL Rev 195.

Curtin, D. 'The Effectiveness of Judicial Protection of Individual Rights' (1990) 27 CML Rev 209.

Green, N., 'Directives, Equity and the Protection of Individual Rights' (1984) 9 EL Rev 295.

Hartley, T., 'International agreements and the Community Legal System; some recent developments' (1983) 8 EL Rev 383.

Pescatore, P., 'The Doctrine of Direct Effect; an infant disease of Community Law' (1983) 8 EL Rev 155.

Prechel, S. 'Remedies after *Marshall*' (1990) 27 CML Rev 451. Shaw, J., 'European Community Judicial Method: its Application to Sex Discrimination Law' (1990) 19 ILJ 228.

Steiner, J., 'Direct Applicability in EEC law: a chameleon concept' (1982) 98 LQR 229.

Steiner, J., 'Coming to terms with EEC Directives' (1990) 106 LQR 144.

Winter, T. A., 'Direct Applicability and Direct Effects' (1972) 9 CML Rev 425.

Wyatt, D., 'Direct Effects of Community Law, not forgetting Directives' (1983) 8 EL Rev 241.

THREE

Principle of supremacy of EEC law

The problem of priorities

The extended application by the Court of Justice of the principle of direct effects, together with the wide scope of the EEC Treaty, covering a number of areas normally reserved to national law alone, have led inevitably to a situation of conflict between national and EEC law. In such a case, which law is to prevail? The way in which that conflict was resolved is of crucial importance to the Community legal order; it was a constitutional problem of some magnitude for member States.

The EEC Treaty is silent on the question of priorities. Perhaps this was a diplomatic omission; perhaps it was not thought necessary to make the matter explicit, since the extent to which Community law might be directly effective was not envisaged at the time of signing the Treaty. In the absence of guidance, the matter has been left to be decided by the courts of member States, assisted by the Court of Justice in its jurisdiction under Article 177 (see chapter 24). As with the concept of direct effects, the Court of Justice has proved extremely influential in developing the law.

The question of priorities between directly effective international law and domestic law is normally seen as a matter of national law, to be determined according to the constitutional rules of the State concerned. It will depend on a number of factors. Primarily it will depend on the terms on which international law has been incorporated into domestic law. This in turn will depend on whether the State is monist or dualist in its approach to international law. If monist, it will be received automatically into national law from the moment of its ratification, without the need for further measures of incorporation. If dualist, international law will not become binding internally, as part of domestic law, until it is incorporated by a domestic statute. In the EEC, France, for example, is monist; Germany, Belgium, Italy and the UK are dualist. But whether received automatically, by process of 'adoption', or whether incorporated by statute, by way of 'transformation', this does not settle the question of priorities. This will depend on the extent to which the State has provided for this, either in its constitution, where it has a written constitution, or, where it has no written constitution, in its statute of incorporation.

There is wide variation in the way in which, and the extent to which, member States of the EEC have provided for this question of priorities. Where States have a written constitution, provision may range from the whole-hearted acceptance of international law of the Dutch constitution (Articles 65-7), which accords supremacy to *all* forms of international law, whether prior or subsequent to domestic law, to Article 55 of the French constitution, which provides that treaties or agreements duly ratified 'have authority superior to that of laws' (thus leaving open the question of secondary legislation), to Article 24 of the German constitution, which provides, rather loosely, that the State 'may transfer sovereign powers' to intergovernmental institutions; or Article 11 of the Italian constitution whereby the State 'consents, on conditions of reciprocity with other States, to limitations of sovereignty necessary for an arrangement which may ensure peace and justice between the nations'. (Under the principle of reciprocity, if one party to an agreement breaches his obligations, the other contracting parties may regard themselves as entitled to be relieved of theirs.)

A State which does not have a written constitution, and which is dualist, such as the UK, must provide for priorities in the statute of incorporation itself. This statute will have the same status as any other statute. As such it will be vulnerable to the doctrine of implied repeal, or *'lex posterior derogat priori'*, whereby any inconsistency between an earlier and a later statute is resolved in favour of the latter. The later statute is deemed to have impliedly repealed the earlier one (see *Ellen Street Estates Ltd* v *Minister of Health* [1934] 1 KB 590).

On a strict application of this doctrine, any provision of a domestic statute passed subsequent to the statute incorporating EEC law, in our case the European Communities Act 1972, which was inconsistent with EEC law, would take priority.

Given the differences from State to State it is clear that if national courts were to apply their own constitutional rules to the question of priorities between domestic law and EEC law, there would be no uniformity of application, and the primacy of EEC law could not be guaranteed throughout the whole Community. Not only would this weaken the effect of Community law, it would undermine solidarity among the member States, and in the end threaten the Community itself.

It is no doubt reasons such as these which led the Court of Justice to develop its own constitutional rules to deal with the problem, in particular the principle of supremacy, or primacy, of EEC law.

The Court of Justice's contribution

The first cautious statement of the principle of supremacy of EEC law came in the case of *Van Gend en Loos* (case 26/62). The principal question in the case was the question of the direct effects of Article 12. The conflict, assuming that Article were found directly effective, was between Article 12 and an *earlier* Dutch law. Under Dutch law, if Article 12 were directly effective it would, under the Dutch constitution, take precedence over domestic law. So the questions referred to the Court of Justice under Article 177 did not raise the issue of sovereignty directly. Nevertheless, in addition to declaring that Article 12 was directly effective, the Court went on to say that:

> . . . the Community constitutes a new legal order in international law, for whose benefit the States have limited their sovereign rights, albeit within limited fields.

The conflict in *Costa* v *ENEL* (case 6/64) posed a more difficult problem for the Italian courts. This case too involved an alleged conflict between a number of Treaty provisions and an Italian statute nationalising the electricity company of which the defendant, signor Costa, was a shareholder, but here the Italian law was later in time. On being brought before the Milan *tribunale* for refusing to pay his bill (the princely sum of L1,925, or approximately £1.10), signor Costa argued that the company was in breach of EEC law. They argued '*lex posterior*'; the Italian Act nationalising the electricity company was later in time than the Italian Ratification Act, the Act incorporating EEC law. Therefore it took priority. The Italian court referred this question of priorities to the Court of Justice. It also referred the matter to its own constitutional court. This time the principle of supremacy was clearly affirmed by the Court of Justice. The Court cited *Van Gend*; the States had 'limited their sovereign rights'. It went further. It looked to the Treaty; it noted that Article 189 indicated that there had been a transfer of powers to the Community institutions; Article 5 underlined States' commitment to observe Community law. The Court concluded:

> The reception, within the laws of each member State, of provisions having a Community source, and more particularly of the terms and of the spirit of the Treaty, has as a corollary the impossibility, for the member State, to give preference to a unilateral and *subsequent* measure against a legal order accepted by them on a basis of reciprocity. . . .
> The transfer, by member States, from their national orders in favour of the Community order of the rights and obligations arising from the Treaty, carries with it a clear limitation of their sovereign right upon which a *subsequent* unilateral law, incompatible with the aims of the Community, cannot prevail. (Emphasis added.)

In the case of *Internationale Handelsgesellschaft mbH* (case 11/70) the Court went even further. Here, the conflict was between not a Treaty provision and a domestic statute, but between an EEC Regulation and provisions of the German constitution. The plaintiff claimed the Regulation infringed, *inter alia*, the principle of proportionality enshrined in the German constitution and sought to nullify the Regulation on those grounds. Normally, any ordinary law in breach of the constitution is invalid, since the constitution is superior in the hierarchy of legal rules to statute law. EEC law had been incorporated into German law by statute, the Act of ratification. There was no provision in the constitution that the constitution could be overridden by EEC law. Article 24 merely provides for 'the transfer of sovereign powers to intergovernmental institutions'. So the question before the German court (Verwaltungsgericht, Frankfurt) was: If there were a conflict between the Regulation and the German constitution, which law should prevail? As in *Costa*, the German judge referred the question to the Court of Justice and his own federal constitutional court (Bundesverfassungsgericht).

The ruling from the Court of Justice was in the strongest terms. The legality of a Community act cannot be judged in the light of national law:

> . . . the law born from the Treaty [cannot] have the courts opposing to it rules of national law *of any nature whatever*. . . . the validity of a Community instrument or its effect within a member State cannot be affected by allegations that it strikes at either the fundamental rights as formulated in that State's constitution or the principles of a national constitutional structure. (Emphasis added.)

If the Court's ruling seems harsh in the light of the importance of the rights protected in a State's constitution, many of which are regarded as fundamental human rights, it is worth adding that the Court went on to say that respect for such rights was one of the principal aims of the Community and as such it was part of its own (albeit unwritten) law (see chapter 4).

The principle of supremacy of Community law applies not only to internal domestic laws, but also to obligations undertaken by States towards third countries. In the *ERTA* case (case 22/70) the Court of Justice held, in the context of a challenge to an international road transport agreement to which the Community was a party, that once the Community, in implementing a common policy, lays down common rules, member States no longer have the right, individually or collectively, to contract obligations towards non–member States affecting these common rules. And where the Community concludes a treaty in pursuance of a common policy, this excludes the possibility of a concurrent authority on the part of the member States. This means that where a State attempts to exercise concurrent authority it will be overridden to the extent that it conflicts with Community law.

Thus as far as the Court of Justice is concerned *all* EEC law, whatever its nature, must take priority over *all* conflicting domestic law, whether it be prior or subsequent to Community law. Given the fact that the Court was approaching the matter *tabula rasa,* there being no provision in the Treaty to this effect, on what basis did the Court justify its position?

The Court's reasoning is pragmatic, based on the purpose, the general aims and spirit of the Treaty. States freely signed the Treaty; they agreed to take all appropriate measures to comply with EEC law (Article 5); the Treaty created its own institutions, and gave those institutions power to make laws binding on member States (Article 189). They agreed to set up an institutionalised form of control by the Commission (under Article 169, see chapter 25) and the Court. The Community would not survive if States were free to act unilaterally in breach of their obligations. If the aims of the Community are to be achieved, there must be uniformity of application. This will not occur unless all States accord priority to EEC law.

The reasoning is convincing. Nonetheless national courts were understandably reluctant to disregard their own constitutional rules and the Italian and German constitutional courts in *Costa v ENEL* [1964] CMLR 425 at p. 430 and *Internationale Handelsgesellschaft mbH* [1974] 2 CMLR 540, adhering to their own traditional view, refused to acknowledge the absolute supremacy of EEC law.

There were other problems too for national courts — problems of application. Even if the principle of primacy of EEC law were accepted in theory, what was a national judge to do in practice when faced with a conflict? No English judge can declare a statute void; in countries with a written constitution only the constitutional court has power to declare a domestic law invalid for breach of the constitution. Must the national judge wait for the offending national law to be repealed or legally annulled before he can give precedence to EEC law?

The Court of Justice suggested a solution to this problem in *Simmenthal SpA (No. 2)* (case 106/77). This case involved a conflict between a Treaty provision, Article 30 on the free movement of goods, and an Italian law passed *subsequent* to the Italian Act incorporating EEC law, a similar clash to the one in *Costa v ENEL* (case 6/64). Following *Costa* the Italian constitutional court had declared that it would be prepared to declare any national law conflicting with EEC law invalid. When the problem arose in *Simmenthal* the Italian judge, the Pretore di Susa, was perplexed. Should he apply EEC law at once to the case before him, or should he wait until his own constitutional court had declared the national law invalid? He referred this question to the Court of Justice. The Court's reply was predictable:

> . . . a national court which is called upon . . . to apply provisions of Community law is under a duty to give full effect to those provisions, if necessary refusing . . . to apply any conflicting provision of national legislation, even if adopted subsequently, and it is not necessary for the court to request or await the prior setting aside of such provision by legislative or other constitutional means.

The reasoning behind the judgment is clear. Unless Community law is given priority over conflicting national law at once, from the moment of its entry into force, there can be no uniformity of application throughout the Community. Thus, according to the Court of Justice, national judges faced with a conflict between national law, whatever its nature, and Community law, must ignore, must shut their eyes to national law; they need not, indeed must not, wait for the law to be changed. Any incompatible national law is automatically inapplicable.

The principle laid down in *Simmenthal SpA (No. 2)* was applied by the Court in *R v Secretary of State for Transport, ex parte Factortame Ltd (No. 2)* (case C 213/89), in the context of a claim before the English courts by a group of Spanish fishermen for an interim injunction to prevent the application of certain sections of the Merchant Shipping Act 1988, which denied them the right to register their boats in the UK, and which the plaintiffs alleged were in breach of EEC law. The question of the 'legality' of the British provisions under Community law had yet to be decided under a separate reference to the Court of Justice. Thus the British courts were being asked to give primacy to a *putative* Community right over an allegedly conflicting national law, and to grant an interim injunction against the Crown, something which they were not permitted to do under national law. Following a reference by the House of Lords asking whether they were obliged to grant the relief in question as a matter of Community law, the Court of Justice pointed out that national courts were obliged, by Article 5 of the EEC Treaty, to ensure the legal protection which persons derive from the direct effect of provisions of Community law. Moreover:

> The full effectiveness of Community law would be . . . impaired if a rule of national law could prevent a court seised of a dispute governed by Community law from granting interim relief in order to ensure the full effectiveness of the judgment to be given on the existence of the rights claimed under Community law. It follows that a court which in those circumstances would grant interim relief, if it were not for a rule of national law, is obliged to set aside that rule' (para 21).

The member States' response

After a shaky start (we have already noted the Italian and German constitutional courts' response in *Costa* and *Internationale Handelsgesellschaft mbH*) the courts of member States seem now to have accepted the principle of supremacy of EEC law provided they regard it as directly effective. They have done so in a variety of ways; in some cases by bending and adapting their own constitutional rules; in others by devising new constitutional rules to meet the new situation.

Great Britain   As a dualist State without a written constitution the status of Community law in the UK derives from the European Communities Act 1972. To what extent does that Act enable our courts to give effect to the principle of supremacy of EEC law?

The most important provisions are sections 2 and 3.

Section 2(1) provides for the direct applicability of EEC law in the UK:

> All such rights, powers, liabilities, obligations and restrictions from time to time created or arising by or under the Treaties, and all such remedies and procedures from time to time provided for by or under the Treaties, as in accordance with the Treaties are without further enactment to be given legal effect or used in the United Kingdom shall be recognised and available in law, and be enforced, allowed and followed accordingly; and the expression 'enforceable Community right' and similar expressions shall be read as referring to one to which this subsection applies.

Section 2(2) provides a general power for the further implementation of Community obligations by means of secondary legislation. This is subject to schedule 2. Schedule 2 lists the 'forbidden' areas, such as the power to increase taxation, to introduce retrospective measures or to create new criminal offences. These areas apart, s. 2(2) thus allows for ongoing domestic legislation over the whole field of objectives of the Treaty.

Section 2(4) is the section relevant to the question of primacy. It does not expressly say EEC law is supreme. Section 2(4) provides (emphasis added):

The provision that may be made under subsection (2) above includes, subject to schedule 2 to this Act, any such provision (of any such extent) as might be made by Act of Parliament, and *any enactment passed or to be passed,* other than one contained in this part of this Act [i.e., an enactment of a non-Community nature], *shall be construed and have effect subject to the foregoing provisions of this section* [i.e., obligations of a Community nature].

Is this sufficient to enable our courts to give priority to EEC law, on *Simmenthal* principles, as the Court of Justice would require? Or does it merely lay down a rule of construction, whereby domestic law must be *construed,* so far as possible, to conform with EEC law? The traditional constitutional view is that our doctrine of parliamentary sovereignty, and particularly the principle of implied repeal, makes entrenchment of EEC law impossible. Parliament is not free to bind its successors. Therefore priority for EEC law cannot be guaranteed, and s. 2(4) can only provide a rule of construction.

An approach based on the jurisprudence of the Court of Justice, particularly *Simmenthal,* would involve a departure from that view.

There was considerable wavering in the early years on the question of primacy. Lord Denning MR in *H. P. Bulmer Ltd* v *J. Bollinger SA* [1974] Ch 401 claimed that the Treaty 'is equal in force to any statute'. In *Felixstowe Dock & Railway Co.* v *British Transport Docks Board* [1976] 2 CMLR 655 he said in the context of an alleged conflict between an imminent statute and Article 86 of the EEC Treaty:

It seems to me that once the Bill is passed by Parliament and becomes a statute, that will dispose of all this discussion about the Treaty. These courts will then have to abide by the statute without regard to the Treaty at all.

In 1979 the Court of Appeal in *Macarthys Ltd* v *Smith* [1979] ICR 785, a landmark case, took the 'European' view. Cumming-Bruce and Lawton LJJ, invoking the European Court in *Costa* (case 6/64) and *Simmenthal* (case 106/77), were prepared, on the basis of the European Communities Act 1972, s. 2(4), to give European law 'priority'. Lord Denning MR preferred to use s. 2(4) as a rule of construction and construed the relevant English legislation (Equal Pay Act 1970) to conform with the principle of equal pay for equal work in Article 119 of the EEC Treaty. However, in doing so he took a rather broader view of 'construction' than is usually taken in construing international agreements. In construing our statutes, he said, 'we are entitled to look to the

Treaty as an aid to its construction: and even more, not only as an aid but as an overriding force'. Moreover he went on to say that 'If . . . our legislation is deficient — or is inconsistent with Community law . . . then it is our bounden duty to give priority to Community law'.

The House of Lords in *Garland* v *British Rail Engineering Ltd* [1983] 2 AC 751 adopted the 'rule of construction' approach to s. 2(4). The case involved a conflict, as in *Macarthys Ltd* v *Smith,* between our own Equal Pay Act 1970 and Article 119 of the EEC Treaty. The relevant section of the Equal Pay Act 1970, s. 6(4), which exempts from the equal pay principle provisions relating to death and retirement, had been broadly construed by the Court of Appeal to the detriment of the plaintiff. He sought therefore to rely directly on Article 119. The House of Lords held that s. 6(4) must be construed to conform with Article 119.

However, in *Garland* it was possible to construe the relevant English legislation to conform with EEC law 'without any undue straining of the words'. The matter would be more difficult were a court to be faced with a clear and patently irreconcilable conflict. What should it do in such a situation? According to Lord Denning in *Macarthys Ltd* v *Smith,* it is its 'bounden duty' to give 'priority' to EEC law. In *Garland* Lord Diplock suggested, whilst refusing to commit himself outright, that national courts must still construe domestic law to conform, 'no matter how wide a departure from the prima facie meaning may be needed to achieve consistency'. This approach was approved and applied in *Pickstone* v *Freemans plc* [1989] AC 66. Here the House of Lords, in contrast to the Court of Appeal, which had been prepared to apply EEC law directly, chose to 'interpret' certain Regulations amending the Equal Pay Act 1970 against their literal meaning, even to the extent of reading certain words into the Regulations in order to achieve a result compatible with EEC law. The provisions, said Lord Keith 'must be construed purposively in order to give effect to the manifest broad intentions of Parliament'. In this case it was clear, from evidence from House of Commons debates on the matter, that the Regulations had been introduced specifically in order to give effect to Community law.

In *Factortame Ltd* v *Secretary of State for Transport* (1989) 2 All ER 692 the House of Lords was prepared to go further. Lord Bridge suggested that the combined effect of Section 2(1) and 2(4) European Communities Act 1972 was 'as if a section were incorporated into Part II (the impugned part) of the Merchant Shipping Act which in terms enacted that the provisions with respect to registration of British fishing vessels were to be without prejudice to the directly enforceable Community rights of nationals of any member state of the EEC'. He suggested that if it were to be found that the British Act was in breach of the plaintiffs' directly effective community rights the latter rights would 'prevail' over the contrary provisions of the 1988 Act.

Subsequently, in applying the Court of Justice's ruling (in case C 213/89 noted above) that national courts must grant interim relief against the Crown where this was necessary to protect individuals' Community rights the House of Lords, unanimously, granted that relief (*R v Secretary of State for Transport, ex parte Factortame (No. 2)* [1991] 1 All ER 106). Here clearly no question of 'interpretation' of national law was possible; the House simply gave 'priority' to Community law.

Most recently, in *McKecknie* v *UBM Building Supplies (Southern) Ltd* [1991] ICR 710, Knox J in the Employment Appeal Tribunal was faced with a claim to redundancy payment based on Article 119 of the EEC Treaty. Since, as he pointed out, there was no national law capable of granting the benefit claimed, the matter could not be resolved by 'construction' of national law 'however purposive or indeed violent'. He had no hesitation in upholding the plaintiff's right to benefit under Article 119 alone, on the basis of the European Communities Act 1972, s. 2(1) and (3). In such a case, he suggested, 'the Community law remedy supplements rather than contradicts national law'.

Thus our courts, led by the House of Lords, have shown a clear willingness to accord supremacy to directly effective Community law, either by a (fictional) 'construction' of domestic law, or, where necessary, by applying EEC law directly, in priority over national law. However, both Lord Denning in *Macarthys Ltd* v *Smith* and Lord Diplock in *Garland* have made it clear that if Parliament were expressly to attempt to repudiate its EEC obligations our courts would be obliged to give effect to Parliament's wishes.

If the time should come when our Parliament deliberately passes an Act – with the intention of repudiating the Treaty or any provision in it – or intentionally of acting inconsistently with it – and says so in express terms – then . . . it would be the duty of our courts to follow the statute of our Parliament (per Lord Denning in *Macarthys Ltd* v *Smith* [1979] ICR 785 at p. 789).

Whilst this is unlikely to happen as long as we remain members of the Community, it was perhaps seen as important that it should remain a theoretical possibility. If our courts have changed in their approach to statutory interpretation in the context of Community law, the principle of parliamentary sovereignty remains intact.

In *Garland*, *Pickstone* and *Factortame* their Lordships' views on the European Communities Act 1972, s. 2(4), were expressed in the context of a conflict between domestic law and *directly effective* Community law. Is it possible to achieve primacy for EEC law when it is not directly effective? In other words, does s. 2(4) of the Act enable our courts to follow *Von Colson* (see chapter 2) and interpret domestic law to comply with EEC law, even when it is not directly effective? In *Duke* v *GEC Reliance Ltd* [1988] AC 618 the House of Lords thought not. The European Communities Act 1972, s. 2(1) and (4), said Lord Templeman, applied, and only applied, to EEC law which was directly effective. 'Section 2(4) of the European Communities Act 1972 does not . . . enable or constrain a British court to distort the meaning of a British statute in order to enforce against an individual a Community Directive which has no direct effect between individuals' (cited with approval by the English Court of Appeal in *Webb* v *EMO Air Cargo (UK) Ltd* [1992] 2 All ER 33). However, as was suggested in chapter 3, a refusal to interpret the Sex Discrimination Act 1975 to comply with Equal Treatment Directive 76/207 was acceptable on the particular facts of the case. In *Litster* v *Forth Dry Dock & Engineering Co. Ltd* [1990] 1 AC 546, in the context of a claim against a 'private' party, the House of Lords interpreted certain UK regulations to comply with EEC Directive 80/777, citing and approving *Pickstone*, and suggesting that where legislation had been introduced specifically in order to implement an EEC Directive, UK courts must interpret domestic law to comply with the Directive, if necessary 'supplying the necessary words by implication' in order to achieve a result compatible with EEC law. No reference was made to *Duke* v *GEC Reliance Ltd*, nor to the fact that the Directive in question was not directly effective.

Thus, in the absence of evidence, such as was adduced in *Duke* v *GEC Reliance Ltd*, that Parliament did not intend to comply with Community law, *Litster* suggests that even where EEC law is not directly effective, 'priority' for EEC law should be ensured by way of interpretation of national law. The Court of Justice in *Marleasing* (case C 106/89) (see chapter 2) has now held that this applies whether the national provision is prior or subsequent to the community law in question. It is only where domestic legislation has not been introduced to implement Community law and existing laws are explicitly incompatible with EEC law that enforcement must be left to the Commission acting under Article 169. The legitimate expectations of individuals must not be infringed (see *Kolpinghuis Nijmegen* (case 80/86), noted chapter 2).

In arguing for the primacy of Community law, support may be provided by the European Communities Act 1972, s. 3(1), which provides that:

> For the purposes of all legal proceedings any question as to the meaning or effect of any of the Treaties, or as to the validity, meaning or effect of any Community instrument, shall be treated as a question of law (and, if not referred to the European Court, be for determination as such in accordance with the principles laid down by and any relevant decision of the European Court or any court attached thereto).

The relevant decisions of the European Court would clearly be *Costa* v *ENEL* (case 6/64), *Internationale Handelsgesellschaft mbH* (case 11/70), *Simmenthal* (case 106/77) and, where the relevant EEC law is not directly effective, *Von Colson* (case 14/83) and *Marleasing* (case C 106/89).

Other member States After some early resistance, the French courts at all levels now seem prepared to give primacy to EEC law. They have done so in some cases by applying Article 55 of the French constitution (e.g., *Vabre* [1975] 2 CMLR 336, Cour de Cassation), in others by invoking the reasoning and case law of the Court of Justice (see *Von Kempis* v *Geldof* [1976] 2 CMLR 152, Cour de Cassation, and Procureur Général Touffait in *Vabre*). More recently the Versailles Cour d'Appel in *Rossi di Montalera* v *Procureur Général* [1984] 1 CMLR 489 declared EEC law to be 'top of the hierarchy of sources of law'. The Conseil d'État, the supreme French administrative court, has been the most reluctant of the French courts to concede the supremacy of EEC law. In

Semoules [1970] CMLR 395 it refused outright to do so. However, in *Nicolo* [1990] 1 CMLR 17 and *Boisdet* [1991] 1 CMLR 3, following a powerful submission from the Commissaire du Gouvernement, it recognised implicitly that Treaty Articles (*Nicolo*) and EEC Regulations (*Boisdet*) must take precedence over (even subsequent) national laws, by examining the latter for their compatibility with Community law. Its judgment in *Boisdet*, unlike that in the earlier case of *Nicolo*, was based neither on the EEC Treaty nor the French constitution but on the case law of the European Court. Whether the Conseil d'État will make the same concessions in respect of Directives and Decisions remains to be seen.

In Italy the constitutional court has moved far from its position in *Costa* v *ENEL* [1964] CMLR 430, and in *Frontini* [1974] 3 CMLR 381, applying Article 11 of the Italian constitution, in a judgment based almost entirely on the reasoning of the European Court, held that any question concerning the legality under the constitution of incorporating Article 189 of the EEC Treaty into the Italian Act of ratification 'must be dismissed'. Since then it has been unequivocal in its support for the principle of the supremacy of EEC law, sometimes advocating the route-by-construction of domestic law (*SpA Comavicola*, noted (1982) 19 CML Rev 455), sometimes following the case law of the Court of Justice (*Granital* (1984) I Giur It 1521; *Beca SpA* (1985) I Giur It 694).

The German federal constitutional court too has modified its view taken in *Internationale Handelsgesellschaft* [1974] 2 CMLR 540. In *Steinike und Weinleg* [1980] 2 CMLR 531 it suggested that any challenge to the constitutionality under German law of EEC law could only be brought by way of challenge to the German Act of ratification itself, and in October 1986, in *Application of Wünsche Handelsgesellschaft* [1987] 3 CMLR 225 its position in *Internationale Handelsgesellschaft* was finally reversed. As long as EEC law itself ensured the effective protection of fundamental rights (see chapter 4) a ruling from the Court of Justice under Article 177 would not, the court held, be subject to review. Similarly, in *Re Kloppenberg* [1988] 3 CMLR 1, in the context of a successful challenge to the Bundesfinanzhof's decision on the direct effect of Directives (see *Re VAT Directive*, noted in chapter 2), it affirmed the principle of the supremacy of Community law in the strongest terms.

The approach of the Belgian courts was novel, and perhaps closest of all in spirit to that of the European Court. As a dualist state, EEC law was incorporated into Belgian law by statute, but the constitution contained no provision (such as Article 55 of the French constitution) giving supremacy to international law. Thus EEC law was particularly vulnerable to the doctrine of *lex posterior*. Nevertheless the Cour de Cassation in the case of *Le Ski* [1972] CMLR 330 refused to accept this argument in the context of a conflict between EEC law and a later Belgian law. Even though EEC law was incorporated by statute the court held that the normal *lex posterior* rule would not apply. That rule was based on the presumption that the legislature in passing a statute wished to amend any earlier conflicting statute. That presumption would not apply in the case of a treaty. A treaty represented a higher legal norm. Because of the nature of international treaty law, in the case of a conflict the treaty must prevail. Similar reasoning was applied by the magistrates' court of Antwerp, in the *Social Funds for Diamond Workers* case [1969] CMLR 315.

Thus in a relatively short space of time the courts of member States, despite their different constitutional rules and traditions, have adapted to the principle of supremacy of EEC law. Credit for their accepting this principle must go to the European Court, which has supplied persuasive reasons for doing so. However, equal credit must go to the courts of member States, which have contrived to embrace the principle of primacy in practice without denying in principle that ultimate political and judicial control remains within the member States.

Further Reading

Bebr, G., 'Agreements concluded by the Community and their possible direct effects; from International Fruit Company to Kupferberg' (1983) 20 CML Rev 35.

Green, N., 'Directives, Equity and the Protection of Individual Rights' (1984) 9 EL Rev 295.

Hartley, T., 'International agreements and the Community Legal System; some recent developments' (1983) 8 EL Rev 383.

Pescatore, P., 'The Doctrine of Direct Effect; an infant disease of Community Law' (1983) 8 EL Rev 155.

Schermans, H., 'The Scales in Balance: National Constitutional Court v Court of Justice' (1990) 27 CML Rev 97.

Steiner, J., 'Direct Applicability in EEC law: a chameleon concept' (1982) 98 LQR 229.

Steiner, J., 'Coming to terms with EEC Directives' (1990) 106 LQR 144.

Tatham, A., 'The Effect of European Community Directives in France' (1991) 40 ICLQ 907.

Winter, T. A., 'Direct Applicability and Direct Effects' (1972) 9 CML Rev 425.

Wyatt, D., 'Direct Effects of Community Law, not forgetting Directives' (1983) 8 EL Rev 241.

FOUR
General principles of law

After the concept of direct effects and the principle of supremacy of EEC law the third major contribution of the Court of Justice has been the introduction into the corpus of EEC law of general principles of law. Although primarily relevant to the final section of this book, to the question of remedies and enforcement of EEC law, a discussion of the role of general principles of law is appropriate at this stage in view of their fundamental importance in the jurisprudence of the Court of Justice as compared with the relatively minor role they play in English law. It is thus important at an early stage to appreciate their significance.

General principles of law are relevant in the context of EEC law in a number of ways. First they may be invoked as an aid to interpretation: EEC law, including domestic law implementing EEC law obligations, must be interpreted in such a way as not to conflict with general principles of law. Secondly, general principles of law may be invoked by both States and individuals in order to challenge Community action, either to annul or invalidate acts of the institutions (under Articles 173, 184, 177 or 179), or to challenge inaction on the part of these institutions (under Article 175 or 179). Thirdly, as a logical consequence of its second role, but less generally acknowledged, general principles may also be invoked as a means of challenging action by a member State, whether in the form of a legal or an administrative act, where the action is performed in the context of a right or obligation arising from *Community* law (see *Klensch* (cases 201 & 202/85); *Hubert Wachauf* v *Bundesamt Ehrnahrung unt Forstwirtschaft* (case 5/88)). This would follow in the UK from the incorporation into domestic law, by s. 2(1) of the European Communities Act 1972, of '*All* such rights, powers, liabilities, obligations and restrictions from time to time created or arising by or under the Treaties'. Finally, general principles of law may be invoked to support a claim for damages against the Community (under Article 215(2)). Where damages are claimed as a result of an illegal act on the part of the Community institutions, it is necessary (but not sufficient) to prove that a sufficiently serious breach of a superior rule of law for the protection of the individual has occurred (*Aktien-Zuckerfabrik Schöppenstedt* v *Council* (case 5/71)).

General principles of law are not to be confused with the fundamental principles of Community law, as expressed in the EEC Treaty, for example, the principles of free movement of goods and persons, of non-discrimination on the grounds of sex (Article 119) or nationality (Article 7). General principles of law constitute the 'unwritten' law of the Community.

The legal basis for the incorporation of general principles into community law is slim, resting precariously on three Articles. Article 173 gives the Court of Justice power to review the legality of Community acts on the basis of, *inter alia*, 'infringement of this Treaty', or '*any rule of law relating to its application*'. Article 215(2), which governs Community liability in tort, provides that liability is to be determined '*in accordance with the general principles common to the laws of the member States*'. And Article 164, governing the role of the Court of Justice, provides that the court 'shall ensure that in the interpretation and application of this Treaty *the law* is observed'.

In the absence of any indication as to the scope or content of these general principles, it has been left to the Court of Justice to put flesh on the bones provided by the Treaty. This function the Court has amply fulfilled, to the extent that general principles now form a substantial element of Community law.

Reasons for, and sources of, general principles of law

The reasons for what has been described as the Court's 'naked law-making' in this area are best illustrated by the case of *Internationale Handelsgesellschaft mbH* (case 11/70). There the German courts were faced with a conflict between an EEC Regulation requiring the forfeiture of deposits by exporters if export was not completed within an agreed time, and a number of principles of the German constitution, in particular, the principle of proportionality. It is in the nature of constitutional law that it embodies a State's most sacred and fundamental principles. Although these fundamental principles were of particular importance, for obvious reasons, in post-war Germany, other States of the Community too had written constitutions embodying fundamental rights. Clearly it would not have done for EEC law to conflict with such principles. Indeed, as the German constitutional Court made clear ([1974] 2 CMLR 540), were such a conflict to exist, national constitutional law would take precedence over EEC law. This would have jeopardised not only the principle of primacy of EEC law but also the uniformity of application so necessary to the success of the new legal order. So whilst the Court of Justice asserted the principle of primacy of EEC law in *Internationale Handelsgesellschaft* it was quick to point out that respect for fundamental rights was in any case part of EEC law.

In fact the Court's first tentative recognition of fundamental human rights as part of EEC law was prior to *Internationale Handelsgesellschaft*, in the case of *Stauder* v *City of Ulm* (case 29/69), Article 177 proceedings. Here the applicant was claiming entitlement to cheap butter provided under a Community scheme to persons in receipt of welfare benefits. He was required under German law to divulge his name and address on the coupon which he had to present in order to obtain the butter. He challenged this law as representating a violation of his fundamental human rights (namely, equality of treatment). The Court of Justice, on reference from the German court on the validity of the relevant Community Decision, held that on a proper interpretation the Community measure did not require the recipient's name to appear on the coupon. This interpretation, the Court held, contained nothing capable of prejudicing the fundamental human rights enshrined in the general principles of Community law and protected by the Court.

The Court of Justice went further in *Internationale Handelsgesellschaft*. There it asserted that respect for fundamental rights forms an integral part of the general principles of law protected by the Court — such rights are inspired by the constitutional traditions common to the member States.

This judgment can be taken as implying that only rights arising from traditions *common to* member States can constitute part of EEC law (the 'minimalist' approach). It may be argued that if the problem of conflict between Community law and national law is to be avoided in *all* member States it is necessary for *any* human right upheld in the constitution of *any* member State to be protected under EEC law (the 'maximalist' approach). In the recent case of *Hoechst* v *Commission* (cases 46/87, 227/88), in the context of a claim based on the fundamental right to the inviolability of the home, the Court, following a comprehensive review by Advocate-General Mischo of the laws of all the member States on this question, distinguished between this right as applied to the 'private dwelling of physical persons', which was common to all member States (and which would by implication be protected as part of Community law), and the protection offered to commercial premises against intervention by public authorities, which was subject to 'significant differences' in different member States. In the latter case the only common protection, provided under various forms, was protection against arbitrary or disproportionate intervention on the part of public authorities. Similarly in *Australian Mining & Smelting Europe Ltd* v *Commission* (case 155/79), in considering the principle of professional privilege, the Court found that the scope of protection for confidentiality for written communications between lawyers and their clients varied from State to State; only privilege as between independent (as opposed to in-house) lawyers and their clients was generally accepted, and would be upheld as a general principle of Community law.

These cases suggest that where certain rights are protected to differing degrees and in different ways in member States, the Court will look for some *common* underlying principle to uphold as part of Community law.

Following *Internationale Handelsgesellschaft* the scope for human rights protection was further extended in the case of *J. Nold KG* v *Commission* (case 4/73), Article 173 proceedings. In this case J. Nold KG, a coal wholesaler, was seeking to challenge a Decision taken under the ECSC as being in breach of the company's fundamental right to the free pursuit of business activity. Whilst the Court did not find for the company on the merits of the case, it asserted its commitment to fundamental rights in the strongest terms. As well as stating that fundamental rights form an integral part of the general principles of law, the observance of which it ensures, it went on to say:

In safeguarding these rights, the Court is bound to draw inspiration from constitutional traditions common to the member States, and it cannot therefore uphold measures which are incompatible with fundamental rights recognised and protected by the constitutions of those States.

Similarly, international treaties for the protection of human rights on which the member States have collaborated or of which they are signatories, can supply guidelines which should be followed within the framework of Community law.

The reasons for this inclusion of principles of certain international treaties as part of EEC law are clearly the same as those upholding fundamental constitutional rights; it is the one certain way to guarantee the avoidance of conflict.

The most important international treaty concerned with the protection of human rights is the European Convention for the Protection of Human Rights and Fundamental Freedoms 1953 (ECHR), to which all member States are now signatories. The Court has on a number of occasions confirmed its adherence to the rights protected therein, and in 1977 the institutions of the Community issued a Joint Declaration expressing their commitment to its principles (OJ No. C103, 27.4.77, p. 1). In *R* v *Kirk* (case 63/83), Article 177 proceedings, in the context of criminal proceedings against Kirk, the captain of a Danish fishing vessel, for fishing in British waters (a matter subsequently covered by EEC Regulations), the principle of non-retroactivity of penal measures, enshrined in Article 7 of the ECHR, was invoked by the Court and applied in Captain Kirk's favour. The EEC Regulation, which would have legitimised the rules under which Captain Kirk was charged, could not be applied to penalise him retrospectively. (See also *Johnston* v *Chief Constable of the Royal Ulster Constabulary* (case 222/84) (ECHR, Article 6, right to judicial process); *Hoechst* (cases 46/87, 227/88); *National Panasonic* v *Commission* (case 136/79) (ECHR Article 8, right to respect for private and family life, home and correspondence – not infringed).)

Thus it seems that any provision in the ECHR may be invoked, provided it is done in the context of a matter of EEC law. In *Kaur* v *Lord Advocate* [1980] 3 CMLR 79, Court of Session of Scotland, an attempt was made to invoke the Convention (Article 8 'respect for family life') by an Indian immigrant seeking to challenge a deportation order made under the Immigration Act 1971. She failed on the grounds that the Convention had not been incorporated into British law. Its alleged incorporation via the European Communities Act 1972 did not enable a party to invoke the Convention before a Scottish court in a matter *wholly unrelated to EEC law.*

Other international treaties concerned with human rights referred to by the Court as constituting a possible source of general principles are the European Social Charter (1971) and Convention 111 of the International Labour Organisation (1958) (*Defrenne* v *Sabena (No. 3)* (case 149/77)).

It remains to consider a number of specific general principles taken from a variety of sources which have come to assume a particular significance in EEC law.

Proportionality

This was the principle invoked in *Internationale Handelsgesellschaft mbH* (case 11/70). The principle, applied in the context of administrative law, requires that the means used to achieve a given end must be no more than that which is appropriate and necessary to achieve that end. The test thus puts the burden on an administrative authority to justify its actions and requires some consideration of possible alternatives. In this respect it is a more rigorous test than one based on reasonableness.

The principle has been invoked on many occasions as a basis of challenge to EEC secondary legislation, often successfully (e.g., *Werner A. Bock KG v Commission* (case 62/70), Article 173 proceedings; *Bela-Mühle Josef Bergmann KG v Grows-Farm GmbH & Co. KG* (case 114/76), Article 177 proceedings). It was applied in *R v Intervention Board for Agricultural Produce (ex parte E.D. & F. Man (Sugar) Ltd* (case 181/84) in the context of a claim by E.D. & F. Man (Sugar) Ltd before the English Divisional Court, on facts very similar to *Internationale Handelsgesellschaft*. Here the plaintiff E.D. & F. Man (Sugar) Ltd, was seeking repayment of a security of £1,670,370 forfeited when it failed to comply with an obligation to submit licence applications to the Board within a specified time-limit. Due to an oversight they were a few hours late. The plaintiff's claim rested on the alleged illegality of the EEC Regulations governing the common organisation of the sugar market. The Regulations appeared to require the full forfeiture of the deposit (lodged by the exporter at the time of the initial offer to export) in the event of a breach of both a *primary* obligation to export goods as agreed with the Commission and a *secondary* obligation to submit a licence application following the initial offer within a specified time-limit. The Court of Justice held, on a reference from the Divisional Court on the validity of the Regulations, that to require the same forfeiture for breach of the secondary obligation as for the primary obligation was disproportionate, and to the extent that the Regulation required such forfeiture, it was invalid. As a result of this ruling, the plaintiff was held entitled in the Divisional Court to a declaration that the forfeiture of its security was unlawful. A significant victory for the plaintiff.

The proportionality principle has also been applied in the context of the EEC Treaty, for example, in the application of the provisions relating to freedom of movement for goods and persons. Under these provisions States are allowed some scope for derogation from the principle of free movement, but derogations must be 'justified' on one of the grounds provided (Articles 36 and 48(3)). This has been interpreted by the Court of Justice as meaning that the measure must be *no more than is necessary* to achieve the desired objective (see chapters 8, 9 (goods), 18 and 20 (persons)).

In *State v Watson and Belmann* (case 118/75) the proportionality principle was invoked in the sphere of the free movement of persons in order to challenge the legality of certain action by the Italian authorities. One of the defendants, Ms Watson, was claiming rights of residence in Italy. The right of free movement of workers expressed in Article 48 of the EEC Treaty is regarded as a fundamental Community right, subject only to 'limitations' which are 'justified' on the grounds of public policy, public security or public health (Article 48(3)). The Italian authorities sought to invoke this derogation to expel Ms Watson from Italy. The reason for their expulsion was that they had failed to comply with certain administrative procedures, required under Italian law, to record and monitor their movements in Italy. The Court of Justice, on reference from the Italian court, held that, whilst States were entitled to impose penalties for non-compliance with their administrative formalities, these must not be disproportionate; and they must never provide a ground for deportation. Here, it is worth noting, it is a member State's action which was deemed to be illegal for breach of the proportionality principle.

Similarly, in the context of goods, in a recent case brought against Germany in respect of its beer purity laws (case 178/84), a German law imposing an absolute ban on additives was found in breach of EEC law (Article 30) and not 'justified' on public health grounds under Article 36. Since the same (public health) objective could have been achieved by other less restrictive means, the ban was not 'necessary'; it was disproportionate.

Equality

The principle of equality means, in its broadest sense, that persons in similar situations are not to be treated differently unless the difference in treatment is objectively justified. This, of course, begs the question of what are similar situations. Discrimination can only exist within a framework in which it is possible to draw comparisons, for example, the framework of race, sex, nationality, colour, religion. The equality principle will not apply in situations which are deemed to be 'objectively different' (see *Les Assurances du Crédit SA* v *Council* (case C 63/89) – public export credit insurance operations different from other export credit insurance operations). The EEC Treaty expressly prohibits discrimination on the grounds of nationality (Article 7) and, to a limited extent, sex (Article 119 provides for equal *pay* for men and women for equal work). In the field of agricultural policy, Article 40(3) prohibits 'discrimination between producers or consumers within the Community'. However, a general principle of equality is clearly wider in scope than these provisions. In the first isoglucose case, *Royal Scholten-Honig Holdings Ltd* v *Intervention Board for Agricultural Produce* (cases 103 & 145/77), Article 177 proceedings, the plaintiffs, who were glucose producers, together with other glucose producers, sought to challenge the legality of a system of production subsidies whereby sugar producers were receiving subsidies financed in part by levies on the production of glucose. Since glucose and sugar producers were in competition with each other the plaintiffs argued that the Regulations implementing the system were discriminatory, i.e., in breach of the general principle of equality, and therefore invalid. The Court of Justice, on a reference on the validity of the Regulations from the English court, agreed. The Regulations were held invalid. (See also *Ruckdeschel* (case 117/76); *Pont-à-Mousson* (cases 124/76 & 20/77).)

Similarly, the principle of equality was invoked in the case of *Airola* (case 21/74) to challenge a rule which was discriminatory on grounds of sex (but not pay), and in *Prais* (case 130/75) to challenge alleged discrimination on the grounds of religion. Neither case at the time fell within the more specific provisions of Community law.

Certainty

The principle of legal certainty was invoked by the Court of Justice in *Defrenne* v *Sabena (No. 2)* (case 43/75), Article 177 proceedings. The principle, which is one of the widest generality, has been applied in more specific terms as:

(a)   The principle of legitimate expectations.
(b)   The principle of non-retroactivity.

The principle of legitimate expectations, derived from German law, means that, in the absence of an overriding matter of public interest, Community measures must not violate the legitimate expectations of the parties concerned. A legitimate expectation is one which might be held by a reasonable man as to matters likely to occur in the normal course of his affairs. It does not extend to anticipated windfalls or speculative profits. In that the principle requires the encouragement of a reasonable expectation, a reliance on that expectation, and some loss resulting from the breach of that expectation, it is similar to the principle of estoppel in English law.

The principle was applied in *August Töpfer & Co. GmbH* v *Commission* (case 112/77), Article 173 proceedings (see chapter 27). August Töpfer & Co. GmbH was an exporter which had applied for, and been granted, a number of export licences for sugar. Under Community law, as part of the common organisation of the sugar market, certain refunds were to be payable on export, the amount of the refunds being fixed in advance. If the value of the refund fell, due to currency fluctuations, the licence holder could apply to have his licence cancelled. This scheme was suddenly altered by an EEC Regulation, and the right to cancellation withdrawn, being substituted by provision for compensation. This operated to Töpfer's disadvantage, and it sought to have the Regulation annulled, for breach, *inter alia*, of the principle of legitimate expectations. Although it did not succeed on the merits, the principle of legitimate expectations was upheld by the Court. (See also *CNTA SA* v *Commission* (case 74/74), monetary compensation scheme ended suddenly and without warning: chapter 30.)

The principle of non-retroactivity, applied to Community secondary legislation, precludes a measure from taking effect before its publication.

In *R* v *Kirk* (case 63/83) the principle of non-retroactivity of penal provisions (activated in this case by a Community Regulation) was invoked successfully.

This principle also has relevance in the context of national courts' obligation to interpret domestic law to comply with Community law when it is not directly effective (the *Von Colson* principle, see chapter 2). In *Pretore di Salo* v *Persons Unknown* (case 14/86) in a reference under Article 177 from the Salo magistrates' court on the compatibility of certain Italian laws with EEC Water

Purity Directive 78/659, which had been invoked against the defendants in criminal proceedings, the Court held that:

A Directive cannot of itself have the effect of determining or aggravating the liability in criminal law of persons who act in contravention of the provisions of the Directive.

The Court went further in *Officier van Justitie* v *Kolpinghuis Nijmegen* (case 80/86), Article 177 proceedings. Here, in response to a question concerning the scope of national courts' obligation of interpretation under the *Von Colson* principle, the Court held that that obligation was 'limited by the general principles of law which form part of Community law and in particular the principles of legal certainty and non-retroactivity'. Thus, where EEC law is not directly effective national courts are not required to interpret domestic law to comply with EEC law in violation of these principles.

Problems also arise over the temporal effects of the Court of Justice's rulings under Article 177.

In *Defrenne* v *Sabena (No. 2)* (case 43/75) the Court, in Article 177 proceedings, held that, given the exceptional circumstances, 'important considerations of legal certainty' required that its ruling on the direct effects of Article 119 should apply prospectively only. Article 119 could not be relied on to support claims concerning pay periods prior to the date of judgment, except as regards workers who had already brought legal proceedings or made an equivalent claim. However, in *Ariete SpA* (case 811/79) and *Meridionale Industria Salumi Srl* (cases 66, 127 & 128/79) the Court affirmed that *Defrenne* was an exceptional case. In a 'normal' case a ruling from the Court of Justice was retroactive; the Court merely declared the law as it always was. This view was approved in *Barra* (case 309/85), Article 177 proceedings. However, in *Blaizot* (case 24/86), Article 177 proceedings, a case decided the same day as *Barra,* 'important considerations of legal certainty' again led the Court to limit the effects of its judgment on the lines of *Defrenne.* It came to the same conclusion in *Barber* v *Guardian Royal Exchange Assurance Group* (case 262/88). These cases indicate that in exceptional cases, where the Court introduces some new principle, or where the judgment may have serious effects as regards the past, the Court will be prepared to limit the effects of its rulings. *Kolpinghuis Nijmegen* may now be invoked to support such a view. However, the Court has insisted that only the Court of Justice can limit the temporal effect of its rulings (see further chapter 24).

Procedural rights

Where a person's rights are likely to be affected by EEC law, EEC secondary legislation normally provides for procedural safeguards (e.g., Regulation 17/62, competition law, chapter 15; Directive 64/221, free movement of workers, chapter 20; Directive 76/207, Article 6, equal treatment for men and women, chapter 22). However, where such provision does not exist, or where there are lacunae, general principles of law may be invoked to fill those gaps.

Natural justice: the right to a hearing   The right to natural justice, and in particular the right to a fair hearing, was invoked, this time from English law, in *Transocean Marine Paint Association* v *Commission* (case 17/74) by Advocate-General Warner. The case, which arose in the context of EEC competition law (see chapter 15), was an action for annulment of the Commission's Decision, addressed to the plaintiff association, that their agreements were in breach of EEC law. The Court, following Advocate-General Warner's submissions, asserted a general rule that a person whose interests are perceptibly affected by a decision taken by a public authority must be given the opportunity to make his views known. Since the Commission had failed to comply with this obligation its Decision was annulled. The principle was affirmed in *Hoffman-La Roche & Co. AG* v *Commission* (case 85/76), in which the Court held that observance of the right to be heard is, in all proceedings in which sanctions, in particular fines and periodic payments, may be imposed, a fundamental principle of Community law which must be respected even if the proceedings in question are administrative proceedings.

The Duty to give reasons   The duty was affirmed in *Union Nationale des Entraîneurs et Cadres Techniques Professionels du Football (UNECTEF)* v *Heylens* (case 222/86), Article 177 proceedings. In this case, M. Heylens, a Belgian and a professional football trainer, was the defendant in a criminal action brought by the French football trainers' union, UNECTEF, as a result of his practising in Lille as a professional trainer without the necessary French diploma, or any qualifications recognised by the French government as equivalent. M. Heylens held a Belgian football trainers' diploma, but his application for recognition of this diploma by the French authorities had been rejected on the basis of an adverse opinion from a special committee, which gave no reasons for its decision. The Court of Justice, on a reference from the Tribunal de Grande Instance, Lille, held that the right of free movement of workers, granted by Article 48 of the EEC Treaty, required that a decision refusing to recognise the equivalence of a qualification issued in another member State should be subject to legal redress which would enable the legality of that decision to be established with regard to Community law, and that the person concerned should be informed of the reasons upon which the decision was based.

Similarly in *Al-Jubail Fertiliser Company (SAMAD)* v *Council* (case C 49/88) in the context of a challenge to a Council Regulation imposing anti-dumping duties on the import of products manufactured by the applicants, the Court held that since the applicants had a right to a fair hearing the Community institutions were under a duty to supply them with all the information which would enable them effectively to defend their interests. Moreover if the information is supplied orally, as it may be, the Commission must be able to prove that it was in fact supplied.

The right to due process   As a corollary to the right to be informed of the reasons for a decision is the right, alluded to in *UNECTEF* v *Heylens* (case 222/86), to legal redress to enable such decisions and reasons to be challenged. This right was established in *Johnston* v *Chief Constable of the Royal Ulster Constabulary* (case 222/84), Article 177 proceedings. The case arose from a refusal by the RUC to renew its contracts with women members of the RUC Reserve. This decision had been taken as a result of a policy decision taken in 1980 that henceforth full-time RUC Reserve members engaged on general police duties should be fully armed. For some years women had not been issued with firearms nor trained in their use. Mrs Johnston, who had been a full-time member of the Reserve for some years and wished to renew her contract, challenged the decision as discriminatory, in breach of EEC Directive 76/207, which provides for equal treatment for men and women in all matters relating to employment. Although the measure was admittedly discriminatory, since it was taken solely on the grounds of sex, the Chief Constable claimed that it was justified, arguing from the 'public policy and public security' derogation of Articles 36 (goods, see chapter 9) and 48 (workers, see chapter 20), and from Article 224, which provides for the taking of measures in the event of, *inter alia*, 'serious internal disturbances affecting the maintenance of law and order'. As evidence that these grounds were made out the Chief Constable produced before the industrial tribunal a certificate issued by the Secretary of State certifying that the act refusing to offer Mrs Johnston further employment in the RUC Reserve was done for the purpose of safeguarding national security and safeguarding public order. Under Article 53(2) of the Sex Discrimination (Northern Ireland) Order a certificate that an act was done for that purpose was 'conclusive evidence' that it was so done. A number of questions were referred to the Court of Justice by the industrial tribunal on the scope of the public order derogation and the compatibility of the Chief Constable's decision with Directive 76/207. The question of the Secretary of State's certificate and the possibility of judicial review were not directly raised. Nevertheless this was the first matter seized upon by the Court. The Court considered the requirement of judicial control, provided by Article 6 of Directive 76/207, which requires States to enable persons who 'consider themselves wronged' to 'pursue their claims by judicial process after possible recourse to the competent authorities'. This provision, the Court said, reflected:

> a general principle of law which underlies the constitutional traditions common to the member States. That principle is also laid down in Articles 6 and 13 of the European Convention for the Protection of Human Rights and Fundamental Freedoms . . ..
>
> It is for the member States to ensure effective judicial control as regards compliance with the applicable provisions of Community law and of national legislation intended to give effect to the rights for which the Directive provides.

The court went on to say that Article 53(2) of the Sex Discrimination (Northern Ireland) Order, in requiring the Secretary of State's certificate to be treated as conclusive evidence that the conditions for derogation are fulfilled, allowed the competent authority to deprive an individual of the possibility of asserting by judicial process the rights conferred by the Directive. Such a provision was contrary to the principle of effective judicial control laid down in Article 6 of the Directive.

Although the Court's decision was taken in the context of a right provided by the Directive it is submitted that the right to effective judicial control enshrined in the European Convention on Human Rights and endorsed in this case could be invoked in any case in which a person's Community rights have been infringed. The case of *UNECTEF* v *Heylens* (case 222/86) would serve to support this proposition.

Thus general principles of law act as a curb not only on the institutions of the Community but also on member States, which are required, in the context of EEC law, to accommodate these principles alongside existing remedies and procedures within their own domestic systems of administrative law. This may result eventually in some modification in national law itself. In *Council of Civil Service Unions* v *Minister for the Civil Service* (the 'GCHQ' case) [1985] AC 374, HL, Lord Diplock, in considering the question of judicial review of the exercise of prerogative powers (resulting, in that case, in the exclusion of trade union membership), alluded to the question of 'legitimate expectations', and even 'the possible adoption in the future of the principle of "proportionality" which is recognised in the administrative law of several of our fellow members of the European Economic Community'. However, hopes that the principle of proportionality would be adopted as a principle of English administrative law were dashed in *R* v *Secretary of State for the Home Department, ex parte Brind* [1991] 1 AC 696, when the House of Lords (Lord Templeman excepted) refused to take 'the first step' in this direction. Lord Bridge and Lord Roskill did not, however, rule out the possibility of 'further development of the law in this respect'.

Conclusions

The above cases illustrate the importance of general principles of law in the judicial protection of individual rights. The success of the European Court's policy in incorporating these principles is demonstrated in *Re Wunsche* [1987] 3 CMLR 225, in which the German Constitutional Court resiled from its position in *Internationale Handelsgesellschaft* [1974] 2 CMLR 540, acknowledging the protection for fundamental human rights provided under Community law. The Community's commitment to fundamental human rights has now been acknowledged in Article F of the Maastricht treaty, which provides that 'The Union shall respect fundamental rights, as guaranteed by the European Convention of Human Rights and Fundamental Freedoms signed in Rome on 4th November 1950 and as they result from the constitutional traditions common to the member States as general principles of Community law.'

However, the fact that a particular principle is upheld by the Court and appears to be breached does not automatically lead to a decision in favour of the plaintiff. Fundamental rights are not absolute rights. As the Court pointed out in *J. Nold KG* v *Commission* (case 4/73), rights of this nature are always subject to limitations laid down in the public interest, and, in the Community context, limits justified by the overall objectives of the Community. They may not, however, constitute a 'disproportionate and intolerable interference, impairing the very substance of those rights' (*Wachauf* (case 5/88) at para. 18).

Thus, where the objectives are seen from the Community standpoint to be essential, individual rights must yield to the common good. In *J. Nold KG* v *Commission* the system set up under an ECSC provision whereby Nold, as a small-scale wholesaler, would be deprived of the opportunity, previously enjoyed, to buy direct from the producer, to its commercial disadvantage, was held to be necessary in the light of the system's overall economic objectives. 'The disadvantages claimed by the applicant', held the Court, 'are in fact the result of economic change and not of the contested Decision'.

A similar example is provided in *Walter Rau Lebensmittelwerke* v *Commission* (case 279, 280, 285 & 286/84), Article 215(2) proceedings. Here the plaintiffs were a group of margarine producers. They were seeking damages for losses suffered as a result of the Commission's 'Christmas butter' policy. This was an attempt to reduce the 'butter mountain' (surplus stocks acquired as a result of the Community's system of intervention buying under the common agricultural policy (CAP) by selling butter stocks at greatly reduced prices to certain groups of the population over the Christmas period. As a basis for their claim the plaintiffs alleged that the Regulations implementing the Christmas butter policy were in breach of the principles of equality and proportionality. Since margarine and butter are clearly in competition with each other it might have been imagined that, following the first isoglucose cases (e.g., *Royal Scholten-Honig Holdings Ltd* v *Intervention Board for Agricultural Produce* (cases 103 & 145/77), they had a good chance of success. But they failed. The Court held that the measure must be assessed with regard to the general objectives of the organisation of the butter market:

. . . taking into consideration the objective differences which characterised the legal mechanisms and the economic conditions of the market concerned, the producers of milk and butter on the one hand and the producers of oils and fats and margarine manufacturers on the other, are not in comparable situations.

The measures were no more than was necessary to achieve the desired objective.

This latitude shown to the Community institutions, particularly where they are exercising discretionary powers in pursuit of common Community policies (most notably the CAP) does not extend to member States in their implementation of Community law. Here general principles of law are strictly enforced. Thus under the guise of the protection of individual rights general principles of law can also serve as a useful (and concealed) instrument of policy.

Further reading

Akehurst, M., 'The Application of General Principles of Law by the Court of Justice of the European Communities', [1981] BYIL 29.
Arnull, A., 'The General Principles of EEC Law and the Individual', (1989) Leicester University Press.
Dallen, R. M. Jr, 'An Overview of EEC Protection of Human Rights' (1990) 27 CML Rev 761.

Dauses, M., 'The Protection of Fundamental Rights in the Community Legal Order', (1985) 10 EL Rev 398.

Jowell, J. and Lester, A., 'Beyond Wednesbury: Substantive Principles of Administrative Law', (1987) PL 368.

McBride, J., and Brown, N., 'The United Kingdom, the European Community and the European Convention on Human Rights', (1981) 1 YEL 167.

Mancini, G. F. 'The Making of a Constitution for Europe' (1989) 26 CML Rev 594.

Mendelson, M., 'The European Court of Justice and Human Rights', (1981) 1 YEL 126.

Schermers, H., 'The European Community Bound by Fundamental Human Rights' (1990) 27 CML Rev 249.

Schermers, H., 'The Scales in Balance: National Constitutional Court v Court of Justice' (1990) 27 CML Rev 97.

Schwartze, J., 'The Administrative Law of the Community and the Protection of Human Rights' (1986) 24 CML Rev 401.

Schwarze, J., 'The Tendency towards a Common Administrative Law in Europe' (1991) 16 EL Rev 3.

Sharpston, E., 'Legitimate Expectations and Economic Reality' (1990) 15 EL Rev 103.

Usher, J., 'The Influence of National Concepts on Decisions of the European Court', (1976) 1 EL Rev 359.

Weiler, J., 'Eurocracy and Distrust: Some Questions Concerning the Role of the European Court of Justice in the Protection of Fundamental Human Rights within the Legal Order of the European Communities', (1986) 61 Washington Law Rev 1103.

PART TWO

Economic and Social Law of the EEC: Aspects of The Internal Market

FIVE
Introduction

The law relating to the free movement of goods is one of the principal pillars of the Internal Market, defined in Article 8A of the EEC Treaty (renumbered 7a by the TEU) as:

> an area without internal frontiers in which the free movement of goods, persons, services and capital is ensured in accordance with the provisions of this Treaty.

The principle of freedom of movement of goods has been described as a fundamental freedom, the 'corner-stone' of the Community. The aim of the free movement provisions of the Treaty is to create within the member States of the Community a single market, free of all internal restrictions on trade, and presenting a common commercial front to the outside world. To this end the Treaty seeks:

(a)   To establish a *customs union* which shall involve (Article 9):
   (i)   'the prohibition between member States of customs duties on imports and exports and of all charges having equivalent effect', and
   (ii)   'the adoption of a common customs tariff in their relations with third countries'.

(b)   The elimination of quantitative restrictions on imports and exports and all measures having equivalent effect (Articles 30 and 34).

In addition States are required:

(c)   To adjust any State monopolies of a commercial character so as to ensure that . . . no discrimination regarding the conditions under which goods are procured and marketed exists between nationals of member States (Article 37).

The provisions relating to free movement of goods, contained in Part 2, Title I of the Treaty, apply to both industrial and agricultural products (save, where agriculture is concerned, as otherwise provided in Articles 39–46 (Article 38(2)), whether originating in member States or coming from third countries which are in free circulation in member States, even where, in the latter case, the goods have been admitted to the original State of import under special dispensation from the Commission under Article 115 (*Levy* (case 212/88) (1991) 1 CMLR 49). Products coming from third countries are regarded as in free circulation in a member State 'if the import formalities have been complied with and any customs duties or charges having equivalent effect which are payable have been levied in that member State, and if they have not benefited from a total or partial drawback of such duties or charges' (Article 10(1)).

Though the terms are used interchangeably, 'goods' and 'products' are not defined in the Treaty. They were interpreted by the Court of Justice in *Commission* v *Italy (re Export Tax on Art Treasures)* (case 7/68), Article 169 proceedings, as anything capable of money valuation and of being the object of commercial transactions. In *R* v *Thompson* (case 7/78), Article 177 proceedings, they were held to include collectors' coins in gold and silver, provided they were not coins in circulation as legal tender. In *Commission* v *Ireland Re Dundalk Water Supply* (case 45/87), Article 169 proceedings, the concept of goods was held to apply not only to the sale of goods per se but to goods and materials supplied in the context of the provision of services.

Although the free movement provisions are addressed to member States all the main Articles have been found to be directly effective and thus may be invoked by individuals, whether in dispute with the State or with another individual.

Because of the fundamental importance of the principle of free movement of goods the Treaty rules in this area have been strictly enforced, and exceptions, where provided, have been given the narrowest scope. In interpreting the rules the Court of Justice looks not to the name of a particular national measure, nor the motive for its introduction, but to its *effect* in the light of the aims of the Treaty; does it create an obstacle to the free movement of goods within the single internal market?

Interpreted in this way, as will be seen, Community law is capable of undermining national measures designed to achieve the most worthy objectives of national social, regional or economic policy. If these objectives are to be achieved without endangering the single market it must therefore be done through agreed action at Community level. This is one of the principal purposes of the extensive Community harmonisation programme to be completed by 31 December 1992.

Also relevant to the free movement provisions, although not contained in the free movement of goods section of the Treaty, are Article 95, which prohibits States from applying discriminatory taxation, and Article 92, which prohibits, subject to exceptions, the granting of State aids which threaten or distort competition. Thus EEC law comprises a whole network of provisions designed to prevent member States from enacting measures which hinder free trade and free competition within the single market.

SIX
Customs union

This is to be achieved by:

(a) the adoption of a common customs tariff towards third countries, and
(b) the prohibition between member States of customs duties on imports and exports and of all charges having equivalent effect (Article 9).

Common customs tariff

As part of its common commercial policy, and in order to ensure equal treatment in all member States for goods imported into the EEC from third countries, thereby enabling *all* goods in circulation within the Community to benefit equally from the free movement provisions, the Treaty provided for the introduction of the common customs tariff (CCT), sometimes known as the common external tariff (CET). The CCT applies to all products imported into the Community from outside the EEC, thus erecting a single tariff wall which no individual State is free to breach.

The operation of the CCT is governed by Articles 18–29. Products are divided into lists, the classifications being derived from the Brussels Convention on Nomenclature for the Classification of Goods. The lists, and the applicable tariff rates, are set out in Annexe I to the EEC Treaty. Tariffs are based on the arithmetical average of the duties applied in the four customs territories comprised in the Community on 1 Janaury 1957 (Article 19(1)). The CCT is published by the Commission and is regularly updated (see OJ L320, 10.12.84, p. 1). The Council, acting by qualified majority on a proposal from the Commission, is empowered to modify or suspend duties within certain limits (Article 28) or grant to individual member States tariff quotas at a reduced rate, or duty free, if production of a given product in the Community is insufficient and if the supply of that product in the State concerned traditionally depends on imports from third countries (Article 25). However, once goods are imported into the Community the free movement provisions of the Treaty apply. Even where goods are imported into a member State under a special tariff quota the Court of Justice has held that a State cannot deny the application of the free movement provisions to the import and export of such goods within the Community, unless the Commission has, under Article 115, authorised derogation in order to avoid a deflection of trade or economic difficulties in one or more member States (see *Donckerwolcke* (case 41/76) and note by J. Usher (1986) 11 EL Rev 210).

Thus the Commission, subject to the Council's approval, has a central role in establishing and administering the CCT. In carrying out its task it is required to balance a number of (often conflicting) economic needs set out in Article 29, in the light of the general aims of the Community.

Prohibition between member States of customs duties on imports and exports and of all charges of equivalent effect

This is governed by Articles 12–17. Article 12 is the 'standstill' provision, prohibiting the introduction of *new* customs duties or charges of equivalent effect on imports and exports; Articles 13–15 provide for the abolition of existing duties (or their equivalent) on *imports* within certain time-limits, known as the transitional period. For all States except Spain and Portugal that period has now expired, and these provisions, like Articles 9 and 12, will be directly effective. Article 16 provides for the abolition of such duties and charges on *exports*. Article 17 provides that Articles 9–15 are to apply to 'customs duties of a fiscal nature'.

The prohibition applies to all duties, whether applied directly or indirectly. In *Van Gend en Loos* (case 26/62), Article 177 proceedings, the product in question had been reclassified under Dutch law, with the result that it became subject to a higher rate of duty. The Court of Justice held that this would constitute a breach of Article 12.

If the meaning of 'custom duties' is clear, what are 'charges having equivalent effect' to a customs duty? It was held by the Court of Justice in the case of *Sociaal Fonds voor de Diamantarbeiders* (cases 2 & 3/69), Article 177 proceedings, in the context of a challenge to a 'tax' imposed on imported diamonds, that it included any pecuniary charge, however slight, imposed on goods by reason of the fact that they cross frontiers. The charge need not be levied at the frontier, as long as it is levied by reason of importation.

A charge of equivalent effect to a customs duty may come in many guises, and is often disguised as a 'tax'. Since genuine taxes fall to be considered under Article 95, it is necessary at the outset to distinguish between a charge, falling within Articles 9 and 12–16, and a genuine tax. A genuine tax was defined in *Commission* v *France, (Re Levy on Reprographic Machines)* (case 90/79), Article 169 proceedings, as one relating 'to a general system of internal dues applied systematically to categories of products in accordance with objective criteria irrespective of the origin of the products' ([1981] ECR 283 at p. 301). Thus to ascertain whether a 'tax' is genuine it must be examined to see whether it fits into an overall system of taxation or whether it has been superimposed on the system with a particular purpose in mind. Provided the tax is genuine, it may be imposed on imports even where the importing State produces no identical or similar product *(Commission* v *France)*. In such a case it will not breach Article 12 but may be examined for its compatibility with Article 95.

A charge, in order to breach Articles 12 et seq., need not be introduced for protectionist reasons. It was pointed out in the *Sociaal Fonds* case that there existed no diamond-mining industry in Belgium, and the proceeds of the charge were used for a most worthy purpose, to provide a social fund for workers in the diamond industry. These factors were held by the European Court to be irrelevant. Such duties are forbidden independently of the purpose for which they are levied and the destination of the charge. In reaching its decision the Court looked at the effect of the measure: any pecuniary charge imposed on goods by reason of the fact that they cross frontiers is an obstacle to the free movement of goods.

A similar conclusion was reached by the Court of Justice in *Commission* v *Luxembourg and Belgium (Re Import on Gingerbread)* (cases 2 & 3/62), Article 169 proceedings, in the context of a compensatory 'tax' on imported gingerbread. The governments claimed the 'tax' was introduced merely to compensate for the competitive disadvantage resulting from a high rate of domestic tax on rye, an ingredient of gingerbread. The purpose of the prohibition on measures of equivalent effect to customs duties, the Court held, was to prohibit not only measures ostensibly clothed with the classic nature of a customs duty but also those which, presented under other names or introduced by the indirect means of other procedures, would lead to the same discriminatory or protective *results* as customs duties. If compensatory 'taxes' of this type were allowed, States would be able to make up for all sorts of taxes at home by imposing a so-called balancing charge on imports. This would ensure that imported goods would lose any competitive advantage they might have as against the equivalent domestic product and thereby frustrate the objectives of the single market.

Even when the charge is levied in order to benefit the importer it may still breach Article 12. In *Commission* v *Italy, (Re Statistical Levy)* (case 24/68), Article 169 proceedings, a levy, applied to all imports and exports, regardless of source, the proceeds of which were used to finance an export statistical service for the benefit of importers and exporters, was found to be in breach of Articles 9–16. The Court of Justice held that the advantage to importers was so general and uncertain that it could not be considered a payment for service rendered (see also *W. Cadsky SpA* (case 63/74)).

This implies that a charge levied for a service rendered to the importer and which is not too general and uncertain would be permissible. This principle has, however, been given the narrowest possible scope. The Court of Justice has held that where an inspection service is imposed in the general interest, for example, for health or safety purposes, or quality control, this cannot be regarded as a service rendered to the importer or exporter to justify the imposition of a charge *(Rewe-Zentralfinanz eGmbH* v *Landwirtschaftskammer Westfalen-Lippe* (case 39/73), Article 177 proceedings). Even when such inspections are expressly *permitted* under EEC law, as in *Commission* v *Belgium (Re Health Inspection Service)* (case 314/82), Article 169 proceedings, the Court held that a charge for such a service cannot be regarded as a service rendered for the benefit of the importer. It is only when such services are mandatory, as part of a common Community regime, or arising from an international agreement into which the EEC has entered (*Bakker Hillegom* (case C 111/89)), that States are entitled to recover the cost, and no more than the cost, of the service *(Bauhuis* v *Netherlands State* (case 46/76), Article 177 proceedings).

Thus, unless a service is required under Community law, it appears that only a service which gives a tangible benefit to the importer, or the imported goods, for example, a finishing or packaging service, will be regarded as sufficient to justify a charge, and even then it will not be permissible if the 'service' is one imposed on the importer in the general interest. Where a genuine service is provided for the benefit of the importer the ECJ has held that the charge must not exceed the value or the cost of the service *(Rewe-Zentralfinanz eGmbH* (case 39/73)), or a sum proportionate to the service provided *(Commission* v *Denmark* (case 158/82)). A charge based on the value of the goods is not permissible *(Ford España SA* v *Spanish State* (case 170/88), Article 177 proceedings).

Where a charge is imposed only upon domestically produced goods, the ECJ appears to take a more lenient view. In *Apple & Pear Development Council* v *K. J. Lewis Ltd* (case 222/82), Article 177 proceedings, a number of growers challenged a compulsory levy imposed on growers of apples and pears in the UK. The proceeds of the levy went to finance the Apple and Pear Development Council, a semi-public body whose functions included research, the compilation of statistics, provision of information, publicity and promotion. The ECJ held that since the levy did not apply to imported products there was no breach of Articles 9–16. The charge would only be illegal if it served to finance activities which were incompatible with EEC law.

All the cases considered so far have concerned unilateral charges, charges imposed only upon imported or exported products and not on the comparable domestic product (or vice versa). Clearly such charges undermine the principle of free trade and free competition within the common market. What about a non-discriminatory charge, applied to a particular product regardless of source? Will this be capable of infringing Arts 9, 12–17? This calls for a more subtle enquiry into:

(a)   the nature of the charge and its mode of calculation, and
(b)   the destination of the charge, i.e., who receives the benefit.

Three situations may be considered:

(a)   If the charge is identical in every respect and levied as part of a general system of taxation it will not fall within Article 12 and will be treated as a fiscal measure, and examined for its compatibility with Article 95 (prohibition on discriminatory taxation).

(b)   If the same charge is levied on a particular product, regardless of source, it will nonetheless breach Article 12 if the charge on the imported or exported product is not imposed in the same way and determined according to the same criteria as apply to the domestic product. This point was made by the ECJ in *Marimex SpA* v *Italian Minister of Finance* (case 29/72), Article 177 proceedings, in the context of a challenge to a 'veterinary inspection tax' imposed on imported meat, live and dead, to ensure that it conformed to Italian health standards. Similar domestic products were subject to corresponding inspections which were also 'taxed', but they were conducted by different bodies according to different criteria. The ECJ, in a reference under Article 177, held that such a tax on imports would be in breach of Article 9.

(c) Even if the charge is levied at the same rate and according to identical criteria it may still breach Articles 9 and 12–17 if the proceeds of the charge are applied to benefit the domestic product exclusively. This point was first made in *Capolongo* v *Azienda Articola Maya* (case 77/72), Article 177 proceedings. In this case the Italians had introduced a charge on imported egg boxes, as part of an overall charge on cellulose products, the aim being to finance the production of paper and cardboard in Italy. Although the charge was imposed on all egg boxes, domestic and imported, the Court held it was in breach of Article 13. Although applied to domestic and imported goods alike, it was discriminatory if it was intended exclusively to support activities which specifically benefited the domestic product.

The scope of *Capolongo* was restricted in the subsequent case of *Fratelli Cucchi* v *Avez SpA* (case 77/76), Article 177 proceedings. Here a dispute arose concerning the legality of a levy on imported sugar. Domestically produced sugar was subject to the same levy. The proceeds of the levy went to finance the sugar industry, to benefit two groups, the beet producers and the sugar-processing industry. The ECJ held that such a charge would be of equivalent effect to a customs duty if three conditions were fulfilled:

(a)   if it has the *sole* purpose of financing activities for the specific advantage of the domestic product;

(b)   if the taxed domestic product and the domestic product to benefit are the same; and

(c)   if the charges imposed on the domestic product are made up *in full*.

If these conditions are not fulfilled the charge will not breach Articles 12–17. However, a grant to a particular industry may be adjudged a State aid in breach of Article 92 or, alternatively, discriminatory taxation in breach of Article 95 (see *Commission* v *Italy Re Reimbursement of Sugar Storage Costs* (case 73/79)).

Thus, the rules concerning charges of equivalent effect to a customs duty are strictly applied by the European Court. Indeed, in its anxiety to ensure that no pecuniary restriction, however small, shall create obstacles to trade, particularly to imports, the Court is even prepared to countenance a degree of reverse discrimination, since States are required themselves to finance measures such as health inspections which may be fully justified in the public interest (see *Rewe-Zentralfinanz eGmbH* (case 39/73). Nor does the Treaty or the Court provide for any exceptions in this field. In *Commission* v *Italy (Re Export Tax on Art Treasures)* (case 7/68), Article 169 proceedings, the Italians argued that the tax was justified in order to protect their artistic heritage. Under Article 36 States are entitled to derogate from the prohibition on imposing quantitative restrictions on imports (Article 30) or exports (Article 34), or measures of equivalent effect, on the grounds of *inter alia*, 'the protection of national treasures possessing artistic, historic or archaeological value'. The Court held that Article 36 could never be invoked to justify a charge (see also *Marimex SpA* (case 29/72)).

Since Articles 9 and 12 et seq. are directly effective, any sums paid under an illegal charge are recoverable. Although repayment must be sought within the framework, and according to the rules, of national law, conditions must not be so framed as to render virtually impossible the exercise of rights conferred by Community law (*SpA San Giorgio* (case 199/82)). The principle of unjust enrichment may be invoked to deny a claim for repayment where the charge has been incorporated into the price of goods and passed on to purchasers (*SpA San Giorgio*). However, national authorities may not impose the burden of proving that a charge has *not* been passed on to those persons seeking reimbursement, nor may restrictive or onerous evidential requirements (such as documentary evidence alone) be imposed. Member States are not entitled to presume that illegal taxes have been passed on (*Commission* v *Italy Re Repayment of Illegal Taxes* (case 104/86)).

SEVEN

Prohibition of discriminatory taxation (Article 95)

Although the prohibition of discriminatory taxation is contained in the tax provisions of the Treaty (Part Three, Title I, Chapter 2), Article 95 may best be considered in the context of the free movement of goods, in particular Articles 9 and 12. In examining those provisions it was pointed out that the Court draws a distinction between a charge having equivalent effect to a customs duty and a genuine tax. A genuine tax is a measure relating to a system of internal dues applied systematically to categories of products in accordance with objective criteria irrespective of the origin of the products *(Commission* v *France (Re Levy on Reprographic Machines)* (case 90/79), Article 169 proceedings). Even what may appear a genuine tax may be treated as a charge if it is earmarked to benefit only the domestic product subject to the tax (see *Fratelli Cucchi* v *Avez SpA* (case 77/76), Article 177 proceedings).

Since the line between a charge and a genuine tax may be hard to draw, and since the Court has held *(Fratelli Cucchi* v *Avez SpA)* that the prohibition of customs duties and charges having equivalent effect and of discriminatory internal taxation are mutually exclusive, it is safer in case of doubt to invoke both Article 12 and Article 95 and leave the Court to define the boundaries.

A 'genuine' tax must comply with Article 95. Article 95 provides that:

No member State shall impose, directly or indirectly, on the products of other member States any internal taxation of any kind in excess of that imposed directly or indirectly on similar domestic products.

Furthermore, no member State shall impose on the products of other member States any internal taxation of such a nature as to afford indirect protection to other products.

Thus while States are free to decide on the rate of taxation to be applied to a particular product they are not free to apply rates which discriminate as between the domestic and imported product or which afford indirect protection to the former.

The Court has held that internal tax may be imposed on imported products even if there is no domestic production of a similar or competing product as long as it applies to the product as a class, irrespective of origin *(Fink-Frucht GmbH* (case 27/67), Article 177 proceedings, applied in *Commission v France* (case 90/79)). However, if in this case the 'tax' is set at such a level as to compromise the free circulation of trade within the Community it cannot be deemed part of a general system of taxation (*Commission v Denmark* (case C 47/88)). It may, however, fall within other provisions of the Treaty.

In assessing the question of discrimination account must be taken of the basis of assessment of the tax and the detailed rules for its collection, and it may be necessary to have regard to taxation levied at earlier stages of manufacture and marketing (*Molkerei-Zentrale Westfalen/Lippe GmbH* (case 28/67)).

Although Article 95 is expressed as applying to the 'products of other member States', the Court has held (*Cooperative Co-Frutta SLR v Amministrazione Delle Finanze dello Stato* (case 193/85)), arguing from *Donckerwolcke v Procureur de la République* (case 41/76), that the prohibition of discriminatory taxation must apply, by analogy with the free movement of goods provisions, to goods from third countries in free circulation within the member States.

'Similar' products

It is clear that products need not be identical to fall within Article 95. What then is a 'similar' product? In the course of a number of judgments, mostly infringement proceedings against member States under Article 169 (see chapter 25), in respect of allegedly discriminatory taxation of alcoholic drinks (e.g., *Commission v France (Re French Taxation of Spirits)*, (case 168/78)) the Court has held that 'similar' must be interpreted widely; similar products are those which meet the same needs from the point of view of consumers, and which are, broadly, in competition with each other. The concept is analogous to that of the relevant product market in competition law (see chapter 14).

In assessing the question of competition the Court has held (*Commission v UK (Re Excise Duties on Wine)* (case 170/78), Article 177 (interlocutory) proceedings) that it is necessary to look not only at the present state of the market but also possible developments, i.e., the possibility of substituting one product for another. Taxation policy must not be allowed to crystallise consumer habits. Thus beer and wine, which were subject to different rates of tax in the UK (not surprisingly wine being more highly taxed!) might be regarded as 'similar' products. In its final judgment in this case [1983] 3 CMLR 512 the Court held that the decisive competitive relationship was between beer and the more 'accessible' wines, i.e., the lightest and cheapest varieties. The increasing popularity of wine bars in the UK over recent years testifies to the change in consumer habits anticipated by the Court.

Different rates of taxation may, however, be applied to what appear to be 'similar' products provided they are based on objective criteria, designed to achieve economic policy objectives which are compatible with EEC law, and are applied in such a way as to avoid discrimination against imports or afford indirect protection to domestic products. This reasoning was applied in

Commission v *France* (case 196/85) in the context of infringement proceedings in respect of a system of differential taxation in which certain wines known as natural sweet wines or liqueur wines, production of which is 'traditional or customary', attracted more favourable tax rates than ordinary wine. The purpose of the special rate was to bolster the economy in areas largely dependent on the production of these wines, to compensate for the relatively rigorous conditions under which they are produced. The Court found the economic policy objectives pursued by the French to be justified. Such rules, it said, may not be regarded as contrary to Community law merely because they may be applied in a discriminatory manner if it is not proved that they have in fact been applied in such a manner. Clearly in this case it felt that neither discrimination nor protectionist motives had been proved.

Taxation affording indirect protection to domestic products

Article 95, para. 2, may render it unnecessary to decide whether the products in question are 'similar'. Internal taxation will be contrary to Article 95 if it affords indirect protection to domestic products. This will be the case if the system of taxation imposes a heavier burden on an imported product than on a domestic product with which it is in competition by reason of one or more economic uses to which it is put (*Fink-Frucht GmbH* (case 27/67)). A number of the alcohol cases were decided on the basis of this paragraph, since in many cases, for example, *Commission* v *France* (case 168/78) (high rate of tax on spirits, low rate on wine), the different rates of taxation were clearly designed to boost the domestic product at the expense of the imported one.

EIGHT

Elimination of quantitative restrictions on imports and exports and all measures having equivalent effect (Articles 30–4)

The abolition of customs duties and charges of equivalent effect alone would not have been sufficient to guarantee the free movement of goods within the common market. In addition to pecuniary restrictions there are other barriers to trade of a non-pecuniary nature, usually in the form of administrative rules and practices, protectionist and otherwise, equally capable of hindering the free flow of goods from State to State. Articles 30–4 are designed to eliminate these barriers.

As will be apparent, Articles 30–4 cover a much wider range of measures than Articles 9 and 12–16, but unlike these latter articles provision is made for derogation under Article 36.

The principle provisions are:

(a)   Article 30, which prohibits quantitative restrictions, and all measures having equivalent effect, on *imports*.
(b)   Article 34, which contains a similar prohibition on *exports*.
(c)   Articles 31–3 which provide for the gradual abolition of import restrictions during the transitional period.

Article 36 provides that the prohibitions in Articles 30–4 will not apply to restrictions on imports and exports which are *justified* on a number of specified grounds.

These Articles are addressed to, and relate to measures taken by, member States. However, 'measures taken by member States' have been interpreted in the widest sense to include the activities of any public body, legislative, executive or judicial, or even semi-public body, such as a quango, exercising powers derived from public law (e.g., *Apple & Pear Development Council* v *K.*

J. Lewis Ltd (case 222/82)). In *R* v *Royal Pharmaceutical Society of Great Britain* (cases 266, 267/87) the Court held that measures adopted by professional bodies, such as the Royal Pharmaceutical Society, on which national legislation has conferred regulatory or disciplinary powers were 'measures taken by member States' subject to Article 30. Nor need the 'measures' concerned be binding measures. This was expressly provided by the Commission in the preamble to its Directive 70/50, and confirmed by the ECJ in *Commission* v *Ireland (Re 'Buy Irish' Campaign)* (case 249/81), Article 169 proceedings. In this case certain activities of the Irish Goods Council, a government-sponsored body charged with promoting Irish goods by, *inter alia*, advertising, principally on the basis of their Irish origin, were held to be in breach of Article 30. Even though no binding measures were involved, the Board's actions were capable of influencing the behaviour of traders and thereby frustrating the aims of the Community.

Although Articles 30–4 are addressed to member States, neither Community institutions nor individuals are free to act in breach of these articles. However, Community institutions may derogate from these provisions where they are expressly authorised to do so by other provisions of the Treaty, for example in implementing the common agricultural policy (Articles 39–46) *(Rewe Zentrale AG* v *Direktor der Landwirtschaftskammer Rheinland* (case 37/83)). But even where a particular activity falls within other provisions of the Treaty, such as the 'Services' provisions, it may still fall foul of Article 30 *(Commission* v *Ireland Re Dundalk Water Supply* (case 45/87); requirement that pipes required under a contract for the supply of services must comply with Irish specifications held in breach of Article 30).

Prohibition, as between member States, of quantitative restrictions on IMPORTS and of all measures having equivalent effect (Article 30)

The prohibition is twofold, embracing:

(a) quantitative restrictions, and
(b) measures of equivalent effect to quantitative restrictions.

Quantitative restrictions   These were interpreted in *Riseria Luigi Geddo* v *Ente Nazionale Risi* (case 2/73) as any measures which amount to a total or partial restraint on imports, exports or goods in transit. They would clearly include a ban, as was found to be the case in *Commission* v *Italy (Re Ban on Pork Imports)* (case 7/61), Article 169 proceedings, and *R* v *Henn and Darby* (ban on import of pornographic materials) (case 34/79), Article 177 proceedings. They would also include a quota system, as in *Salgoil SpA* v *Italian Minister of Foreign Trade* (case 13/68), Article 177 proceedings.

A covert quota system might operate by means of an import (or export) licence requirement. A licensing system might in itself amount to a quantitative restriction, or, alternatively, a measure of equivalent effect to a quantitative restriction. It was held in *International Fruit Co. NV* v *Produktschap voor*

Groenten en Fruit (cases 51–4/71) that even if the granting of a licence were a pure formality the requirement of such a licence to import would amount to a breach of Article 30. In that case it was deemed to be a measure of equivalent effect to a quantitative restriction.

Measures having equivalent effect to quantitative restrictions   The concept of measures having equivalent effect to quantitative restrictions is altogether wider in scope than that of quantitative restrictions, and has few equivalents in other trade treaties. Perhaps to the surprise of member States, it has been interpreted very generously by both the Commission and the Court, to include not merely overtly protective measures or measures applicable only to imports or exports ('distinctly applicable' measures), but measures applicable to imports (or exports) and domestic goods alike ('indistinctly applicable' measures), often introduced (seemingly) for the most worthy purpose. Such measures range from regulatory measures designed to enforce minimum standards, for example, of size, weight, quality, price or content, to tests and inspections or certification requirements to ensure that goods conform to these standards, to any activity capable of influencing the behaviour of traders such as promoting goods by reason of their national origin, as was the case in *Apple & Pear Development Council* v *K.J. Lewis Ltd* (case 222/82) and *Commission* v *Ireland (Re 'Buy Irish' Campaign)* (case 249/81).

To offer States guidance as to the meaning and scope of 'measures having equivalent effect' to quantitative restrictions, the Commission passed Directive 70/50. Although passed under Article 33(7) and therefore applicable only to measures to be abolished during the transitional period, it has been suggested that the Directive may still serve to provide non-binding guidelines to the interpretation of Article 30. Article 2(3) of the Directive provides a non-exhaustive list of measures capable of having equivalent effect to quantitative restrictions. These are divided into:

(a)   'measures, *other than those applicable equally to domestic or imported products*', i.e., 'distinctly applicable' measures, 'which hinder imports which could otherwise take place, including measures which make importation more difficult or costly than the disposal of domestic production' (Article 2(1)), and

(b)   measures *'which are equally applicable to domestic and imported products'*, i.e., 'indistinctly applicable' measures (Article 3). These measures are only contrary to Article 30 'where the restrictive effect of such measures on the free movement of goods exceeds the effects intrinsic to trade rules', that is where 'the restrictive effects on the free movement of goods are out of proportion to their purpose', or where 'the same objective cannot be attained by other measures which are less of a hindrance to trade' (Article 3). Thus, indistinctly applicable rules appear to be acceptable provided that they comply with the principle of proportionality.

The Court of Justice, in 1974, in the case of *Procureur du Roi* v *Dassonville* (case 8/74), Article 177 proceedings, introduced its own definition of measures having equivalent effect to quantitative restrictions. This definition, now known as the *'Dassonville* formula', has since been applied consistently, almost verbatim, by the Court. According to the formula:;

> All trading rules enacted by member States which are capable of hindering, directly or indirectly, actually or potentially, intra-Community trade are to be considered as measures having an effect equivalent to quantitative restrictions.

Thus it is not necessary to show an actual hindrance to trade between member States as long as the measure is capable of such effects. Unlike the competition provisions of Articles 85 and 86, which require an *'appreciable effect'* on trade and competition between member States, the Court has held that Article 30 is not subject to a *de minimis* rule (*Van de Haar* (case 177/82)). It does, however, require proof of a *hindrance* to trade. A measure which is not capable of hindering trade between member States, which merely affects the flow of trade *within* a member State, will not breach Article 30. In *Oebel* (case 155/80) a Belgian law banning the production and delivery to consumers and retail outlets of bakery products during the night hours, designed to protect workers in small and medium-sized bakeries, was held not to breach Article 30, because, although delivery of imported products through some outlets was precluded, 'trade within the Community remained possible at all times' (see also *Blesgen* (case 75/81)). In *Quietlynne Ltd* v *Southend Borough Council* (case C 23/89) a licensing requirement for the sale of sex appliances by sex shops was held not to breach Article 30, since the goods in question, which included imported goods, 'could be marketed through other channels'. However, the case law of the Court has not been consistent on this point. In *Torfaen Borough Council* v *B & Q plc* (case 145/88) the Court found that a ban on Sunday trading in England and Wales under the Shops Act 1950, the effect of which was to restrict the volume of imports to the shops trading in breach of the rules, was prima facie contrary to Article 30, even though alternative outlets for the sale of these goods existed during the working week (see also *Conforama* (case C 312/89) and *Marchandise* (case C 332/89), to be discussed later).

A measure falling within the *Dassonville* formula but which operates solely to the disadvantage of domestic production will not fall foul of Community law. The ban in Oebel on the production of bakery products during the night, which prevented Belgian bakers from benefiting from the early morning trade in adjacent member states, was found not to breach Articles 7, 30 or 34. The Court held that it was not contrary to Article 7 (principle of non-discrimination on grounds of nationality) for States to apply national rules where other States apply less strict rules to similar products.

The Court took the same view of a Dutch regulation concerning the permitted ingredients of cheese, which was only applicable to cheese produced in Holland (*Jongeneel Kaas BV* v *Netherlands* (case 237/82)) and of a French law requiring French retailers to adhere to a minimum selling price for books, provided it was not applied to books which, having been exported, were reimported into France *(Association des Centres Distributeurs Édouard Leclerc* v *'Au Blé Vert' Sàrl* (case 229/83)). In this respect, as in other areas (e.g., free movement of workers), the Court is prepared to accept a measure of reverse discrimination. Whilst member States must be compelled, in the interests of the common market, not to discriminate against, or in any way prejudice, imports, it seems that they may be safely left to act themselves in order to protect their own interests. There is now a consistent line of authority from the ECJ to this effect.

The measure in issue in *Dassonville* was a requirement, under Belgian law, that imported goods should carry a certificate of origin issued by the State in which the goods were manufactured. Dassonville imported a consignment of Scotch whisky from France. Since the seller was unable to supply the required certificate he attached a home-made certificate of origin to the goods and appeared before the Belgian court on a forgery charge. In his defence, he claimed that the Belgian regulation was contrary to EEC law. On a reference from the Belgian court under Article 177, the ECJ, applying the *Dassonville* formula, found the measure was capable of breaching Article 30.

In the cases of *Tasca* (case 65/75), Article 177 proceedings, and *Van Tiggele* (case 82/77), Article 177 proceedings, the *Dassonville* test was applied in the context of a domestic law imposing maximum and minimum selling prices respectively. The laws were indistinctly applicable. In both cases the issue of Article 30 arose in criminal proceedings against the defendants for breach of these laws. Tasca was accused in Italy of selling sugar above the permitted national maximum price; Van Tiggele in Holland of selling gin below the national minimum price. Both pleaded that the measures were in breach of EEC law. Applying the *Dassonville* test the ECJ found that both measures were capable of breaching Article 30. Regarding the maximum price the Court held a maximum price does not in itself constitute a measure equivalent in effect to a quantitative restriction. It becomes so when fixed at a level such that the sale of imported products becomes if not impossible more difficult. The maximum price in *Tasca* could have that effect, in that importers of more highly priced goods might have to cut their profit margins or even be forced to sell at a loss. In *Van Tiggele* the minimum price also acted as a hindrance to imports, since it would prevent the (possibly) lower price of imported goods from being reflected in the retail selling price. The Court suggested, however, that a prohibition on selling below cost price, or a minimum profit margin, would be acceptable, since it would have no adverse effect on trade between member States (principle applied in *Commission* v *Italy* (*Re Fixing of Trading Margins*) (case 78/82)).

In applying the *Dassonville* formula in these three cases, the Court did not distinguish between distinctly and indistinctly applicable measures, and ignored the proportionality test laid down for the latter in Directive 70/50. The breadth of the formula, especially when applied 'mechanically', looking to the *effect* of the measure on intra-Community trade rather than to the question of *hindrance*, bore harshly on member States, particularly where the measure was indistinctly applicable and might be justified as in the public interest.

Perhaps taking heed of criticisms on this account, the Court took a decisive step in the case of *'Cassis de Dijon' (Rewe-Zentral AG v Bundesmonopolverwaltung für Branntwein* (case 120/78), Article 177 proceedings), and paved the way for a distinction between distinctly and indistinctly applicable measures. The question before the ECJ in *Cassis* concerned the legality under EEC law of a German law laying down a minimum alcohol level of 25% for certain spirits, which included cassis, a blackcurrant-flavoured liqueur. German cassis complied with this minimum, but French cassis, with an alcohol content of 15–20%, did not. Thus although the German regulation was indistinctly applicable, the result of the measure was effectively to ban French cassis from the German market. A number of German importers contested the measure, and the German court referred a number of questions to the ECJ under Article 177.

The ECJ applied the *Dassonville* formula, but went on to add that:

> Obstacles to movement within the Community resulting from disparities between the national laws relating to the marketing of the products in question must be accepted in so far as those provisions may be recognised as being necessary in order to satisfy mandatory requirements relating in particular to the effectiveness of fiscal supervision, the protection of public health, the fairness of commercial transactions and the defence of the consumer.

This principle ('the first *Cassis* principle'), that certain measures, though within the *Dassonville* formula, will not breach Article 30 if they are necessary to satisfy mandatory requirements, has come to be known as the 'rule of reason', a concept borrowed from American anti-trust law and occasionally applied in EEC competition law (see chapter 13).

Prior to *Cassis*, it was assumed that any measure falling within the *Dassonville* formula would breach Article 30 and could be justified only on the grounds provided by Article 36. Since *Cassis*, at least where indistinctly applicable measures are concerned, courts may apply a rule of reason to Article 30. If the measure is necessary in order to protect mandatory requirements, it will not breach Article 30 at all. Distinctly applicable measures on the other hand will normally breach Article 30, but may be justified under Article 36.

This distinction is significant, since the mandatory requirements permitted under *Cassis* are wider than the grounds provided under Article 36, and, unlike Article 36, are non-exhaustive. In *Oebel* (case 155/80) it was not disputed that the improvement of working conditions could constitute a mandatory requirement, although it was not necessary to the judgment, since the Court found the rules in any case compatible with Article 30. In *Cinéthèque SA* (cases 60 & 61/84), Article 177 proceedings, Advocate-General Slynn suggested — in the context of a non-discriminatory French law prohibiting the marketing of videograms of films within 12 months of first showing, designed to protect the cinema industry — that cultural activities could constitute a mandatory requirement. Without expressly endorsing that statement the Court found that the rule, designed to encourage the creation of cinematographic works, was justified on *Cassis* principles and did not breach Article 30. In *Commission* v *Denmark (re disposable Beer Cans)* (case 302/86) the protection of the environment was held to constitute a mandatory requirement, and in *Torfaen*

Borough Council v *B & Q plc* (case 145/88) measures such as the English and Welsh Sunday trading rules, designed to protect 'national or regional socio-cultural characteristics' were held to be justifiable under the rule of reason. The Court of Justice has, however, refused to contemplate a justification based on purely economic grounds (see *Duphar BV* v *Netherlands* (case 238/82), Article 177 proceedings).

It should be noted that the rule of reason as laid down in *Cassis* was not in terms confined to indistinctly applicable measures. Although shortly after *Cassis* in *Gilli and Andres* (Italian cider vinegar case) (case 788/79), Article 177 proceedings, the Court suggested (para. 14) that the principle applied only where national rules apply *without discrimination* to both domestic and imported products, it has not insisted on this distinction, and, perhaps because the line between the two is not always clear, has not infrequently considered the question of justification of indistinctly applicable measures not on *Cassis* principles but under Article 36 (see *Sandoz BV* (case 174/82)). There appear to be two possible reasons for this approach: in some cases the Court is merely responding to questions submitted by national courts under Article 177; in others, where the 'mandatory requirement' falls under one of the specific heads of derogation provided by Article 36, the Court may prefer to rely on the express provisions of that Article (see e.g. *Commission* v *Germany Re German Sausages* (case 274/87) (health justification)).

In applying the rule of reason to the facts in *Cassis* the Court found that the German law was in breach of Article 30. Although the measure fell within the categories suggested, being allegedly enacted in the interests of public health (to prevent increased consumption resulting from lowering the alcoholic content of cassis) and the fairness of commercial transactions (to avoid giving the weak imported cassis an unfair advantage over its stronger, hence more expensive, German rival), the measure was not *necessary* to achieve these ends. Other means, such as labelling, which would have been less of a hindrance to trade, could have been used to achieve the same ends. Thus the word 'necessary' has been interpreted to mean no more than is necessary, i.e., subject to the principle of proportionality. With *Cassis* the Court of Justice appears finally to have fallen in line with Directive 70/50.

The Court established a second important principle in *Cassis* ('the second *Cassis* principle'). It suggested that there was no valid reason why 'provided that [goods] have been lawfully produced and marketed in one of the member States, [they] should not be introduced into any other member State' (para. 14).

Is this not in conflict with its *first* principle, the rule of reason? It is submitted that it is not. It merely gives rise to a presumption that goods which have been lawfully marketed in another State will comply with the 'mandatory requirements' of the importing State. This can be rebutted by evidence that further measures are *necessary* to protect the interest concerned.

That presumption will however be hard to rebut; the burden of proving that a measure is necessary is a heavy one, particularly when, although justifiable in principle, it clearly operates as a hindrance to intra-Community trade. Although in theory it is for national courts to *apply* the proportionality principle, the Court of Justice, in interpreting Community law in the light of the relevant national rules, and offering guidance to national courts on its application, has applied the proportionality principle rigorously, excluding all measures that go beyond what is strictly necessary to achieve the desired end. In *Walter Rau Lebensmittelwerke* v *De Smedt PVBA* (case 261/81) a Belgian law requiring margarine to be packed in cube-shaped boxes, allegedly introduced in the interests of consumers, to enable them to distinguish margarine from butter, was held to be in breach of Article 30. The same objective could have been achieved by other means, such as labelling, which would be less of a hindrance to trade. Similar arguments have been used successfully to challenge national rules, allegedly in the interest of public health and consumer protection, concerning the permitted ingredients of pasta (*Drei Glöcken* (case 407/85)) and sausages (*Commission* v *Germany* (case 274/87)).

In *Prantl* (case 16/83), Article 177 proceedings, Article 30 was invoked in the context of criminal proceedings against Prantl for breach of a German law designed to prevent unfair competition. He had imported wine from Italy in bulbous-shaped bottles which closely resembled a German bottle known as a 'Bocksbeutel'. The *Bocksbeutel* was protected under German law as denoting a quality wine from a particular region of Germany. The Italian bottle was a bottle traditional to Italy. Although the measure was arguably justifiable under *Cassis* in the interests of fair trading ('the fairness of commercial transactions') and consumer protection, the Court held that as long as the Italian wine was in accord with fair and traditional practice in its State of origin there was no justification for its exclusion from Germany.

Similarly in *Miro BV* (case 182/84), Article 177 proceedings, it was held that a generic name such as *'jenever'*, reserved in Holland for gin with a minimum alcohol content of 35%, could not be restricted to one national variety provided the imported product, in this case Belgian *jenever*, with a 30% alcohol content, had been lawfully produced and marketed in the exporting State. This was despite the fact that Dutch *jenever* was subject to a higher rate of tax because of its high alcohol content and would be at a competititve disadvantage *vis-à-vis* the imported product. (See also *Ministre Public* v *Deserbais* (case 286/86) re minimum fat content for Edam cheese.)

It seems moreover that where a defence is based on the rule of reason the genuineness of the justification proffered by member States will be closely scrutinised by the Court in the light of existing knowledge. In a case concerning the German beer purity laws, *Commission* v *Germany* (case 178/84), Article 169 proceedings, the Court held, in the context of a ban in Germany on the use of additives in beer, that the use of a certain additive, permitted in another member State, must be authorised for a product imported from that State where, having regard to the results of international scientific research, in particular the work of the FAO (Food and Agriculture Organisation) and WHO (World Health Organisation), and to eating habits in the member State of importation, that additive does not constitute a danger to public health and it meets a real need, in particular a technological need. States wishing to prove their standards are necessary must prove that those of the State from which the goods are imported are inadequate.

In this case, although the drinking habits of the German population might have justified a selective exclusion of certain additives the exclusion of all additives was found on the evidence to be disproportionate.

By comparison, in the earlier case of *Sandoz BV* (case 174/82), Article 177 proceedings, the existing state of scientific knowledge was not such as to undermine a justification for a measure prohibiting, on public health grounds, the use of certain vitamin additives in food without prior authority. Provided the national authorities could prove a 'real need' for the measure, it would be permitted under Article 36.

The extent to which member States are now limited, in the interests of the single market, in their ability to introduce indistinctly applicable and seemingly justifiable measures is illustrated by the case of *Commission v UK (Re Origin Marking of Retail Goods)* (case 207/83), Article 169 proceedings. Here the Commission claimed that a British regulation requiring certain goods (e.g., clothing, textiles) sold retail to indicate their country of origin was in breach of Article 30. The British government argued that the measure was justified on *Cassis* principles in the interest of consumers, who regarded the origin of goods as an indication of their quality. The Court refused to accept this argument. It held that the regulation merely enabled consumers to assert their prejudices, thereby slowing down the economic interpenetration of the Community. The quality of goods could as well be indicated on the goods themselves or their packaging, and the protection of consumers sufficiently guaranteed by rules which enabled the use of false indications of origin to be prohibited. Whilst manufacturers remained free to indicate their own national origin it was not necessary to compel them to do so. The regulation was in breach of Article 30.

Problems arising from the rule of reason

Although the rule of reason has allowed States a welcome latitude to enact or maintain indistinctly applicable measures which are capable of hindering trade between member States in order to protect important national interests, the rule has not been without its problems. Principally it has encouraged a lax, 'mechanical' application of the *Dassonville* formula, requiring measures which might affect the volume of imports overall, but with little potential to *hinder* imports, to be justified under the rule of reason. Defence lawyers in member States have been quick to exploit the 'Euro-defence' of Article 30 to charges involving a wide range of regulatory offences. Examples of such defences include challenges to Dutch laws restricting the use of free gifts for promotional purposes (*Oosthoek's Uitgeversmaatschappij BV* (case 286/81)); to French laws prohibiting the door-to-door selling of educational materials (*Buet v Ministère Public* (case 382/87)); to English laws requiring the licensing of sex shops for the sale of sexual appliances (*Quietlynn Ltd v Southend Borough Council* (case C 23/89)); and a number of cases such as *Torfaen Borough Council v B & Q plc* (case 145/88) pleading the illegality under Article 30 of the Sunday trading rules. The latter cases particularly have drawn criticism, as representing an 'abuse' of EEC law. The defendant shops have been accused of deliberately protracting legal proceedings by invoking Article 30 in order to buy lucrative Sunday trading time, to the detriment of their smaller more 'law-abiding' rivals. In *Torfaen Borough Council* v *B & Q plc*, the Court of Justice had held that the rules in question might be justified to ensure that working hours be arranged to accord with 'national or regional socio-cultural characteristics', and directed the referring magistrates' court to examine the rules in the light of their proportionality. Unfortunately the precise grounds of justification permitted to protect such socio-cultural characteristics were not spelt out; nor was any guidance offered on the question of proportionality. Thus different British courts in different cases came to different conclusions. Courts which concluded that the socio-cultural purpose of the rules was to protect workers who did not want to work on Sunday not surprisingly concluded that the rules were disproportionate (e.g., *B & Q Ltd* v *Shrewsbury & Atcham Borough Council* [1990] 3 CMLR 535); those which saw the rules as designed to 'preserve the traditional character of the British Sunday' legitimately concluded otherwise: the rules were not more than was necessary to achieve that end (e.g., *Wellingborough Borough Council* v *Payless DIY Ltd* [1990] 1 CMLR 773). Despite a clear ruling from the Court in two cases subsequent to *Torfaen Borough Council* v *B & Q plc* (*Conforama* (case C 312/89); *Marchandise* (case C 332/89)) that similar rules would be permissible under the rule of reason the question of the legality of the English Sunday trading rules has yet to be conclusively decided, and awaits a further ruling from the European Court in 1992 (*Stoke-on-Trent City Council* v *B & Q plc* referred by the House of Lords in May 1991).

It has been suggested (see articles by White, Mortelmans, Steiner) that the Court should adopt a new, more rigorous approach to Article 30, and distinguish between those national measures which pose a real threat to the single market, such as the German beer purity laws (case 178/84), which require justification under the rule of reason, and those which do not. As Advocate-General Van Gerven pointed out in *Torfaen Borough Council* v *B & Q plc*, national courts are 'having to decide in an increasing number of cases on the reasonableness (i.e. proportionality) of policy decisions of member States in innumerable spheres where there is no question of direct or indirect, factual or legal, discrimination against imported products'. Clearly measures which make importation of a particular product more difficult or costly or burdensome or, *a fortiori*, impossible will breach Article 30, and require justification, as will rules which clearly deter imports, such as the restrictions on the sale of video recordings in *Cinéthèque* (cases 60 & 61/84). But measures such as the Sunday trading rules, which simply restrict the volume of imports, as they restrict the volume of sales of domestic goods, *by certain undertakings,* arguably should not require justification under the rule of reason.

One solution would lie in a less 'mechanical' application of the *Dassonville* rule. In order to raise a prima facie case of breach of Article 30 a clear *hindrance* to imports of the products in question should be proved. Where a national measure requires justification under the rule of reason it is to be hoped that the Court of Justice will give clear guidance both on the grounds for justification and their proportionality, as it did in *Cassis*.

These problems apart, *Cassis* remains a landmark judgment. Its twin principles formed the basis for the Commission's new approach to the freeing of the internal market within the 31 December 1992 deadline, outlined in its White Paper of 1985. Relying on the presumption that goods lawfully marketed in one State are to be freely admitted into other member States, the Commission proposed henceforth to concentrate its efforts on harmonisation measures designed to provide *essential* guarantees to safeguard the 'mandatory requirements' of member States. As a result of this new approach, and greatly assisted by the change from unanimity to qualified majority voting under Article 100A EEC, introduced by the Single European Act 1986, a large number of measures in the field of health and safety and environmental and consumer protection have been adopted in this area in recent years. These areas were expressly incorporated into the EEC Treaty by the Single European Act.

Prohibition, as between member States, of quantitative restrictions on EXPORTS and of all measures having equivalent effect (Article 34)

All the principles relating to imports under Article 30 will also apply to exports under Article 34, with one important exception. Measures which are *indistinctly applicable* will not breach Article 34 merely because they are capable of hindering, directly or indirectly, actually or potentially, intra-Community trade. The *Dassonville* test does not apply. To breach Article 34 such measures must have as their specific object or effect the restriction of patterns of exports and thereby the establishment of a difference in treatment between the domestic trade of a member State and its export trade in such a way as to provide a particular advantage for national production or for the domestic market of the State in question, at the expense of the production or of the trade of other member States. In other words, they must be overtly or covertly protectionist.

This principle was established in *P. B. Groenveld BV* (case 15/79), Article 177 proceedings. Here, a ban on the possession of horse meat by manufacturers of meat products, designed to safeguard exports of such products to countries which prohibit the sale of horseflesh, was found, applying the above test, not to breach Article 34, although, as Advocate-General Capotorti pointed out, it presented an almost insuperable obstacle to exports. The Court's judgment represented a clear departure from the opinion of the Advocate-General. He had approached the matter along the lines of Article 30; he applied the *Dassonville* test, and *Cassis,* and found that the measure was not justified since other, less restrictive measures, such as labelling, could have been used to achieve the same ends.

In *Oebel* (case 155/80), Article 177 proceedings, the restriction on night working and delivery hours for bakery products, although undoubtedly a barrier to exports, since it precluded Belgian bakers from selling bread in adjacent member States in time for breakfast, was found, following *P. B. Groenveld BV,* not to breach Article 34.

On the other hand measures which are *distinctly applicable* and which discriminate against exports *will* be subject to the *Dassonville* test, and will normally breach Article 34. In *Bouhelier* (case 53/76), Article 177 proceedings, the requirement in France of an export licence, following a quality inspection, for watches destined for export was held to breach Article 34 since the same inspection and licences were not required for watches sold on the domestic market.

The principles of both *P. B. Groenveld BV* and *Bouhelier* were applied in *Jongeneel Kaas BV* (case 237/82), Article 177 proceedings. Here Dutch rules, indistinctly applicable, regulating the quality and content of cheese produced in the Netherlands were found not to breach Article 34, even though domestic producers were thereby at a competitive disadvantage *vis-à-vis* producers from other States not bound by the same standard of quality, since they did not fall within the *P. B. Groenveld BV* criteria, whereas a distinctly applicable rule requiring inspection documents for exports alone was, following *Bouhelier,* in breach of Article 34.

This tolerance towards indistinctly applicable, non-protective restrictions on exports introduced in *P. B. Groenveld BV* is in line with the Court's attitude, noted above, towards reverse discrimination. Clearly where there is no danger of protectionism the Court can afford to take a more lenient view. Restrictions on imports, on the other hand, will always raise a suspicion of protectionism.

Since only protective or discriminatory measures will breach Article 34 it is submitted that a rule of reason will not be applied and justification can only be sought under Article 36. This will be discussed in the next chapter.

Further reading

Arnull, A., 'What shall we do on Sunday?' (1991) 16 EL Rev 112.

Barents, R., 'New Developments in Measures Having Equivalent Effect' 18 (1981) CML Rev 271.

Diamond, P., 'Dishonourable Defences: The Use of Injunctions and the EEC Treaty; Case Study of the Shops Act 1950' (1991) 54 MLR 72.

Mortelmans, K., 'Article 30 of the EEC Treaty and Legislation Relating to Market Circumstances: Time to Consider a New Definition?' (1991) 28 CML Rev 115.

Oliver, P., 'Measures of Equivalent Effect: a Reappraisal' (1982) 19 CML Rev 217.

Quinn, M. & McGowan, N., 'Can Article 30 Impose Obligations on Individuals?' (1987) 12 EL Rev 163.

Steiner, J., 'Drawing the Line: Uses and Abuses of Article 30 EEC' (1992) 29 CML Rev.

White, E., 'In Search of Limits to Article 30 of the EEC Treaty' (1989) 26 CML Rev 235.

NINE

Derogation from Articles 30–4 (Articles 36, 100A(4), 103, 108, 109, 115 and 223)

The principle provision for derogation from Articles 30-4 is Article 36, which provides:

> The provisions of Articles 30 to 34 shall not preclude prohibitions or restrictions on imports, exports or goods in transit justified on grounds of public morality, public policy or public security; the protection of health and life of humans, animals or plants; the protection of national treasures possessing artistic, historic or archaeological value; or the protection of industrial and commercial property. Such prohibitions or restrictions shall not, however, constitute a means of arbitrary discrimination or a disguised restriction on trade between member States.

Since indistinctly applicable measures restricting imports will now be subject to the rule of reason under *Cassis* (case 120/78), it will normally only be necessary to apply Article 36 to distinctly applicable measures in breach of Articles 30 and 34. However, where indistinctly applicable measures are clearly discriminatory in their effect on imports or fall within one of the heads of derogation of Article 36, the Court may consider the question of justification under Article 36. (See *Royal Pharmaceutical Society of Great Britain* (cases 266, 267/87); *Commission* v *UK (Re UHT Milk)*, (case 124/81) to be discussed later.) Distinctly applicable measures, on the other hand, can never be justified under *Cassis*.

This was tried in *Commission* v *Ireland (Re Restrictions on Importation of Souvenirs)* (case 113/80), Article 169 proceedings. Here the Irish government sought to justify, on *Cassis* principles, an Order requiring that imported souvenirs be marked 'foreign', or with their country of origin, arguing that the measure was necessary in the interests of consumers and fair trading — to enable consumers to distinguish the 'genuine' (home-produced) souvenirs from the (imported) 'fakes'. The Court held that since the measure applied only to imported souvenirs it could not be judged on *Cassis* principles. It could only be justified on the grounds of Article 36. Moreover since Article 36 created an exception to the principle of free movement of goods it could not be extended to cases other than those specifically laid down. Thus the measure could not be justified in the interests of consumer protection.

Although the grounds listed in Article 36 appear extensive they have been narrowly construed. The Court has held on many occasions that the purpose of Article 36 is not to reserve certain matters to the exclusive jurisdiction of the member States; it merely allows national legislation to derogate from the principle of free movement of goods to the extent to which this is and remains justified in order to achieve the objectives set out in the Article *(Commission v Germany (Re Health Control on Imported Meat)* (case 153/78), Article 169 proceedings). A measure is 'justified' if it is necessary, and no more than is necessary, to achieve the desired result (the proportionaltiy principle). Moreover, Article 36 cannot be relied on to justify rules or practices which, though beneficial, are designed primarily to lighten the administrative burden or reduce public expenditure, unless in the absence of such rules or practices the burden or expenditure would exceed the limits of what can reasonably be required *(De Peijper* (case 104/75)).

As well as being necessary, measures must comply with the second sentence of Article 36; they must not 'constitute a means of arbitrary discrimination or a disguised restriction on trade between member States'. Discrimination will be regarded as arbitrary if it is not justified on objective grounds. Thus, the enquiry under Article 36 is very similar to that conducted in applying the rule of reason and, as with the application of that rule, the presumption in favour of goods lawfully marketed in one of the member States of the Community means that a State seeking to rebut that presumption must itself prove that the conditions for the application of Article 36 are satisfied.

Public morality

The public morality ground was considered in two English cases, *R v Henn and Darby* (case 34/79), Article 177 proceedings, and *Conegate Ltd v Customs and Excise Commissioners* (case 121/85), Article 177 proceedings. In *R v Henn and Darby,* Article 36 was invoked to justify a ban on the import of pornographic materials. To a certain extent the ban was discriminatory, since not all pornographic material of the kind subject to the ban was illegal in the UK. In the UK it was only illegal if likely to 'deprave or corrupt', whereas under UK customs legislation, import was prohibited if the goods were 'indecent or obscene'. On a reference from the House of Lords the ECJ found that the ban was in breach of Article 30 but was justified under Article 36. Although it was discriminatory, the discrimination was not arbitrary; nor was it a disguised restriction on trade between member States; there was no lawful trade in such goods in the UK. The measure was genuinely applied for the protection of public morality, not for the protection of national products. It was for each State to determine in accordance with its own scale of values the requirements of public morality in its territory.

The court took a stricter view in *Conegate Ltd* v *Customs and Excise Commissioners*. Here Article 36 was invoked to justify the seizure by HM Customs and Excise of a number of inflatable rubber dolls euphemistically described as 'love dolls' together with other exotic and erotic articles imported from Germany, on the grounds that they were 'indecent and obscene'. The importers claimed the seizure was in breach of Article 30, and, since there was no ban on the manufacture and sale of such items in the UK (the sale was merely restricted), it was discriminatory. Their argument succeeded before the Court of Justice. The Court held that the seizure was not justified under Article 36, since, unlike *R* v *Henn and Darby,* there was no general prohibition on the manufacture and marketing of such goods in the UK; nor had the State adopted serious and effective measures to prevent the distribution of such goods in its territory. (Similar reasoning has been applied in the sphere of free movement of persons, see chapter 20.)

Public policy

This ground, potentially wide, has been strictly construed, and has rarely succeeded as a basis for derogation under Article 36. However, in *R* v *Thompson* (case 7/78) a restriction on the import and export of gold collectors' coins was held to be justified on the grounds of public policy, since the need to protect the right to mint coinage was one of the fundamental interests of the State. (For a similar approach to public policy derogation in the context of free movement of persons, see chapter 20.) But it has been repeatedly stated that it cannot provide a clause of general safeguard (*Commission* v *Italy (Re Ban on Pork Imports)* (case 7/61), Article 169 proceedings) and can never be invoked to serve purely economic ends (*Commission* v *Italy* (case 95/81), Article 169 proceedings). Nor can it be invoked on the grounds that the activities it seeks to curb carry criminal sanctions (*Prantl* (case 16/83)). Indeed, as in *Prantl,* there are many cases where the free movement provisions have provided a valid defence to a criminal charge. Even in what could be a legitimate case, such as *Campus Oil Ltd* (case 72/83), Article 177 proceedings (to be discussed later), where Advocate-General Slynn was prepared to accept a public policy justification, the Court preferred to base its judgment on other grounds. It seems that public policy will be an exception of last resort.

Public security

This ground was successfully invoked in *Campus Oil Ltd* to justify an Irish order requiring importers of petroleum oils to buy up to 35% of their requirements of petroleum products from the Irish National Petroleum Co. (INPC), at prices to be fixed by the minister. The measure was clearly discriminatory and protective. The Irish government argued that it was justified on public policy and public security grounds, to maintain a viable refinery which would meet essential needs in times of crisis. The Court found it in breach of Article 30 but, contrary to the view of the Commission, justifiable on public security grounds, since its purpose was to maintain the continuity of essential oil supplies. Petroleum products, the Court held, are of fundamental importance to the country's existence, since they are needed not only for the economy, but for the country's institutions, its vital services, and the survival of its inhabitants. The Court stressed that purely economic objectives would not provide justification under Article 36, but provided the measure was justified on other grounds the fact that it might secure economic objectives did not exclude the application of Article 36. As to whether the measures were necessary, the Court held that a compulsory purchase requirement would only be justified if the output of the INPC refinery could not be freely disposed of at competitive prices, and the compulsory prices only if they were competitive in the market concerned; if not the financial loss must be borne by the State, subject to the application of Articles 92 and 93 (prohibition on State aids, see chapter 11).

Protection of the health and life of humans, animals and plants

Discriminatory measures for which justification may be sought on health grounds may include bans, tests and inspections of imports to ensure that domestic standards are met, and licensing or documentary requirements to provide evidence of this fact. To succeed on this ground it is necessary to prove a real health risk (see also *Duphar BV,* (case 238/82)). This will not be the case where the exporting State maintains equivalent standards and those standards are adequate to meet that risk. Thus, in *Commission* v *UK (Re UHT Milk)* (case 124/81), Article 169 proceedings, the Court found that a requirement that UHT Milk should be marketed only by approved dairies or distributors (allegedly to ensure that milk was free from bacterial or viral infections) which necessitated the repacking and retreating of imported milk, was not justified, since there was evidence that milk in all member States was of similar quality and subject to equivalent controls. (Although the measure was prima facie indistinctly applicable the Court considered it to be discriminatory in effect and examined it for its compatibility with Article 36.)

By contrast, in *Rewe-Zentralfinanz eGmbH* (case 4/75), Article 177 proceedings, a plant health inspection applied only to imported apples, designed to control a pest called San Jose scale, which was clearly in breach of Article 30, was found to be justified on health grounds, since the imported apples constituted a real risk which was not present in domestic apples. Although discriminatory, the discrimination was not arbitrary. (Although the inspection was justified it will be remembered from chapter 6 that the charge for the inspection was not, since Article 36 is not available to justify a charge: *Rewe-Zentralfinanz eGmbH* (case 39/73).)

The health justification has often failed on proportionality grounds, or because it constitutes 'arbitrary discrimination or a disguised restriction on trade between member States'. In the *UHT Milk* (case 124/81), in addition to the marketing restrictions, UHT milk coming into the UK required a specific import licence. The Court found both requirements disproportionate; it was not necessary to market the products in that way, and the information gleaned from processing the licensing applications could have been obtained by other less restrictive means, for example, by declarations from importers, accompanied if necessary by the appropriate certificates. For similar reasons in *Commission v UK (Re Imports of Poultry Meat)* (case 40/82), Article 169 proceedings, a specific import licence requirement for poultry and eggs, allegedly designed to prevent the spread of Newcastle disease, was found not to be justified. Yet in *Commission v Ireland (Re Protection of Animal Health)* (case 74/82), Article 169 proceedings, a similar import licence requirement was permitted under Article 36 on account of the exceptionally high health standards of Irish poultry, a standard which was not matched by British flocks. The Court said it was necessary in each case to weigh the inconvenience caused by the administrative and financial burden against the dangers and risks to animal health. Thus it may be difficult to predict when a specific import licence requirement will or will not be justified.

In the first Newcastle disease case, *Commission v UK* (case 40/82), Article 169 proceedings, the same licensing system was found to result in a total ban on imports from six member States. The Court found that the measure did not form part of a seriously considered health policy and operated as a disguised restriction on trade between member States.

Similar protectionist motives were discovered in *Commission v France (Re Italian Table Wines)* (case 42/82), Article 169 proceedings. Here the Court found excessive delays in customs clearance of wine imported from Italy into France, pending analysis of the wine to ensure it complied with French quality standards. Whilst it conceded that some analysis in the form of random checks, resulting in minor delays, might be justified, the measures taken by the French, which involved systematic checks greatly in excess of those made on domestically produced wine, were both discriminatory and disproportionate.

More recent cases have shown a greater leniency on the part of the Court, especially when the public health justification is convincing and there is no evidence of a protectionist motive. In *R v Royal Pharmaceutical Society of Great Britain* (cases 266, 267/87) the Court found that the rules of the Society prohibiting the substitution by pharmacists of other equivalent drugs for proprietary brands prescribed by doctors, although clearly discriminatory in the effect on imports, were justified to maintain patients' confidence and to avoid the 'anxiety factor' associated with product substitution.

Protection of national treasures possessing artistic, historic or archaeological value

So far these grounds have not been used to provide a basis for derogation under Article 36, but it was suggested in *Commission v Italy (Re Export Tax on Art Treasures)* (case 7/68) that a desire to prevent art treasures leaving the country would have justified a quantitative restriction, even though it could not justify a charge. It is thought that it would normally apply to restrictions on exports.

Protection of industrial and commercial property

The exception provided by Article 36 for industrial and commercial property must be read in conjunction with Article 222, which provides that:

This Treaty shall in no way prejudice the rules in member States governing the system of property ownership.

Together these provisions would appear to ensure that national laws governing industrial property remain intact. However, since industrial property law by its very nature tends to contribute to a partitioning of the market, usually along national lines, its exercise inevitably restricts the free movement of goods and conflicts with the principle of market integration so fundamental to the Community. The competition provisions of the Treaty, Articles 85 and 86 (see chapters 13, 14 and 16), may be invoked to prevent this partitioning, but they are not in themselves sufficient to deal with all the situations in which industrial property law may be used to compartmentalise the market. So the Commission, and more particularly the Court, since the Commission has no power, as it has under Articles 85 and 86, to enforce the free movement of goods provisions against individuals, have solved the problem by the application of Articles 30 and 36. As a result, despite the prima facie protection offered to industrial property rights by Articles 36 and 222, these rights, protected under national law, have undoubtedly been curtailed.

The scope of Article 36 was considered in *Deutsche Grammophon Gesellschaft mbH* v *Metro–SB–Grossmärkte GmbH & Co. KG* (case 78/70), Article 177 proceedings. Here Deutsche Grammophon (DG) were seeking to invoke German copyright law to prevent the defendant wholesalers from selling DG's Polydor records, previously exported to France, in Germany. Since a prohibition on reimport would clearly breach Article 30, the matter fell to be decided under Article 36. Arguing from the second sentence of Article 36, that 'prohibitions or restrictions shall not . . . constitute a means of arbitrary discrimination or a disguised restriction on trade between member States' the Court concluded that Article 36 permitted prohibitions or restrictions on the free movement of goods only to the extent that they were justified for the protection of the rights that form the *specific subject-matter of the property*. The Court drew a distinction between the *existence* of industrial property rights, which remains unaffected by Community law, and their *exercise,* which may come within the prohibition of the Treaty. If copyright protection is used to prohibit, in one member State, the marketing of goods brought on to the market by the holder of the rights, or with his consent, in the territory of the other member State (i.e., to prevent what are known as 'parallel' imports) *solely* because the marketing has not occurred in the domestic market, such a prohibition, maintaining the isolation of the national markets, conflicts with the essential aim of the Treaty, the integration of the national markets into one uniform market. Thus it would constitute an improper *exercise* of the property right in question and would not be justified under Article 36.

The specific subject-matter of the property, to protect which property rights may be legitimately exercised under EEC law, was expressed in *Centrafarm BV* v *Sterling Drug Inc.* (case 15/74) and *Centrafarm BV* v *Winthrop BV* (case 16/74), Article 177 proceedings, in the context of a claim for infringement of patents and trade marks respectively, as a guarantee that the owner of the trade mark or patent has the exclusive right to use that trade mark or patent, for the purposes of putting into circulation products protected by the trade mark or patent *for the first time;* either directly, or by the grant of licences to third parties.

Thus, once the protected product has been put on the market in a particular State by or with the consent of the owner, either directly, or by the grant of a licence to third parties, he can no longer rely on national property rights to prevent its import from that State into other member States. His rights have been exhausted.

This doctrine of 'exhaustion of rights', has been applied by the Court to trade marks (*Centrafarm BV* v *Winthrop BV* (case 16/74)), patents (*Centrafarm BV* v *Sterling Drug Inc.* (case 15/74)), copyright (*Musik Vertrieb Membran GmbH* v *GEMA* (cases 55 & 57/80), Article 177 proceedings) and industrial designs (*Keurkoop BV* v *Nancy Kean Gifts BV* (case 144/81)). It is thought that plant breeders' rights too would be subject to the principle, since they were held in *L. C. Nungesser KG* v *Commission* (case 258/78), Article 173 proceedings, to fall within the concept of industrial and commercial property.

In *Merck & Co. Inc.* v *Stephar BV* (case 187/80), Article 177 proceedings, the exhaustion principle was applied where the patent owner had sold his product in Italy, where there existed no system of patent protection. The Court held that having allowed the goods to be sold in Italy he must accept the consequences as regards free circulation in the Community.

However, where a product has been sold under a compulsory licence without the consent of the owner, the latter is entitled under Article 36 to rely on his property right to prevent the import of goods resulting from the exploitation of the compulsory licence, since, not having consented to its use, he is still entitled to enjoy the substance of his exclusive licence (*Pharmon BV* v *Hoechst AG* (case 19/84). See also *Thetford Corp.* v *Fiamma SpA* (case 35/87)). Similarly, where the manufacturing or marketing of a product is lawful in a member State, *not* through the owner's consent but because of the expiry of the protection period provided for industrial property rights under the law of that State, a person with exclusive rights in that product in another State may prevent the import of the protected product into the State in which he holds these rights (*EMI Electrola GmbH* v *Patricia* (case 341/87), Article 177 proceedings: re rights of reproduction and distribution of musical works).

Where a product has been put lawfully on the market in a particular State with the owner's consent and the period of protection permitted under national law in that State has *not* expired, its import into another member State may not be restrained, even though the purpose of an attempt to prevent importation is to prevent parties taking advantage of different price levels in different member States, whether the reason for the price differences be government policy, legislation, or ordinary market forces (*Centrafarm, GEMA*).

There have been a number of cases involving pharmaceuticals in which importers have sought to take advantage of these price differences and the exhaustion principle, but, because the same product has been marketed in different States under different guises, they have needed to repackage or relabel the goods to establish their identity in the State of import. The Court has held that persons seeking to rely on trade-mark rights to prevent the import of such goods may do so in order to avoid confusion as to the identity of the product, and to ensure that the consumer can be certain that the trade-marked product has not been subject to interference by a third party. However, it was decided in *Hoffman-La Roche & Co. AG* v *Centrafarm* (case 102/77), Article 177 proceedings, that an attempt to prevent the import of the trade-marked goods would constitute a disguised restriction on trade between member States (thus bringing it outside Article 36) where:

(a)   the marketing system for the products adopted by the owner of the trade-mark rights involves an artificial partitioning of the market; and where

(b)   the repackaging cannot adversely affect the condition of the product,

(c)   the proprietor receives prior notice of the marketing of the repackaged product, and

(d)   it is stated on the new package that the product has been repackaged.

The Court added that these principles were not confined to medical products.

Similar reasoning underlay the decision in *Centrafarm BV* v *American Home Products Corporation* (AHPC) (case 3/78), Article 177 proceedings, about whether the importer, Centrafarm (again!) could change the name of the product it was seeking to import from the UK into Holland from Serenid D, under which it was marketed in the UK, to Seresta, the name under which a near-identical drug from the same manufacturer (AHPC) was marketed in Holland. The Court held that the proprietor of a trade mark was entitled to rely on his property rights to prevent the unauthorised fixing of trade marks on to the goods. However, whilst it might be lawful for a manufacturer to use different trade marks in different States, where a trade-mark system is used in order to partition the market along national lines a prohibition on the unauthorised fixing of labels would constitute a disguised restriction on trade between member States, thereby falling outside Article 36.

The importer in *Pfizer Inc.* v *Eurim-Pharm GmbH* (case 1/81), Article 177 proceedings, did its homework. Prior to importing Vibramycin tablets, manufactured by Pfizer Ltd in the UK, into Germany, Eurim-Pharm repackaged the tablets in packets resembling those used for Vibramycin tablets of German manufacture without tampering with the individual tablets; the new packages had windows through which the trade names 'Vibramycin' and 'Pfizer' could be seen. The pack stated that the tablets had been produced by Pfizer Ltd of Great Britain and had been repackaged and imported by Eurim-Pharm. And they had informed the plaintiff, Pfizer Inc. (USA), the parent company which owned the Vibramycin and Pfizer trade marks in Europe, in advance of what they were intending to do. The Court held that the plaintiff could not rely on its trade-mark rights and Article 36 to prevent the import of the tablets into Germany under those circumstances.

The free movement of goods has, at least until recently, taken precedence over national industrial property rights by reason of another doctrine introduced by the Court — the doctrine of common origin, introduced in the case of *Van Zuylen Frères* v *Hag AG* (case 192/73), Article 177 proceedings. The case arose from an attempt by Van Zuylen Frères, who owned the trade mark for Hag coffee in Belgium and Luxembourg, to prevent the import into Luxembourg of 'Hag' decaffeinated coffee made by Hag AG in Germany. The trade mark 'Hag' had been owned originally by a German Company, Hag AG, which had operated in Luxembourg and Belgium through its subsidiary company, Hag Belgium. After the Second World War Hag Belgium was sequestrated and sold to a Belgian family. Its Hag trade mark was eventually transferred to Van Zuylen Frères. Thus Hag AG and Van Zuylen Frères legitimately owned the same mark. Could Van Zuylen Frères invoke their rights to prevent Hag AG from exercising its? There was no question of exhaustion of rights, since Hag AG had clearly not consented to the original transfer of its trade mark. The Court held that they could not. Drawing a distinction between the existence of trade-mark rights and their exercise the Court concluded that it was not possible to rely on a trade mark to prohibit, in one member State, goods lawfully produced in another member State under an identified mark which has the same origin.

However, the ruling in *Van Zuylen Frères* was reconsidered by the Court in a second case, *SA CNL- SUCAL v Hag GF AG* (case C 10/89) in a reverse fact situation, Hag (Belgium) having changed hands and Hag (Germany) seeking to restrain import of the former's coffee into Germany. Following its ruling in *Pharmon BV v Hoechst AG* (case C 19/84) the Court held that in the absence of an element of *consent* on the part of the trade-mark owner to the product being manufactured or marketed in another member State the owner was entitled to protect his product against imported goods which could be confused with his but for which he was not responsible.

Where goods have no common origin but have been manufactured and marketed independently it has always been possible to invoke trade-mark rights to prevent imports of goods with the same or similar trademarks where this might lead to the confusion of the customer, even though marketing of these goods under their respective marks may be quite lawful and even protected in their country of origin. In *Terrapin (Overseas) Ltd v Terranova Industrie C. A. Kapferer & Co.* (case 119/75), Article 177 proceedings, a German firm, proprietors of the trade name Terranova, sought to prevent an English company from registering its trade name Terrapin in Germany, since the products of both firms (building materials) were similar, and would, the German company argued, lead to confusion amongst consumers. The Court of Justice held that Article 36 could be invoked to prevent the import of goods marketed under a name giving rise to confusion where these rights have been acquired by different proprietors under different national laws as long as they do not operate as a means of arbitrary discrimination or disguised restriction on trade between member States.

A similar situation, involving not trade marks but a registered design, arose in *Keurkoop BV v Nancy Keane Gifts BV* (case 144/81). Here Keurkoop BV, the proprietor in Holland of a registered design for a particular style of handbag, sought to prevent the import into Holland of an identical bag, manufactured in France to a design registered in France by a different owner. The court held that it would be entitled under Article 36 to exercise its property rights in order to prevent the bags being imported from France, since these bags had not been marketed in France by it or with its consent; the rights had arisen independently of each other. The Court did, however, suggest that the matter should be examined to ensure that there was no agreement or concerted practice between the parties concerned which might infringe Article 85 (competition law, see chapter 13).

Keurkoop v *Nancy Keane* was followed in *Consorzio Italiano della Componentistica de Ricambio per Autoveicoli* v *Régie Nationale des Usines Renault* (case 53/87), Article 177 proceedings. Here Renault was held entitled under Article 36 to invoke its registered patent rights in ornamental designs for car body parts to prevent the plaintiff association's members from manufacturing copies of Renault's parts in Italy, or marketing such parts following their manufacture in other member States, *without Renault's consent* (see also *AB Volvo* v *Eric Veng* (case 238/87)).

In both the above cases, the property rights were being invoked in order to protect the owner's legitimate property in his *product*. Where the owner seeks to invoke his rights to prevent the import of goods solely because the public *may be misled as to their national origin* the court has held (*Theodor Kohl KG* v *Ringelhan and Rennett SA* (case 177/83), Article 177 proceedings) that national trade-mark law may not be relied upon in the absence of evidence of unfair competition.

The limited protection offered by Article 36 to trade marks will not it seems extend to the more amorphous 'property' rights which are often protected under national law in order to prevent unfair competition. It will be remembered from chapter 8 that in *Prantl* (case 16/83), the German authorities were not entitled to rely on German law against unfair competition to prevent the import of a wine from Italy in bottles very similar in shape and appearance to the protected *Bocksbeutel,* since the Italian wine had been produced in accordance with fair and traditional practice in Italy. It is submitted that the position might and should be different if the Italian bottle had not also been a traditional design but had been deliberately produced to pass itself off as the *Bocksbeutel.* This would surely be unfair competition against which national law protecting industrial property should legitimately be exercised.

Because of the wide disparity in national trade-mark rules the first Trade Marks Directive, Directive 89/104, was passed in 1989 ((1989) OJ L 40/1). Its aim was to approximate those aspects of trade-mark law which most directly affect the functioning of the common market, and ensure protection for trade-mark owners. The Directive defines trade-mark rights and the rights attached to trade-mark ownership, as well as its limitations. The Directive provides common grounds for refusal of registration, invalidity and loss or exhaustion of rights. In other respects national trade-mark law remains unaffected.

The principles outlined above will only apply to trade within the Community. Where parties seek to assert their property rights to prevent goods from third countries from entering the Community the free movement provisions of Articles 30 and 36 do not apply (*EMI Records Ltd* v *CBS United Kingdom Ltd* (case 51/75), Article 177 proceedings).

The case law of the ECJ, as examined above, represents an uneasy and often unsatisfactory compromise between the single market principle and the need to safeguard legitimate industrial and commercial property rights protected under national law. A similar tension arises in the field of competition law (see chapters 12–16). The Court's more recent decisions indicate a greater willingness to safeguard the interests of creativity and originality protected by intellectual property law, and to encourage and reward the taking of commercial risks. This is evidenced by a more generous approach to the question of the permitted *exercise* of property rights protected under national law (e.g. *EMI Electrola* v *Patricia* (case 341/87)) and by limiting the scope of the exhaustion principle (e.g. *EMI Electrola*; *Warner Brothers Inc.* v *Christiansen* (case 158/86): rights to sale of video cassettes exhausted; rights to hire not exhausted). The Court's decision in *SA CNL-SUCAL NV* v *HAG GF AG* (case C 10/89) provides another example. And now the Trade Marks Directive, which was due to be implemented by 29 December 1991, will provide further protection for industrial property rights in the Community.

Articles 30 and 36 and the common organisation of the market: Article 100A(4)

Once a common organisation for a particular product has been set up (and many agricultural products are now subject to common organisation), member States are no longer entitled to maintain in force provisions or adopt practices which are incompatible with the scheme of common organisation or which jeopardise its aims or functioning (*Tasca* (case 65/75), Article 177 proceedings). Thus in each case it is necessary to examine the common provision to ascertain whether the field is occupied. If so, any national measure conflicting with the common provision will be illegal. If not, national measures are permissible provided they do not impair the effective functioning of the common organisation or run counter to Article 30. In this case derogation may still be permissible under Article 36.

The same principles apply where harmonisation has occurred at Community level. Indeed, the Court seemed to go further in *Tedeschi* v *Denkavit Commerciale Srl* (case 5/77), Article 177 proceedings, in the context of a dispute concerning a Community Directive regulating the use of food additives, when it claimed that where in the application of Article 100, Community Directives provide for harmonisation of the measures necessary to the free movement of goods, recourse to Article 36 is no longer justified. (See also *Ratti* (case 148/78), Article 177 proceedings.)

Where matters relate to harmonisation for the purposes of the internal market, these will now be governed by Article 100A(4) EEC. This Article, introduced by the Single European Act 1986, provides that where harmonising legislation has been passed by qualified majority, member States seeking to 'apply national provisions on grounds of major needs referred to in Article 36, or relating to the protection of the environment or the working environment' must notify the Commission. The Commission may then 'confirm' the provisions after having verified that they do not constitute a means of 'arbitrary discrimination or disguised restriction on trade between member States'. The

Commission or any other member State may bring the matter before the Court of Justice if it considers that a State is making improper use of these powers.

Thus member States are not free to act unilaterally in breach of this Article; any derogation will now be subject to the Commission's approval, or, ultimately, the consent of the Court. The protection of the environment and the working environment have been added to the grounds of Article 36.

Although expressed to apply only where harmonisation measures have been enacted by qualified majority, it has been suggested that the same procedure should be available where legislation has been passed unanimously; the Article 100A(4) procedure is not in terms limited to States which have *not* agreed to the measure in question, and some scope for derogation should be available to meet emergencies not foreseen at the time when the legislation was passed. Moreover, in an emergency, it should not be necessary for a State to obtain *prior* approval for its actions from the Commission, provided that the need for action is genuine and urgent and the Commission is notified at the earliest possible time.

Derogation provisions other than Article 36

In addition to the rule of reason and Article 36 there are further specific provisions of the Treaty allowing for derogation from the principles of Articles 30 and 34, mainly in the field of economic and commercial policy; hence the Court's refusal to allow Article 36 to justify purely economic measures. These comprise:

(a)   measures to meet *short-term economic difficulties* ('conjunctural policy') (Article 103),

(b)   measures to meet *balance of payment difficulties* (Articles 107, 108 and 109), and most important of all,

(c)   measures to meet:

(i)   *deflections of trade* which might obstruct the execution of Community commercial policy, or

(ii)   *economic difficulties in any member State* resulting from the implementation of commercial policy (Article 115) (see *Donckerwolcke* v *Procureur de la République* (case 41/76)).

Article 115 applies only in the context of the common commercial policy, i.e., to goods originating from third countries which are in free circulation within the EEC, and is necessary, since deflections of trade or economic difficulties may well arise as a result of differences in regimes between member States, permitted under the Community's common commercial policy.

Measures taken under the above Articles are required to be taken either by the Commission or the Council (on a proposal from the Commission), or, if taken by member States, subject to authorisation or approval by the Commission. They are thus subject to strict Community control. As with measures taken under Article 36, they must comply with the proportionality principle.

Derogation is also permitted *in the interests of national security* (Articles 223 and 224). Under Article 223, a State 'may take such measures as it considers necessary for the protection of the essential interests of its security which are connected with the production of or trade in arms, munitions and war material', provided that such measures do not adversely affect competition within the common market regarding products which are not intended for military purposes. Under Article 224, States may consult with each other and take steps to counteract measures taken by a member State in the event of war or the threat of war or serious internal disturbances, or to carry out obligations undertaken for the purpose of maintaining peace or international security. Should the Commission or a member State consider that a State is making improper use of its powers under Articles 223 and 224 they may bring that State before the Court under Article 225.

Further reading

Flynn, J., 'How well will Article 100A(4) work? A comparison with Article 93' (1987) 24 CML Rev 689.

TEN

State monopolies of a commercial character (Article 37)

Complementary to Articles 30 and 34 is Article 37, which requires member States to 'adjust any State monopolies of a commercial character so as to ensure that when the transitional period has ended no discrimination regarding the conditions under which goods are procured and marketed exists between nationals of member States'.

States must also refrain from introducing any new measure contrary to the above paragraph or which restricts the scope of Articles 12, 30 and 34 (Article 37 (2)).

State monopolies are clearly capable of obstructing the free movement of goods since their position in a particular market enables them to control the flow of goods in and out of the country as well as the conditions under which trade in such goods takes place.

To qualify as a monopoly it is not necessary to exert total control of the market in particular goods; it is sufficient if the bodies concerned have as their object transactions regarding a commercial product capable of being the subject of trade between member States, and play an *effective* part in such trade (*Costa* v *ENEL* (case 6/64), Article 177 proceedings).

The aim of Article 37 is not to abolish monopolies *per se* but to ensure that they do not operate in a discriminatory manner, thereby obstructing the free movement of goods and distorting competition within the Community. Even if the rules of a commercial monopoly are not on their face discriminatory they will be condemned if they are liable in fact to have a discriminatory effect and to distort competition between member States.

Article 37 only applies to State monopolies in the provision of goods. It does not apply to services. However, discrimination in the monopoly provision of services may be caught by Article 7, together with the services provisions of the Treaty (Part Two, Title III, Chapter 3, Articles 59–66), or by Article 86 (competition provision — abuse of a dominant position).

Although not expressly stated in the Article the Court has held that an exclusive right to import or export particular goods falls within the scope of Article 37 (*Manghera* (case 59/75)).

However, the Article only applies to activities which are intrinsically connected with the specific business of the monopoly (*SA des Grandes Distilleries Peureux* (case 119/78)). The activities must be capable of affecting trade between member States.

ELEVEN

Restrictions on State aids
(Articles 92–4)

State aids, like State monopolies, pose a threat to the free movement of goods, since by conferring a benefit on a particular undertaking or industry, they distort competition between member States and interfere with the functioning of the single market. With the completion of the internal market, and the intensification of competition likely to result therefrom, it is even more important that State aid to industry be strictly controlled. The line between State aids, discriminatory taxation and measures equivalent to charges or quantitative restrictions is often a fine one. Therefore, although included under the competition provisions of the Treaty and logically belonging there, for practical purposes they may more usefully be considered in advance, alongside and in conjunction with the provisions relating to the free movement of goods.

However, if they pose a threat to the Community interest, State aids represent for member States a vital instrument of economic and social policy, necessary to the economic health of a region or to whole sectors of the economy, particularly in times of economic difficulty and high unemployment. The regulation of State aids is thus a sensitive area, requiring a balancing of the interests of member States and of the Community.

The EEC Treaty attempts to achieve that balance by laying down a broad prohibition on the granting of State aid 'which distorts or threatens to distort competition by favouring certain undertakings or the production of certain goods' in so far as it affects trade between member States (Article 92(1)), subject to express and extensive derogation to protect a number of legitimate economic and social goals (Article 92(2) and (3)). Article 92(2) lays down the categories of aid that '*shall* be compatible with the common market'; these comprise:

(a) aid having a social character, granted to individual consumers, provided that such aid is granted without discrimination related to the origin of the products concerned;

(b) aid to make good the damage caused by natural disasters or exceptional occurrences;

(c) aid granted to the economy of certain areas of the Federal Republic of Germany affected by the division of Germany, in so far as such aid is required in order to compensate for the economic disadvantages caused by that division.

Article 92(3) lists those aids which *may* be compatible with the common market. These comprise:

(a) aid to promote the economic development of areas where the standard of living is abnormally low or where there is serious underemployment;

(b) aid to promote the execution of an important project of common European interest or to remedy a serious disturbance in the economy of a member State;

(c) aid to facilitate the development of certain economic activities or of certain economic areas, where such aid does not adversely affect tråding conditions to an extent contrary to the common interest [Followed by special provision for aids granted to shipbuilding];

(d) such other categories of aid as may be specified by decision of the Council acting by a qualified majority on a proposal by the Commission.

Machinery for the application of Article 92 is provided by Articles 93 and 94. Under Article 93(1) the Commission is required, 'in cooperation with member States', to 'keep under constant review all systems of aid existing in those States ["existing aid"]'. Under Article 93(3) the Commission must 'be informed, in sufficient time to enable it to submit its comments, of any plans to grant or alter aid ["new aids"]'.

With regard to existing aids, if the Commission finds, after giving notice to the parties concerned to submit their comments, that aid granted by a member State is not compatible with the common market, or is being misused, it may require the State to abolish or alter such aid within a specified time-limit (Article 93(2)). If no time-limit is specified a two-month limit will normally be appropriate (*Gebrüder Lorenz GmbH* v *Germany* (case 120/73)). If the member State fails to comply with the Commission's Decision the Commission may refer the matter to the Court of Justice (Article 93(2)).

As to proposals for new aids, if the Commission, having been informed, finds that the plans are not compatible with the common market it must initiate the procedure outlined in Article 93(2). The State 'shall not put its proposed measures into effect until this procedure has resulted in a final decision' (Article 93(3)).

In exceptional circumstances a member State may apply to the Council for a Decision, which must be unanimous, that in derogation from Article 92 or Article 94, an aid which it is granting (existing aid) or intends to grant (new aid) is compatible with the common market. In this case where proceedings have already been initiated by the Commission under Article 93(2) they will be suspended until the Council has made its attitude known (Article 93(2), paras 3 and 4). It may be noted that under Article 92(3)(d) the Council has the power to extend the categories of aid for which dispensation is allowed.

Finally, under Article 94 the Council, acting by qualified majority on a proposal from the Commission, is empowered to make Regulations concerning the application of Articles 92 and 93.

The Commission insists on strict compliance with the procedures of Article 93, namely member States' duty to inform the Commission of plans to grant or alter aid (Article 93(3)). Since States not infrequently flouted this requirement, or, having notified the Commission, went ahead without giving the Commission time to respond, the Commission, in a practice note issued in November 1983 (OJ No. C318, 24.11.83, p. 3) expressed its intention to 'use all the measures at its disposal' to ensure compliance by member States with Article 93(3). Henceforth States which had granted aid illegally, i.e., without informing the Commission, or precipitately, would be required to recover such aid from recipients, and, in the agricultural sector, would be refused advance payments from the EAGGF (European Agriculture Guidance and Guarantee Funds). Since then the Commission has taken many decisions requiring the repayment of aid. In July 1990 British Aerospace was required to repay £44.4 million worth of 'sweeteners' it received when acquiring the Rover car group in 1988 (decision successfully challenged on procedural grounds in January 1992: the Commission has announced its intention to institute new proceedings for the recovery of this sum).

In a number of cases a decision requiring repayment has been challenged on the grounds of breach of the plaintiff's legitimate expectations. In *RSV Maschinefabrieken & Scheepswerven NV* v *Commission* (case 223/85), Article 173 proceedings, a Commission Decision ordering repayment of aid granted to RSV to write off financial losses was annulled at the suit of the recipient, since the Decision was issued, without justification for the delay, some 26 months after the aid had been granted. However, in *Commission* v *Germany* (case C 5/89), the Court, endorsing its decision in *Commission* v *Germany* (case 94/87), held that save in exceptional circumstances firms in receipt of State aid could not have legitimate expectations concerning the lawfulness of aid unless it had been granted in accordance with the procedures of Article 93. The diligent recipient of aid would make sure that these procedures had been complied with. Nor could the State plead the legitimate expectations of recipients in order to evade its obligation to comply with the Commission's decision requiring the recovery of aid. To ensure 'transparency' the Commission now publishes an annual survey of its aid proceedings in the *Official Journal*, and warns potential recipients of the legal consequences of repayment decisions. It also publishes a section on State aids in its annual report on competition policy. In the light of these practices a defence based on legitimate expectations is only likely to succeed in exceptional circumstances such as those obtaining in *RSV* (case 223/85).

Thus all aids granted by member States are subject either to the dispensation of the Council, or, more normally, the strict supervision and control of the Commission, with ultimate recourse to the Court, either in annulment proceedings under Article 173 (see chapter 27) or in proceedings under Article 93(2).

Meaning of State aids

State aids comprise any advantages granted directly or indirectly through State resources. The aid may be granted 'in any form whatsoever' (Article 92(1)), through any central or local government body or any agency subject to the control of the State. It is not necessary that the benefit should be paid out of public funds as long as the State plays a part in initiating or approving the aid. No distinction is made between aid granted directly by the State or by public or private bodies established and operated by it to administer that aid (*Steinike und Weinleg* (case 78/76)). In *Kwekerij Gebroeders van der Kooy BV & Others v Commission* (cases 67, 68/85, 70/85), Article 173 proceedings, a power company created under private law but controlled by the State through a 50% shareholding, and whose prices were subject to government control, was held to be equivalent to the State for the purpose of establishing State aid under Article 92(1). To constitute State aid in breach of Article 92 it must distort or threaten competition by favouring certain undertakings or the production of certain goods, and it must be capable of affecting trade between member States. These questions will be determined according to the principles developed under the competition provisions of Articles 85 and 86 (see chapters 13 and 14).

Aid can take many forms, and can include, as well as actual payments, preferential tax treatment, preferential interest rates, grants to cover redundancy costs, investment grants and subsidies, financial incentives to privatisation (e.g., British Aerospace), or special prices for land, plant or power (e.g. *Kwekerij Gebroeders van der Kooy* (cases 67, 68 and 70/85), power company supplying natural gas at special reduced prices to the horticulture industry). It will be judged not by its name or aims but its effect (*Italy v Commission (Re Aids to the Textile Industry)* (case 173/73)). It does not include a system of minimum prices, since this is not an advantage granted to favour an undertaking or to benefit certain goods and will normally be applied to all goods irrespective of origin. (The latter will, however, be judged under Article 30 — see *Van Tiggele* (case 82/77), discussed in chapter 8.)

Policy of the Commission

Whether aid is new or existing, whether it falls allegedly within Article 92(2) or 92(3), apart from the exceptional case under Articles 92(3)(d) and 93(2), which will be decided by the Council, it is the Commission, subject to final adjudication by the Court, which decides whether it is in fact compatible with Community law. Clearly if it falls squarely within Article 92(2) it must be allowed. If it falls within the permitted exceptions of Article 92(3) (a) to (c) the Commission has a discretion, both in permitting the exemption and in determining its scope (*Walloon Regional Executive & Glaverbel SA v Commission* (case 67/87), Article 173 proceedings; modernisation aid granted to Glaverbel (Belgian glass manufacturers) not an important project of common European interest under Article 92(3)(b); to constitute the latter must form part of a transnational European programme).

The exercise of this discretion, as the Court commented in *Philip Morris Holland BV* v *Commission* (case 730/79), Article 173 proceedings, involves economic, political and social assessments which must be made in the Community context, the determining factor being the Community interest. As a general rule aid will only be allowed if it promotes recognised Community objectives and does not frustrate the move to the single market (*20th Report on Competition Policy*). The Court will only question the exercise of the Commission's discretion in extreme cases.

In permitting *regional* aid under Article 92(2)(a) (to counter underemployment) and (c) (to assist development) the Commission looks not to national levels of employment and income but to the standard of the Community as a whole. As a result eligibility for such benefit will depend on the State's position relative to the Community average.

In allowing *sectoral aid* (e.g., to agriculture, transport, particular industries) under Article 92(3)(c) the Commission's main concern is to prevent the grant of State aid from exacerbating existing problems or from transferring them from one State to another. The Commission will not allow aid which strengthens the power of an undertaking compared with other undertakings competing in intra-Community trade. Thus, in *Philip Morris* the plaintiff failed to obtain the annulment of a Commission Decision refusing to allow the Dutch government to grant aid to increase the production capacity of a Dutch cigarette manufacturer, who was in competition in Europe with a number of other manufacturers.

Nor will the Commission allow States to 'shore up obsolete structures' (*16th General Report*, 1982, 104), to grant relief to rescue firms which are incapable of adjusting to conditions of competition (*15th Report on Competition Policy*, 1981, 103). Aid will only be permitted which will lead to sound economic structures to enable an industry to become competitive, to resolve underlying problems, not to postpone or shift the solution.

The majority of aids, notably regional and sectoral aids, for example, aids to the textile industry, to shipbuilding and to the film industry, have been granted under Article 92(3) (c) — 'to facilitate the development of certain economic activities or of certain economic areas'. Regional aids, i.e., national as opposed to Community aid granted pursuant to its regional policy, have been subject to progressive coordination since the first formal guidelines were adopted in 1971 (First resolution on Regional Aids, (1971) JO C111/1).

Exceptions under Article 92(3)(b) must relate to projects of common *European*, as opposed to national interest. Aid has been permitted under this head to enable firms to bring their plant into line with environmental standards.

Since German unification there is no longer any justification for continuing to subsidise areas of East Germany under Article 92(2)(c) although the Commission has recognised that some State aid will be necessary to ease East Germany's transition to a market economy.

General aids as opposed to 'special' aids normally fall outside Article 92. General schemes may exceptionally be permitted for short periods to counter 'a serious disturbance in the economy of a member State' (Article 92(3) (b)).

The Commission has taken the view that the provisions on State aids apply to both private and public undertakings. In a communication issued in 1991 (OJ C 273/2) it expressed its concern at the volume of aid granted by States to public undertakings which had not been notified under Article 93(3) (£3.5 billion between 1985 and 1990). It stressed the need for the development of a policy for public undertakings, which had not hitherto been sufficiently subject to State aid disciplines. Aid granted to public undertakings *must* be notified in advance to the Commission. Such aid would be judged according to the 'market economy investor principle' adopted in the private sphere: namely 'where the State provides finances to a company that would not be acceptable to an investor operating under normal market economy conditions state aid is involved'.

The Commission also stressed the need for 'transparency'. In order to achieve transparency, States would be required to submit annual reports to the Commission, setting out the details of all State intervention measures. These principles apply only to the manufacturing sector; but the Commission is not precluded from applying them outside this sector.

Relationship between State aids and other provisions of the Treaty

State aid that is permitted under Article 92 cannot in itself fall within Article 30 or Article 37. To that extent the provisions are mutually exclusive. However, some aspects of State aid, not necessary for the attainment of its object, may be incompatible with other provisions of the Treaty, even though they may not invalidate the aid as a whole (*Ianelli & Volpi SpA* v *Ditta Paola Meroni* (case 74/76), Article 177 proceedings). Therefore, if the aid goes beyond what is necessary to achieve a particular legitimate objective it may infringe Article 30. Similarly, if it is applied to activities which are incompatible with Article 30 (e.g., 'Buy Irish' campaign sponsored by the Irish Goods Council: *Commission* v *Ireland*, (case 249/81), Article 169 proceedings). On the same principle the operations of a State-owned monopoly are not exempt from Article 37 by reason of the fact that they may classify as aids.

Even when the activities of a State monopoly are linked with a grant to producers subject to the monopoly they must still comply with the non-discrimination requirements of Article 37 (*Ianelli & Volpi SpA* v *Ditta Paolo Meroni* (case 74/76)).

Enforcement by individuals

Articles 92 and 94, both being dependent on the exercise of discretion by Community institutions, are not directly effective (*Ianelli & Volpi SpA* v *Ditta Paola Meroni* (case 74/76)). So in the absence of a Decision from the Commission or Court of Justice, a national court has no power to decide whether a State aid is compatible with Article 92. However, the procedural obligations of Article 93(3) are directly effective, and as such, as the Commission pointed out in its practice note of 1983, are amenable to assessment by national courts. Thus an individual, provided he has *locus standi* under English law, may challenge in his domestic courts a grant of aid by national authorites in breach of Article 93(3). Also, as the ECJ noted in *Ianelli & Volpi SpA* v *Ditta Paolo Meroni*, if Article 92 is invoked before domestic courts in the context of directly effective provisions such as Article 30 and Article 37, questions relating to State aids may, along with other questions, be referred to the Court of Justice for preliminary ruling (under Article 177 (see chapter 24)).

In proceedings before national courts, actions by national authorities taken in breach of Article 93(3) cannot be legalised by a subsequent finding by the Commission that the aid is compatible with EEC law (*Fédération Nationale du Commerce Extérieur des Produits Alimentaires* v *France* (case C 354/90)). However, a failure to notify the granting of aid does not automatically lead to nullity (*France* v *Commission* (case C 301/87)).

Once a Decision in respect of State aid has been issued, a recipient or potential recipient may challenge that Decision before the ECJ under Article 173; however, where a Decision affects a whole industry the Court has held that individual members have no standing to sue, although an organisation created to represent those members, if it took part in the proceedings relating to the granting of aid, may (*Kwekerij Gebruders van der Kooy*). In addition, any interested party who suspects that aid is being granted in breach of Article 92 may complain to the Commission and request the Commission to act, and, providing he acts in time, may challenge any action or inaction on the part of the Commission resulting from his complaint (*Irish Cement Ltd* v *Commission* (case 166/88), Article 173, 175 proceedings; see chapters 27, 28).

Where repayment of aid is ordered, recovery will be governed by the domestic law of the State in question, provided that the rules do not render recovery 'practically impossible' (*Commission* v *Germany* (case 94/87)). Interest will be payable from the date on which the unlawful aid was paid. Since the Court has decided that undertakings in receipt of State aid must be deemed to be aware of the rules regarding the recovery of illegally granted aid it is unlikely that a person in receipt of such aid can claim damages against the State, either on the basis of tort (see *Bourgoin SA* v *Ministry of Agriculture, Fisheries & Food* [1986] QB 716 in chapter 23) or under *Francovich* v *Italian State* (cases C 6 & 9/90) (see chapters 2, 23, and 25); arguably, in a 'normal' case he could be seen as having caused his own loss.

Further reading

Commission's Annual Reports on Competition Policy.
Cownie, F., 'State aids in the Eighties' (1986) 11 EL Rev 247.
Evans, A., and Martin, M., 'Socially Acceptable Distortions of Competition: Community Policy on State Aid' (1991) 16 EL Rev 79.
Flynn, J., 'How well will Article 100A(4) work? A comparison with Article 93' (1987) 24 CML Rev 689.
Hellingman, K., 'State participation as State aid under Article 92 of the EEC Treaty: The Commission's guidelines' (1986) 23 CML Rev 111.
Quigley, C., 'The notion of a State Aid in the EEC' (1988) 13 EL Rev 242.

Ross, M., 'Challenging State Aids – the effect of recent developments' (1986) 23 CML Rev 867.
Slot Piet, Jan, 'Procedural Aspects of State Aids: the Guardians of Competition versus the Subsidy Villains' (1990) 27 CML Rev 741.

TWELVE

Introduction

The competition policy of the Community is based on Article 3(f) of the EEC Treaty, requiring: 'the institution of a system ensuring that competition in the common market is not distorted', and Articles 85-94 (Part Three, Title I, Chapter 1). Articles 92-4, relating to State aids, have already been discussed in the context of free movement of goods (chapter 11); the question of whether State aids 'distort or threaten competition' (Article 92(1)) will be assessed according to the principles developed by the Commission and the Court in interpreting and applying Articles 85 and 86. The present section is concerned with Articles 85 and 86, and the secondary legislation enacted by the Council and the Commission under Article 87 to give effect to the principles contained therein.

After agriculture, competition policy is perhaps the most highly developed of the Community's common policies, with the greatest impact on undertakings situated both inside and outside the common market. It is an essential complement to the fundamental provisions of the Treaty designed to create the common market. The obligations imposed on member States to ensure the free movement of goods and services and freedom of establishment within the Community would be of little effect if parties were free to engage in restrictive practices such as concerted price fixing or market sharing which inhibit the free play of market forces within the common market, particularly when such practices tend to partition the market along national lines.

Broadly speaking, the purposes of EEC competition policy, which is spelt out in detail in the Commission's annual reports on competition policy, is to encourage economic activity and maximise efficiency by enabling goods and resources to flow freely amongst member States according to the operation of normal market forces. The concentration of resources resulting from such activity functioning on a Community, rather than a national, scale is intended to increase the competitiveness of European industry in a world market. In addition to this primary goal, and sometimes conflicting with it, Community competition policy seeks to protect and encourage small and medium-sized enterprises so that they too may play their full part in the competitive process.

In order to understand and evaluate the policies pursued by the Commission it is necessary briefly to examine the economic theory underlying competition policy.

The theory of competition

The original concept of competition, dating from the 18th century, and Adam Smith's *Wealth of Nations* (1776), merely meant the absence of legal restraints on trade. Modern economic theory, however, which stems from the late 19th century, and led to the first anti-trust legislation, the Sherman Act, in the USA in 1890, is based on the model of 'perfect competition'. This is an idealised concept, based on a number of assumptions. It assumes that there are in the market a large number of buyers and sellers, the latter all producing identical or homogeneous products; that consumers have perfect information, and always act in order to maximise utility; that resources flow freely from one area of economic activity to another, and that there are no impediments to the emergence of new competition ('barriers to entry'); and that business people always maximise profits. A system of 'pure' or 'perfect' competition guarantees the maximum efficiency, the optimum allocation of resources. It is the polar opposite to the monopoly.

The 'traditional' view, adopted by the early economists, was that the real world did not correspond to this model of perfect competition. Practices which stood in the way of the achievement of perfect competition, which restricted the freedom of buyers and sellers, must therefore be curtailed. It was necessary to regulate the market in order to bring it close to the ideal. Intervention was also seen as necessary to keep open opportunities for competitive activity, particularly for small and medium-sized firms, and to preserve real choice for consumers. Early anti-trust law, e.g., the Sherman Act (1890, USA), was thus designed to make capitalism work more effectively.

Anti-trust law in Western Europe, which only became widespread after the Second World War, was based on this traditional view. The influence of this view was particularly strong in Germany, where concentrations of industrial power in pre-war Germany were seen as having contributed to a concentration of political power. It was this German inheritance, together with the appeal of the traditional view following the Second World War, that shaped EEC competition law. French law too, though in much smaller degree, influenced EEC law, particularly in its concern to protect the small business person.

Opposed to the traditional view is the view of the Chicago school of economists. Although implicit in the *laissez-faire* view of the early 19th century it has only recently emerged and has been rapidly gaining ground over the traditional view, particularly in the USA. According to the Chicago school the real world approximates quite well to the model of perfect competition; even monopolies are not in themselves anti-competitive as long as there are no barriers to entry, i.e., as long as other business people are not prevented from entering the field as competitors. This will only occur if the minimum efficient scale of the operation is such as to make entry virtually impossible. Thus the Chicago school believes that only the minimum intervention is needed, and then only to curb the most blatant forms of anti-competitive activity.

In the absence of empirical evidence as to the correctness of the views of either school it is a matter of faith, or fashion, or more significantly, politics, which view is espoused. EEC law has been criticised as excessively traditional and interventionist, both in its drafting and its interpretation by the Commission and the Court. In its concern to strike down all restrictions on competition it is said that the Commission fails adequately to distinguish between 'vertical' agreements (agreements between parties at different levels in the chain of distribution, e.g., between manufacturer and his selected dealer, or between dealer and retailer) which carry many economic advantages, and 'horizontal' agreements (agreements between parties at the same level in the economic chain, e.g., cartels between manufacturer and manufacturer, between dealer and dealer), which are potentially much more damaging to competition. Nor does it distinguish sufficiently between *ancillary restraints,* i.e., restraints which are attached to some pro-competitive transaction, and *naked restrictions* on competition, clothed with no desirable transaction at all. Whilst the latter are never justifiable, the former may be judged according to whether they are necessary in order to make the (desirable) transaction viable.

The Commission has also been criticised for subordinating other goals, such as overall economic efficiency, to the supreme goal of market integration. Thus, in order to protect the single market, *intra-brand* competition (competition between undertakings dealing in the *same* product, e.g., between rival Ford car dealers) is protected at the expense of *inter-brand* competition (competition between undertakings dealing in *competing* products, e.g., between Ford dealers (or manufacturers) and Citroën dealers (or manufacturers)). The effect of this may be to reduce the competitiveness of the industry as a whole. It has also been suggested that by elevating the single market principle above all other considerations the Commission and the Court have failed to take into account other Community objectives relevant to the application of competition law, such as the need to counter regional or structural imbalances and to safeguard employment and the environment.

These criticisms may be kept in mind when specific cases fall to be examined. Approval or disapproval of Community policies will ultimately depend on one's view of its economic, social and political priorities. No doubt it was essential that market integration should come first during the Community's formative years. Equally it is not surprising that as the Community has become more closely integrated there has been a greater recognition on the part of the Commission and the Court of the need to promote economic efficiency, to enable European industry to compete more effectively in the world market. Looking to the future the completion of the internal market in 1992 is likely to have regional, social and environmental repercussions which may necessitate the weighing of other wider policy considerations within the context of the application of EEC competition rules, as will the Community's growing links with the newly independent states of central and eastern Europe and its role in their industrial regeneration.

Enforcement of EEC competition law

Enforcement of EEC law has been entrusted to the Commission under Regulation 17/62, the principal Regulation concerned with competition policy. Decisions of the Commission made pursuant to its policy may, however, be challenged under Article 173 (see chapter 27) and a failure to take such a decision may be challenged under Article 175 (see chapter 28). These matters are now dealt with by the Court of First Instance. Since Articles 85 and 86 have been declared directly effective *(BRT* v *SABAM* (case 127/73), Article 177 proceedings), member States may be called upon to apply EEC competition law, although as will be seen later, there are important limits to their powers.

Unlike the provisions considered so far, a breach of Articles 85 or 86 may give rise to sanctions in the form of heavy fines and penalties. This is rare in EEC law.

Although the obligations of Articles 85 and 86 are imposed on 'undertakings' and do not prima facie concern the laws and regulations of member States, Article 90(1) expressly provides that EEC competition law applies to 'public undertakings and undertakings to which member states grant special or exclusive rights', subject to limited exceptions provided under Article 90(2), which have been narrowly interpreted. As the Court held in *BNIC* v *Clair* (case 123/83):

> The legal framework within which agreements are made or decisions are taken and the classification (i.e. public or private) given to that framework are irrelevant as far as the applicability of Community rules on competition are concerned.

Even where there is no agreement or behaviour on the part of a public (or semi-public) body such as to give rise to liability under Articles 85 and 86, the Court has held that a State may not adopt or maintain in force any measures which deprive Articles 85 or 86 of their effectiveness. Any public measure which endorses or encourages action in breach of Articles 85 or 86 will be deemed unlawful *(GB-INNO* v *ATAB* (case 13/77)). Thus a public body, depending on its actions and the measures concerned, may, in the context of anti-competitive action, incur liability under other Articles of the Treaty (e.g. Articles 5, 30–34 (goods), 59 (services)) *or* Articles 85 and 86. Where doubt exists as to which Articles are appropriate, all relevant articles should be pleaded.

A number of areas, such as transport, were originally excluded from EEC competition law. The scope of these exclusions has been considerably reduced in recent years, as the Commission has introduced specific legislation in the field of communications, postal services, transport, insurance and audiovisual media, with a view to further increasing competition in these spheres. Also, in order to achieve the benefits of free competition within the single market in the important field of public procurement, the Community has issued Directives governing the award of public supply and public works contracts, laying down detailed procedures for the advertising (in the *Official Journal*) and award of such contracts, including the payment of damages by authorities acting in breach of these procedures (see Directive 89/665 OJ No. L 395, 30. 12. 89, p. 33).

In the external sphere the Commission has stepped up its attempts to extend the application of its competition policy amongst the Communities' trading partners. In September 1990 it concluded an agreement with the US government for increasing cooperation and mutual coordination in the enforcement of competition law (see *20th Annual Report on Competition Policy*).

So pervasive is the influence of EEC competition law, and so severe are the sanctions for its breach, that businesses, whatever their size, whether or not their operations are currently confined to their domestic market, cannot afford to ignore Community law. Indeed, in the UK a knowledge of EEC competition law may well become essential, since in 1989 the UK government published a White Paper outlining its proposals for a wide ranging reform of domestic law on restrictive trade practices, modelled largely on EEC competition law.

Further reading

Commission's Annual Reports on Competition Policy.
European Competition Law Review.
Van Gerven, W., 'Twelve Years of EEC Competition Law (1962–1973) revisited' (1974) 11 CML Rev 38.
Gyselen, L., 'State Action and the Effectiveness of the EEC's Competition Provisions' (1989) 26 CML Rev 33.
Hornsby, S., 'Competition Policy in the 80s: More Policy Less Competition?' (1987) 12 EL Rev 79.
Korah, V., 'EEC Competition Policy: Legal Form or Economic Efficiency' (1986) 39 Current Legal Problems 85.
Snyder, F., 'Ideologies of Competition in European Community Law' (1989) 52 MLR 149.

THIRTEEN
Article 85

Article 85: the general scheme

Article 85(1) prohibits:

> all agreements between undertakings, decisions by associations of undertakings and concerted practices which may affect trade between member States and which have as their object or effect the prevention, restriction or distortion of competition within the common market.

A number of examples of the types of agreements covered by Article 85(1) are provided in Article 85(1) (a) to (e).

Article 85(2) provides that any agreement or decision in breach of Article 85(1) 'shall be automatically void'.

Under Article 85(3), Article 85(1) may, however, be declared 'inapplicable' to agreements or decisions fulfilling a number of specified criteria.

Thus, Article 85(1) provides a very broad base of liability subject to the possibility of exemption under Article 85(3).

Under Regulation 17/62 (Article 9(1)) the Commission has the *sole* power to grant exemption under Article 85(3). In order to obtain exemption, parties must notify their agreements or decisions to the Commission (Regulation 17/62, Article 4). Once notified, even if the agreement is subsequently found in breach of Article 85(1) and not eligible for exemption, parties obtain immunity from fines (Article 15(5) (a)). However, except in the case of 'old' agreements (pre-accession, or those entered into prior to the entry into force of Regulation 17/62) which have provisional validity during the notification period, notification cannot prevent agreements from being void *ab initio* should the Commission eventually decide that they infringe Article 85(1) and do not merit exemption under Article 85(3) *(Brasserie de Haecht* v *Wilkin No.2)* (case 48/72), Article 177 proceedings). It is possible for an agreement to be held void in part only, if the offending clauses can be severed and are not sufficiently serious to vitiate the whole.

As an alternative to exemption, parties can seek 'negative clearance' from the Commission, i.e., a Decision that their agreement or decision does not infringe Article 85(1) at all (Regulation 17/62, Article 2). It is possible, and common, for undertakings to apply for both negative clearance and exemption on the same form A/B.

The breadth of Article 85(1) and the severity of the consequences of breach inevitably led to uncertainty. There was a risk that many desirable, pro-competitive agreements would fall foul of its provisions; certainly many would require exemption under Article 85(3). There was thus a strong incentive for business people to play safe and notify. This resulted in an increasing work-load for the Commission which in turn resulted in long delays. It might take years before a final Decision was taken by the Commission. A Decision that an agreement was void could have disastrous consequences for all the parties concerned. There was thus a fear that business people might be deterred from entering into beneficial, pro-competitive agreements for fear of the consequences.

In order to solve these problems the Commission has, over the years, issued a number of 'notices' and 'block exemptions'. The notices merely provide non-binding guidelines as to the kinds of agreement which will *not* breach Article 85(1) (e.g., Notice concerning minor agreements (1986) OJ No. C 231/02). The block exemptions, which are enacted by Regulation, apply to agreements which *do* breach Article 85(1) but, because of their beneficial nature, are exempt *'en bloc'* on the grounds of Article 85(3). Agreements falling within these notices and block exemptions need not be notified. However, notices, as non-binding measures, cannot guarantee immunity, and, to obtain the benefit of a block exemption, an agreement must contain *no* anti-competitive clauses additional to those allowed under the exemption, even though they may seem to be justifiable.

Article 85(1): elements of an infringement

Article 85(1) contains three essential elements. There must be:

(a) an agreement between undertakings, or a decision by an association of undertakings or a concerted practice,

(b) which may affect trade between member States, and

(c) which must have as its object or effect the prevention, restriction or distortion of competition within the common market.

Agreements between undertakings, decisions by associations of undertakings and concerted practices

Undertakings   In the absence of a definition, the word 'undertaking' has been interpreted in the widest possible sense to include any legal or natural person engaged in some form of economic or commercial activity, whether in the provision of goods or services, including cultural or sporting activities (*9th Report on Competition Policy*, 116), banking (*Züchner* v *Bayerische Vereinsbank AG* (case 172/80)), insurance (*Verband der Sachversicherer eV* v *Commission* (case 45/85)) (*13th Report on Competition Policy*) and transport (*Commission* v *Belgium* (case 156/77)). It is not necessary that the activity be pursued with a view to profit.

Although air and sea transport were treated as special cases and excluded from the enforcement provisions of Regulation 17/62, legislation has now been introduced with a view to achieving full and free competition in these areas by 1 January 1993.

Article 85(1) also applies in the sphere of agriculture (*The Community* v *Milchförderungs fonds* [1985] 3 CMLR 101, Commission Decision), coal and steel, and atomic energy, provided the matter falls outside the scope of existing provision in these areas. It applies to undertakings in the public as well as the private sphere (Article 90(1) and *Re British Telecom*, Commission Decision 82/861 [1983] 1 CMLR 457, upheld by ECJ in *Italy* v *Commission* (case 41/83)). In *Re UNITEL* [1978] 3 CMLR 306 an individual, in the form of an opera singer, was found to be an undertaking!

Agreements   Agreements are not confined to binding agreements. A 'gentleman's agreement' will suffice. In view of the wide scope of 'concerted practices' there is clearly no need for a narrow interpretation.

Decisions by associations of undertakings   Clearly the effect of such decisions, i.e., of trade associations, may be to coordinate behaviour amongst undertakings with anti-competitive effects, without any need for actual agreement; hence their inclusion in Article 85(1).

This provision has been widely interpreted, and is not confined to binding decisions. It was held in *NV IAZ International Belgium* v *Commission* (case 96/82), Article 173 proceedings, that even a non-binding recommendation from a trade association which was normally complied with could constitute a decision within Article 85(1). In *Re the Application of the Publishers' Association* [1989] 4 CMLR 825 the Association's Code of Conduct was found by the Commission to have the character of a recommendation to its members and customers, and as such was to be considered as a decision of an association of undertakings, despite its non-binding character. As well as the association itself, its members may be liable for fines if they comply, even unwillingly, with a decision in breach of Article 85(1).

Article 85(1) also applies to decisions by associations of associations (*NV IAZ International Belgium* v *Commission*).

Concerted practices   These are altogether wider than 'agreements' and 'decisions by associations of undertakings'. The concept of a concerted practice was borrowed from US anti-trust law; when the EEC Treaty was signed the competition rules of the signatory States contained no rules against such practices. A concerted practice was defined in *Imperial Chemical Industries Ltd* v *Commission* (Dyestuffs) (case 48/69), Article 173 proceedings, as a form of cooperation between undertakings which, without having reached the stage where an agreement properly so-called has been concluded, knowingly substitutes practical cooperation between them for the risks of competition.

To constitute a concerted practice, it is not necessary to have a concerted plan. It is enough that each party should have informed the other of the attitude they intended to take so that each could regulate his conduct safe in the knowledge that his competitors would act in the same way.

Clearly such practices can be just as damaging to competition as agreements or decisions by associations, and are much harder to prove.

Imperial Chemical Industries Ltd v *Commission* centred on three uniform price increases introduced by a number of leading producers (including ICI) of aniline dyes, almost simultaneously, in 1964, 1965 and 1967. The increases covered the same products. Between 7 and 10 January 1964 there was a 10% increase; between 14 October and 28 December 1964 a 10-15% increase was announced, to come into effect on 1 January 1965. At a meeting in Basle in August 1967 one of the producers announced an 8% increase to take effect from 16 October. Two other producers subsequently announced a similar increase of 8%. The Commission issued a Decision that they were engaged in concerted practices in the fixing of price increases, and imposed heavy fines on them (*Re Aniline Dyes Cartel* JO (1969) L195/11, [1969] CMLR D23). ICI sought annulment of that Decision, arguing that the price increases were merely examples of parallel increases common in oligopolistic situations (an oligopoly exists where the market is dominated by a small number of large concerns). The argument failed. The Court held that whilst parallel behaviour does not in itself constitute a concerted practice it provides strong evidence of such a practice if it leads to conditions of competition which do not correspond to the normal conditions of the market. This aspect of the decision has been criticised. Whilst a finding of concerted practices was acceptable on the facts (the market was found to be divided on national lines; the prior meetings and announce-ments eliminated all uncertainty between the parties; the increases were general and uniform and covering the same products), it is submitted that a decision based solely on the 'normal conditions of the market' would be incapable of proof, and could render oligopolies highly vulnerable to a charge of concerted practices in the event of quite 'normal' parallel price increases.

However, fears on this account have not been borne out. Subsequent decisions (e.g., *Züchner* (case 172/80); *Zinc Producers' Group* [1985] 2 CMLR 108) indicate that the Commission does distinguish between 'innocent' parallel conduct by independent firms and concerted practices. It seems it is only when parallel action occurs amongst parties within a particular distribution system that the Commission is willing to conclude, usually with good reason, that concerted practices exist (e.g., *AEG-Telefunken AG* v *Commission* (case 107/82), Article 173 proceedings; *Re Italian Flat Glass* Commission Decision (1989) OJ No.L 33/34 – decision annulled in part, *SIV* v *Commission* (cases T68/89, T77/89, T78/89)).

In *AEG-Telefunken* the parties had notified their distribution agreements for AEG products and obtained negative clearance from the Commission. AEG was subsequently found in breach of Article 85(1) for having *operated* the agreements in such a way as to restrict competition by systematically refusing to allow dealers into its network who did not comply with the (unofficial) pricing policy apparently observed by existing members. Moreover, since

AEG had acted outside the framework of its agreement as notified, notification did not bring it immunity from fines.

AEG-Telefunken illustrates too that what may look like a unilateral act in the form of a refusal to supply may be found to breach Article 85(1) because of the *context* in which it operates, i.e., as part of a deliberate concerted plan to partitition the market, usually on national lines, in order to reduce or eliminate competition.

Similarly, in *Ford Werke AG* v *Commission* (case 25/84), Article 173 proceedings) the Court approved the Commission's refusal to grant clearance for what appeared to be a perfectly acceptable standard distribution agreement because Ford was refusing to supply existing distributors in Germany with right-hand-drive cars for export in England, apparently in order to maintain an artificial partitioning of the market and thereby different price levels in different member States. Although there was no clear evidence of concerted action, certainly none of any agreement, the Court held that Ford's decision to cease supplies formed part of the contractual relations between Ford Werke AG and its dealers. Admission to Ford's dealer network implied acceptance by the contracting parties of the policies pursued by Ford. This case shows how far the Commission and the Court are prepared to go to suppress practices which are against the spirit, even if they seem to be within the letter, of EEC competition law. *AEG-Telefunken and Ford Werke* were followed in *Sandoz* (1987) OJ No. L 222/28 and *Tipp-Ex* (1987) OJ No. L 222/1 (decision confirmed by the Court: *Tipp-Ex GmbH & Co. KG* v *Commission* (case C 279/87)).

Public authorities

Where public bodies are concerned it seems that a distinction must be drawn between agreements or concerted practices entered into in the course of commercial activities, which are clearly capable of falling within Article 85(1), and executive measures which merely permit or encourage such action which, although illegal under other provisions of the Treaty such as Articles 30–34 (see e.g. *GB–INNO* v *ATAB* (case 13/77)), will not in themselves breach Article 85(1). In *Bodson* v *Pompes Funèbres* (case 30/87) a licensing arrangement, whereby the local authority granted exclusive rights in respect of certain funeral services to the Société des Pompes Funèbres, was held not to constitute an 'agreement between undertakings' within Article 85(1); but had the municipality imposed a certain level of prices on the licensees the Court suggested it would have been subject to EEC competition rules.

Field of application of Article 85(1)

Article 85(1) applies to agreements or decisions of associations or concerted practices on a vertical level (e.g., between manufacturer and dealer) as well as a horizontal level (e.g., between manufacturer and manufacturer) (*Établissements Consten SA* v *Commission* (cases 56 & 58/64), Article 173 proceedings). The undertakings must, however, be independent of each other. An agreement between a parent and its subsidiary will not breach Article 85(1) unless the subsidiary enjoys full independence of action, the reason being that competition between them cannot be restricted by the agreement, since they were never in competition with each other. However, a parent as well as its subsidiary may be liable for acts of the subsidiary *vis-à-vis* third parties in breach of Article 85(1) where the subsidiary has acted as a result of the parent's promptings; and an agreement between parent and (non-independent) subsidiary may fall within Article 86 if it constitutes an abuse of a dominant position (*Béguelin Import Co.* v *GL Import-Export SA* (case 22/71), Article 177 proceedings). Similarly members of an 'economic unit' comprising bodies with identical interests and subject to common control may be liable under Article 85 or Article 86 (*Hydrotherm* v *Compact* (case 170/83) [1984] ECR 2999). The same principles as apply to parents and subsidiaries apply to agreements between principal and agent. However, the Commission will scrutinize the relationship between the parties to ascertain its true nature (see e.g. *Pittsburg Corning Europe* [1973] CMLR D2; description of concession agreement as a commercial agency 'mere colouring').

An undertaking situated outside the EEC may be liable under Article 85(1) provided that the effects of its agreements or practices are felt inside the common market (*Béguelin Import Co.* v *GL Import-Export SA*). In *Imperial Chemical Industries Ltd* v *Commission* (case 48/69), ICI (UK) was held liable for the acts of its subsidiary in Holland although the UK was not yet a member of the EEC. In *Wood Pulp* [1985] 3 CMLR 474, Commission Decision, a number of firms, all from ouside the EEC, who were not acting through subsidiaries in the EEC but who supplied two thirds of the EEC consumption of wood pulp, were fined for concerted practices in breach of Article 85(1). The Court has now confirmed the Commission's decision ([1988] 4 CMLR 901, Article 173 proceedings). In assessing the applicability of EEC competition rules the determining factor, the Court held, is the place where the agreement is implemented.

'Which may affect trade between member States'

The agreement or decision by associations of undertakings or concerted practice must be one which may affect trade between member States to breach Article 85(1). In the absence of an effect on inter-State trade any restriction on competition is a matter for national law alone. However, the question of whether trade between member States may be affected has been broadly interpreted by the Commission and the Court. In *Société Technique Minière* v *Maschinenbau Ulm GmbH* (case 56/65), Article 177 proceedings, the Court held that an agreement was capable of affecting trade between member States if, on the basis of objective legal or factual criteria, it allows one to expect that it will exercise a direct or indirect, actual or potential effect on the flow of trade between member States. The test is thus very similar to the *Dassonville* test applied in the context of Article 30, but broader, since it requires simply an *effect* on, not a *hindrance* to, trade between member States (see chapter 8). Clearly the most obvious effect on trade between member States occurs when parties attempt to partition the market along national lines by means of restrictions on 'parallel' imports or exports (i.e., restrictions, usually agreed between manufacturers and appointed dealers, on dealers' powers to import or export goods across national frontiers). But an effect on trade between member States can occur even when an agreement takes place wholly within a member State and appears to concern only trade within that State. This is so particularly in the case of decisions of associations of national agreements which are intended to operate across the whole national market. As the court pointed out in *Vereeniging van Cementhandelaren* v *Commission* (case 8/72), Article 173 proceedings — in the context of a challenge to a Commission Decision that cement dealers' price-fixing scheme, limited to the Dutch market, infringed Article 85(1) — an agreement extending over the whole of the territory of a member State by its very nature has the effect of reinforcing the compartmentalisation of markets on a national basis, thereby holding up the economic interpenetration which the Treaty is designed to bring about and protecting domestic production. The Court has on several occasions held that Article 85(1) applies to agreements between undertakings in the same State. For example in *Re Vacuum Interrupters Ltd* [1977] 1 CMLR D67 a joint venture agreement between three UK manufacturers to design and develop switch-gear apparatus in the UK was held capable of affecting trade between member States, since in the absence of such agreement they would have attempted to develop the apparatus independently and to market it in other member States. (See also *Re Italian Flat Glass* [1982] 3 CMLR 366 (agreement between Italian producers and wholesalers of glass representing more than half of the Italian market); *Salonia* v *Poidomani* (case 126/80), Article 177 proceedings (national selective distribution system for newspapers capable of affecting trade between member States).)

In the case of a domestic agreement between individuals it may be necessary to examine the agreement in the context of other similar agreements, to ascertain whether, taken as a whole, they are capable of affecting trade between member States (*Brasserie de Haecht SA* v *Wilkin (No. 1)* (case 23/67), Article 177 proceedings (Belgian tied-house agreement part of a network of similar agreements)).

Since only a *potential* effect of trade need be proved the enquiry is not limited to existing patterns of trade; the Commission is prepared to speculate as to possible future patterns of trade. Thus in *Pronuptia* (case 161/84), Article 177 proceedings, the Court accepted the Commission's finding that a franchising agreement between Pronuptia in France (the franchisor) and its franchisee in Germany, which restricted the franchisee's power to operate outside a particular territory was capable of affecting inter-State trade even though there was no evidence, and indeed it seemed highly unlikely, that the franchisee had any intention of extending its activities to other member States.

The question of effect on trade between member States is not concerned with the increase or decrease of trade which might result from an agreement; all that is required to be shown is a deviation (actual or potential) from the 'normal' pattern of trade which might exist between member States (*Établissements Consten SA* v *Commission* (cases 56 & 58/64)). In assessing this question it is not necessary to examine every clause in the agreement as long as the agreement as a whole is capable of affecting trade between member States.

'Which have as their object or effect the prevention, restriction or distortion of competition within the common market'

As with the question of effect on trade between member States, EEC competition law is not concerned with the question of increase in trade between member States but with whether there is a distortion of the 'normal' competition which should exist within the common market. Moreover, it is concerned not only with 'horizontal' agreements (i.e., between competing manufacturers, or competing wholesalers — the 'classic' cartel), which clearly restrict competition, but also with 'vertical' agreements (i.e., between manufacturer and distributor, between distributor and retailers, parties not competing with each other) which are often economically beneficial, since they streamline the distribution process and concentrate promotional activity, to the eventual benefit of consumers. These principles were established in *Établissements Consten SA* v *Commission* (cases 56 & 58/64), Article 173 proceedings.

This case concerned an exclusive dealership agreement between Grundig, a German company manufacturing electronic equipment, and Consten SA in France. Under the agreement Consten was appointed Grundig's sole distributor in France and granted exclusive rights to Grundig's trade mark, GINT, in France. Consten agreed not to re-export Grundig's products to any other EEC country; Grundig agreed to obtain similar assurances from its dealers in other member States. There was thus a total ban on parallel imports and exports in Grundig products, reinforced by the GINT trade mark. Consten discovered that another French firm, UNEF, had bought Grundig products from German traders and was selling them in France at prices below those charged by Consten. Consten brought an action against UNEF for infringement of its trade mark; UNEF applied to the Commission for a decision that the Consten-Grundig agreement was in breach of Article 85(1) and the Commission subsequently issued a Decision to that effect (*Re Grundig's agreement* [1964] CMLR 489). In cases 56 & 58/64 the parties sought to annul that Decision. The plaintiffs argued that the effect of their agreement was not to reduce trade between member States but to increase it. The agreement served to concentrate and streamline the distribution of Grundig products in France, and trade in Grundig products had in fact increased. Moreover, Grundig faced lively competition from other rival producers. The Court rejected these arguments. The fact that trade in Grundig products had increased was irrelevant; the agreement might nonetheless affect trade between member States and harm the object of the Treaty, namely the creation of the single market. Competition law was concerned not only with agreements which restricted competition amongst competing manufacturers (inter-brand competition). The object of the agreement was to eliminate competition in Grundig products at the wholesale level (intra-brand competition). Moreover, the parties could not rely on their trade-mark rights in these circumstances. To use them merely in order to partition the market constituted an abuse of such rights. However the Court was not prepared, as was the Commission, to declare the whole agreement void. Only the offending clauses were severed.

The decision in *Établissements Consten SA v Commission* has been criticised, but it must be acknowledged that restrictions on intra-brand competition, contained in vertical agreements, whilst they may carry economic benefits, are often used, as they were in the Consten-Grundig agreement, to partition the market, usually along national lines, in order to insulate the distributor in each State from competition from parallel imports from States where price levels are low. Artificially high price levels may thus be maintained. As has been noted in chapter 9, industrial property rights have been used to the same purpose.

Because of these dangers the Commission prefers to maintain the prohibition under Article 85(1) on these agreements, with the possibility of block exemption under Regulation 1983/83 (exclusive distribution) or Regulation 1984/83 (exclusive purchasing) for the more innocuous agreements, or individual exemption under Article 85(3). This approach ensures the maximum supervision and control.

'Object or effect'   If the object of an agreement is to prevent or restrict or distort competition, for example, a naked price-fixing or market-sharing agreement between competing manufacturers, there is no need to prove its effect. Unless the agreement is clearly incapable of affecting competition, an anti-competitive effect will be presumed. Where the agreement is not designed to restrict competition, for example, a standard distribution agreement, a detailed economic analysis of its effects on the particular market will be necessary before a breach of Article 85(1) can be proved.

The scope of the analysis required was considered in *Société Technique Minière v Maschinenbau Ulm GmbH* (case 56/65), Article 177 proceedings.

The case involved an exclusive distribution agreement between a German manufacturer of heavy earth-moving equipment, Maschinenbau Ulm GmbH (MU), and a French distributor, Société Technique Minière (STM), similar to the Consten-Grundig agreement, but without its undesirable features. It contained no restrictions on parallel imports or exports, and no abusive use of trade marks. STM sought to resile on its agreement, claiming it was in breach of Article 85(1). On a reference from the Paris Cour d'Appel under Article 177, the Court of Justice held that in order to ascertain whether an agreement is capable of preventing, restricting or distorting competition a number of factors must be examined, i.e.:

(a)   *The nature and quantity of the products concerned* (i.e., the product market, and the parties' combined share in that market). The greater the market share held by the parties, the more damaging its impact on competition.

(b)   *The position and size of the parties concerned* (i.e., their position in the market). The bigger they are, in terms of turnover and *relative* market share, the more likely it is that competition will be restricted.

(c)   *The isolated nature of the agreement or its position in a series* (see also *Brasserie de Haecht SA* v *Wilkin* (case 23/67)). This is particularly relevant in the case of distribution agreements, which in themselves may appear insignificant, but which often form part of a network of similar agreements.

(d)   *The severity of the clauses.* The more severe the clauses the more likely they will be deemed in breach of Article 85(1). However, any clause that is more than is necessary to achieve the desired (beneficial) result will risk infringing Article 85(1) (*L'Oréal NV* v *De Nieuwe AMCK PVBA* (case 31/80), Article 177 proceedings).

(e)   *The possbility of other commercial currents acting on the same products* by means of reimports and re-exports (i.e., parallel imports or exports). Thus any agreement which attempts to ban or even limit parallel imports or exports will normally breach Article 85(1).

The agreement between STM and MU was found on the facts not to breach Article 85(1).

Thus the enquiry needed to ascertain whether an agreement has the potential to prevent, restrict or distort competition within the common market is a wide-ranging one, often involving all the factors outlined above, *always* involving the first two. As will be seen, the Commission is equipped with wide investigative powers to undertake this analysis. National courts, on the other hand, particularly those with an accusatorial system such as ours, *a fortiori* our lower courts (e.g., *Potato Marketing Board* v *Robertsons* [1983] 1 CMLR 93, Oxford County Court) will have more difficulty in fulfilling this task.

The *de minimis* principle

All agreements between business people curtail to some extent each other's freedom of action in the market-place. Clearly not all such agreements are capable of preventing, restricting or distorting competition to any noticeable extent. Always it is a question of size and scale, as the criteria of *Société Technique Minière* v *Maschinenbau Ulm GmbH,* particularly points (a) and (b), indicate, whether in fact they do so. Hence the importance in EEC law of the *de minimis* principle.

The principle was introduced in the case of *Völk* v *Établissements Vervaecke Sprl* (case 5/69), Article 177 proceedings. The agreement in question was an exclusive distribution agreement between Völk, a small-scale manufacturer of washing machines in Germany, and Vervaecke, a Dutch distributor of electrical goods. Vervaecke was to enjoy an exclusive right to distribute Völk's machines in Belgium and Luxembourg. Völk agreed, *inter alia,* to block all sales of his machines into Vervaecke's territory by third parties (i.e., parallel imports). They were thus seeking absolute territorial protection for Vervaecke in relation to Völk's machines in Belgium and Luxembourg. Subsequently the parties disputed the terms of the agreement and a ruling was sought from the Court of Justice from the Munich Oberlandesgericht on the legality of the agreement under EEC law. In assessing this question, the Court asked, must courts have regard to Völk's share in the markets of member States, particularly in the States where his products have absolute territorial protection? (In fact Völks production of washing machines was between 0.2 and 0.5% of the German market, and his share in the Belgian and Luxembourg market was minute.)

In reply the Court ruled that in order to come within Article 85(1) competition must be affected to a noticeable extent; there must be a sufficient degree of harmfulness. Therefore it was necessary to take into account the position of the parties on the market for the product in question. In the case under referral the effect of Völk-Vervaecke's agreement on the washing-machine market in Belgium and Luxembourg was insignificant.

Thus the size of the parties, and even more important, their share in the relevant product market, will be an essential factor in determining liability. However, if the parties are powerful in a particular market (e.g., alcoholic drinks), they cannot rely on the *de minimis* rule for any of their products within that market (e.g., Pimms (No. 1)) even though they may represent a negligible share of the market in other member States (*Distillers Co. Ltd v Commission* (case 30/78), Article 173 proceedings).

If an agreement falls within the *de minimis* principle, even if it contains the most blatantly anti-competitive clauses (e.g., price-fixing), even if the parties *intend* to restrict competition (clearly the aim of the territorial protection clause in *Völk v Vervaecke*) there will be no breach of Article 85(1). Thus, in assessing the question of breach of Article 85(1), some economic and market assessment will have to be made in every case, although agreements which do not have the object of restricting competition will require a more thorough analysis to prove that they are capable of that effect.

The principle of *Völk v Vervaecke* can at its best only provide a guideline serving to exclude agreements whose effect on competition is negligible. No figures were suggested as to the size of the market share needed to bring the principle into play. In *Miller International Schallplatten GmbH v Commission* (case 19/77), Article 173 proceedings, the Court held that a 5% share in the product market did *not* come within the *de minimis* principle. A Notice issued by the Commission in 1986 on Agreements of Minor Importance ((1986) OJ No.C 231/02) has now provided that, as a general rule, agreements between undertakings engaged in the production and distribution of goods and services which do not represent more than 5% of the total market for such goods and services in the area affected by the agreement, and with an aggregate turnover of no more than 200 million ecus, will not fall within Article 85(1). But according to paragraph 3 these figures are not to be regarded as an 'absolute yardstick'. Agreements between firms which exceed these limits may have a negligible effect on competition. Conversely, an agreement between firms falling below these limits may exert an appreciable effect if the market is highly fragmented. Much will depend on the structure of the market. However, paragraph 5 of the Notice provides that where, owing to exceptional circumstances, an agreement covered by the Notice falls within Article 85(1), the Commission will not impose fines. So, in assessing the question of breach of Article 85(1), the first question which should be asked is does the *de minimis* principle apply?

Agreements capable of preventing, restricting or distorting competition

Examples of agreements likely to breach Article 85(1) are provided in Article 85(1)(a) to (e). Any agreement falling within these categories will raise a prima facie case of breach of Article 85(1), provided that it does not fall within the *de minimis* principle and that competition within the common market is affected. The Community dimension is essential, but, since it is subject to the same principles as the question of 'effect on trade between member States', not hard to prove.

Although it is always a question of size and scale whether or not a breach of Article 85(1) has occurred, it is possible from the approach of the Commission and the Court to the types of agreement listed in Article 85(1) to distinguish between 'excusable' and 'inexcusable' restrictions. The inexcusable restrictions will breach Article 85(1) and are unlikely to obtain exemption under Article 85(3). Excusable restrictions fall into one of two categories. *Either* they are found not to breach Article 85(1) at all, or they are found in breach of Article 85(1) but eligible for exemption under Article 85(3). The distinction is significant.

Article 85(1) (a): Agreements which directly or indirectly fix purchase or selling prices or other trading conditions

(a) *Price fixing.* Price-fixing agreements, because of their obvious anti-competitive effects, are almost always inexcusable. The Court of Justice was, however, in *Centres-Leclerc* v *'Au Blé Vert' Sàrl* (case 229/83), Article 177 proceedings, prepared to accept that French legislation allowing a system of retail price maintenance for books, the prices to be fixed by publishers, was compatible with Article 85(1). The government had claimed that the measure was indispensable to protect books as a cultural medium against the negative effects of fierce price competition and to maintain the existence of specialist bookshops. Evidence was adduced that most member States operated some form of price maintenance for books. In the absence of common Community provision in the area, clearly a sensitive one, the Court was prepared to let these arguments prevail. However, in *Re the Application of the Publishers Association* [1989] 4 CMLR 825 the Commission found that the Publishers Association's Code of Conduct, which applied to books sold throughout the UK as well as to exports and reimports, and which provided, *inter alia*, for a system of *collective* price maintenance, was in breach of Article 85(1) and not eligible for exemption under Article 85(3).

Minimum prices are regarded in the same light as fixed prices. In *Hennessy/Henkell* [1981] 1 CMLR 601, Commission Decision, a clause in an exclusive distribution agreement between Hennessy, the producer, in France, and Henkell, the distributor in Germany, setting maximum and minimum price limits for Hennessy's products, was found by the Commission to be in breach of Article 85(1), and not eligible for exemption under Article 85(3). A similar finding was made and approved by the Court, in the case of recommended prices circulated amongst dealers in *AEG-Telefunken* (case 107/82), Article 173 proceedings. However, it was clear in *AEG-Telefunken* that the recommended prices were used to enable the parties to engage in concerted pricing policies. In *Pronuptia* v *Schillgalis* (case 161/84), Article 177 proceedings, the Court ruled that recommended prices issued in the context of a distribution franchising system would not breach Article 85(1) as long as they did not lead to concerted practices and the franchisee remained free to fix his own selling prices. In this area parallel pricing will provide strong evidence of concerted practices. In its subsequent Decision on the *Pronuptia* agreement ([1989] 4 CMLR 355) the Commission found the provision for recommended *maximum* prices to be acceptable.

(b) *Other trading conditions.* A manufacturer will often seek to impose trading conditions on his distributors (or retailers) in order to ensure that the premises are suitable, or that adequate after-sales service is provided. He may insist that his distributor holds minimum stocks or that he engages in specific promotional activities. In return for his efforts, a distributor may seek to safeguard his investment through protection from competition within his particular territory. To what extent are these arrangements compatible with EEC law?

The first principle, laid down in *Metro-SB-Grossmärkte GmbH & Co. KG* v *Commission* (case 26/76), Article 173 proceedings, is that selective distribution systems will not breach Article 85(1) provided that dealers are chosen on the basis of objective criteria of a *qualitative* nature relating to the technical qualifications of the dealer and his staff and the suitability of his trading premises, and that such conditions are laid down uniformly and not applied in a discriminatory manner.

In *L'Oréal* (case 31/80), Article 177 proceedings, the court followed *Metro,* adding that the qualitative criteria must not go beyond what is necessary. What is regarded as necessary will depend on the nature of the product. In *Re Ideal/Standard Agreement* [1988] 4 CMLR 627 the Commission found that the characteristics of plumbing fittings were not sufficiently technically advanced to necessitate a selective distribution system in which wholesalers were required to be specialists in the sale of plumbing fittings and sanitary ware and to have a department specialising in the sale of such products. The products were too 'banal' to warrant such a system. With regard to *quantitative* criteria, such as, in *L'Oréal*, requirements that the distributor should guarantee a minimum turnover and hold minimum stocks, these were held to exceed the requirements of a selective distribution system, and were thus in breach of Article 85(1), although it was suggested that they might be exemptible under Article 85(3). However, in *Pronuptia* v *Schillgalis*, in addition to a number of qualitative restrictions relating to layout, shop fittings, advertising and promotion, the Court did allow, as compatible with Article 85(1), a requirement that the franchisee should buy 80% of its wedding dresses from Pronuptia and the remainder only from suppliers approved by Pronuptia. This requirement, like the qualitative requirements, was found essential in a franchising agreement to protect the know-how and reputation of the franchisor. The Commission confirmed in its Decision on *Pronuptia* that certain quantitative restrictions, including an obligation to hold minimum stocks, were permissible as essential to a franchising agreement, at the same time stressing that retail franchising agreements were different in kind from distribution agreements. It is submitted that apart from franchising agreements, quantitative restrictions will still require individual exemption.

Conditions in the form of import and export restrictions, designed to partition the market and to protect the distributor from (intra-brand) competition within his particular territory, as in *Consten/Grundig*, will always breach Article 85(1) and will rarely qualify for exemption under Article 85(3). The hard line taken by the Commission, with the qualified approval of the Court, is illustrated by its attitude to patent licensing agreements. in *L.C. Nungesser KG* v *Commission* (case 258/78), Article 173 proceedings, in the context of a licensing agreement assigning plant breeder's rights, the Court drew a distinction between an 'open' exclusive licence (restricting the grantor's right to grant other licences to the licensee's territory or to compete there himself), which was compatible with Article 85(1), and a 'closed' exclusive licence (restricting the rights of third-party importers or licensees in other territories to import into the licensee's territory), which was not. Nor did the latter qualify for exemption under Article 85(3), since the condition was not regarded as indispensable to the agreement. In *Hennessy/Henkell* a covert attempt by Jas. Hennessy & Co. to protect Sektellereien Henkell & Co. from competition from parallel imports by means of lowering their selling prices when 'infiltration' was threatened resulted in the striking down of the agreement as a whole. However, in *Pronuptia* there was a suggestion by the Court that a restriction on franchisees' rights to open up on other franchisees' territory, although in breach of Article 85(1), might be justified under Article 85(3) in order to protect franchisees' investment in the business. This has now been confirmed in the *Pronuptia* Decision, and followed in a Decision on the *Computerland Europe SA* franchising agreement [1989] 4 CMLR 259. Thus, a degree of territorial protection has now been permitted in franchising agreements. This has now been incorporated in the Block Exemption on franchising agreements.

Article 85(1)(b): Agreements which control production, markets, technical developments or investments These agreements, which are normally horizontal agreements, will invariably breach Article 85(1). 'Naked' restrictions of this nature will rarely, if ever, qualify for exemption. However, where the restriction is ancillary to some desirable, pro-competitive agreement, such as a specialisation agreement between small and medium-sized firms, or a research and development agreement, it is likely to qualify for exemption — either block exemption, under Regulation 417/85 (specialisation) or Regulation 418/85 (research and development), or individual exemption. In *Re Vacuum Interrupters Ltd* [1977] 1 CMLR D67 the parties obtained individual exemption for such an agreement (research and development). (See also *Clima Chapée/Buderus* [1970] CMLR D7; *ACEC/Berliet* [1968] CMLR D35.)

Article 85(1) (c): Agreements to share markets or sources of supply These too will normally be horizontal agreements in breach of Article 85(1). A market-sharing agreement may qualify for exemption if ancillary to some beneficial agreement on the same principles as apply to Article 85(1) (b), provided it does not attempt to establish absolute territorial protection for the product in question in the markets concerned. An agreement to share sources of supply would require exemption, and would be difficult to justify.

Article 85(1) (d): Agreements which apply dissimilar conditions to equivalent transactions with other trading parties, thereby placing them at a competitive disadvantage Concerted discriminatory treatment will always breach Article 85(1) and will rarely if ever be eligible for exemption under Article 85(3). However, agreements imposing dissimilar conditions will only breach Article 85(1) if the transactions are 'equivalent'; there will be no breach if the difference in treatment is objectively justified (see *Metro-SB-Grossmärkte GmbH & Co. KG* v *Commission* (case 26/76)). Thus an agreement to charge different (but not fixed) prices to different customers would be permissible if the prices charged genuinely reflected different (e.g., transport) costs; it would not if they were based on what the market would bear. Similarly, 'quantity' discounts (discounts for bulk purchases), if they genuinely reflect cost savings, are permissible, whilst 'fidelity' or 'loyalty' rebates, which are tied to the volume of business transacted, are not.

Article 85(1) (e): Agreements which make the conclusion of contracts subject to acceptance by other parties of supplementary obligations which, by their nature and/or according to commercial usage, have no connection with the subject-matter of such contracts Such agreements, or, rather, such clauses in an agreement, will always breach Article 85(1) and will require individual exemption under Article 85(3). However, it is a matter of judgment whether an obligation is deemed to have the requisite connection with the subject-matter of the contract. Agreements guaranteeing exclusivity, such as exclusive supply agreements (*Hennessy/Henkell, Pronuptia*) or exclusive licensing agreements (*Nungesser*) are seen as essential to the subject-matter of the contract; attempts at territorial protection are not. Trading conditions based on necessary objective qualitative criteria are essential, those based on quantitative criteria are not (*Metro, L'Oréal*), although certain 'essential' quantitative restrictions may be imposed in franchising agreements (*Pronuptia*) at least if expressed in percentage terms. In *Hennessy/Henkell* a clause prohibiting Henkell & Co. from dealing in products competing with Hennessy's was found acceptable as essential to the exclusive distribution agreement; a clause prohibiting them from dealing in any other products at all was not, nor was it justifiable under Article 85(3). 'Non-competition' clauses, i.e., restraint of trade clauses attached on the sale of a business have been found by the Commission to be essential to the main contract, since the know-how and goodwill of a business protected by a non-competition clause are seen to constitute a substantial part of the assets transferred (*Reuter/BASF AG* [1976] 2 CMLR D44; approved by the court in *Remia BV* v *Commission* (case 42/84), Article 173 proceedings). However, the restraints must be no more than is necessary to preserve the value of the bargain. Thus in *Reuter/BASF AG* a non-competition clause of eight years' duration and extending to non-commercial research was found excessive, and not justifiable under Article 85(3), and in *Remia BV* a 10-year restriction on competition was reduced to four.

Other agreements   The above list of agreements capable of preventing, restricting or distorting competition is not exhaustive. In *AEG-Telefunken* (case 107/82) and *Ford Werke AG* (case 25/84) a refusal to supply was found in breach of Article 85(1) where that refusal was made in the context of existing agreements in order to enable anti-competitive practices to continue. In *British American Tobacco (B.A.T.) and Reynolds* v *Commission* [1988] 4 CMLR 24, Article 173 proceedings, the Court of Justice held for the first time that Article 85(1) applied to mergers. The case arose from a proposed merger between Philip Morris Inc. and Rembrandt Ltd, which would have given Philip Morris a controlling interest in one of its principal competitors, Rothmans Tobacco (Holding) Ltd, in the EC cigarette market. The Commission had been alerted to the proposed merger by the parties' competitors, B.A.T. and Reynolds. Subsequently the agreement was modified by a Decision from the Commission reducing Philip Morris's shareholding in Rothmans Ltd, and thereby ensuring that the relationship between them remained competitive. The Decision was challenged by B.A.T. and Reynolds. Whilst the Decision was upheld by the Court, the Court affirmed that Article 85(1) could apply in principle to mergers. Whilst the acquisition of an equity interest in a competitor did not in itself restrict competition, it might serve as an instrument to that end.

This Decision paved the way for the acceptance by member States of a Regulation on merger control which had been languishing for many years. The final version of the Regulation, Regulation 4064/89 (corrected version OJ No. L 257, 21.9.90, p. 13) was adopted in December 1989, after much debate amongst member States on the appropriate turnover and market share thresholds required to bring the Regulation into operation. Under the Regulation any cross-border mergers between undertakings with a combined worldwide aggregate turnover of more than ecus 5,000m and with an aggregate EEC turnover of more than ecus 250m must notify the Commission of their merger plans and obtain the Commission's approval. Exemption will be granted to mergers which are indispensable to the attainment of a Community priority. Substantial fines may be imposed on firms acting in breach of the Regulation. The Regulation is due to come into effect in October 1990 (see further chapter 14). The Regulation applies to concentrative, not cooperative joint ventures, which remain subject to Article 85 (see Commission Notice OJ No. C 203, 14.8.90, p. 10).

Although neither the Commission nor the Court expressly distinguishes between naked and ancillary restrictions on competition, it is safe to say that naked restrictions in any of the above categories will breach Article 85(1) and will be unlikely to obtain exemption under Article 85(3).

Where ancillary restrictions are concerned, the approach of the Commission and the Court is not entirely consistent. Certain restrictions, contained in exclusive distribution agreements (*Metro-SB-Grossmärkte, L'Oréal, Hennessy/Henkell*), or exclusive licensing agreements (*Nungesser*), or franchising agreements (*Pronuptia, Computerland*), or attached to the sale of a business (*Reuter/BASF, Remia BV*), although apparently falling within the wide words of Article 85(1), have been construed as essential to the main agreement, and as such not in breach of Article 85(1) at all. Similarly, in *Bayer AG* v *Sullhofer* (case 65/86) Advocate-General Darmon suggested that a no-challenge clause in a licensing agreement would be acceptable if it was *crucial* to the equilibrium of the licensing agreement, the object and effect of which is not shown to be specifically restrictive of competition. The Court confined itself to stating more narrowly that a no-challenge clause would not breach Article 85(1) where the licence was granted for no consideration or, although granted for consideration, it related to some outdated procedure. Other restrictions in these same types of agreement, although not blatantly anti-competitive, and arguably regarded by one, if not both of the parties, as necessary to the transaction as a whole, have been found in breach of Article 85(1) although possibly exemptible under Article 85(3). And in other kinds of agreement, for example, research and development or specialisation agreements, restrictions (e.g., within Article 85(1) (b)) which are clearly justifiable in the context of the agreement as a whole have rarely been regarded by the Commission as acceptable *per se;* they must be given exemption under Article 85(3). However, in *Elopak/Metal Box-Odin* (OJ L 209/15 1990), the Commission granted negative clearance to a joint venture between Elopak/Metal Box and Odin for the purposes of research and development: this may indicate a change of approach on the part of the Commission towards agreements which are clearly beneficial overall.

The former approach, where clauses which are to a certain extent restrictive of competition are permitted under Article 85(1) as necessary to the agreement as a whole is said to be an application of the rule of reason.

The rule of reason

The concept of 'rule of reason' originated in US anti-trust law, where it was applied in interpreting s.1 of the Sherman Act 1890. This section, which condemns every contract in restraint of trade, does not contain any definition of restraint of trade nor any provision for exemption for beneficial agreements on the lines of Article 85(3). It was left to the courts to decide whether or not a restraint of trade had occurred. In 1911 the US Supreme Court held, in *US* v *American Tobacco* (1911) (221 US 106 at p. 179), that not every contract in restraint of trade was illegal; it would only be illegal if it was unreasonable in that it operated to the prejudice of the public interest by *unduly* restricting competition. Thus, in applying this 'rule of reason', the US courts attempt to balance the pro and anti-competitive effects of an agreement in order to assess whether a breach of s. 1 has occurred.

The structure of Article 85 is quite different. It was clearly intended that this weighing of the pro and anti-competitive effects of an agreement was to take place not under Article 85(1) but under Article 85(3), the Commission alone having exclusive power to grant exemption under Article 85(3) (Regulation 17/62, Article 9(1)). In this way uniformity of interpretation, and the maximum supervision and control by the Commission, would be guaranteed.

This scheme, however, had its drawbacks. The need to notify agreements to obtain exemption and the resulting work-load on the Commission led to long delays. If this created uncertainty for business people, it created even greater difficulties for national courts, since they were required to apply Article 85(1) but not empowered to grant exemption under Article 85(3). Nor could Article 177 help here, since in the absence of a Decision from the Commission the Court of Justice has no power to declare an agreement exempt under Article 85(3).

One solution to this problem, adopted by the Commission, was to pass block exemptions. If parties structured their agreements to comply with the exemptions they would be free of risk. Another possible solution lay in the application of a rule of reason. Under the 'European' rule of reason, which is undoubtedly narrower than its US progenitor, only restrictions which constitute an *essential* element of the agreement, without which the agreement would be emptied of its substance, and which pose no real threat to competition or to the functioning of the single market, are deemed compatible with Article 85(1). Non-essential restrictions, or restrictions which might interfere with the functioning of the common market, are left to be decided under Article 85(3). Many of the agreements discussed above (e.g., *Metro-SB-Grossmärkte, L'Oréal, Hennessy/Henkell, Nungesser, Pronuptia, Reuter v BASF AG, Remia BV*) provide examples of both essential and non-essential restrictions. A similar two-tiered approach has already been noted in the Court's interpretation of quantitative restrictions under Articles 30 and 36, although in the case of Article 30 justification under the *Cassis* rule of reason is more explicit (see chapter 8).

However, a continued reliance on Article 85(3) for non-essential restrictions which are nonetheless justifiable, for example, in research and development agreements, ignores the central structural weakness of the exemption procedure, namely, the inability of national courts to apply Article 85(3). Even the Court of Justice overlooked this problem when it suggested in *Pronuptia* that the clauses seeking territorial protection for the franchisees could be examined in the light of Article 85(3). (See also *L'Oréal*, Court's comments regarding quantitative restrictions.)

But there is no doubt that the Commission and, more particularly, the Court (in *Nungesser* the Commission regarded even the open exclusive licence as in breach of Article 85(1), although exemptible under Article 85(3)) have been moving tentatively towards a rule of reason approach, although neither has acknowledged the rule as such. However, in view of the clear role of Article 85(3) in the framework of Article 85 as a whole there are obvious limits to the application of the rule of reason, and it would be wise, where an agreement appears to fall within Article 85(1) but has not yet been subjected to a rule of reason, to structure the agreement to fit within a block exemption or to seek negative clearance or individual exemption under Article 85(3).

Article 85(3): exemption

Under Article 85(3), Article 85(1) may be declared inapplicable to any agreement or category of agreement between undertakings, or any decision or category of decision by associations of undertakings:

... which contributes to improving the production or distribution of goods or to promoting technical or economic progress, while allowing consumers a fair share of the resulting benefit, and which does not:

(a) impose on the undertakings concerned restrictions which are not indispensable to the attainment of these objectives;
(b) afford such undertakings the possibility of eliminating competition in respect of a substantial part of the products in question.

In order to take advantage of these provisions, agreements *must* be notified (Regulation 17/62, Article 4(1)). In the absence of notification exemption will not be granted (*Distillers Co. Ltd* v *Commission* (case 30/78), Article 173 proceedings). Once the Commission has decided whether an agreement as notified is eligible for exemption or not it will issue a Decision to the parties to that effect. This Decision must be published in the *Official Journal* (Regulation 17/62, Article 21) and as a binding act it may be challenged before the Court of First Instance under Article 173 (see chapter 27). The parties concerned must be given an opportunity to be heard before a Decision is taken (Regulation 17/62, Article 19(1)), as may persons who can show a 'sufficient interest' (Article 19(2)). A Decision may be annulled if these essential procedural requirements are breached.

To obtain exemption under Article 85(3) the agreement or decision must satisfy four essential criteria.

It must contribute to improving the production or distribution of goods or to promoting technical or economic progress Thus the agreement as a whole must show positive benefits. These are expressed in the alternative, although the more benefits that are proved the greater the likelihood of exemption. Different kinds of agreement will produce different benefits.

(a) *Production.* Benefits in production are most likely to accrue from specialisation agreements. Specialisation enables each party to concentrate its efforts and achieve the benefits of scale; it avoids wasteful duplication. In *Clima Chappée/Buderus* [1970] CMLR D7 the Commission granted exemption to a specialisation and reciprocal supply agreement between Clima Chappée in France and Buderus in Germany. Both were engaged in the manufacture of air-conditioning and ventilation systems and central-heating apparatus in their own countries. They agreed each to manufacture a certain range of products exclusively, and to supply the other exclusively with these products in the other's own country. Clearly there was some reduction in competition in the common market since they were potential competitors. Nonetheless the gains in production and distribution were clear, and the agreement contributed to both technical and economic progress. The other elements of Article 85(3) too were satisfied. The agreement would result in fair shares for consumers because there was sufficient inter-brand competition to ensure that the parties would pass on the benefit of their agreement to the consumers. Nor had they imposed on each other restrictions which were not indispensable; they were not obliged to purchase the other's products unless they were competitive. And there was no possibility of eliminating competition in respect of a substantial part of the products in question. Even combined, the parties were subject to strong inter-brand competition for the products in question.

(b) *Distribution*.   Benefits in distribution occur principally through vertical agreements in the form of exclusive supply or dealership or distribution agreements. The benefits result from the streamlining of the distribution process and the concentration of activity on the part of the distributor, whether it be in the provision of publicity, technical expertise, after-sales service, or simply the maintenance of adequate stocks. These factors were important in the *Transocean Marine Paint Association* Decision [1967] CMLR D9. The agreement here was between a number of small and medium-sized manufacturers and distributors of marine paint from inside and outside the EEC. The purpose of their collaboration was to produce and market marine paints to identical standards and to organise the sale of these products on a world-wide basis. They hoped thereby to compete with the giants of the paint world. The paints were sold under a single trade mark, though members were free to add their own name and mark. Markets were to be divided up on national lines, and members were free to sell in each other's territory only on payment of a commission. There was thus a degree of territorial protection. (Their original plan to prohibit sales on each other's territory was dropped at the request of the Commission.) The advantage claimed for the agreement was the achievement of a world-wide distribution network for the same interchangeable product. Alone each manufacturer would be too small to offer adequate stocks and expertise.

Exemption was granted. The Commission agreed that the system did improve distribution; it streamlined the service to customers and led to a specialised knowledge of the market. Even the clauses granting limited territorial protection were permitted since they avoided fragmentation of the market, especially important during the launching period. Whilst competition between members was restricted, on an international scale it was greatly increased. The use of the trade mark too was permitted, since it was used in order to identify the product, not to partition the market.

(c) *Technical progress*.   Technical progress is most likely to result from specialisation agreements, particularly those concerned with research and development. The *ACEC/Berliet* Decision [1968] CMLR D35 concerned an agreement between ACEC, who were manufacturers, *inter alia*, of electrical transmission systems for commercial vehicles, and Berliet, who manufactured buses in France. They wished to collaborate to produce a new prototype bus. ACEC was to develop a new transmission system for the bus; Berliet agreed to buy the system only from ACEC; ACEC to supply only Berliet in France and not more than one outlet in any other member State. ACEC also undertook to give Berliet 'most favoured treatment', and agreed not to reveal to any other manufacturer information acquired from Berliet. Despite these many restrictions the Commission granted them exemption. There were clear gains in production and technical progress.

In *Re Vacuum Interrupters (No. 2)* [1981] 2 CMLR 217 an agreement in the form of a joint venture between the three leading British companies engaged in the manufacture of switch gear for research and the development of vacuum interrupters was exempted. It was found to lead to benefits on all four fronts, but particularly technical progress (see also *I.C.I./B.P.* [1985] 2 CMLR 330).

(d) *Economic progress.* Rather surprisingly economic progress has received scant attention in Decisions concerning exemption. It is normally presumed if improvements in production or distribution or technical progress are achieved. However, it did form the basis of a Decision granting exemption to an agreement regulating the holding of trade fairs in *Cecimo* [1969] CMLR D1 on the grounds that it tended to rationalise the operation and avoided wasteful duplication of time and effort.

The agreement must allow consumers a fair share in the resulting benefit Provided there is sufficient (inter-brand) competition from other producers in the relevant market the improvements achieved will inevitably enure to the benefit of consumers, either in the form of a better product, or a better service, or greater availability of supplies or lower prices. If the parties fail to pass on the benefits to consumers they risk losing out to their competitors. Thus the parties' market share, both in absolute terms and in relation to their competitors, will be crucial. In all the cases considered above where exemption was granted the parties faced lively competition.

The agreement must not impose on the undertakings concerned restrictions which are not indispensable This is the familiar proportionality principle, the downfall of many an otherwise-exemptible agreement, a trap to catch the greedy. The Commission will examine each clause in an agreement to see if it is necessary to the agreement as a whole. Fixed prices, even fixed maximum and minimum price limits, as in *Hennessy/Henkell* will rarely be indispensable. Likewise clauses seeking absolute territorial protection (*Consten/Grundig* (cases 56 & 58/64), *Hennessy/Henkell, Nungesser* (case 258/78)). But even these restrictions may occasionally be justified. In the *Transocean Marine Paint Association* Decision some limited territorial protection in the form of a commission payable by the parallel importer to the appointed distributor in the territory in question was deemed to be necessary to avoid fragmentation of the market during the initial launching period. When the agreement was renewed five years later, when the product was launched and the parties had grown in size and strength, that clause was required to be dropped; it was no longer indispensable. In *Pronuptia* (case 161/84) there was a suggestion by the Court that some territorial protection for the franchisee might be justified. If the agreement is a desirable one, pro-competitive overall, even quite severe restrictions may be deemed indispensable. In *ACEC/Berliet*, ACEC's undertaking not to divulge to any other customer confidential information received from Berliet, even their agreement to give Berliet 'most favoured' (i.e., discriminatory) treatment was considered no more than was necessary to safeguard their investment in the light of the mutual confidence needed and the burden or risk involved in the enterprise.

In the *Carlsberg Beers* agreement [1985] 1 CMLR 735 a cooperation agreement of 11 years' duration between Carlsberg Brewery Ltd (UK) and Grand Metropolitan plc, whereby Grand Metropolitan agreed to buy 50% of its lager supplies from Carlsberg, was granted exemption. The agreement was necessary to enable Carlsberg to establish itself in the UK market and build up its own independent distribution network.

The agreement must not afford such undertakings the possibility of eliminating competition in respect of a substantial part of the products in question In all the cases in which exemption has been granted, the parties have been subject to substantial inter-brand competition, whether from producers inside the common market or from outside (e.g. *Re Vacuum Interrupters,* parties faced competition from the Americans and Japanese). It seems that, in the case of new products the market will not be too narrowly defined. in *ACEC/Berliet* the product market, in which the parties were competing, was found to be buses, not buses with special transmission systems. In assessing this question the parties' market share and the structure of the market in which they are competing will be significant.

Block exemptions

Because the Commission was unwilling, or felt unable, to apply a rule of reason to many restrictions on competition which were clearly justifiable on the principles outlined above, it chose to solve the twin problems of uncertainty (for business people) and work-load (for itself) by means of block exemptions. Thus many agreements for which it would have been necessary to seek individual exemption no longer need to be notified. Indeed, the block exemptions were passed in order to avoid the need for individual appraisal by the Commission, in the hope that parties would tailor their agreements to fit within their confines. In many cases this has now become standard practice. These block exemptions, being enacted by Regulation, may be applied by national courts.

The areas selected for block exemption are those which, although restrictive of competition within the wide meaning of Article 85(1), are on the whole economically beneficial, and pose no real threat to competition. Since this is now a highly technical area of law it is not possible in a book of this nature to examine each block exemption in detail. Instead, the general scope of the exemptions, and their limitations, will be considered.

A large number of Regulations have now been passed granting block exemption to certain categories of agreement, the most important being:

(a) *Exclusive distribution* agreements (Regulation 1983/83, OJ No. L173, 30.6.83 p. 1).

(b) *Exclusive purchasing* agreements (with special provisions relating to beer and petrol) (Regulation 1984/83, OJ No. L173, 30.6.83, p.5).
(These two replaced an earlier Regulation concerning exclusive dealing agreements, Regulation 67/67 (JO No. 57, p. 849/67; OJ English Special Edition 1967, p. 10).)

(c) *Specialisation* agreements (Regulation 417/85, OJ No. L53, 22.2.85, p. 1, replacing former Regulation 2779/72).

(d) *Research and development* agreements (Regulation 418/85, OJ No. L53, 22.2.85, p. 5).

(e) *Patent licensing* agreements (Regulation 2349/84, OJ No. L219, 16.8.84, p. 15).

(f) *Motor vehicle distribution* agreements (Regulation 123/85, OJ No. L15, 18.1.85, p. 16).

(g) *Franchising* agreements (Regulation 4078/88 OJ No. (1988) L 359/46).

(h) *Know-how licensing* agreements (Regulation 556/89 OJ No. (1989) 61/1).

Further block exemptions have now been agreed (e.g. shipping conferences, certain air transport agreements) or are in the process of gestation (e.g., insurance, computer software agreements).

The regulations follow a similar pattern. First, they lay down the kinds of restrictions which are permitted, the 'white' list, the restrictions which are deemed 'essential' to the agreement in question; this is followed by the 'black' list — the kind of clauses which will not be permitted. With the *patent licensing* Regulation the Commission introduced a third category, the 'grey' restrictions. These are subject to a special procedure, known as the 'opposition' procedure. Under this procedure the grey restrictions must be notified to the Commission, but if they are not opposed within six months, they are deemed to be exempt. This procedure was incorporated into the new *research and development* Regulation (418/85), and the *specialisation* Regulation (417/85), although it was applied here in a rather different context, only where the turnover ceiling limiting the application of the Regulation was exceeded. The procedure has also been incorporated in the franchising and know-how Regulations.

Exemption under the *specialisation* Regulation depends on the parties' combined turnover and their market share in the goods covered by the agreement. These figures have been raised each time the Regulation has been renewed. The current turnover limit is 500 million ecu, with a market share of 20%. The opposition procedure may be applied where this turnover limit is exceeded.

Exemption under the *research and development* Regulation is also limited to parties with a combined market share of 20%, this figure too having been regularly increased. There is no turnover limit. Concessions to size are also made in the *exclusive distribution* Regulation (1983/83, Article 3(b)).

The *franchising* Regulation applies to distribution and servicing, but not to manufacturing franchises. The franchise system is described as based on the exploitation of intangible property rights such as trade marks or names and know-how, for the purpose of selling goods or providing services in premises of uniform appearances and with the same business methods (Article 1(2)). Know-how, to be covered by the *know-how licensing* Regulation, must be 'secret and substantial, and described in sufficient detail to allow the technology which is transferred to be identified' (Article 1(3)).

In selecting its white and black lists, the Commission has drawn on its earlier Decisions and the jurisprudence of the Court. Thus in exclusive distribution and purchasing agreements exclusivity is permitted, but absolute territorial protection is not. Distributors may be required not actively to seek business outside their territory, but they may not be prohibited from selling there. In patent licensing agreements, open exclusive licences are permissible, closed exclusive licences are not. Non-competition clauses are permissible, unreasonable tie-ins are not. However, conessions have been made in the field of patent licences, in that a five-year ban of 'passive' sales (i.e., licensee may not *respond* to unsolicited orders from other territories) is allowed. Time will run from the date when the goods in question were first put on the market in the common market (Regulation 2349/84, Article 1(1) (b)).

Since any clause which is not included in the white list or allowed under the opposition procedure will remove an agreement from the benefit of the block exemption, parties will still need to seek individual exemption if they wish to exceed the permissible limits. The opposition procedure increases flexibility, but agreements such as *Transocean Marine Paint Association, ACEC/Berliet* and *Re Vacuum Interrupters* might still require individual exemption, either because the parties are too big, or because the clauses (*Transocean Marine Paint Association ACEC/Berliet*) exceed the permissible limits, or because the parties are competing manufacturers (*Re Vacuum Interrupters Ltd*). Block exemption under the research and development Regulation does not apply to manufacturers of competing products (Article 3). The *exclusive purchasing* Regulation has been held not to apply to obligations which are less than exclusive; thus a 90% purchasing obligation has been held not to fall within Regulation 1984/83 (Commission's 17th Report on Competition Policy, p. 36). Thus these agreements will still require individual exemption (see *Distillers Co. plc* [1986] 2 CMLR 664). In case of doubt as to whether an agreement falls within a block exemption it is wise to play safe and notify.

Comfort letters

Apart from introducing block exemptions, and a limited application of the rule of reason, the Commission has further attempted to reduce its work-load, and at the same time speed up its decision-making processes, by the issuing of 'comfort' letters. Originally issued in response to applications for negative clearance, their scope was expanded in 1983 (OJ No. C295, 2.11.83, p. 6) to cover applications for exemption under Article 85(3). A comfort letter is a communication from the Commission to the effect that, in its opinion, the agreement *either* does not infringe Article 85(1) at all ('soft' negative clearance), *or* that it infringes Article 85(1) but is of a type that qualifies for exemption. Following this, the file is normally closed.

Unlike a formal Decision, which will only be issued following procedures laid down in Regulation 17/62, after lengthy investigation and consultation with all the parties concerned, a comfort letter represents a quick, informal way of providing assurance for the parties concerned. However, it may be 'cold comfort', since, as the Court of Justice pointed out in the *Perfume cases* (case 253/78; case 99/79), Article 177 proceedings, comfort letters are merely 'administrative letters' issued outside the framework of Regulation 17/62, and as such are not binding on national courts. Moreover, as non-binding measures, they cannot be challenged before the Court of Justice in annulment proceedings, either by the parties concerned or by a third party who is directly and individually concerned (see chapter 27). It has been suggested that, since the practice is an evasion of the procedures laid down in Regulation 17/62 it is itself *ultra vires*. The same shortcomings and criticisms apply to the Commission's new opposition procedures.

However, it could be argued that both practices were expedients necessary to avoid the excessive delays of the more formal procedures whilst at the same time ensuring that the Commission retained control. Where comfort letters are concerned the Commission has attempted to remedy the procedural deficiencies by publishing a notice of its intentions in order to give third parties an opportunity to comment prior to its issuing the final letter (e.g., *Volvo/Sauer* [1985] 1 CMLR 663). As far as national courts are concerned it is most unlikely that they would override or ignore a comfort letter, and even if it were subsequently revised (by the Commission) or invalidated (by the Court of Justice) which in either case is theoretically possible, it is likely that the principle of legitimate expectations could be invoked to shield the parties concerned from any adverse consequences, provided they had acted in good faith in reliance on the letter.

Further reading

See reading for chapter 12 and:

Forrester, I. and Norall, C., 'The Laicization of Community Law; Self Help and the Rule of Reason' (1984) 21 CML Rev 11.
Green, N., 'Article 85 in perspective' [1988] ECLR 190.
Steindorff, E., 'Article 85 and the Rule of Reason' (1984) 21 CML Rev 639.
Venit, J., 'The Commission's Opposition Procedure – Legal Consequences and Tactical Considerations' (1985) 22 CML Rev 167.
Whish, R. and Sufrin, B., 'Article 85 and the Rule of Reason' (1987) 7 Yearbook of European Law 1.

FOURTEEN
Article 86

The prohibition

Article 86 provides that:

Any abuse by one or more undertakings of a dominant position within the common market or in a substantial part of it shall be prohibited as incompatible with the common market in so far as it may affect trade between member States.

The prohibition is followed by a list of examples of abuse.

Whereas Article 85 is concerned with the dangers to competition arising from the grouping together of otherwise independent organisations, Article 86 is aimed at individual undertakings and the special problems raised by market power. If an agreement between independent undertakings which is merely capable of restricting or distorting competition is prohibited, *a fortiori* this must apply to abusive behaviour on the part of a dominant undertaking, which will have a much more profound effect on competition; indeed its very position may enable it to eliminate competition altogether.

As its wording makes clear the scope of Article 86 is not limited to monopolies or single organisations enjoying substantial market power. It applies also to undertakings within the same corporate or economic group which, when combined, together create a position of dominance. Where parent companies are acting in close conjunction with their subsidiaries they will often be treated as a single undertaking (see *Eurofix & Bauco* v *Hilti AG* [1989] 4 CMLR 677).

It was thought originally that Article 86 did not apply to undertakings which were independent of each other, and could not therefore be used to control oligopolies. This has not proved to be the case. In *Re Italian Flat Glass* ((1989) OJ No.L 33/44) the Commission held that three Italian producers of flat glass, who between them held a 79% to 95% share of the Italian market in flat glass, had a *collective* dominant position in these markets and had abused that position. Whilst the decision was annulled in part in *SIV* v *Commission* (cases

T68/89, T77/89, T78/89) for lack of proof of dominance, the application of Article 86 to oligopolies was not disputed by the court. Nevertheless the implications of the decision for oligopolies are not clear. In *Re Italian Flat Glass* the parties were engaged in concerted price-fixing and market-sharing practices in breach of Article 85(1). It remains to be seen whether Article 86 could be invoked to control oligopolistic practices which are not in breach of Article 85(1), but which nevertheless undermine the competitive structure in a particular market. Nevertheless, it seems that Articles 85 and 86 are not mutually exclusive; where doubt exists as to which Article is applicable, both should be pleaded.

Undertakings

The term 'undertakings' is subject to the same broad interpretation as is applied to Article 85, and covers the same activities, both public and private. As the Court held in *Italy* v *Commission* (case 41/83), Article 173 proceedings, in the context of a challenge to a Commission Decision that certain activities of British Telecom were in breach of Article 86, the fact that the enterprise has statutory rule-making powers does not prevent EC competition law from applying to such powers. Similarly, the Commission pointed out in the *Belgian Telemarketing* Decision [1986] 2 CMLR 558 that the fact the dominant (in this case monopoly) position is brought about or encouraged by provisions laid down by law is no bar to the application of Article 86.

   Like Article 85, Article 86 applies to undertakings engaged in the provision of goods or services, and can apply to any undertaking in the world as long as the effects of the abuse are felt inside the common market. The most vulnerable under Article 86 are the large multinationals. The Commission will not hesitate to take into account the economic strength of other members of a group or to fix them with liability if they are implicated in the abusive behaviour. The most obvious example is the case of *Europemballage Corp. and Continental Can Co. Inc.* v *Commission* (case 6/72), Article 173 proceedings. However, the scope of Article 86 is not limited, as will be seen, to very large concerns.

   Article 86 contains 3 essential ingredients. There must be:

(a)   a dominant position,
(b)   an abuse of that position, and
(c)   the abuse must affect trade between member States.

The principle of dominance

Dominance was defined in *United Brands Co.* v *Commission* (case 27/76), Article 173 proceedings, at para. 65, as:

   a position of economic strength enjoyed by an undertaking which enables it to prevent effective competition being maintained on the relevant market by giving it the power to behave to an appreciable extent independently of its competitors, customers, and ultimately of its consumers.

To this the Commission added in *AKZO Chemie BV* [1986] 3 CMLR 273 at para. 67 that:

> The power to exclude effective competition is not . . . in all cases coterminous with independence from competitive factors but may also involve the ability to eliminate or seriously weaken existing competitors or to prevent potential competitors from entering the market.

In order to assess whether an undertaking has sufficient economic strength to behave independently of, or even exclude, competitors, it is necessary first to ascertain the relevant market in which competition is said to exist. As the Court pointed out in *Europemballage Corp. and Continental Can Co. Inc.* v *Commission* (case 6/72), a position can be dominant within the meaning of Article 86 only if it is dominant in a relevant product market.

The relevant product market (RPM)

This is defined by the Commission and the Court in terms of product substitution. The relevant product market is one in which products are substantially interchangeable (*Istituto Chemicoterapico Italiano SpA* v *Commission* (cases 6 & 7/73), Article 173 proceedings). It includes identical products, or products considered by consumers to be similar by reason of their characteristics, price or use. Two questions are central to this enquiry:

(a) To what extent is the customer, or importer, or wholesaler, able to buy goods *similar* to those supplied by the dominant firm, or *acceptable as substitutes?* This is known as cross-elasticity of demand.

(b) To what extent are other firms *able to supply, or capable of producing* acceptable substitutues? This is known as cross-elasticity of supply.

These questions may be assessed by reference to the characteristics of the product, its price, or the use to which it is to be put. Although the principles are expressed in terms of goods or products they apply equally in the context of services.

Ascertaining the relevant product market is no easy matter. Its difficulties are illustrated in the case of *Europemballage Corp. and Continental Can Co. Inc.* (case 6/72). This case involved the proposed takeover of a large Dutch packaging firm, Thomassen & Drijver-Verblifa NV (TDV) by Europemballage Corporation, a company registered in the USA, held and controlled by another US company, Continental Can Co. Inc. Continental Can was a powerful organisation engaged in packaging operations throughout the world. It held an 86% share in a German packaging company, Schmalbach–Lubeca–Werke AG (SLW), prominent in Germany in the manufacture of, *inter alia*, light metal containers for meat and fish and bottle-sealing machines. Continental Can proposed to transfer its interest in SLW to Europemballage. Thus the whole deal would result in Europemballage and, indirectly, Continental Can, holding significant market power in Europe. The Commission issued a

Decision that the takeover of TDV by Continental Can via Europemballage constituted a breach of Article 86.

Continental Can, through its holding in SLW, was alleged to be dominant in Germany in three separate product markets:

(a) light metal containers for meat products,
(b) light metal containers for fish products, and
(c) metal closures for glass containers.

The acquisition of TDV by Europemballage would have further increased its dominance in these markets, since it would have removed an important potential competitor to SLW. Continental Can and Europemballage sought to annul the Commission's Decision. Although the Court agreed with the Commission in principle that the takeover could constitute an abuse, it found that the Commission had failed to prove the plaintiffs' dominance in the relevant product market. The Commission had failed to explore the question of product substitution. In order to be regarded as a distinct market, the Court held, the products in question must be individualised not only by the mere fact that they are used for packing certain products, but by particular characteristics of production which make them *specifically suitable for this purpose*. The Commission had also failed to consider the question of substitution on the supply side, i.e., whether other potential competitors might not be able to enter the market by simple adaptation.

The Commission was more thorough in *United Brands Co.* v *Commission* (case 27/76). In this case the Commission claimed that United Brands, one of the world's largest banana empires, producer of 'Chiquita' bananas, was abusing its dominant position in a number of ways. The question was whether the relevant product market was bananas, branded and unbranded, as the Commission claimed, or fresh fruit, as United Brands claimed. Clearly it was in the Commisson's interest to define the market as narrowly, and in the interest of United Brands to define it as widely, as possible. The Commission produced research from the Food and Agriculture Organisation which revealed that the existence of other fruit had very little influence on the price and consumption of bananas. Moreover, bananas occupied a special place in the diet of the very young, the sick, and the old. For them other fruits were not acceptable as substitutes. This time the Court accepted the Commission's view of the relevant product market.

It has been argued that the relevant product market could have been defined even more narrowly, either as branded bananas, or as bananas bought for the old, the sick or the very young, since there was evidence that customers continued to buy branded bananas even when they were considerably more expensive than unbranded bananas, thus showing little cross-elasticity of demand, whilst for the old, the sick and the very young, there was practically no cross-elasticity at all.

On the question of cross-elasticity, both the Commission and the Court will scrutinize the evidence with care, and will not necessarily agree with the experts. In *Eurofix & Bauco* v *Hilti AG* [1989] 4 CMLR 677, in the context of a finding of abuse against Hilti, a firm dominant in the market for cartridge strips and nails compatible with Hilti nail guns, the Commission rejected an econometric study produced by Hilti which purported to show significant cross-elasticity between nail guns and power drills, finding that the methodology of the study 'needed further refinement'. Moreover, the findings of the study were inconsistent with the way in which the market operated. The decision in *Hilti* was approved by the Court (*Hilti* v *Commission* (case 98/88), Article 173 proceedings).

The relevant product market, and the question of substitutability, is not necessarily defined by reference to consumers. In *Istituto Chemicoterapico Italiano SpA* v *Commission* (cases 6 & 7/73), Article 173 proceedings, the abuse alleged against Commercial Solvents Corporation (CSC), an American company, and its Italian subsidiary, Istituto Chemicoterapico Italiano SpA (ICI), was a refusal to supply an Italian company, Zoja, with a particular chemical, aminobutanol, which CSC had supplied to Zoja in the past through ICI. The chemical was required for processing into ethambutol, a drug used for the treatment of tuberculosis. CSC had a near monopoly in aminobutanol, which was widely used as the best, and cheapest, for the manufacture of ethambutol. CSC refused to supply Zoja with aminobutanol in order that it might itself manufacture ethambutol in Italy through ICI. However, ethambutol was not the only drug suitable for treating tuberculosis. There existed a number of others, based on different raw materials. Thus there was a substitutable end product. Moreover, ethambutol could be made from other raw materials. So was the relevant product market aminobutanol, CSC's raw material, as the Commission decided — in which case CSC was undoubtedly dominant — or was it raw materials for making ethambutol — in which case CSC was probably not dominant — or was it, as CSC claimed, the end product, a drug for the treatment of tuberculosis — in which case CSC was undoubtedly not dominant? In an action before the Court for annulment of the Commission's decision, CSC argued that what mattered was whether consumers had a choice of drugs for tuberculosis. Article 86 was aimed at abuses which prejudiced the interests of consumers. The Court disagreed. Article 86 was concerned not only with abuses which prejudiced consumers directly. It was also aimed at abuses which prejudiced consumers indirectly by impairing the competitive structure. The effect of CSC's refusal to supply Zoja was to eliminate one of the principal manufacturers of ethambutol in the common market. Nor was the Court prepared to accept that Zoja could switch to other raw materials for the manufacture of ethambutol. The Court found that it was not feasible for Zoja to adapt its production in this way. Only if other raw materials could be substituted *without difficulty* for aminobutanol could they be regarded as acceptable substitutes. Since they could not the relevant product market was aminobutanol.

The hard line taken in this case illustrates that the Commission and the Court are not concerned merely with the immediate protection of the consumer; they are conerned to protect competition at the manufacturing level and in particular to prevent the smaller firm from suffering at the hands of its more powerful competitors. Similar thinking lay behind the Commission and the Court's approach in *Établissements Consten SA* v *Commission* (cases 56 & 58/64). Both reflect the influence of French and German competition policy on EEC law.

In the above cases the relevant product market was a substantial one and the parties alleged to be dominant in that market wielded considerable power. But the relevant market, whether in goods or services, can be quite small, and provided an undertaking is dominant in that market it does not need to be generally powerful to fall foul of Article 86. In *Hugin Kassaregister AB* v *Commission* (case 22/78), Article 173 proceedings, a Swedish firm, Hugin, which manufactured cash registers, supplying them to Liptons Cash Registers and Business Equipment Ltd in the UK through its British subsidiary, Hugin Cash Registers Ltd, was found to be dominant in the supply of spare parts for Hugin machines to independent repair businesses. (See also *AB Volvo* v *Erik Veng* (case 238/87).) In *British Brass Band Instruments* v *Boosey & Hawkes Interim measures* [1988] 4 CMLR 67 the relevant product market, in which Boosey & Hawkes held a 90% share, was held to be instruments for *British style* brass bands. The fact that the market, or in this case the sub-market, was defined in narrow terms, did not, the Court said, exclude the application of Article 86. 'The essential question is whether the sub-market is sufficiently distinct in commercial reality.' Similarly certain activities of a firm which seem quite insignificant may constitute a relevant market in which that firm may be dominant. In *General Motors Continental NV* [1975] 1 CMLR D20 the issuing of test certificates for second-hand imports of Opel cars, carried out exclusively by General Motors in Belgium, constituted the relevant market, even though in one year (1973) only five cars were involved, and in the *British Leyland plc* Decision [1984] 3 CMLR 92 BL was found to be dominant in the provision of national type-approval certificates for its vehicles since it alone had the right to issue these certificates. The Decision was approved by the Court in *British Leyland plc* v *Commisson* (case 226/84), Article 173 proceedings.

Dominance in fact

Once the relevant market is established it is necessary to ascertain whether the parties concerned are dominant within that market. When will an undertaking be regarded as dominant? The Commission suggested in *United Brands Co.* [1976] 1 CMLR D28 that:

> Undertakings are in a dominant position when they have the power to behave independently without taking into account, to any substantial extent, their competitors, purchasers and suppliers. Such is the case where an undertaking's market share, either in itself or when combined with its know-how, access to raw materials, capital or other major advantage such as trade-mark ownership, enables it to determine the prices or to control the production or distribution of a significant part of the relevant goods. It is not necessary for the undertaking to have total dominance such as would deprive all other market participants of their commercial freedom, as long as it is strong enough in general terms to devise its own strategy as it wishes, even if there are differences in the extent to which it dominates individual submarkets.

Thus the question of dominance requires a wide-ranging economic analysis of the undertaking concerned and of the market in which it operates. According to the Commission the significant factors will be:

(a) *Market share.* This will be of the first importance. In *Instituto Chemicoterapico Italiano SpA* (cases 6 & 7/73), CSC (according to the Commisson; this was not found proved by the Court) held a virtual monopoly in aminobutanol. In *Europemballage Corp. and Continental Can Co. Inc.* (case 6/72) SLW, owned by Continental Can, held a 70-80% share in the RPM in Germany. But such a high figure is not essential. United Brands held only a 40-45% share in the banana market in a substantial part of Europe. Where the share is less than 50%, the structure of the market will be important, particularly the market share held by the next largest competitor. In *United Brands* (case 27/76) the nearest competitors held 16% and 10% shares in the market. Where the market is highly fragmented the Commission has even suggested that a share of 20-40% could constitute dominance (*10th Report on Competition Policy*). The Court has held that the existence of lively competition does not rule out a dominant position (*United Brands*).

(b) The *length of time* during which a firm has held its position in the relevant product market. This point was stressed in *Istituto Chemicoterapico Italiano* and *United Brands*. The firm cannot be dominant unless it is dominant *over time*. Clearly the longer a firm has been dominant, the greater the barriers to entry for potential competitors.

(c) *Financial and technological resources.* A firm with large financial and technological resources will be in a position to adapt its market strategy in order to meet and drive out competitors. It may indulge in predatory pricing, selling below cost if necessary to undercut rivals (see *AKZO Chemie BV* Decision [1986] 3 CMLR 273); it can maintain demand for its product by heavy advertising, thereby reducing cross-elasticity of demand, as was clearly the case in *United Brands*. Technological resources will enable a firm to keep ahead of potential competitors.

(d) *Access to raw materials and outlets.* The greater the degree of vertical integration (i.e., control over businesses up and downstream in the marketing process) the greater a firm's power to act independently. However powerful Zoja may have been as a manufacturer of ethambutol, it was dependent on CSC for its raw materials. CSC on the other hand controlled both raw materials and outlets via ICI. United Brands enjoyed an even greater degree of vertical integration. Its empire extended virtually from the plantation to the table. They owned plantations, fleets of refrigerated vessels and refrigerated warehouses in key ports throughout Europe.

(e) *Behaviour.* The Commission suggested in *United Brands* that an undertaking's behaviour can in itself provide evidence of dominance. In *United Brands* the firm's discriminatory rebate system was taken, inter alia, as an indicium of independence. In *Eurofix & Bauco* v *Hilti* the Commission regarded Hilti's discriminatory treatment of its customers as 'witness to its ability to act independently and without due regard to other competitors or customers'.

Economists have questioned the validity in economic terms of some of these criteria, and even more so their application by the Commission in particular cases. For example, although United Brands had large financial and technological resources and enjoyed a high degree of vertical integration there was evidence that it faced fierce competition from time to time and its share of the market was falling. Moreover its banana operations were not showing steady profits. These factors would not seem to indicate a power to behave independently of competitors.

The relevant geographical market

To fall within Article 86 an undertaking must be dominant 'within the common market or in a substantial part of it'. Thus the question of dominance must be assessed also in the context of the relevant geographical market. The relevant geographical market is the one in which the 'objective conditions of competition are the same for all traders' (*United Brands Co.* v *Commission* (case 27/76)). It is the market in which available and acceptable substitutes exist, described, helpfully, by Overbury as 'the area in which consumers are willing to shop around for substitute supplies or in which manufacturers are willing to deliver'. This will depend on the cost and feasibility of transportation as well as consumer habits and preferences. Where goods are homogeneous and easily and cheaply transportable the relevant geographical market may be large. The Commission suggested in the *AKZO Chemie BV* Decision [1986] 3 CMLR 273 that in certain circumstances the whole of the common market may constitute the relevant geographical market. In *Eurofix & Hilti* the whole of the EEC was found to constitute the relevant geographical market in the nail cartridge market. Where goods are differentiated, or where consumer tastes are inflexible, or where transportation is difficult or costly, a single State or even part of a State may constitute the relevant market. Where a service is only needed within one particular State, as in *General Motors Continental NV* [1975] 1 CMLR D20 or *British Leyland plc* v *Commission* (case 226/84) clearly that State will represent the relevant market. As the Court commented in *United Brands*, in order to ascertain whether a particular territory is large enough to amount to a substantial part of the market, the pattern and volume of the production and consumption of the products as well as the habits and economic opportunities of vendors and purchasers must be considered.

Useful guidance on the relevant geographical market has been provided by the Commission's Notice on Agreements of Minor Importance ((1986) OJ No.C 231/2, paras 13 and 14). The cost of transport is noted as being particularly important. In deciding in *Hilti* that the relevant market was the whole of the EEC, the Commission took into account the fact that nail cartridges could be transported throughout the Community at relatively little cost. Clearly geographical markets have been growing and will continue to grow as the barriers to the single internal market are removed.

In considering the relevant geographical market the Commission has been criticised for failing adequately to take into account the possibility of countries outside the EEC forming part of the market, even though in the case of certain products (e.g., vitamins) a world market may exist. For this reason a firm may be treated as dominant even though it is subject to substantial competition world-wide. However, in *SIV v Commission Re Italian Flat Glass* (cases T68/89, T77/89, T78/89) the Commission's Decision was annulled in part on the grounds, inter alia, that the Commission had failed to take into account imports of flat glass from non-member States.

The temporal market

In assessing the question of dominance the temporal aspect of the market should also be considered. It has been suggested that the Commission in *United Brands* should have defined the relevant product market by reference to the particular time of the year (e.g. the winter months), when there was little opportunity for product substitution. The Commission did take the temporal element into account in *Re ABG Oil* [1977] 2 CMLR D1 in limiting the market for oil to the period of crisis following the OPEC action in the early 1970s.

Abuse

It is not dominance *per se* but the abuse of a dominant position that brings Article 86 into play. Examples of abuse are provided by Article 86.
They comprise:

(a)   directly or indirectly imposing unfair purchase or selling prices or unfair trading conditions;

(b)   limiting production, markets, or technical development to the prejudice of consumers,

(c)   applying dissimilar conditions to equivalent transactions with other trading parties, thereby placing them at a competitive disadvantage,

(d)   making the conclusion of contracts subject to acceptance by the other parties of supplementary obligations which, by their nature or commercial usage, have no connection with the subject of such contracts.

These are merely examples; the list is not exhaustive.

A glance back to Article 85 will reveal that the kinds of abuse prohibited under Article 86 run in close parallel to the examples of concerted behaviour likely to breach Article 85(1). As far as most forms of behaviour are concerned, the difference between Article 85 and Article 86 is a difference in degree rather than in kind. The existence of a dominant position merely makes the conduct more dangerous; thus there is no possibility of exemption for a breach of Article 86.

Abuses prohibited under Article 86 have been divided into two categories, the exploitative abuses and the anti-competitive abuses. Exploitative abuses occur when an undertaking seeks to take advantage of its position of dominance by imposing oppressive or unfair conditions on its trading partners. Examples of these are provided under (a), (c) and (d) above, and some behaviour under (b). Anti-competitive abuses are those which, whilst not in themselves unfair or oppressive, are damaging because they reduce or eliminate competition. Such behaviour would arise under paragraph (b) above, and certain practices falling under paragraph (d). Many kinds of behaviour fall into both categories (e.g., *Istituto Chemicoterapico Italiano SpA* (cases 6 & 7/73).

Exploitative abuses

United Brands Co. v *Commission* (case 27/76) provides a number of such abuses.

(a) *Unfair prices.* According to the Commission, United Brands Co. was charging excessively high prices for its branded bananas. Although this point was not found proved by the Court, the Court agreed with the Commission on the matter of principle. An excessive price was defined by the Court as one which bears no reasonable relation to the economic value of the product. This test was applied in *General Motors Continental NV* [1975] 1 CMLR D20 to prices charged by General Motors for its exclusive inspection service for second-hand Opel cars imported into Belgium The Commission decided that it had charged excessive rates on the service for five Opel cars in 1973. The Court, in annulment proceedings (case 26/75), applying the 'reasonable relation to economic value' test, found that GM's charges were excessive. The charge of abuse was, however, not sustained, as GM had amended its charges and reimbursed the five customers for the excessive charge.

In *British Leyland plc* v *Commission* (case 226/84), Article 173 proceedings, the fees charged for the type-approval certificates for left-hand drive cars (when issued) were found to be excessive and discriminatory.

Problems arise over the question of 'economic value'. Deciding the economic value of a product or a service is a complex accounting exercise which leaves ample scope for differences of opinion. Economists would disagree as to what constituted the economic value of a product, and indeed, whether it can be accurately ascertained at all. What uniformity, then, can be hoped for from national courts when called upon to apply Article 86?

(b) *Unfair trading conditions.* United Brands was found to be imposing unfair conditions by refusing to allow importers to resell bananas while they were still green. This meant that only wholesalers with the correct storage and ripening facilities were able to handle the bananas. The fact that the consumer might thereby be assured of obtaining a better, more standardised product did not prevent the Commission and the Court from finding that this requirement constituted an abuse. Again we find EEC competition law protecting the 'middleman'.

(c) *Discriminatory treatment.* United Brands was charging prices with a difference of, in some cases, more than 100% in different common market countries, not, apparently, according to objective criteria, but according to what the market would bear. This constituted discriminatory treatment. Similarly *British Leyland* (case 226/84) charged different prices for type-approval certificates for left-hand drive cars, without objective justification.

(d) *Refusal to supply.* United Brands refused to supply one of its most important wholesalers, who had constructed special facilities to store and ripen the bananas, in retaliation for his taking part in an advertising campaign for a competitor. This was found to be an abuse. A refusal to supply which is not retaliatory would fall into the category of anti-competitive abuses, to be discussed next.

Anti-competitive abuse

This kind of abuse is less easy to detect than the exploitative abuse. Here the dominant firm uses its position in such a way as to undermine or even eliminate existing competitors, thereby reinforcing or increasing its dominance. A number of examples may be considered:

(a) *Tying-in*. A good example of tying-in practices is provided by the case of *Hoffman-La Roche & Co. AG* v *Commission* (case 85/76), Article 173 proceedings. La Roche was the largest pharmaceutical company in the world, with a dominant position in seven separate vitamin markets. The alleged abuses lay in a number of tying-in practices. Customers undertook to buy all or most of their requirements from La Roche ('requirements contracts'); as a reward they were entitled to 'fidelity' rebates (discounts). The agreement also contained 'English' clauses. These provided that if customers found other suppliers offering similar products at cheaper prices they should ask La Roche to 'adjust' their prices. If La Roche failed to respond they were free to buy elsewhere. None of these clauses was oppressive as far as La Roche's customers were concerned. But the Commission (approved by the Court) found the practices to be abusive. The tying-in system limited their customers' freedom to buy from competing suppliers; the English clauses were unacceptable because they enabled La Roche to identify competitors and take pre-emptive action, e.g., by dropping its prices to its competitors' levels, thereby nipping potential rivals in the bud. Similar tying-in practices were condemned in *Hilti*.

(b) *Predatory pricing*. This is a strategy whereby prices are reduced, below cost if necessary, in order to drive potential competitors out of the market. In *AKZO Chemie BV* [1986] 3 CMLR 273, Commission Decision, AKZO, a firm dominant world-wide in the production of organic peroxides, was found to be engaged in such practices. However, as the Commisson pointed out, it may be necessary to examine a firm's costs and motives in order to ascertain whether its low prices are predatory or merely the result of efficiency. Where low pricing is susceptible of several explanations evidence of an anti-competitive intent may be needed. Indeed, the lowering of prices may even be evidence of weakness. In *Hoffman-La Roche* the Court suggested that the fact that an undertaking is compelled by the pressure of its competitors' price reductions to lower its prices is in general incompatible with that independence which is the hallmark of dominance. The Court, in its first decision on predatory pricing (*AKZO Chemie* v *Commission* (case 62/86), Article 173 proceedings) agreed with the Commission. There was a distinction, in competition law terms, between lowering prices in order to win new customers and trying to eliminate a competitor. In the case of *AKZO* the firm's 'avowed intention' had been to eliminate one of its competitors.

(c)   *Refusal to supply.* Where supplies (or services) are refused in order to reduce or eliminate competition, such a refusal will constitute abuse. This appeared to be the case in *Istituto Chemicoterapico Italiano SpA* (cases 6 & 7/73) where it was intended that CSC's subsidiary, ICI, would take over production of ethambutol previously undertaken by Zoja (see also *Hugin Kassaregister AB* v *Commission* (case 22/78)). Boosey & Hawkes' cessation of supplies to BBI was designed deliberately to prevent them entering into the market as competitors. Similarly BL's covert purpose in refusing type-approval to imports of left-hand drive cars was to keep imports out, thus maintaining an artificial partitioning of the market. However, a refusal to supply either an existing or a new customer will not necessarily be abusive. Arguing from *Metro-SB-Grossmärkte GmbH & Co. KG* v *Commission* (case 26/76), a refusal may be permissible if it is non-discriminatory and objectively justified. However, a refusal of supplies, particularly to an existing customer, will require cogent justification, and any signs of an anti-competitive motive will be fatal.

(d)   *Exclusive reservation of activities.* Similar principles to those applicable to a refusal to supply will apply where a dominant undertaking reserves certain activities to itself. This occurred in *Italy* v *Commission* (*Re British Telecommunications* (case 41/83), Article 173 proceedings) where BT reserved for itself exclusive rights to its telex forwarding services, and in *Belgian Telemarketing* (case 311/84), Article 177 proceedings, in which a telephone marketing service was channelled exclusively through RTL's agent. The Court pointed out in *Belgian Telemarketing* that there was no 'objective necessity' for its so doing. This implies, in line with *Metro*, that the exclusive reservation of certain activities by a dominant undertaking, whether for itself or for an appointed agent, might be permissible if it were necessary and objectively justified. However the Court was not prepared to accept that the preservation of RTL's image constituted a 'necessity'.

(e)   *Import and export bans.* In view of the hard line of the Commission and the Court over such restrictions under Article 85 it is no surprise that import and export bans have been held to constitute abuse under Article 86 (*Suiker Unie* v *Commission* (case 40/73), Article 173 proceedings). Apart from when industrial property rights are legitimately exercised to this end it is hard to imagine a situation in which such a ban would not be deemed an abuse.

(f)   *Mergers and takeovers.* In all the examples of anti-competitive behaviour considered so far, there has existed an element of exploitation; the parties have used their dominance, if not unfairly or oppressively, in order to reduce or eliminate competition. Perhaps the most surprising development came in the case of *Continental Can (Europemballage Corp. and Continental Can Co. Inc.* v *Commission* (case 6/72), Article 173 proceedings). Here the Commission had applied Article 86 in the context of a proposed merger, namely, the proposed takeover by Continental Can, which owned an 86% share in SLW in Germany, of TDV in Holland, the entire package to be held by Continental Can's subsidiary Europemballage. The Commission issued a Decision that the proposed takeover constituted an abuse of their dominant position within the common market (viz. Germany). In annulment proceedings Continental Can argued that such action could not be regarded as an abuse. Article 86 was concerned only with behaviour detrimental to consumers. Moreover, it required some causative link between the position of dominance and abuse. Neither Continental Can nor Europemballage had used their power to effect the merger. The Court, in annulment proceedings, disagreed. Article 86, the Court said, cannot allow mergers which eliminate competition. Prejudice under Article 86 does not mean affecting consumers directly but also prejudice through interference with the structure of competition itself. Nor was it necessary to prove a causal link between the dominance and the abuse. The mere fact of dominance rendered the proposed takeover an abuse. Although the Court annulled the Commission's Decision on the grounds that the relevant product markets had not been fully proved, the principle was established.

Continental Can and Article 86 remained the basis on which the Commission exercised control over mergers until the Court decided for the first time, in *BAT & Reynolds* v *Commission* (cases 142, 156/84), Article 173 proceedings, that mergers could also fall within Article 85(1) (see chapter 13). This widened the scope of the Commission's control, since its jurisdiction no longer depended on the need to prove dominance. *BAT & Reynolds* v *Commission* provided the impetus for the passing of the Merger Regulation, Regulation 4064/89 (corrected version OJ No. L 257 21.9.90), proposals for which had been circulating for many years.

The Merger Regulation

Regulation 4064/89, which came into effect on 30 October 1990, applies to mergers, acquisitions and certain joint ventures, between firms with a combined worldwide turnover of more than 5,000 million ecus, where at least two of the firms have a combined turnover of more than 250 million ecus in the EC but do not earn more than two-thirds of their turnover in a single member State (Article 1). A distinction is made between cooperative and concentrative joint ventures; only the latter will fall within the Regulation. A joint venture will be concentrative if it forms an autonomous economic entity and does not result in the coordination of its parents' other activities.

The principle underlying the Regulation is that of the 'one-stop shop'. Concentrations falling within the Regulation will be subject to the exclusive jurisdiction of the Commission (Article 21) and must be notified to the Commission (Article 4). A failure to notify or to supply correct or exact information may result in fines of from 1,000 to 50,000 ecus (Article 14). Concentrations falling outside the Regulation's thresholds will be subject to control by the relevant national authority. However, a member State may ask the Commission to intervene in respect of a concentration falling outside the Regulation which will 'significantly impede' competition within its own territory (Article 22(3)). Similarly the Commission may refer a matter notified to it to the relevant national authority where it is thought to be appropriate.

A concentration will be permitted if it does not 'create or strengthen a dominant position as a result of which effective competition would be impeded in the common market or a substantial part of it' (Article 2(2)). In making its decision the Commission must take into account the 'need to preserve and develop effective competition within the common market' (Article 2(1)). The Commission has one month in which to decide whether to investigate the matter and four months from the date on which proceedings are initiated in which to reach a final Decision (Article 10).

Procedures governing notification and detailed provision in respect of hearings and time-limits are laid down in Regulation 2367/90 (OJ No. L 219 14.8.90). This Regulation replaces Regulation 17/62 in respect of *all* concentrations (Article 22(2)). As a result the Commission's competence to apply Articles 85 and 86 to concentrations is significantly reduced, and individuals' right to complain to the Commission under Article 3 of Regulation 17/62 in respect of these matters is excluded. These factors, and the high thresholds set by Regulation 4064/89, whereby a concentration is deemed to have a 'community dimension' have been criticised as introducing a weakness into EEC competition law. The thresholds were to be reviewed by the Council, acting by qualified majority, after four years; the Commission is hoping to achieve a substantial reduction by the end of 1993. However, at the time of writing, only one out of a flood of concentrations notified under the Regulation has failed to obtain approval (*Aerospatiale/Alenia/De Havilland* (EEC Bulletin No. 10 (1991), 1.2.24). This indicates that the thresholds may not be set too high.

Since Articles 85 and 86 are directly effective individuals remain free despite the Regulation to raise questions concerning *any* concentration, whatever its dimensions, before their national courts. Thus it cannot be guaranteed that concentrations falling outside the Regulation will not be found to breach these Articles. This problem apart, the Regulation has introduced a welcome degree of certainty in an area likely to be subject to ever-increasing activity as firms both within and outside the Community seek to take advantage of the opportunities offered by the single EEC market.

The abuse must affect trade between member States

As with Article 85, there must be some effect on trade between member States for Article 86 to apply, but such an effect is not hard to establish. The Court held in *British Leyland plc* v *Commission* (case 226/84) that it was not necessary to establish any specific effects, as long as there was evidence that a particular activity *might* affect trade between member States. Thus a theoretical possibility will be sufficient.

However, in *Hugin Kassaregister AB* v *Commission* (case 22/78), Article 173 proceedings, the Court annulled the Commission's Decision ([1978] 1 CMLR D19) that Hugin had acted in breach of Article 86. Although it agreed with the Commission on the questions of the relevant product market and abuse, it found that Hugin's refusal to supply Liptons with spares did not affect trade between States. Hugin was a Swedish firm and thus outside the common market, and Liptons was functioning in London on a purely local scale.

An effect on trade between member States was held in *Istituto Chemicoterapico Italiano SpA* (cases 6 & 7/73) to include repercussions on the competitive structure within the common market.

This was approved and followed by the Court in *Bodson* v *Pompes Funèbres* (case 30/87) and an effect on trade between member States found despite the Commission's view that a monopoly in funeral services granted to Ms Bodson by the municipality of Charleville-Mèziéres did not affect trade between member States.

The relative ease with which an effect on trade between member States may be established is particularly important in the UK, since under UK law the decision to investigate a merger or a monopoly situation under the Fair Trading Act 1973, or anti-competitive practices under the Competition Act 1980, is a discretionary one, and, as such, does not give rise to rights or remedies for individuals. Article 86, on the other hand, is directly effective, and gives rise to rights and obligations for individuals. Thus, provided the matter is seen to have the requisite Community dimension, an individual may challenge behaviour, and obtain remedies, in a situation in which he would have no remedy under national law (see chapter 15).

Negative clearance and exemption

There is no provision for exemption from liability under Article 86. Thus a party cannot notify and obtain exemption from fines. However, parties may apply for negative clearance under Article 2 of Regulation 17/62 in order to obtain a Decision that their proposed action provides no ground for action under Article 86.

Further reading

De Jong, H., 'Unfair and Discriminatory Pricing under Article 86' [1980] ECLR 297.

Elland, W., 'The Mergers Control Regulation and its effect on National Merger Control and the Residual Application of Articles 85 and 86' [1991] ECLR 19.

Flint, J., 'Abuse of a collective dominant position' [1978] 2 LIEI 21.

Fuller Baden, 'Economic Analysis of a Dominant Position: Article 86 of the Treaty' (1979) 4 EL Rev 423.

Gyselen & Kyriazio, 'Article 86: "The Monopoly Power Measurement Issue Revisited"' (1990) 27 CML Rev 7.

Korah, V., 'Concept of a dominant Position within the meaning of Article 86' (1980) 17 CML Rev 395.

Lever & Lasok, 'Mergers and Joint Ventures in the EEC' (1986) 6 YEL 121.

Overbury, C., 'First Experiences of European Merger Control', (1991) European Law Review Competition Law Checklist 1990 p. 79.

Pathak, 'EEC Concentration Control: the Foreseeable Uncertainties' [1990] ECLR 119.

Scott James, M., 'Concept of Abuse in EEC Competition Law - an American view' (1976) 92 LQR 242.

Sharpe, T., 'Predation' [1987] ECLR 53.

Siragusa, M., and Subiotto, R., 'The EEC Merger Control Regulation: the Commission's Evolving Case Law' (1991) 28 CML Rev 877.

Smith, P., 'The Wolf in Wolf's clothing; the Problem of Predatory Pricing' (1989) 14 EL Rev 209.

Temple Lang, J., 'Monopolies and the definition of abuse of a dominant position under Article 86 EEC Treaty' (1979) 16 CML Rev 345.

Vajda, C., 'Article 86 and a refusal to supply' [1981] ECLR 97.

Vogelenganz, P., 'Abuse of a dominant position in Article 86; the problem of causality and some applications' (1976) 13 CML Rev 61.

FIFTEEN

Enforcement of Articles 85 and 86: powers and procedures

In all matters except concentrations, as defined in the Merger Control Regulation 4064/89, Article 3, which are governed by Regulation 2367/90, the powers and procedures governing EEC competition law are laid down in Regulation 17/62. It is the Commission which has the central role in enforcing Articles 85 and 86, through the department responsible for competition policy, Directorate-General (D/G) IV, although national courts, and even individuals, have some part to play.

In order to fulfil its tasks the Commission enjoys substantial powers; at the same time it is subject to strict procedural requirements under Regulation 17/62 and to a general duty of confidentiality (*AKZO Chemie BV* v *Commission* (case 53/85), Article 173 proceedings). A breach of these duties can result in the annulment of its Decision by the Court of Justice, or now the Court of First Instance, and even a successful action for damages (*Adams* v *Commission* (case 145/83), Article 215 proceedings). The Court may order interim measures pending its final decision (Article 185, 186 EEC; see *Publishers' Association* v *Commission Re Net Book Agreement* (case 56/89R)).

Powers and duties of the Commission

Powers of dispensation   As has already been noted, it is the Commission's task to monitor agreements with a view to granting negative clearance or exemption. Whilst national courts may apply Article 85(1) and Article 86, only the Commission can grant exemption under Article 85(3), and individual exemption can only be granted following notification of the parties' agreements (or proposed course of action) in the prescribed manner (form A/B). Although notification cannot prevent an illegal agreement from being declared void (under Article 85(2)), it can result in immunity from fines (Regulation 17/62, Article 15(5)(a)). However, under Article 15(6) the Commission may withdraw that immunity by Decision if after a preliminary examination the agreement is found in breach of Article 85(1) and not eligible for exemption under Article 85(3).

Before taking a final Decision *adverse to* the applicant the Commission must give him an opportunity to be heard on the matters to which he objects (Regulation 17/62, Article 19(1)). Applications for a hearing by persons who show a 'sufficient interest' must also be granted (Regulation 17/62, Article 19(2)).

Before taking a Decision *favourable* to the applicant the Commission must publish a summary of the relevant application or notification and all interested parties must be invited to submit their comments (Regulation 17/62, Article 19(3)).

All final Decisions granting or refusing negative clearance or exemption must be published in the *Official Journal* (Regulation 17/62, Article 21).

Since a final decision concerning negative clearance or exemption may require an extensive analysis of the economic context in which the agreement operates in order to assess its effect on competition within the common market, some years may elapse before such a Decision is issued. Because of this, and because of the volume of notifications received, and a lack of resources to deal formally with all the cases brought to its attention, the Commission has resorted to a number of short cuts (see chapter 13). Many cases are now settled informally; block exemptions have been issued, thus obviating the need for notification. Where agreements are notified, comfort letters may be issued giving soft clearance or exemption, following only brief investigation and enquiry. The extension of the opposition procedure has increasingly relieved the Commission of the need to issue even an informal reply. These developments have no doubt speeded up the decision-making process, and given some security to the parties concerned, but they have been criticised as lacking the essential safeguards of the prescribed procedures. Although the Commission has tightened up its procedures in recent years, the lack of a formal Decision from the Commission has deprived interested parties of both the certainty to which they were entitled under Regulation 17/62 and the chance of judicial review by the Court, since only binding Decisions are capable of annulment.

Investigative powers If the Commission is to undertake a market analysis adequate to enable it to make a Decision concerning negative clearance or exemption, it must be able to obtain the necessary information. *A fortiori* if it is to fulfil its main task, carried out through D/G IV, of rooting out agreements or practices in breach of Article 85 and 86 which have not been notified, with a view to bringing them to an end by formal Decision (Regulation 17/62, Article 3). To these ends it has been given extensive powers:

(a) *Requests for information* (Regulation 17/62, Article 11). The Commission may obtain from the Governments of member States and competent authorities of member States, and from undertakings and associations of undertakings, all information which is 'necessary' to enable it to carry out its task of enforcing Articles 85 and 86.

(b) *Inquiry into sectors of the economy* (Regulation 17/62, Article 12). The Commission may conduct general inquiries into whole sectors of the economy if economic trends suggest that competition in the common market is being restricted or distorted. To achieve this task it may request every undertaking in the sector concerned to supply details of agreements, decisions or concerted practices considered exempt, and undertakings or groups of undertakings which may be dominant to supply information concerning their structure and practices.

(c) *Investigations by the Commission* (Regulation 17/62, Article 14). The Commission may undertake all necessary on-the-spot investigations.

These include the power to enter premises, to examine books or business records, to take copies of such records, and to conduct oral examinations. Investigations may be 'voluntary', under Article 11(2), or 'compulsory', under Article 11(3). Before undertaking such investigations Commission officials are required to produce written authorisation in the form of a Decision specifying the subject-matter and purpose of the investigation (Article 14(3)). The Decision 'shall appoint the date on which the investigation is to be made'. In *National Panasonic (UK) Ltd* v *Commission* (case 136/79), Article 173 proceedings, National Panasonic sought to annul the Commission's Decision of authorisation required by Article 14. The Commission's officials had arrived at dawn, unannounced but bearing their authorisation, and had conducted their search and seizure operations before Panasonic could summon its lawyers to the scene. Panasonic argued that Article 14(3) required that some prior warning should have been given, as required for a request for information under Article 11. The Court disagreed; looking for support to the preamble to Regulation 17/62 (eighth recital) it found the Commission was entitled to undertake 'such investigations as are necessary' to bring to light any breaches of Article 85 or 86.

As a result of its investigations the Commission discovered that National Panasonic and its distributors were engaged in concerted practices in breach of Article 85(1) (see [1983] 1 CMLR 497).

In *Hoechst* v *Commission* (cases 46/87, 227/88) Hoechst sought likewise to challenge the legality of the Commission's 'dawn raid'. Hoechst claimed that the search breached the fundamental principle of the inviolability of the home, and that the Commission's Decision of authorisation under Article 14(3) lacked precision, as a result of which they had been deprived of their right to a fair hearing. The ECJ held that whilst EEC law provided protection against arbitrary or disproportionate intervention on the part of public authorities (see chapter 4), there was no evidence that these principles had been breached. Moreover, it was for the Commission (subject to the control of the Court), and not for national courts, to decide on the necessity of the investigation, although the Commission must respect the procedural guarantees provided under national law for the purposes of such investigations. As to the lack of precision of the grounds of the Commission's Decision, the Court held that the Commission is not required to provide the addressee with 'all the information at its disposal with regard to the alleged infringement or to provide a rigorous classification of those infringements', as long as it 'clearly indicates the suspicions which it is seeking to verify'. The Court found that although the Commission's statement of reasons was drafted in very general terms, it contained the essential information required by Article 14(3). The reasoning in *Hoechst* was followed in *Dow Benelux NV* v *Commission* (case 85/87) and *Dow Chemical Ibérica SA* v *Commission* (cases 97–99/87).

(d) *Investigations by the authorities of member States* (Regulation 17/62, Article 13). The Commission may request the competent authorities of the member States to undertake the investigations which it considers necessary under Article 14(1) or which it has ordered under Article 14(3). In the latter case they too must produce written authorisation. Normally officials of the competent authority in the member State where the investigation takes place will accompany the Commission's officials.

Undertakings are bound to comply with the (legitimate) demands of the Commisson under Articles 11, 12 and 14. If they fail to do so, or give false or misleading information, they are liable to penalties (Regulation 17/62, Articles 15 and 16). The Commission imposed a periodic penalty of 1,000 ecus per day on Hoechst as a result of their refusal to submit to the Commission's searches. This too was found by the Court to be legitimate. It was originally thought, on the basis of Advocate-General Warner's comments in *Australian Mining & Smelting Europe Ltd* v *Commission* (case 155/79), Article 173 proceedings, that information cannot be withheld even if it is self-incriminating. However, in *Orkem* v *Commission* (case 374/87), Article 173 proceedings, the Court held that the Commission, although entitled under Article 11 of Regulation 17/62 to compel an undertaking to provide all necessary information relating to facts of which it might have knowledge, could not compel the undertaking to incriminate itself by admitting to infringements of competition rules. To do so would infringe the undertaking's right to a fair hearing, which was a fundamental principle of Community law. It was for the Commission to prove that a breach of Article 85 or 86 had occurred (see also *Solvay & Cie* v *Commission* (case 27/88) decided on the same day).

There is also limited scope for claiming privilege. According to *Australian Mining & Smelting Europe Ltd* certain correspondence between a client and an independent lawyer based in the EEC or with an establishment in the EEC, principally correspondence dealing with the defence of the client after the initiation of proceedings by the Commission, is privileged, whilst similar dealings with an in-house lawyer are not. Such discrimination is hard to justify (but see chapter 4).

Confidential information

The Commission is subject to a duty of confidentiality. Under Regulation 17/62, Articles 19(2), 20(2) and 21(2), it must have regard to the 'legitimate interests of undertakings in the protection of their business secrets'. In *AKZO Chemie BV* v *Commission* (case 53/85), Article 173 proceedings, the Court held that it was for the Commisson to decide whether a particular document contained business secrets. However, before communicating documents allegedly containing business secrets to third parties the Commission must, by Decision, inform the undertaking whose alleged secrets are to be revealed, and give it an opportunity to challenge that Decision before the Court of Justice.

The duty to protect business secrets expressed in Regulation 17/62 is a specific application of a general duty 'not to disclose information of the kind covered by the obligation of professional secrecy' imposed by Article 214 of the EEC Treaty. In *Adams* v *Commission* (case 145/83), Article 215 proceedings, the applicant, Mr Adams, obtained damages for breach of this duty, in exceptional, and tragic, circumstances. As a senior executive working for Hoffman-La-Roche in Switzerland, he had secretly and voluntarily passed to the Commission documents about La Roche's business activities, as a result of which La Roche was eventually fined 300,000 ecus for breach of Article 86 ((case 85/76), Article 173 proceedings; fine reduced to 200,000 ecus by Court). Adams had asked for his identity to be kept secret. The Commisson did not reveal his identity, but in the course of its investigations it passed the documents to La Roche, albeit doctored, and as a result Adam's identity as informer was discovered. La Roche subsequently brought criminal proceedings against Adams, who was found guilty of industrial espionage under Swiss law and sentenced to one year's imprisonment. During this time his wife committed suicide. In his subsequent claim against the Commission for damages the Court held that the Commission's duty of confidentiality under Article 214 applied to information supplied even on a voluntary basis. It was in breach of that duty since it had not taken care to prevent his identity becoming known, and had not taken steps to warn Adams when it learned that La Roche was contemplating criminal action against him. However, damages were reduced by 50% on account of Adams's contributory negligence. (He had failed to give the Commisson his precise address; failed to warn it that the documents might give a clue to his identity, and had returned to Switzerland knowing that in doing so he risked arrest.) A cautionary tale.

Sanctions

Fines and penalties   The Commission has power to impose fines for breaches of Articles 85 or 86 of up to 1 million ecu (the value of the ecu is determined according to a basket of European currencies, normally fluctuating in the UK around 70 pence) on an undertaking, or 10% of its turnover, whichever is the greater (Regulation 17/62, Article 15(2)). In the latter case, fines are calculated on the basis of group turnover in the relevant sector, not only in the countries where the offence took place but globally (*Re Benelux Flat Glass Cartel* [1985] 2 CMLR 350). The size of the fine will depend on a number of criteria (see *Re Benelux Flat Glass Cartel*). These are:

(a)   The nature of the infringement. It is the 'classic' type — e.g., market sharing, price fixing?

(b)   The economic importance of the undertakings and their share of the relevant market.

(c)   The duration of the infringements.

(d)   Whether the infringements are deliberate, i.e., intended to restrict competition, or inadvertent.

(e)   Whether the party has already been found to have infringed Articles 85 or 86.

(f)   Whether the behaviour is open or underhand. In *Re Benelux Flat Glass Cartel* the parties had observed the letter of their written undertaking to the Commission, but indulged in practices against its spirit.

Where it is clear that the parent companies in a group are the main culprits they will be fined more heavily than their subsidiaries.

The Commisson has not hesitated to use its powers to the full. In *Re 'Pioneer' Hi-Fi Equipment* [1980] 1 CMLR 457 it imposed fines of almost 7 million ecus on four firms for concerted market-sharing practices in breach of Article 85(1). *Pioneer* was approved by the Court of Justice in annulment proceedings (cases 100-3/80), although the fines were reduced by approximately 2,500,000 ecus overall, due to an incorrect assessment on the part of the Commission as to the duration of the offences. In *Re Peroxygen Cartel* [1985] 1 CMLR 481 fines totalling 9 million ecus were imposed for breach of Article 85(1) on a number of companies, all major producers world-wide of peroxide products, in respect of a market-sharing and price-fixing cartel of extreme gravity and long duration. In *Re Polyethylene* ((1989) OJ No.L 74/21) 17 undertakings were fined a total of 60 million ecus for similar concerted price-fixing and market sharing practices in the low density polyethylene industry. (See also *Re Polypropylene Cartel;* and *Community* v *ICI* [1988] 4 CMLR 347.) And in *Tetra Pak* (1991) the Commission fined the Swiss-based packaging company Tetra-Pak 75 million ecus in respect of pricing policies (including predatory pricing) and market-sharing practices which were deliberately designed to eliminate actual or potential competitors in the aseptic and non-aseptic markets in machinery and cartons. Tetra-Pak is appealing against the fine.

As has been noted, the Commission also has power to fine undertakings from 100 to 5,000 ecus for intentionally or negligently failing to supply the information required under Articles 11, 12 or 14 of Regulation 17/62, or for supplying false or misleading information (Regulation 17/62, Article 15(1)).

In addition the Commission may impose periodic penalty payments of from 50 to 1,000 ecus per day for a failure to comply with a Commission Decision requiring parties to end infringements under Articles 85 or 86 or for failure to cooperate in enquiries and investigations under Article 11(5) or Article 14(3) (Article 16). Hoechst was fined 1,000 ecus per day under these provisions.

The Court of Justice, under Article 172, and now the Court of First Instance, has unlimited jurisdiction in regard to fines. It will not, however, substitute its discretion for that of the Commission. The matter will normally be determined in the context of proceedings for annulment under Article 173, and according to the same principles (see chapter 27).

As many of the cases examined in the context of Articles 85 and 86 indicate, it is not uncommon for undertakings to seek annulment of the Commission's Decisions. Whilst annulment is rare, fines are frequently reduced. Until the case of *AEG-Telefunken* (case 107/82), Article 173 proceedings, there had been further incentive to try for annulment. Unsure of its powers in this area the Commission had not charged interest on fines for the period prior to commencement of review proceedings. There was some evidence that parties were embarking on annulment actions as a tactical manoeuvre. Any possibility of doing so came to an end with *AEG-Telefunken,* when the Court held that the Commission had power to demand interest from the date of the Decision itself.

Interim measures   Although Regulation 17/62 gives the Commission no express power to issue interim measures, the Court of Justice in *Camera Care Ltd* v *Commission* (case 792/79R), Article 173 proceedings, decided that the Commission does have that power, implied in Article 3 of Regulation 17/62. The case came before the Court as a result of the Commission's Decision refusing to make an interim order at the request of Camera Care, a retail photographic business, requiring Hasselblad to supply Camera Care with its cameras. The Commission believed it had no power to do so. On a very broad interpretation of Article 3 of Regulation 17/62, the Court held, in annulment proceedings, that the Commission could take interim measures provided they were:

(a)   indispensable,
(b)   urgent,
(c)   to avoid serious or irreparable damage to the party seeking its adoption *or* in a situation which is intolerable to the public interest.

In exercising this power the Commission must observe the essential procedural safeguards of Article 19 of Regulation 17/62 (hearings of parties and third parties), *and* the interim measure must be open to challenge before the Court of Justice. The Court has held that damage is not serious and irreparable if it is purely financial and can, in the event of success in the main action, be wholly recouped (*Cargill* v *Commission; interim measures* (case 229/88R)).

The scope of *Camera Care* was reduced somewhat in *Ford of Europe Inc.* v *Commission* (cases 228 & 229/82), Article 173 proceedings. Here the Court held that an interim order can only be granted if it falls within the framework of the final Decision. Thus the Commission's interim order requiring that Ford Germany continue to supply right-hand drive cars to German distributors was annulled, since the final Decision was to be a Decision in response to its application for negative clearance or exemption.

Concentrations

As noted in chapter 14, the Merger Control Regulation 4064/89 repealed Regulation 17/62 in respect of *all* concentrations. Concentrations falling within the Merger Regulation will be subject to the powers and procedures laid down in Regulations 4064/89 and 2367/90, which are broadly similar in scope to those of Regulation 17/62. The Commission now has no power to act in respect of concentrations falling outside the Merger Regulation, unless it is requested to do so by a member State (see chapter 14).

The role of national courts

Article 88 of the EEC Treaty gave the 'authorites in member States' the power to administer the competition provisions of the Treaty until these powers were taken over by the Commission in Regulation 17/62.

According to Article 9(3) of Regulation 17/62:

As long as the Commission has not initiated any procedure under Articles 2 [negative clearance], 3 [investigation either on application of third parties or on own initiative], or 6 [exemption], the authorities of the member States shall remain competent to apply Article 85(1) and Article 86.

Initial uncertainties as to the meaning of, 'authorities in member States' and the limitations of Article 9(3) were dispelled in *BRT* v *SABAM* (case 127/73), Article 177 proceedings. Here the Court held that the competence of national courts to apply Articles 85 and 86 derived from the direct effects of those provisions, and not from Article 88 or Regulation 17. Thus, Article 9(3) of Regulation 17 could not operate to deprive individuals of rights held under the Treaty itself. Where the Commission has instituted parallel proceedings, a national court faced with a problem of Article 85 or 86 may stay proceedings until a Decision has been made; but it is not obliged to do so.

Since Articles 85 and 86 are directly effective, they can be invoked before any domestic court in matters to which they are relevant. Both the Commission and the Court of Justice have encouraged national courts to apply EEC competition law, no doubt in the hope of lessening the Commission's administrative burden. In the *Perfume* cases (e.g., *Lancôme* (case 99/79), Article 177 proceedings) the Court held that even the issuing of a comfort letter could not deprive national courts of their freedom to apply Articles 85 and 86. Despite the passing of the Merger Regulation and the principle of one-stop shopping, national courts remain competent to apply Articles 85 and 86 to *all* concentrations.

Yet allowing national courts to apply these Articles raises formidable problems.

Exemptions   National courts, at all levels, are free to make a finding of infringement of Articles 85 and 86 or no infringement. They may rely on a comfort letter, but they do not need to do so. Where Article 85 is concerned they may apply the block exemption. But they have no power to grant individual exemption under Article 85(3), no matter how strong the justification. What is a national court to do faced with an agreement in breach of Article 85(1) which seems to merit exemption? Three possibilities may be considered:

(a)   If a rule of reason has already been applied by the Commission or the Court in similar circumstances, the national court can safely conclude that there has been no breach of Article 85(1).

(b)   If not, where the Commission has instituted parallel proceedings, the national court may stay proceedings until a Decision is made, as suggested in BRT v *SABAM* (case 127/73).

(c)   If neither (a) nor (b) applies the only possible remedy lies in a reference to the Court of Justice under Article 177; that Court has no power to grant exemption under Article 85(3), but it may be persuaded to apply a rule of reason.

The inability of national courts to apply Article 85(3) has led to demands that they themselves should be encouraged to apply the rule of reason. However, to allow them to do so without prior authority from the Commission or the Court of Justice would greatly endanger the uniform application of EEC competition law.

Remedies   Where a national court finds an agreement in breach of Article 85(1) or Article 86 it may declare that agreement void, but it has no power to order fines. What remedies should it provide? In the absence of common Community provision the Court of Justice has held that member States must make available the same remedies as are available for comparable breaches of National law (*Rewe-Zentralfinanz-Landwirtschaftskammer für das Saarland* (case 33/76), Article 177 proceedings), and that the remedies must be real and effective (*Harz* v *Deutsche Tradax GmbH* (case 79/83), Article 177 proceedings). But it is not immediately clear which remedies are appropriate. EEC law is *sui generis*. Competition policy in the UK is enforced mainly through administrative procedures. Whilst an injunction or a declaration would clearly be appropriate, the matter is less clear with regard to damages. In *Garden Cottage Foods Ltd* v *Milk Marketing Board,* in interlocutory proceedings, the Court of Appeal ([1982] QB 1114) and the House of Lords ([1984] AC 130) considered whether a breach of Article 86 could give rise to a remedy in damages. Both courts were divided on the issue. Although the majority in both thought that a remedy in damages was available and Lord Diplock suggested that a remedy might lie in tort for breach of statutory duty, it is submitted that that matter was not finally decided. The tort of breach of statutory duty is a notoriously unpredictable remedy, particularly inappropriate where the damage suffered, as is the case with breaches of Articles 85 and 86, is likely to be economic. In this area the economic torts might provide a more appropriate remedy. It is submitted that the courts of member States should approach the question of damages with caution, since, in the absence of common Community provision, unequal treatment as between competing undertakings could undermine the very principles of free and fair competition which Articles 85 and 86 seek to uphold.

Application of Articles 85 and 86   Although the legal principles applicable to Articles 85 and 86 are reasonably clear, their application to the facts involve what is primarily an economic assessment. Questions of market size and structure, of the relevant product market, the relevant geographical market, of the effect of an agreement on competition or on trade between member States, or whether prices or trading conditions are 'unfair', or, in the case of concentrations, whether they may undermine or impede effective competition within the common market, require the analysis of an extensive array of economic data, and the application by lawyers of complex economic criteria. The relevant information and expertise will not always be available to national courts, and if they are there is ample scope for differences of opinion in their application. The problem is particularly acute in adversarial systems such as that of the UK, where the gathering of evidence and the conduct of the investigation lies in the hands of the parties. A ruling from the Court of Justice under Article 177 will merely provide guidance on the law; it will not assist in its application to the facts. If there are likely to be differences between one court and another, there will be even greater differences from State to State. As with the question of damages, the result could be to endanger rather than advance the cause of competition.

The role of individuals

Since Articles 85 and 86 are directly effective, vertically and horizontally, individuals are free to invoke these provisions either as a sword or a shield before their national courts. They should thus be able to obtain an injunction to prevent a breach of these Articles, or damages in lieu of an injunction, or a declaration. If a definitive tort can be proved tortious damages may be obtained.

In addition to these rights, individuals have been given a special place in the enforcement of EEC competiton law under Regulation 17/62. Under Article 3(2) any natural or legal person who can claim a 'legitimate interest' may apply to the Commission to investigate and terminate alleged infringements of Articles 85 or 86. The question of 'legitimate interest' has been widely interpreted. It would certainly include any trader who feels he has been unfairly treated or excluded in breach of these Articles. In the case of concentrations, with the repeal of Regulation 17/62, this right under Article 3(2) has now been removed.

Because a person with sufficient interest has a right to request action from the Commission under Article 3(2) he also has a right to be heard (Article 19(2)). The Court has held that this does not entitle the complainant to an oral hearing; written observations may be sufficient (*British American Tobacco Co. Ltd* v *Commission* (cases 142 & 156/84), Article 173 proceedings). A complainant also has limited rights of discovery, subject to the Commission's duty to protect business secrets. In *AKZO Chemie BV* v *Commission* (case 53/85), Article 173 proceedings, the Court held that the obligation of professional secrecy is mitigated in regard to third parties on whom Article 19(2) confers a right to be heard. The Commission may communicate to such a party certain information covered by the obligation of professional secrecy in so far as it is necessary to do so for the proper conduct of the investigation. However, the Court drew a distinction between 'obligations of professional secrecy' and 'business secrets'. Business secrets require exceptional protection. Third parties may not in any circumstances be given access to documents containing business secrets. How and where the Commission is, in its discretion, to draw the line between 'obligations of professional secrecy' and 'business secrets' is not clear.

An individual may request the Commission to act under Article 3(2) of Regulation 17, but he cannot compel it to do so. However, if the Commission issues a Decision as a result of an application under Article 3(2), the complainant may challenge that Decision before the Court of Justice, whether or not the Decision is addressed to himself (*Metro-SB-Grossmärkte GmbH & Co. KG* v *Commission* (case 26/76), Article 173 proceedings (see chapter 27)).

The right of individuals to apply to the Commission under Article 3(2) is a valuable means of enforcement of EEC competition law; many infringements have come to light via this route. Clearly for individuals this route is cheaper than a direct action before a national court, since the Commission shoulders the burden of enquiry. It may too be more effective, since the threat of fines may act as a deterrent to wrongdoers. *Camera Care* (case 792/79R) has opened up the possibility of obtaining interim orders from the Commission to prevent damage occurring. In *Brass Band Instruments* v *Boosey & Hawkes; interim measures* (case iv/32.279) Brass Band Instruments were successful in obtaining such an order, requiring Boosey & Hawkes to continue supplying them with brass band instruments, thereby avoiding irreparable damage. On the other hand, as Sir Neil Lawson observed in *Cutsforth* v *Mansfield Inns Ltd* [1986] 1 CMLR 1, English High Court, 'the wheels of Brussels (can) grind very slow indeed'. The plaintiffs in *Cutsforth* v *Mansfield Inns Ltd* were suppliers of pin tables and gaming machines to pubs and clubs in the Humberside area of England. The defendants were brewers who had taken over a group of tied houses in that area. Under their new tenancy agreements tenants were required to install in their pubs only pin tables and gaming machines on the defendants' approved list. The plaintiffs, who had supplied the pubs in the past, were not on that list. They complained to the Commission. They also applied for an interim injunction in the English High Court to prevent the defendants from enforcing their agreements. Sir Neil Lawson considered there was a serious case to be tried, and granted them the injunction. There was no time to wait for Brussels to decide.

By contrast, Lord Jauncey (in *Argyll Group plc* v *Distillers Co. plc* [1986] 1 CMLR 764 Outer House of the Court of Session) refused to grant an interim interdict to prevent a merger between Distillers and Guinness. He was not convinced (it is submitted correctly) that a prima facie case had been made out.

Thus it appears that if the case is reasonably clear, and urgent, an action seeking interim relief before domestic courts may produce the best results. *A fortiori* if the plaintiff seeks damages, since the Commission has no power to award compensation to those injured as a result of breaches of EEC competition law. But if there is no urgency, and little prospect of a successful claim for damages, and certainly if the case is a complex or difficult or doubtful one, a complaint to the Commission would be preferable. Where substantial sums are at stake firms would be advised to hedge their bets and proceed both ways.

Further reading

Davidson, J., 'Action for Damages in the English Courts for Breach of EEC Competition Law' (1985) 34 ICLQ 178.
Harris, B., 'Problems of Procedure in EEC Competition Law' (1989) NLJ 1452.
Hunnings, N., 'The Stanley Adams Affair; the Biter Bit' (1987) 24 CML Rev 65.
Jacobs, F. 'Damages for Breach of Article 86" (1983) EL Rev 353.

Steiner, J., 'How to make the Action Fit the Case; domestic remedies for breach of EEC Law' (1987) 12 EL Rev 102.
Waelbroek, D. 'Is Regulation 17 falling into abeyance?' (1986) 11 EL Rev 268.
See also further reading for chapter 23.

SIXTEEN

Articles 85 and 86
and industrial property rights

The exercise of industrial and commercial property rights such as trade marks, patents and copyright must inevitably restrict competition; indeed their very purpose is to give their owner some protection against competition as a reward for his creative endeavour or acquired goodwill in his product. These rights are recognised in Articles 36 and 222 (see chapter 9). But, as was pointed out in chapter 9, the Court of Justice has drawn a distinction between the *existence* of industrial property rights and their *exercise*. The mere existence of industrial property rights cannot infringe Articles 85 or 86; an improper or abusive exercise of these rights can. Thus in *Établissements Consten SA v Commission* (cases 56 & 58/64, Article 173 proceedings, Consten could not rely on its trade mark rights to prevent parallel imports of Grundig products from other member States. The purpose of the GINT trade mark was not to protect the owner's legitimate rights in his product, for example, to prevent other goods being passed off as Grundig's, but to partition the market and ensure absolute territorial protection for Grundig products in France. Thus its exercise in the context of Grundig's dealer agreement was in breach of Article 85(1).

The same principle has been applied to patents and copyright. In *Parke, Davis & Co.* v *Probel* (case 24/67), Article 177 proceedings, the Court held that an 'improper exploitation' of patent rights in the context of agreements, decisions of undertakings or concerted practices or by firms in a dominant position could breach EEC competition law.

In *Re GEMA* [1971] CMLR D35 the Commission found that GEMA, an authors' rights' society holding a dominant position in authors' copyright in Germany was improperly exploiting its rights in breach of Article 86.

The exploitation of industrial or commercial property rights will be improper if these rights are used in order to defeat Community law on restrictive practices (*Consten*). Any concerted attempt or attempt by a dominant undertaking to use these rights to partition markets, or to maintain artificial price levels, or to impose discriminatory or unfair conditions on trading partners is liable to fall foul of Article 85 or Article 86. In *Re GEMA*,

GEMA was exploiting its copyrights by discriminatory practices; it was discriminating against nationals from other member States, who could not become full members; it paid supplementary fees, 'loyalty bonuses', only to some of its members from a fund to which all had contributed, without objective justification. It was imposing unfair conditions on its members, by extending its contractual rights to non-copyright works, and claiming rights to future works. All these practices went beyond what was necessary to protect GEMA's legitimate property rights.

Similarly, in *Windsurfing International Inc.* v *Commission* (case 193/83), Article 173 proceedings, WSI, the owners of patent licences in a special sail rig (comprising mast, mast foot, sail and pair of curved booms) for use with windsurfing boards, was seeking in its licensing agreements to impose unnecessary restrictions on its licensees in breach of Article 85(1). For example, licensees were required to exploit the patents (for the rigs) *only* for the manufacture of sailboards using hulls which had been given WSI's prior approval; to pay royalties for rigs made under the patent on the basis of the selling price of the *complete* sailboard; to manufacture only in a specified manufacturing plant; and they were not permitted to challenge the licensed patents. These provisions were all found to constitute improper exploitation.

Thus in placing limitations on the exercise of industrial property rights the Commission, supported by the Court, has curtailed the very substance of these rights. These rights can now only be exercised to protect what the Commission regards as the 'specific subject-matter' of the property concerned.

The specific subject-matter of the property, to protect which industrial property rights may legitimately be exercised, has been narrowly defined. For patents, it is to ensure, to the holder, so as to recompense the creative effort of the inventor, the exclusive right to use an invention (*Centrafarm BV* v *Sterling Drug Inc.* (case 15/74), Article 177 proceedings). Patent rights clearly merit protection if the Community wishes to encourage creative endeavour. Thus whilst patent licensing agreements have generally been held in breach of Article 85(1) the Commission has been prepared to grant exemption under Article 85(3) (e.g., *Davidson Rubber Co.* [1972] CMLR D52). The Commission's attitude to these agreements has been embodied in its block exemption on patent licensing (Regulation 2349/84). However, the block exemption contains an extensive black list in Article 3, and has drawn the line at allowing licensees full territorial protection. *Windsurfing International Inc.* v *Commission* (case 193/83) and *L. C. Nungesser KG* v *Commission* (case 258/78) would still fall outside its protection.

The specific subject-matter of a trade-mark right is to protect the owner from competitors who would take unfair advantage of the position and reputation of the mark by selling goods improperly bearing the mark (*Centrafarm BV* v *Winthrop BV* (case 16/74), Article 177 proceedings). Thus, trade-mark rights cannot be used to prevent parallel imports, even to protect a firm's or a distributor's investment in a particular territory from 'free riders' (i.e., parallel importers who seek to take advantage of the product's goodwill, built up by the promotional efforts of others). It is only rights *in the product* which are protected.

The Court has refrained from defining the specific subject-matter of copyright, no doubt due to the diversity of national laws in this area. But it is clear from *Re GEMA* that any conditions embodied in an agreement or practice or imposed by a dominant undertaking which go beyond what is necessary to protect the owners' *existing* property, and certainly any discriminatory treatment, risk infringing Articles 85 or 86. In *Ministre Public v Tournier* (case 395/87), in the context of a reference concerning the compatibility of reciprocal arrangements between copyright management societies with Articles 30, 85 and 86, the Court held that contracts entered into with users would not infringe Article 85 unless the practices at issue exceeded the limits absolutely necessary for the attainment of the legitimate copyright objective of safeguarding the rights and interests of their members *vis-à-vis* users of the protected property, in this case recorded music.

It must be emphasised that such protection as is offered to protect the specific subject-matter of the property concerned has been significantly reduced by the doctrine of exhaustion of rights discussed at length in chapter 9. Any rights claimed in the context of agreements or practices within Articles 85 or 86 which are not permitted under this doctrine will risk infringing EC competition law. Since *SA CNL-SUCAL NV v HAG GF AG* (case C 10/89) the doctrine of common origin has lost its sting (see chapter 9).

Finally, the fact that an industrial property right such as an exclusive licence falls within a block exemption cannot protect an undertaking acquiring a business in possesion of such a right from liability in so doing for abuse of a dominant position under Article 86 (*Tetra Pak* (case T 51/89)).

SEVENTEEN

Introduction

The basic principle of free movement of persons is contained in Article 3(c) of the EEC Treaty, which requires 'the abolition, as between member States, of obstacles to freedom of movement for persons'. This is fleshed out in Articles 48-51 (Part Two, Title III, Chapter 1 'Workers'), Articles 52-8 (Chapter 2, 'Rights of establishment') and Articles 59-66 (Chapter 3, 'Services'). These provisions have in their turn been further substantiated by secondary legislation.

Thus the right to freedom of movement has been granted under the Treaty to workers and those exercising rights of establishment and providing services within the Community. They must, in addition, be nationals of one of the member States of the Community. Nationality is determined according to the law of each individual member State.

With one exception (social security, Regulation 1408/71) neither the Treaty nor the secondary legislation enacted thereunder attempts to define the word 'worker'. Although a distinction is drawn between 'workers', covered principally by Article 48, and the self-employed, covered principally by Articles 52 (establishment) and 59 (services), the Court of Justice, no doubt wisely in view of the fine and uncertain line between the two, has held that comparison of these different provisions shows that they are based on the same principles in so far as they concern the entry into and residence in the territory of member States of persons covered by Community law and the prohibition of all discrimination based on nationality (*Procureur du Roi* v *Royer* (case 48/75), Article 177 proceedings). Thus, too much should not be made of the distinction between the two. Although families are not expressly catered for under the Treaty many of the rights available to the worker or the self-employed person have been extended by secondary legislation to their families. Members of the family do not have to be nationals of a member State to be eligible.

The rights of free movement granted under the Treaty are subject to express derogation on the grounds of public policy, public security and public health (Articles 48(3) and 56; Directive 64/221). Exception has also been made for employment in the public service (Article 48(4)) and activities connected with the exercise of official authority (Article 55).

The principle of free movement of persons is regarded by the Court of Justice as a fundamental principle, designed not merely to serve the economic ends of the Treaty by providing a single market in labour as in goods, but as an important social right in itself. The migrant worker is regarded not as a mere source of labour but as a human being (per Advocate-General Trabucchi in *Mr and Mrs F v Belgian State* (state 7/75), Article 177 proceedings). Thus the provisions of the Treaty and of secondary legislation in this sphere have been very generously interpreted by the Court of Justice, and exceptions have been given the narrowest scope. In seeking to promote freedom of movement, and to remove all obstacles to freedom of movement of persons within the Community, the Court has been prepared to sacrifice the letter of the law to what it sees as the spirit of the Treaty. This spirit is exemplified in the preamble to the Treaty, which expresses member States' determination 'to lay the foundations of an ever closer union among the peoples of Europe' and by 'pooling their resources to preserve and strengthen peace and liberty'; and by Article 2, which pledges the Community to 'an accelerated raising of the standard of living and closer relations between the States belonging to it'. The Court draws similarly on the statements of intent contained in the preambles to secondary legislation.

Also extremely important in the application of the free movement of persons' provisions is Article 7 of the EEC Treaty, which provides that:

Within the scope of application of this Treaty, and without prejudice to any special provisions contained therein, any discrimination on grounds of nationality shall be prohibited.

This Article has often been invoked in conjunction with other provisions of the Treaty, or with secondary legislation, in order to resolve ambiguities or fill lacunae, invariably in order to extend the rights of workers and their families. However, Article 7 applies only 'within the scope of application of this Treaty'. It was held in *Walrave and Koch v Association Union Cycliste Internationale* (case 36/74), Article 177 proceedings, in the context of a challenge to the cycling association's rules relating to 'pacemaker' cyclists, which were clearly discriminatory, that the prohibition of discrimination on the grounds of nationality contained in Article 7 does not apply to sports teams which have nothing to do with economic activity. The practice of sport is subject to Community law *only in so far as it constitutes an economic activity* within Article 2 of the Treaty. Thus, just as the rights of free movement are only granted to workers and the self-employed and their families (albeit, as will be seen, very liberally interpreted), so, in order to invoke the principle of non-discrimination of Article 7 in this context, there must be some economic nexus. The claimant must be a worker or self-employed person or a member of the family of such a person. Some inroads have now been made into this principle following the case of *Gravier* v *City of Liège* (case 293/83) in the context of vocational training and *Cowan* v *French Treasury* (case 186/87), to be discussed in chapter 19.

The prohibition of discrimination on the grounds of nationality applies to all forms of discrimination, direct and indirect. It will often take the form of a residence or length of residence requirement. In *Sotgiu* v *Deutsche Bundespost* (case 152/73), Article 177 proceedings, the plaintiff was an Italian national employed by the German post office in Germany. His family lived in Italy. Following the issue of a circular, post office workers separated from their families in Germany were to be paid an increased 'separation' allowance whilst workers who were living abroad at the time of recruitment would continue to be paid at the same rate. Thus the rule was not overtly discriminatory, since it applied to all workers, regardless of nationality. But clearly its effects could fall more heavily on foreigners. The Court, on a reference from the Bundesarbeitsgericht held that the prohibition of discrimination (expressed here in Article 7(1) of Regulation 1612/68, but equally applicable to Article 7 of the EEC Treaty) prohibited all covert forms of discrimination which, by the application of criteria other than nationality nevertheless led to the same result. A residence criterion thus *could* have a discriminatory effect, prohibited by the Treaty and the Regulation. It would be different only if the difference in treatment took into account objective differences in the situation of workers.

To obtain the benefit of Community law, the claimant must be or have been a *migrant* worker. In *Moser* v *Land Baden-Württemberg* (case 180/83), Article 177 proceedings, the plaintiff, a German, sought to invoke EEC law to challenge a law of Baden-Württemberg (Germany) enabling the authorities to reject his application for a postgraduate teachers' training course on the grounds of his former membership of the Communist party. He argued that the rule would prevent him from obtaining his full qualifications and thus from exercising his right of free movement in the Community. His argument failed. EEC law, the Court held, had no application to situations which were wholly internal. (See also *R* v *Saunders* (case 175/78); *Ministre Public* v *Gauchard* (case 20/87) (establishment)). The principle operated extremely harshly in *Morson* v *Netherlands* (cases 35 & 36/82), Article 177 proceedings. Here two mothers from Surinam wished to join their children in Holland, on whom they were dependent. The children had Dutch nationality and were working in Holland. Since the mothers were not entitled to join them under Dutch law the mothers sought to rely on EEC law. They failed. The Court held that EEC rules on freedom of movement for workers cannot be applied to cases which have no factor linking them with Community law. A similar approach has been noted in the context of free movement of goods (see chapters 6 & 7). Thus in both cases an element of reverse discrimination is permitted under EEC law.

Although the ECSC and Euratom Treaties contain their own specific provisions for workers in the industries they cover, EEC law relating to the free movement of persons will apply to those workers and their families in so far as their position is not governed by those Treaties.

The general provisions relating to free movement of persons apply throughout the territories of the member States of the Community. In *Tilmant* v

Groupement des Assédies de la Région Parisienne [1991] 2 CMLR 317 the French Cour de Cassation held, no doubt correctly, that the principle of non-discrimination applies also to EEC workers working outside the EEC where the legal relationship of employer and employee is situated in the Community, whether by reason of the place where it is established or by reason of the place where it takes effect. Although sea and air transport were excluded from the common transport policy, the rules applicable to persons apply equally in these areas (see *Commission* v *France (Re French Merchant Seamen)* (case 167/73), Article 169 proceedings; *Defrenne* v *Belgium (No. 1)* (case 80/70), Article 169 proceedings).

All the main EEC Treaty provisions and most of the secondary legislation concerning freedom of movement of persons, as well as Article 7 itself, have been held to be directly effective. They thus form a fertile source of rights for individuals. Although many of the obligations contained in the secondary legislation will fall on the authorities of member States, some of them (e.g., Regulation 1612/68) will be vertically and horizontally effective, and all the main Treaty provisions, including Article 7, will be vertically and horizontally effective.

If the social provisions of the EEC Treaty were designed originally to complement and promote the Community's economic goals, the second half of the 1980s saw a growing movement to develop the 'social dimension' of the Community by creating a 'Citizens' Europe'. Under an agreement signed at Schengen in 1990, five member States (FRG, France and the Benelux countries, later joined by Italy) agreed to remove all checks on the movement of people crossing their borders. The Single European Act 1986 provided for the enactment of measures to remove all barriers to the free movement of persons within the Community by 31 December 1992 (EEC Treaty, Article 8A renumbered 7a by the TEU). However, problems over security and the control of crime and immigration from outside the Community, exacerbated in the latter case by the increasing flow of economic and political migrants from eastern Europe and the old USSR, render agreement on these matters unlikely within the anticipated time-scale. The Maastricht Treaty has now provided for cooperation in the fields of justice and home affairs (Title VI, Articles K and K.1 to K.9) with a view, *inter alia*, to achieving common action by member States on immigration and asylum policies. It has also introduced into the EEC Treaty the concept of European citizenship (new Article 8). New Article 8a(1) provides that:

Every citizen of the Union shall have the right to move and reside freely within the territory of the Member States, subject to the limitations and conditions laid down in this Treaty and by the measures adopted to give it effect.

Such measures are to be passed unanimously and with the assent of the European Parliament. Thus given the political will there is ample scope for future development.

Meanwhile some progress has been made with the passing of three Directives in 1990, Directives 90/364, 90/365 and 90/366 (OJ No. L 180,

13.7.90, pp. 26, 28, 30), giving rights of free movement to persons of independent means, to retired persons and students respectively, and to members of their families, insofar as they do not enjoy these rights under other provisions of Community law. Persons claiming under the Directives must be covered by medical insurance and must have sufficient financial resources to avoid becoming a burden on the host state. The Directives entered into force on 30 June 1992. It remains to be seen whether such persons who are not economically active will be entitled to be treated on a basis of equality with nationals of their host State. The significance of this point will be revealed in the following chapters.

Fundamental rights: The move towards a 'People's Europe'

The law relating to the free movement of persons represents one aspect of the Community's social policy. The Single European Act, followed by the 'Social Charter' have led to increasing social legislation, particularly in the field of education and training and employment protection. Measures relating to health and safety may be enacted under Article 118A of the EEC Treaty by qualified majority; Article 100A provides for measures directed at the establishment and functioning of the internal market; these too may be by qualified majority vote except where they relate to the free movement of persons or the rights and interests of employed persons, in which case they require unanimity. Clearly a precise line between measures requiring a qualified majority and those requiring unanimity cannot be drawn. Much social legislation has been passed under these provisions. And now 11 member States (the UK excepted) have signed an Agreement on Social Policy in a protocol attached to the Maastricht Treaty, with a view to 'continuing along the path laid down in the 1989 Social Charter'. The agreement has as its objectives: 'the promotion of employment, improved living and working conditions, proper social protection, dialogue between management and labour, the development of human resources with a view to lasting high employment and the combating of exclusion' (Article 1). To this end the Community and member States are required to implement measures which take into account 'the diverse forms of national practices, in particular in the field of contractual relations, and the need to maintain the competitiveness of the Community economy' (Article 1).

Apart from the law relating to the free movement of persons and sex discrimination, which is included because it is already highly developed and has had a significant impact on UK employment law, much EC social law must at present remain outside the scope of this book.

Further reading

O'Higgins, J., 'The Family and European Law' (1990) NLJ 1643.
O'Keefe, D. 'The Free Movement of Persons and the Single Market' (1992) 17 EL Rev 3.
Pickup, D., 'Reverse Discrimination and Freedom of Movement for Workers' (1989) 23 CML Rev 135.

Schutte, J., 'Schengen: its Meaning for the Free Movement of Persons in Europe' (1991) 29 CML Rev 549.
Watson, P., 'The Community Social Charter' (1991) 28 CML Rev 37.
For EEC Social Legislation generally see *Directory of Community Legislation in Force*, ch. 05.

EIGHTEEN

Free movement of workers

The principal Treaty provision governing the free movement of workers is Article 48:

1. Freedom of movement for workers shall be secured within the Community by the end of the transitional period at the latest.
2. Such freedom of movement shall entail the abolition of any discrimination based on nationality between workers of the member States as regards employment, remuneration and other conditions of work and employment.
3. It shall entail the right, subject to limitations justified on grounds of public policy, public security or public health:

  (a) to accept offers of employment actually made;
  (b) to move freely within the territory of member States for this purpose;
  (c) to stay in a member State for the purpose of employment in accordance with the provisions governing the employment of nationals of that State laid down by law, regulation or administrative action;
  (d) to remain in the territory of a member State after having been employed in that State, subject to conditions which shall be embodied in implementing Regulations to be drawn up by the Commission.

4. The provisions of this Article shall not apply to employment in the public service.

As required under Articles 48(3)(d) and 49, secondary legislation was introduced to give further substance to the above principles. The principal measures are:

  (a) Directive 68/360, governing rights of entry and residence.
  (b) Regulation 1612/68, governing access to, and conditions of, employment.

(c)   Regulation 1251/70, governing rights to remain in the territory of a
member State after having been employed there.

(d)   Directive 64/221, governing member States' right to derogate from the
free movement provisions on the grounds of public policy, public security or
public health.

These measures, as the Court held in *Procureur du Roi* v *Royer* (case 48/75),
Article 177 proceedings, merely determine the scope and detailed rules for the
exercise of rights conferred directly by the Treaty.

Personal scope

The rights granted under Article 48 and the secondary legislation implementing Article 48 are granted to workers and their families. The fact of
employment provides the requisite economic nexus to bring these provisions
into play. The families' rights derive from their relationship with the worker.

Workers   As the Court of Justice held in *Levin* v *Staatssecretaris van Justitie*
(case 53/81), Article 177 proceedings, the concept of 'worker' is a Community
concept, not dependent for its meaning on the laws of member States. In
Lawrie-Blum v *Land Baden-Württemberg* (case 66/85), Article 177 proceedings, the Court of Justice suggested that the 'essential characteristic' of a
worker is that during a certain period of time he performs services for and
under the direction of another in return for remuneration. He or she must be
a national of one of the member States. Nationality is determined according to
the domestic law of the member State concerned. Where a state has acceded to
the EC but is still subject to transitional arrangements, a national of that State
may claim rights as a 'favoured EC national' only insofar as that status ensues
from the transitional provisions, unless he has been lawfully employed in the
territory of one of the old member States (*Lopes da Veiga* (case C9/88)).

The term 'worker' has been generously construed. In *Hoekstra (née Unger)*
v *BBDA* (case 75/63), Article 177 proceedings, the Court held that it extended
not merely to the present worker, but to one who, having lost his job, is capable
of taking another. As will be seen, Directive 68/360 expressly provides that a
worker's right of residence cannot be withdrawn merely because he is
temporarily incapable of work, either as a result of illness or accident or
involuntary unemployment (Article 7(1)).

In *Levin* (case 53/81) the Court of Justice held, in response to a request for
a preliminary ruling from the Dutch Raad van State that the term 'worker'
applied even to those who worked to a limited extent (i.e., part-time), provided
that the work was 'real' work, and not nominal or minimal. The rights only
attach to those who perform or wish to perform an activity of an economic
nature. The Court went on to say, in response to the Dutch court's question,
that this principle applied whether the worker was self-supporting or whether
he wished to make do with less than the national minimum income. Thus it
was able to side-step the problem of the part-time worker who relies on public
funds for his support.

This issue was squarely faced in *Kempf* v *Staatssecretaris van Justitie* (case 139/85). Kempf was a German, a part-time music teacher working in the Netherlands from 1981 to 1982. During this time he was in receipt of Dutch supplementary benefit, both sickness benefit and general assistance. In November 1981 he applied for a Dutch residence permit. He was refused on the grounds that he was not a 'favoured EC citizen', since his income from his work was not sufficient to meet his needs. He challenged that decision before the Dutch courts. The Raad van State referred to the Court of Justice the question whether a part-time worker such as Kempf, whose income was below subsistence level and who did not have sufficient means of support was a 'worker' entitled to benefit under Community law. The Court replied that he was. Freedom of movement of workers was, it held, one of the fundamental freedoms, and must, as such, be defined broadly; a person who pursued a genuine and effective activity as an employed person, even on a part-time basis, could not be excluded from the scope of Community rules merely because he sought to supplement his income, which was lower than the means of subsistence, by other lawful means of subsistence. It was irrelevant whether the income was supplemented out of a private income or from public funds.

The boldness of this judgment will be more apparent when the full extent of the rights flowing from the status of 'worker' or 'favoured Community citizen' is appreciated.

Following *Kempf,* in *Steymann* v *Staatssecretaris van Justitie* (case 196/87), Article 177 proceedings, the Court held that the claimant's occupation as part of a religious community, entitling him to his 'keep' and pocket money, but not to formal wages, constituted a genuine and effective activity where commercial activity is an inherent part of membership of that community. By contrast, in *Battray* v *Staatssecretaris van Justitie* (case 344/87), Article 177 proceedings, paid activity provided by the State as part of a drug rehabilitation programme under its social employment law was held by the Court not to represent 'real and genuine economic activity'. Thus, in order to give rise to the status of 'worker', the work performed must fulfil, or derive from, some *economic* purpose. It has been suggested, however, that the principle of *Battray* does not apply to 'ordinary' sheltered employment. The undertaking in *Battray* existed solely for the purpose of rehabilitation and re-education of the persons employed therein.

Families Families are defined in Regulation 1612/68 (Article 10(1)) as a worker's 'spouse and their descendants who are under the age of 21 years or are dependants', and 'dependent relatives in the ascending line of the worker and his spouse'.

(a) *'Spouse'.* In *Netherlands State* v *Reed* (case 59/85), Article 177 proceedings, the Court of Justice, on a reference from the Dutch Supreme Court, was asked whether the term 'spouse' included a cohabitee. The case concerned Ms Reed's right to reside in Holland with her English cohabitee of five years' standing, who was working in Holland. Ms Reed, who was English, was not herself a worker. The Court held that in the present state of

Community law the term spouse referred to marital relationships only. However, this did not mean that Ms Reed was not entitled to remain in Holland. Since her cohabitee was a worker in Holland, and since aliens with stable relationships with *Dutch* nationals were entitled under similar circumstances to reside in Holland, it would be discriminatory, in breach of Articles 7 and 48 of the EEC Treaty (also Article 7(2) of Regulation 1612/68) not to accord him the same treatment as national workers. Thus Ms Reed was not entitled to remain as a 'spouse' but she was entitled to remain on account of her cohabitee's rights under EEC law.

Another question which arises, and has yet to be decided by the Court of Justice, is whether a divorced spouse is entitled to claim rights as a 'spouse' under EEC law. In *Diatta* v *Land Berlin* (case 267/83), Article 177 proceedings, the Court held that a separated spouse (in this case a Senegalese national), who intended to obtain a divorce and who was living apart from her husband, a worker in Germany, did not lose her rights of residence in Germany merely because she did not live under the same roof as her husband. The marital relationship is not dissolved, the Court held, when spouses live separately. Since the matter came before the Court on a reference for interpretation under Article 177 it was not necessary for the Court to decide on the effect of divorce on a spouse's rights.

In *R* v *Secretary of State for the Home Department (ex parte Sandhu)* [1982] 2 CMLR 553 Comyn J in the English High Court took the view that separation and divorce did not automatically put an end to non-EEC spouse's rights. In this case Sandhu, an Indian, had married a German lady and settled with her in England, where they produced a son. He obtained a steady job. Subsequently the marriage broke down, and his wife returned to Germany with their son. In 1976 he went to visit them in Germany. When he returned to England he was informed that he was no longer entitled to remain in England. His rights had come to an end on the departure from England of his wife. He appealed against the decision.

In a remarkable judgment, very close to the Court of Justice in its approach and reasoning, Comyn J pointed out that if an EEC worker could remove the 'cloak of protection' from a non-EEC spouse by deserting or divorcing him, or by leaving the country, 'this would add a new terror to marriage'. Arguing from the purpose of EEC provisions of freedom of movement for workers, and from Regulation 1251/70, by analogy with the family's right to remain after the death of the worker (see below) and taking into account Sandhu's steady job, his son in Europe, and his duties of maintenance towards him, Comyn J concluded that he was entitled to remain. Unfortunately for Mr Sandhu neither the Court of Appeal ([1983] 3 CMLR 131) nor the House of Lords (*The Times,* 10 May 1985) agreed. On a literal interpretation of the relevant EEC legislation and following an earlier Immigration Appeal Tribunal case (*Grewal* v *Secretary of State for the Home Department* [1979-80] Imm AR 119) the Court of Appeal concluded that Sandhu's right of residence ceased when his wife returned to Germany. The court refrained from considering the effect of separation or divorce in a case where the EEC worker remains in the same country as his spouse (or ex-spouse). The House of Lords agreed with the

Court of Appeal and refused to seek an interpretation on the matter from the Court of Justice. Their Lordships considered that the matter had already been covered, to Sandhu's detriment, by *Diatta* (case 267/83).

Yet, as has been demonstrated, the questions considered by the Court of Justice in *Diatta* were quite different, and were resolved in the separated spouse's favour. Were the Court to be faced with the problem in *Sandhu*, its conclusions, it is submitted, would be closer to Comyn J's than those of the Court of Appeal or House of Lords. The policy reasons in favour of giving some security of residence to divorced or abandoned spouses of a bona fide marriage, especially when there may be children of the marriage who will still remain members of the worker's family surely require that the law be construed to ensure that a spouse's EEC rights do not necessarily cease on divorce or when the worker leaves the country.

The problem is particularly acute where the spouse is not a national of a member State, as in *Sandhu* and *Diatta*. A spouse who has EEC nationality can always become a worker in her own right, and, after *Kempf*, (case 139/85) even for a spouse with family responsibilities this should not prove too daunting a prospect.

(b) *Dependants and descendants* Similar problems as arose in *Sandhu* could arise for a spouse's dependent relatives. If they, like the spouse, are not EEC nationals, they too risk losing their status as 'favoured Community citizens' on the separation or divorce of their relative.

For the children of the marriage, or the worker's dependent relatives, problems should not arise. Even after divorce they will remain members of the worker's family.

Although families are expressed in terms of 'descendants' it would be in keeping with the Court of Justice's approach to take a broad view of the rights of children of the family. It would not be likely to deny favoured EEC citizen status to children who had been treated as children of the family even though they were not, strictly speaking, descendants.

A family member threatened with loss of EEC rights in a case such as *Sandhu's* could invoke the principle of respect for the right to family life expressed in Article 8 of the European Convention of Human Rights, which in the context of the application of Community law must be respected by the authorities of member States (see chapter 4).

Material scope

Rights of entry and residence (Directive 68/360) These rights are regulated by Directive 68/360: they comprise, for the worker and his family (as defined above: Regulation 1612/68, Article 10(1)(a)), the right:

(a) To leave their home State in order for the worker to pursue activities as an employed person in another member State (Directive 68/360, Article 2).

(b) To enter the territory of another member State 'simply on production of a valid identity card or passport' (Article 3(1)). Entry visas (or their equivalent) may not be demanded except for members of the family who are not nationals of a member State. Member States are required to accord to such persons every facility for obtaining the necessary visas (Article 3(2)).

(c)   To obtain a residence permit, on production of, for the worker:

(i)   the document with which he entered the territory, and
(ii)   a confirmation of engagement from the employer or a certificate of employment (Article 4(3)(a) and (b));

and, for members of the family:

(i)   their documents of entry,
(ii)   a document proving their relationship with the worker, to be issued by the competent authority of the State of origin or the State whence they came and, if they are dependent on the worker,
(iii)   a document issued by the same authorities testifying that they are dependent on the worker or that they live under his roof in that country (Article 4(3)(c), (d) and (e)).

The residence permit must be valid throughout the territory of the member state which issued it; it must be valid for at least five years from the date of issue; and it must be automatically renewable (Article 6(1)). This may be described as the right to 'settled' or 'lawful' residence.

Breaks in residence not exceeding six consecutive months and absence on military service shall not affect the validity of a residence permit (Article 6(2)).

A valid residence permit may not be withdrawn from a worker solely on the grounds that he is no longer in employment, either because he is temporarily incapable of work as a result of illness or accident, or because he is involuntarily unemployed (Article 7(1)). When the residence permit is renewed for the first time the period of residence may be restricted (but not to less than 12 months) if the worker has been involuntarily unemployed for more than 12 consecutive months (Article 7(2)).

Temporary workers (working from three to 12 months) are entitled to a temporary residence permit for the duration of their employment (Article 6(3)). Seasonal workers and those working for less than three months are entitled to reside during the period of their employment without a residence permit (Article 8).

These provisions are generous, and have been even more generously interpreted by the Court of Justice. In *Procureur du Roi* v *Royer* (case 48/75) [1976] ECR 497, [1976] 2 CMLR 619 the Court held that the right of entry granted by Article 3 included the right to enter *in search of work*. The Court did not suggest the length of time appropriate to such a search, but it had been thought that a period of three months would be allowed, since EEC legislation on social security (Regulation 1408/71, Article 69) allows for the payment of unemployment benefit for up to three months in another member State while the claimant is looking for work. In *R* v *Immigration Appeal Tribunal, ex parte Antonissen* (case C 292/89), the Court of Justice was asked to rule on the legality of English immigration rules which permit the deportation of migrants after six months if they have failed to find employment. The Court held that there was 'no necessary link' between the right to unemployment benefit under Regulation 1408/71 and the right to stay in a State for the purpose of seeking work. A State could, however, deport an EEC migrant if he had not found employment after six months unless he provided evidence that he was continuing to seek employment and that he has a genuine chance of being engaged. Significantly the Court chose not to impose a specific time-limit.

If the right to enter a member State in search of work is available to all EEC citizens, the right to a residence permit is, it seems, conditional on the finding of employment. However, once in employment, the Court has held (*Royer*) that a worker's right to reside in the State where he is employed is not dependent on his possession of a residence permit. The right of residence is a fundamental right, derived from the Treaty itself (Article 48) and not from implementing legislation nor from documents issued by national authorities. Thus neither a worker nor his family can be denied entry to, or be deported from, a member State merely because they do not possess a valid residence permit (see also *R v Pieck* (case 157/79), Article 177 proceedings). As long as the worker has a right of residence as a worker, he will be entitled to reside as long as he would have been entitled had he been in possession of a residence permit, i.e., in normal circumstances, five years plus a minimum of one further year. And as long as he is entitled to stay, his family will also be entitled to stay.

A State is, however, entitled to demand that migrant workers and their families comply with its administrative formalities on immigration, and can even impose penalties in the form of fines for non-compliance, provided that the penalties are not disproportionate. In *Messner* (case C 265/88) a time-limit of three days from crossing the frontier in which aliens were required to register their presence with the Italian police, sanctioned by criminal penalties, was found to be unreasonable. A failure to comply with such formalities can never be a ground for deportation (*Royer; Watson and Belmann* (case 118/75), Article 177 proceedings; *Commission v Belgium* (case 321/87)).

Although Directive 68/360, Article 7(1), specifically provides that a valid residence permit cannot be withdrawn if the worker becomes incapable of work through illness or accident or involuntary unemployment, Article 7(1) implies that that right will be lost if he is *voluntarily* unemployed. The question of whether unemployment is voluntary or involuntary may be confirmed by the 'competent employment office' (Article 7(1)).

This distinction between voluntary and involuntary unemployment was described as 'critical' by the Immigration Appeal Tribunal in *Giangregorio v Secretary of State for the Home Department* [1983] 3 CMLR 472. It was suggested in that case that whilst the Secretary of State might rely on evidence as to whether the unemployment was voluntary or involuntary, a worker seeking to establish that his unemployment was involuntary must himself prove it to be so.

Since the rights of the family are 'parasitic', in that they depend on their relationship with the worker, their rights of residence will be coterminous with his, unless they are EEC citizens who qualify in their own right as workers, or have acquired the right to remain as his survivors under Regulation 1251/70.

Directive 68/360 makes special provision for temporary and seasonal workers. A temporary worker who works from three to 12 months in another member State is entitled to a temporary residence permit in that State, to coincide with the expected period of his employment (Article 6(3)). Those who work for less than three months in another State, or who work only seasonally, are entitled to reside in that State during the period of employment, but are not entitled to a residence permit (Article 8).

All the above rights may be denied to a worker, whether temporary or long term, and to a member of his family, on the grounds of public policy, public security and public health (Article 10).

The question of whether a worker or a member of his family is entitled to 'settled' residence in a member State is of fundamental importance because, as will be seen, their right to equal treatment in the host State, and all that that involves, has been held to flow not so much from the claimant's status as a worker, although it originates there, as from the worker's, and his family's, 'lawful residence' in a member State.

Access to employment; equality of treatment (Regulation 1612/68)   Regulation 1612/68 was passed to implement Articles 48(2) and 48(3) (a) and (b) of the EEC Treaty. As stated in the preamble to Regulation 1612/68, the attainment of the objective of freedom of movement for workers requires, in additon to rights of entry and residence, 'the abolition of any discrimination based on nationality between workers of the member States as regards employment, remuneration and other conditions of work and employment' (first recital). It also requires, in order that the right of freedom of movement may be exercised 'in freedom and dignity', equality of treatment in 'all matters relating to the actual pursuit of activities as employed persons' and that 'obstacles to the mobility of workers shall be eliminated, in particular as regards the worker's right to be joined by his family and the conditions for the integration of that family into the host country' (fifth recital). The Court of Justice has drawn heavily on this preamble in interpreting this Regulation and other measures in this field.

Regulation 1612/68 is divided into several parts. Part I, which is of principal concern here, is entitled 'Employment and workers' families'. Title I, 'Eligibility for employment' covers a worker's rights of access to employment; Title II, 'Employment and equality of treatment', covers his right to equality of treatment not only in all matters relating to employment, but also to 'social advantages', including matters of housing. Title III, 'Workers' families' deals with families' rights. The remaining parts of the Regulation provide for the setting up of machinery and institutions for the clearance and coordination of vacancies and applications for employment.

Eligibility for employment (Articles 1-6)   Any national of a member State has the right to take up activity as an employed person, and pursue such activity, in the territory of another member State under the same conditions as nationals of that state (Article 1).

A member State may not discriminate, overtly or covertly, against non-nationals, by limiting applications and offers of employment (Article 3(1)), or by prescribing special recruitment procedures or limiting advertising or in any other way impeding recruitment of non-resident workers (Article 3(2)). Member States must not restrict by number or percentage the number of foreign nationals to be employed in any activity or area of activity (Article 4; see *Commission* v *France (Re French Merchant Seamen)* (case 167/73), Article 169 proceedings — ratio of three French to one non-French imposed under Code du Travail Maritime 1926 on crew of French merchant ships held in breach of EEC law).

Member States must offer non-national applicants the same assistance in seeking employment as are available to nationals (Article 5).

States are, however, entitled to permit the imposition on non-nationals of conditions 'relating to linguistic knowledge required by reason of the nature of the post to be filled' (Article 3(1)). In *Groener* v *Minister for Education* (case 397/87), Article 177 proceedings, the ECJ held that a requirement of Irish law that teachers in vocational schools in Ireland should be proficient in the Irish language would be permissible under Article 3(1) in view of the clear policy of national law to maintain and promote the use of the Irish language as a means of expressing national identity and culture. The Irish language was the national language and the first official language of Ireland. Such a requirement must not, however, be disproportionate to the objectives pursued. The case may be seen as an example of the Court in its current more conciliatory mood. An employer may require a non-national to undergo a vocational test provided he expressly requests this when making his offer of employment (Article 6(2)). These provisions may not however be used as a means of covert discrimination.

Employment and equality of treatment (Articles 7-9) These rights are expressly granted to workers. However, as will be seen, some of these rights have now been extended to benefit the families of workers.

(a) *Conditions of work.* Article 7(1) provides that:

A worker who is a national of a member State may not, in the territory of another member State, be treated differently from national workers by reason of his nationality in respect of any conditions of employment and work, in particular as regards remuneration, dismissal, and should he become unemployed, reinstatement or re-employment.

This Article covers all forms of discrimination, direct and indirect. In *Ugliola* (case 15/69), Article 177 proceedings, a condition whereby a German employer took into account, for the purposes of calculating seniority, employees' periods of national service *in Germany,* thereby prejudicing an employee such as Ugliola, who was required to perform his national service in Italy, was held unlawful under this Article. Similarly in *Sotgiu* v *Deutsche Bundespost* (case 152/73), Article 177 proceedings, the German post office's decision to pay increased separation allowances only to workers living away from home in Germany, was held to be *capable* of breaching Article 7(1) (see chapter 17).

(b) *Social and Tax advantages.* Article 7(2) packs perhaps the largest punch of all EEC secondary legislation in this area. It entitles the migrant worker to 'the same social and tax advantages as national workers'. The term 'social advantages' has been interpreted in the widest sense.

In *Fiorini v SNCF* (case 32/75), Article 177 proceedings, the Court was faced with a claim by an Italian lady living in France, the widow of an Italian who had worked in France, for a special fare reduction card issued by the French railways to parents of large families. Her husband had claimed it while he was alive. She had been refused the card on the grounds that she was not of French nationality. She claimed discrimination in breach of Article 7 of the EEC Treaty and Article 7(2) of Regulation 1612/68. The French tribunal took the view that Article 7(2) was not applicable, since it was concerned only with advantages granted to citizens within the ambit of work or by virtue of work as employed persons. On a reference by the Paris Cour d'Appel the Court of Justice took a different view. It held that, although certain provisions of Article 7(1) refer to relationships deriving from the contract of employment, there are others which have nothing to do with such relationships. Article 7(2) covers all social and tax advantages, whether or not attached to contracts of employment. Moreover, these rights continue even if the advantages are sought after the worker's death to benefit the family remaining. Since the family had a right under Community law (Regulation 1251/70) to remain in France, they were entitled under Article 7(2) to equal 'social advantages'.

Subsequently, in *Even* (case 207/78), Article 177 proceedings, the Court held, following *Fiorini,* that the social advantages covered by Article 7(2) were 'those which, whether or not linked to a contract of employment, are generally granted to national workers primarily because of their objective status as workers *or by virtue of the mere fact of their residence on national territory*' (emphasis added). This formula, the *'Even'* formula, has since been applied in a number of cases in the context of claims by both workers and the members of their families to a wide range of social benefits.

In *Reina v Landeskreditbank Baden-Württemberg* (case 65/81), Article 177 proceedings, an Italian couple, living in Germany, the husband being a worker in Germany, invoked Article 7(2) to claim a special childbirth loan, State-financed, from the defendant bank. The loan was payable under German law only to German nationals living in Germany. The bank argued that the loan was not a 'social advantage' within Article 7(2), since the loan was granted not as a social right, but rather in the field of political rights, for demographic purposes, i.e., to increase the birth rate in Germany. Granting of the loan was, moreover, discretionary. It argued also that the difference in treatment was justified on account of the practical difficulties of recovering loans from workers who return to their own countries. Despite these persuasive arguments the Court of Justice found, on a reference from the Stuttgart Verwaltungsgericht, that since the loan was granted by reason of the claimant's objective status as a worker or by virtue of the mere fact of residence it was a 'social advantage' within Article 7(2). Social advantages covered not only benefits granted as of right but also those granted on a discretionary basis.

In *Castelli v ONPTS* (case 261/83), on similar reasoning, an Italian mother, who, on being widowed, went to live with her son in Belgium (the son having been a worker and retired there), was held entitled to claim a guaranteed income (not a social security benefit) paid to all old people in Belgium. Since she had a right under Article 10 of Regulation 1612/68 to install herself with her son, she was entitled to the same social and tax advantages as Belgian workers and ex-workers. The Court again applied the *Even* formula; the old-age benefit was one granted to national workers primarily because of their objective status as workers or by virtue of their residence of national territory.

The same reasoning was applied in *Hoeckx* (case 249/83), and *Scrivner* (case 122/84), to claims in Belgium for a minimum income allowance, the 'minimex', by a member of the family of a worker and an unemployed worker respectively. (See also *Frascogna* (case 256/86); *Deak* (case 94/84), 'tiding over' allowance paid to young job-seekers a 'social advantage'.) Similarly in *Matteucci* v *Communauté Française de Belgique* [1989] 1 CMLR 357, Article 177 proceedings, a scholarship to study abroad arising under a reciprocal arrangement between Belgium and Germany was held to constitute a social advantage to which the child of an Italian, established as a worker in Belgium, was entitled.

Thus the right to the same social advantages as nationals of the host state has come to depend not so much on the claimant's status as a worker or even as a member of the family of a worker, but on his lawful residence in that State. Hence the crucial importance, stressed in the context of Directive 68/360 (see above), of the initial enquiry as to whether the claimant is entitled under Directive 68/360, or Regulation 1251/70 (see below) or under the parallel provision for the self-employed (see chapter 19) to reside there.

Perhaps sensing that it had gone far enough, perhaps in response to criticisms of judicial activism, the Court of Justice, in keeping with its current more 'conservative' mood, has become more cautious in this area in recent years. An important limitation was placed on Article 7(2) in *Centre Public de l'Aide Sociale de Courcelles* v *Lebon* (case 316/85), in the context of a claim by a French national, Ms Lebon, for the Belgian minimex. She was living in Belgium and her claim was based, *inter alia*, on the fact that she was looking for work in Belgium. The Court of Justice held, in answer to one of several questions referred by the Mons Cour de Travail, that the right to equality of treatment in the field of social and tax advantages granted by Article 7(2) enured for the benefit only of workers and not for nationals of member States who migrate in search of employment.

Thus in *Lebon*, for the first time, the Court drew a distinction between those who are lawfully resident as a result of obtaining employment, and those who are permitted temporary rights of residence in order to search for work. Only the former will be entitled to full equality of treatment. This is an important development, with implications also for persons who move within the Community in order to receive services (see chapter 19 and *Gravier* v *City of Liège* (case 293/83), Article 177 proceedings).

A second important limitation was placed on Article 7(2) in the recent cases of *Brown* (case 197/86) and *Lair* (case 39/86). These will be discussed shortly.

(c)   *Access to training in vocational schools and retraining centres.* Article 7(3) entitles workers to access, under the same conditions as national workers, to training in vocational schools and retraining centres.

Although Article 7(3) is expressed in terms of access, it seems likely that the Court of Justice will take a broad view of what is meant by access. In *Casagrande* v *Landeshauptstadt München* (case 9/74), Article 177 proceedings, the Court held, in the context of a claim by a child, under Article 12 of Regulation 1612/68, that the right to be *admitted* to the host State's educational, apprenticeship and vocational training courses included not only admission but 'general measures to facilitate attendance', which in Casagrande's case, included a grant. Since grants and loans would now appear to be included in the category of 'social advantages' under Article 7(2) there is perhaps no need for special pleading for their inclusion in Article 7(3). This was the view taken by the Court in *Brown* and *Lair*. In a claim for a university maintenance grant based on Article 7(2) and 7(3), the Court opted for a restrictive interpretation of Article 7(3), holding that the term 'vocational school' applied only to institutions offering sandwich or apprenticeship courses, whilst pointing out that the claim could constitute a 'social advantage' under Article 7(2). Article 7(2) and 7(3) were not mutually exclusive.

This question of equal rights to grants to pursue educational, apprenticeship or vocational training courses had given rise to particular anxiety in member States. Although the rights are only available to migrant workers and their families who are legitimately resident in the host State, it seemed that all that might be necessary to obtain 'legitimate residence' was initially to secure a job: following *Levin* (case 53/81) and *Kempf* (case 139/85), it need not be full-time, as long as it was a real job. If the worker then lost his job, or gave it up, was he then to be entitled to equal access to any course, and any grant of his choice, either because it constituted 'vocational training' within Article 7(3) or a 'social advantage' under Article 7(2)? If this were the case, would not member States, particularly those which were generous in their social provision, be vulnerable to exploitation?

These questions arose before the English courts in several cases (*MacMahon* v *Department of Education and Science* [1982] 3 CMLR 91, High Court; *R* v *Inner London Education Authority (ex parte Hinde)* [1985] 1 CMLR 716, High Court) and, in all but one case (*Hinde*, University LLB course held not to be vocational training), were decided in the claimant's favour. But since these courts did not refer to the Court of Justice for an interpretation there existed no authoritative ruling from that Court on this important question until the matter was raised in *Brown* (case 197/86) and *Lair* (case 39/86).

In both these cases the parties, having obtained a place at university, Brown at Cambridge, to study engineering, and Ms Lair at the University of Hanover, to study languages, were claiming maintenance grants from the UK and German authorities respectively. Although Brown had dual French/English nationality, he and his family had for many years been domiciled in France; Lair was a Frenchwoman. Prior to taking up his place at Cambridge, Brown had obtained university sponsorship from, and worked for, Ferranti in Scotland. The job was clearly intended as a preparation for his university studies, and had lasted for eight months. Lair had worked intermittently in

Germany for over five years, with spells of involuntary unemployment. Both parties were refused a grant and sought to challenge that refusal on the basis of, *inter alia*, Regulation 1612/68, Articles 7(2) and 7(3) (their claim based on Article 7 of the EEC Treaty and 'vocational training' will be discussed in chapter 19, in the context of *Gravier* (case 293/83)).

Advocate-General Sir Gordon Slynn submitted that both courses were capable of constituting vocational training within Article 7(3); if not, they would in any case fall under Article 7(2), as 'social advantages'. The crucial question, therefore, was whether Brown and Lair were 'workers', entitled to claim under these provisions. Brown had come to the UK primarily to prepare for his engineering studies at Cambridge; he had obtained his place at Cambridge prior to taking up work in the UK. Lair on the other hand had undoubtedly come to Germany many years before, intending to work. The Advocate-General suggested that a distinction might be drawn between persons who migrate genuinely in the capacity of a worker and those who move to another State for other purposes, e.g., in order to become a student, or to gain some work experience before their studies begin. Only the former, he suggested, could invoke Article 7(2) and (3) of Regulation 1612/68. Whilst he did not think States could prescribe a minimum residence period before entitlement to benefits under the Article could arise (under German law five years' continuous employment was required for foreigners), the length of time during which a claimant had been in residence in a member State, as well as what he was doing during that time, could be taken into account in deciding whether he was there in the capacity of a genuine worker. He suggested that a year's residence might provide a guideline as to the genuineness of the work, although even this would not be a watertight test.

The Court, which delivered judgments in both cases on the same day, took a rather different approach. As has been noted, it chose to interpret Article 7(3) narrowly, with the result that neither course would constitute 'training in vocational schools'. If the parties were to succeed it could only be on the basis of Article 7(2). A grant to cover university education was undoubtedly a 'social advantage'. But were the applicants 'workers'? The Court did not agree with the Advocate-General that the grant of social advantages might be subject to a minimum residence period, as a measure of the genuineness of the claimant's status as a worker. The concept of worker, the Court held, must have a community meaning. Nevertheless, in Brown's case, although he might be regarded as a worker, he was not entitled to claim the grant as a social advantage because he had acquired the status of worker exclusively as a result of his having been accepted for admission to university. The employment was merely ancillary to the studies to be financed by the grant. With regard to Lair's claim, the Court draw a distinction between a claim by a migrant worker who was *in*voluntarily unemployed, who, if legitimately resident, was entitled to the same treatment as regards reinstatement or re-employment as national workers, and one who gave up his work in order to undertake further training in the host State. In the latter case, he might only claim a grant for such a course if there was some link between the studies to be pursued and his previous work activity.

Thus the Court chose to base its decision in both cases on fine factual distinctions rather than on the 'genuineness' of the claimant's status as a worker, although it did add in *Lair,* in response to the expressed worries of member States as to the possibility of abuse, that 'insofar as a worker has entered a member State for the sole purpose of enjoying, after a very short period of work activity, the benefit of the student assistance system in that State, it should be observed that such abuses are not covered by the community provisions (i.e. Article 7(2) and 7(3)) in question' (para. 43). It is regrettable that in its concern to appease the anxiety of member States it chose in *Lair* to limit the scope of Article 7(2) by denying a right to 'social advantages' in the form of grants to migrant workers who have not become unemployed but who genuinely want to improve their prospects by retraining in a *new* field of activity. In an era of rapid technological and economic change such as will inevitably occur if the single internal market becomes a reality, flexibility in the work force is surely to be encouraged. This limitation in *Lair* was however endorsed in *Raulin* (case 357/87) and *Bernini* (case 3/90).

(d) *Trade union rights; rights of respresentation and management.* Under Article 8 of Regulation 1612/68 a migrant worker is entitled to equality of treatment as regards 'membership of trade unions and the exercise of rights attaching thereto'. This applies also to membership of bodies which carry out similar functions defending or representing the interests of workers (*Association de Soutien aux Travailleurs Immigrés* v *Chambre des Employés Privés* (case C 213/90). He may be excluded from the 'management of bodies governed by public law and from holding an office governed by public law', but he is eligible to sit on workers' representative bodies in such undertakings.

(e) *Housing.* A migrant worker is entitled to enjoy 'all the rights and benefits accorded to national workers in matters of housing, including ownership of the housing he needs' (Article 9; see *Commission* v *Greece* (case 305/87), restrictions on foreigners' right to acquire property held unlawful). The right extends to public and private housing. Lord Denning MR was reluctant to apply this principle in *De Falco* v *Crawley Borough Council* [1980] QB 460, Court of Appeal, in the context of a claim under the Housing (Homeless Persons) Act 1977. It is submitted that all statutory protection in this field must apply equally to 'favoured EEC citizens', i.e., those who are lawfully resident. These rights would also constitute 'social advantages' under Article 7(2).

Workers' families (Articles 10-12)

(a) *Residence.* Members of a workers' family are defined as:

(i)   the worker's spouse and their descendants who are under the age of 21 or are dependants; and
(ii)   dependent relatives in the ascending line of the worker and his spouse.

Members of a worker's family have a right to install themselves with the migrant worker (who must be an EEC national) 'irrespective of their nationality' (Article 10(1)).

States are required to facilitate the admission of any member of the family not falling within the above definition if they are 'dependent on the worker ... or living under his roof in the country whence he comes' (Article 10(2)). Once admitted and installed it is submitted that such members attain the status of favoured EC citizens. In *Lebon* (case 316/85) the Court held, in the context of a claim for the Belgian minimex by the adult child of a retired French worker living in Belgium, that the status of dependency resulted from a purely factual situation, i.e., support provided by the worker; it did not depend on objective factors indicative of a need for support.

However, *Lebon* also established that once a worker's children reach the age of 21 they will cease to be 'members of the family' unless they are still dependent on the worker. They will thus lose their rights as favoured community citizens until they themselves become 'workers'.

In order that the family may install themselves with the worker he must have available for his family 'housing considered as normal for national workers in the region where he is employed' (Article 10(3)). The Court has held (*Commission* v *Germany* (case 249/86)) that as long as the family is living in appropriate housing conditions when the worker begins his working life in the host State, member States may not require this condition to be satisfied throughout the entire duration of their residence. To do so would infringe the fundamental principle of respect for family life enshrined in Article 8 of the Convention for the Protection of Human Rights and protected as part of Community law. Thus a German law which made the granting of a residence permit conditional on the worker's continuing compliance with Article 10(3) was in breach of Community law.

(b) *Employment.* By article 11:

Where a national of a member State is pursuing an activity as an employed or self-employed person in the territory of another member State, his spouse and those of the children who are under the age of 21 years or dependent on him shall have the rights to take up any activity as an employed person throughout the territory of that same state, even if they are not nationals of any member State.

This Article was invoked in *Gül* (case 131/85), Article 177 proceedings, by the Turkish-Cypriot husband of an English woman working as a hairdresser in Germany. He had qualified as a doctor of medicine at Istanbul University, and taken further qualifications in anaesthetics in Germany. He had worked there on a temporary basis for some years. When he applied for permanent authorisation to practise in Germany he was refused on account of his nationality. He sought to annul this decision as in breach of EEC law. The Court of Justice, in response to a request for a preliminary ruling, held that as long as he had the qualifications and diplomas necessary for the pursuit of the occupation in question in accordance with the legislation of the host State, and observed the specific rules governing the pursuit of that occupation, he was entitled under Article 11, as the spouse of an EEC worker, to practise his profession in that State, even though he did not have EEC nationality. Thus in the case of a spouse seeking to practise a profession it will be ncessary to establish whether the spouse's qualifications are recognised as equivalent, which in Gül's case they were. (For a fuller discussion of this matter see chapter 19.)

In *Diatta* (case 267/83) the Court held that a spouse's right under Article 11 to take up employment in the host State gave her the right to install herself in that State even under a separate roof from her husband, since it might be necessary to live apart from her husband in order to exercise her right to work. Article 11 did not, however, itself give rise to a right of residence independent of her position as a spouse.

(c) *Children: access to educational apprenticeship or vocational training courses* (Article 12). As was mentioned in the context of workers' rights under Article 7(3), the case of *Casagrande* (case 9/74) established that this Article entitled children not merely to admission to such courses but also to general measures to facilitate attendance, including grants. This right has been held to extend to a grant to study abroad provided it is available to nationals of the host State (case C 308/89)). In *Commission* v *Belgium* (case 42/87) the Court held that the children of migrant EEC workers are entitled to full national treatment as regards *all* forms of State education, even if the working parent has retired or died in that State. The Court went further in *Moritz* v *Netherlands Minister for Education* (case 390/87). This case involved a claim for an educational allowance from the Dutch authorities by the child of a migrant worker, a German, who had left Holland and returned to his native country. His son sought to return to Holland to complete his studies there since he could not do so in Germany, there being no coordination of school-leaving certification as between the two countries. The Court held, in a reference under Article 177, that in such a case, having regard to the need to ensure the integration of migrant workers in the host State, and the need for continuity in their children's education, a child was not to be regarded as having lost its status as a 'child of the family' benefiting from the provisions of Regulation 1612/68 merely because his family had moved back to its State of origin. It may be presumed that his rights under Regulation 1612/68 would cease when the course was concluded.

Despite the fact that Article 12 does not give a spouse the right to equal access to educational, apprenticeship or vocational training courses, a spouse was successful in claiming such a right in *Forcheri* v *Belgian State* (case 152/82), Article 177 proceedings. Mrs Forcheri was the wife of an Italian working as a Community official in Brussels. She applied for admission to a social work training course in Brussels. She was accepted, but required to pay a special fee, the *'minerval'*, required of all students who were not Belgian nationals. She claimed that the fee was discriminatory, in breach of Articles 7 and 48 of the EEC Treaty and Article 12 of Regulation 1612/68. The Court of Justice, on a reference from the Brussels Juge de Paix, drawing support from the fifth recital in the preamble to Regulation 1612/68, held that to require of a national of another member State, *lawfully established* in the first member State, an enrolment fee which is not required of its own nationals constitutes discrimination by reason of nationality which is prohibited by Article 7 of the Treaty.

Thus, in Mrs Forcheri's case, the right was deemed to arise not from Article 12 of Regulation 1612/68, from which she was clearly excluded, but from Article 7 of the EEC Treaty. Her position as a favoured EEC citizen, as the spouse of a worker, brought her 'within the scope of application of this Treaty' (Article 7 of the EEC Treaty).

In the light of developments in the past few years it would now be permitted to base such a claim for fees levied at the lower, Belgian rate on Article 7(2), as a social advantage.

However, it should be borne in mind, as was made clear in *Lebon* (case 316/85), that members of the worker's family are only *indirect* beneficiaries of the right to equal treatment accorded to the worker under Article 7(2) of Regulation 1612/68; social advantages can only be granted to members of the family under Article 7(2) as advantages to the *worker*. This is a subtle distinction, but an important one.

Rights to remain in the territory of a member State after having been employed in that State (Regulation 1251/70) This Regulation implements Article 48(3)(d) of the EEC Treaty. As stated in the preamble to Regulation 1251/70, 'the right of residence acquired by workers in active employment has as a corollary the right . . . to remain in the territory of a member State after having been employed in that State' (first recital); moreover, 'the exercise by the worker of the right to remain entails that such right shall be extended to members of his family; [and], in the case of the death of the worker during his working life, maintenance of the right of residence of the members of his family must also be recognised' (seventh recital).

Regulation 1251/70 thus provides for the right of the worker and his family to remain permanently in the State in which he has worked on retirement, incapacity, or, in the case of the family, the death of the worker. It also makes special provision for the 'frontier' worker, i.e., one who lives in one, and works in an adjacent, state.

Members of the family are defined as in Regulation 1612/68, Article 10.

(a) *Workers* (Article 2(1)). Article 2(1) provides that:

The following shall have the right to remain permanently in the territory of a member State:

(a) *Retirement* a worker who, at the time of termination of his activity, has reached the age laid down by the law of that member State for entitlement to an old-age pension and who has been employed in that State for at least the last 12 months and has resided there continuously for more than three years.

(b) *Incapacity* a worker who, having resided continuously in the territory of that State for more than two years, ceases to work there as an employed person as a result of permanent incapacity to work. If such incapacity is the result of an accident at work or an occupational disease entitling him to a pension for which an institution of that State is entirely or partially responsible, no condition shall be imposed as to length of residence.

(c) *Frontier workers* a worker who, after three years' continuous employment and residence in the territory of that State, works as an employed person in the territory of another member State, while retaining his residence in the territory of the first State, to which he returns, as a rule, each day or at least once a week.

Periods of time spent working in another member State are to be considered as spent working in the State of residence for the purposes of satisfying the employment requirements of subparagraphs (a) and (b).

If the worker's spouse is a national of the State concerned, or has lost her nationality through marriage to the worker, the residence and employment requirements of subparagraphs (a) and (b) will not apply (Article 2(2)).

(b) *Members of the family* (Article 3). Members of the worker's family will be entitled to remain permanently under two sets of circumstances:

(i)   If the worker has himself acquired the right to remain (Article 3(1)).

(ii)   If the worker dies during his working life before having acquired the right to remain and either:

(1)   the worker has resided continuously in that State for at least two years, or

(2)   his death resulted from an accident at work or an occupational disease, or

(3)   the surviving spouse is a national of that State of residence or has lost the nationality of that State by marriage to the worker (Article 3(2)).

Article 4 provides that continuity of residence as required under Article 2 and 3 will not be affected by temporary absences not exceeding three months per year, nor longer absences due to compliance with obligations of military service: and periods of involuntary unemployment, duly recorded by the competent employment office, and absences due to illness or accident, are to be considered as periods of employment for the purposes of Article 2 (Article 4(2)).

Thus, provision is generous, and designed to provide the maximum security for the migrant worker and his family.

The beneficiaries of these rights are given two years, from the time when they first became entitled, to exercise them. During this time they may leave the territory concerned without forfeiting their rights (Article 5).

Persons exercising their right to remain are entitled to a residence permit which must be valid (throughout the territory of the State concerned) for at least five years, and must be automatically renewable (Article 6). As stated in *Royer* (case 48/75), their right of residence will not depend on the residence permit; the permit will merely provide proof of their right of residence.

Persons exercising their rights to remain in a member State under Regulation 1251/70 will be entitled to equality of treatment as established by

Regulation 1612/68 (Article 7). Thus they may claim all 'social advantages' provided by that State on the same basis as nationals.

Regulation 1251/70, Article 3(2), was invoked, *inter alia*, in the case of *R* v *Secretary of State for the Home Department (ex parte Sandhu)* [1982] 2 CMLR 553 in order to argue for a right of permanent residence in the UK for Mr Sandhu when his EEC wife left him to return to Germany. It was argued that separation and divorce could be regarded in the same light as the death of the worker. To deny a spouse security of residence in the case of separation or divorce would equally create an obstacle to the free movement of workers. The argument succeeded before Comyn J, but not before the Court of Appeal ([1983] 3 CMLR 131) or the House of Lords (*The Times*, 10 May 1985). It is a convincing argument which deserves to be revived.

'Employment in the public service' (Article 48(4))

In the field of employment rights, member States are entitled under Article 48(4) of the EEC Treaty to deny or restrict access to 'employment in the public service' on the basis of a worker's nationality. Given the potential breadth of this provision, it is not surprising that it has been exploited by member States nor that the Court of Justice has given it the narrowest scope.

The German post office sought to rely on this exclusion in *Sotgiu* v *Deutsche Bundespost* (case 152/73) to counter Sotgiu's allegations that the post office's rules granting extra allowances to workers living apart from their families in Germany were discriminatory. On a reference from the Bundesarbeitsgericht the Court of Justice held that the exception provided by Article 48(4) did not apply to all employment in the public service. It applied only to 'certain activities' in the public service, connected with the exercise of official authority. Moreover, it applied only to conditions of *access;* it did not permit discriminatory conditions of employment once access had been granted.

The matter was further clarified in *Commission* v *Belgium (Re Public Employees)* (case 149/79). This was an infringement action against Belgium under Article 169 for breach of Article 48. Under Belgian law, posts in the 'public service' could be limited to Belgian nationals. This was applied to all kinds of posts: unskilled workers, railwaymen, nurses, plumbers, electricians and architects, employed by both central and local government. The city of Brussels (seat of the EEC Commission!) was one of the chief offenders. The Belgian government (supported by France and Germany intervening) argued that all these jobs were 'in the public service' within Article 48(4). The Court of Justice disagreed. The concept of public service was a Community concept; it applied only to the exercise of official authority, and was intended to apply only to employees *safeguarding the general interests of the State.* The fact that higher levels of a post might involve the exercise of official authority would not justify assimilating the junior levels to that status. Belgium was in breach of EEC law.

Similar proceedings were brought, and upheld, against France in *Commission* v *France (Re French Nurses)* (case 307/84) against a French law limiting the appointment of nurses in public hospitals to French nationals.

When a particular job will involve 'the exercise of official authority' is not altogether clear. It certainly does not apply to civil servants generally. In *Lawrie-Blum* v *Land Baden-Württemberg* (case 66/85), Article 177 proceedings, the Court held that access to certain posts could not be limited by reason of the fact that in a given member State persons appointed to such posts have the status of civil servants. To make the application of Article 48(4) dependent on the legal nature of the relationship between the employer and the administration would enable member States to determine at will the posts covered by the exception laid down in that provision. To constitute employment in the public service, employees must be charged with the exercise of powers conferred by public law or must be responsible for *safeguarding the general interests of the State* (approved by ECJ in *Allué & Coonan* v *Università degli studi di Venezia* (case 33/88), teachers in State university not 'employees in the public service' within Article 48(4)).

On these criteria it seems that the derogation provided by Article 48(4) will be of limited use, confined, as has been suggested, to posts which presume, on the part of persons occupying them, a special allegiance to the State, occupations such as the judiciary and the higher echelons of the civil service, the armed forces and the police. Article 48(4) needs to be viewed in conjunction with Article 55, which provides that the freedom of establishment permitted under EEC law 'shall not apply, so far as any given member State is concerned, to activities which in that State are connected, even occasionally, with the exercise of official authority'. Identical principles will apply to the interpretation of both provisions.

Since most of the posts in the above cases may not be denied to non-nationals, access to these posts by way of examination or training must be open, on equal terms, to workers (or their families) who are non-nationals. Thus in *Lawrie-Blum* (case 66/85) a practical training scheme for teachers, organised in Baden-Württemberg within the framework of the civil serivce, was not within Article 48(4) and could not be confined to German nationals.

In view of the widespread practice among member States of excluding non-nationals from a wide range of occupations in the public service on the basis of Article 48(4) (e.g. *Allué & Coonan* noted above), the Commission published a Notice in 1988 (OJ No.C 72/2) announcing that it proposed to review certain sectors of employment which it considered to be for the most part 'sufficiently remote from the specific activities of the public sphere as defined by the European Court that they would only in rare cases be covered by the exception of Article 48(4)'. These comprise:

(a) public health care services,
(b) teaching in State educational establishments,
(c) research for non-military purposes in public establishments, and
(d) public bodies responsible for administering commercial services.

These are still under review. It has been suggested that the review should result in the opening up of many posts which in many member States are currently reserved for nationals, representing a 'tremendous leap forward in the attainment of a true community-wide labour market' (see Watson, noted below).

Derogation on grounds of public policy, public security or public health (Article 48(3))

The rights of entry and residence and the right of permanent residence granted by the Treaty to migrant workers and their families are not absolute. States remain free to deny these rights to migrant workers or their families on grounds of 'public policy, public security or public health'. Because of the importance of this principle and the fact that Directive 64/221, passed to implement the principle, applies to all categories of migrant workers, employed and self-employed, it will be dealt with separately in chapter 20.

Further reading

Handoll, J., 'Article 48(4) EEC and non-national access to public employment' (1988) 13 EL Rev 223.
Hartley, T., 'Free Movement of Students in European Community Law' (1989) Cahiers de Droit Européen.
Lonbay, J., 'Education and Law; the Community Context' (1989) 14 EL Rev 363.
Steiner, J., 'The Right to Welfare: Equality and Equity under Community Law' (1985) 10 EL Rev 21.
Watson, P., Notes on Free Movement of Workers (1985) 9 EL Rev 335; (1989) 14 EL Rev 415.

NINETEEN

Freedom of establishment; freedom to provide services; freedom to receive services

The freedoms granted to workers under Article 48 were also granted by the Treaty to the self-employed in the form of a right of establishment (Part Two, Title III, Chapter 2, Articles 52-8) and a right to provide services (Chapter 3, Articles 59-66). The principal Articles are Article 52 (establishment) and Articles 59 and 60(3) (services).

Establishment

Article 52 provides:

> Within the framework of the provisions set out below, restrictions on the freedom of establishment of nationals of a member State in the territory of another member State shall be abolished by progressive stages in the course of the transitional period. Such progressive abolition shall also apply to restrictions on the setting up of agencies, branches or subsidiaries by nationals of any member State established in the territory of any member State.
>
> Freedom of establishment shall include the right to take up and pursue activities as self-employed persons and to set up and manage undertakings, in particular companies and firms within the meaning of the second paragraph of Article 58, under the conditions laid down for its own nationals by the law of the country where such establishment is effected, subject to the provisions of the Chapter relating to capital [Chapter 4].

'Companies or firms' means 'companies or firms constituted under civil or commercial law, including cooperative societies, and other legal persons governed by public or private law, save for those which are non-profit-making' (Article 58(2)).

Companies or firms formed in accordance with the law of a member State and having their registered office, central administration or principal place of business within the Community shall, for the purposes of this Chapter, be treated in the same way as natural persons who are nationals of member States (Article 58(1)).

Services

Articles 59 and 60(3) provide:

Within the framework of the provisions set out below, restrictions on freedom to provide services within the Community shall be progressively abolished during the transitional period in respect of nationals of member States who are established in a State of the Community other than that of the person for whom the services are provided (Article 59).

Without prejudice to the provisions of the Chapter relating to the right of establishment [Chapter 2], the person providing a service may, in order to do so, temporarily pursue his activity in the State where the service is provided, under the same conditions as are imposed by that State on its own nationals (Article 60(3)).

These rights too are granted to companies or firms formed in accordance with the law of a member State (Article 66).

'Services' are defined as those 'normally provided for remuneration, in so far as they are not governed by the provisions relating to freedom of movement for goods, capital and persons' (Article 60(1)). Services in the field of transport are 'governed by the provisions of the Title [Part Two, Title IV] relating to transport' (Article 61). Article 60 provides a non-exhaustive list of examples of services.

Thus, the right of establishment and the right to provide services are accorded under the Treaty to EEC nationals and to companies formed according to the law of one of the member States. Where in the latter case the central management or principal place of business lies outside the Community the company's activities must have an 'effective and continuous link with the economy of a member State, excluding the possibility that this link might depend on nationality, particularly the nationality of the partners or the members of the managing or supervisory bodies, or of persons holding the capital stock' ('General programme for the abolition of restrictions on freedom to provide services', *Common Market Reporter,* para. 1546; JO 1962, 32). This link is the price exacted for valuable access to the Community market. To benefit from the freedom to provide services, an EEC national must be established in a member State.

The difference between the right of establishment and the right to provide services is one of degree rather than of kind. Both apply to business or professional activity pursued for 'profit' or 'remuneration'. A right of establishment is a right to install oneself, to 'set up shop' in another member State, permanently or semi-permanently, whether as an individual, a partnership or a company, for the purpose of performing a particular activity there. The right to provide services, on the other hand, connotes the provision of services in one State, on a temporary or spasmodic basis, by a person established in another State. In the latter case it is not necessary to reside, even temporarily, in the State in which the service is provided.

In the German insurance case (*Commission* v *Germany (Re Insurance Services)*) (case 205/84), Article 169 proceedings, the Court suggested that an enterprise would fall within the concept of 'establishment' even if its presence is not in the form of a branch or agency but consists merely of an office managed by the enterprise's own staff or by a person who is independent but is authorised to act on a permanent basis for the enterprise.

In view of the fine line between 'establishment' and 'provision of services', and the fact that the general principles applicable to both are the same (as they are to workers, see *Royer* (case 48/75) discussed in chapter 18), too much emphasis should not be placed on the difference between the two. However, in certain circumstances, to be discussed later in this chapter, the distinction may be important.

In addition to the Treaty, secondary legislation has now been enacted granting rights of entry and residence to the self-employed in near-identical terms to those applicable to workers. In the case of services the right of residence is 'of equal duration with the period during which the services are provided' (Directive 73/148, Article 4(2)). The legislation comprises:

(a)   Directive 73/148 (rights of entry and residence; equivalent to Directive 68/360).

(b)   Directive 75/34 (right to remain permanently in a member State after having been self-employed there; equivalent to Regulation 1251/70).

Regulation 1612/68, being expressed in terms of the situation of employment, has no parallel for the self-employed. Hence the special importance in this area of Article 7 of the EEC Treaty, the principle of non-discrimination on the grounds of nationality. Where the self-employed or their families are 'lawfully resident' in a member State, Article 7 may be invoked to ensure that they receive equal treatment in the form of 'social' or any other advantages with nationals of the host State. Certainly this would apply to persons or businesses established in the host State. In the case of the provider of services, the matter is less clear. Whilst he is undoubtedly able to claim full equality as regards access to, and conditions of, work within the host State it is unlikely that he can claim for himself and his family social advantages in the wider sense in which the term has been interpreted in the context of workers. It is submitted, although it has yet to be decided by the Court, that these should be claimed from the State in which he is permanently established. An analogy could perhaps be drawn here with the person migrating in search of employment, who, according to *Lebon* (case 316/85) has no entitlement to the social advantages provided by the host State (see chapter 18).

Both the right of establishment and the freedom to provide services are subject to derogation on the grounds of 'public policy, public security or public health' (Articles 56 and 66; Directive 64/221; see chapter 20). Both are expressed not to apply to 'activities which in that State are connected, even occasionally, with the exercise of official authority' (Articles 55 and 66).

The right of establishment and the right to provide services have been described by the Court of Justice as 'fundamental Community rights'. The principle on which these rights are based is the principle of non-discrimination on grounds of nationality, whether arising from legislation, regulation or administrative practice. The principle is binding on all competent authorities as well as legally recognised professional bodies (*Steinhauser* v *City of Biarritz* (case 197/84) (Article 52); *Walrave* v *Association Union Cycliste Internationale* (case 36/74) (Article 59)).

Limitations on the freedoms

The right of establishment and the freedom to provide services provided under Articles 52 and 59 are not absolute. Apart from the express derogations of Articles 55, 56 and 66, they are subject to one important limitation. The right to equality of opportunity provided by Articles 52(2) and 60(3) can only be exercised 'under the conditions laid down for its own nationals by the law of the country where such establishment is effected' (Article 52(2) or 'under the same conditions as are imposed by that State on its own nationals' (Article 60(3)).

The difficulty for non-nationals seeking to establish themselves or provide services in another member State is that they may not be able to satisfy the conditions laid down in that State for the practice of the particular trade or profession which they wish to exercise. The relevant conditions are those prescribed by trade or professional bodies, normally reinforced by law, relating to:

(a) the education and training required for qualification for the job, and
(b) rules of professional conduct.

Both of these vary greatly in scope and content and quality from State to State. The need to comply with these conditions has thus provided a potent barrier to freedom of movement for the self-employed; it has also hindered the free movement of workers, since they too may wish to work as employees in a trade or profession which is subject to regulation at national level.

Because of these difficulties the Treaty provided for the abolition of existing restrictions on freedom of establishment and freedom to provide services to be achieved in progressive stages during a transitional period. During the first stage the Council, acting on a proposal from the Commission, was to draw up a general programme on the abolition of restrictions on freedom of establishment (Article 53) and on the freedom to provide services (Article 63). In addition these institutions were required, during the first stage, to 'issue Directives for the mutual recognition of diplomas, certificates and other evidence of formal qualifications' (Article 57(1)) and, before the end of the transitional period, to 'issue Directives for the coordination of the provisions laid down by law, regulation or administrative action in member States concerning the taking up and pursuit of activities as self-employed persons' (Article 57(2)).

The general programmes were adopted in 1961 (*Common Market Reporter* paras 1335 and 1546; JO 1962, 36, 32). Although not binding, they provide valuable guidelines in the interpretation of the Treaty, and have been invoked on a number of occasions by the Court (e.g., *Steinhauser* (case 197/84) and *Gravier* (case 293/83) both to be discussed later in this chapter). The issuing of Directives under Article 57(1) and (2) has proved a more difficult task. National professional bodies have understandably been reluctant to compromise on long-established principles and practices, and although many Directives have been passed (for full range see *Encyclopedia of European Community Law*, vol. C, part C12) in areas ranging from wholesaling to hairdressing to medicine, progress has been slow. The architects' Directive alone took 17 years to pass.

Since the right of establishment and the right to provide services provided under Articles 52 and 59 appeared to be conditional on the issuing of Directives under Article 57(1) and (2) it was thought that these rights could not be invoked by individuals until such Directives had been passed. This matter was tested in *Reyners* v *Belgian State* (case 2/74), Article 177 proceedings. Reyners was a Dutchman, born, educated and resident in Belgium, and a doctor of Belgian law. He was refused admission to the Belgian Bar since he was not of Belgian nationality. He challenged this decision, claiming that it was in breach of Article 52. The Belgian government argued that Article 52 was not directly effective, since it depended for its effect on the issuing of Directives under Article 57. On a reference for interpretation from the Belgian Conseil d'État on this point, the Court of Justice held that Article 52 was directly effective from the end of the transitional period. The provisions of Article 57 were complementary to Article 52; they were not a necessary precondition. The purpose of Article 57 was merely to facilitate the increase of freedom of establishment; Article 57, together with Article 7, required that the actual conditions imposed could not be stricter than those imposed on the State's own nationals.

The same principle was applied in the context of services in *Van Binsbergen* (case 33/74), Article 177 proceedings. The plaintiff, Van Binsbergen, a Dutchman, qualified as an advocate in Holland, sought to invoke Articles 59(1) and 60(3) in order to challenge a rule of the Dutch Bar that persons representing clients before certain tribunals must reside in the State in which that service is supplied. Van Binsbergen had been living and working in Holland, but had moved to Belgium. As a result he was denied the right, which he had previously enjoyed, to represent clients before social security tribunals in the Netherlands. As in *Reyners*, no harmonising Directives had been passed. Nevertheless, on a reference from the Dutch Social Security Court, the Court of Justice held he was entitled to rely on Articles 59(1) and 60(3); they were directly effective from the end of the transitional period.

Thus even though recognition and harmonisation have not been achieved in a particular profession by the issuing of Directives under Article 57, once the transitional period has expired Articles 52, 59 and 60, together with Article 7, may be invoked to challenge a national rule, whether in the form of a nationality or a residence requirement, which is discriminatory. This principle applies to both direct and indirect discrimination, and relates not only to the taking up of an activity but to pursuit of that activity in the widest sense. This principle was confirmed in *Steinhauser* v *City of Biarritz* (case 197/84), Article 177 proceedings. Steinhauser was a German, a professional artist resident in Biarritz. He applied to the Biarritz authorities to rent a *'crampotte'*, a fisherman's hut of a type used locally for the exhibition and sale of works of art. He was refused on the grounds of his nationality; under the city's regulations *crampottes* could only be rented by persons of French nationality. He challenged that decision, and the Court of Justice, on reference from the Pau administrative tribunal, held that freedom of establishment provided under Article 52 related not only to the taking up of an activity as a self-employed person but also the pursuit of that activity in the widest sense.

Thus, citing the general programme on the abolition of restrictions on freedom of establishment (1962 JO 36), the right to equal treatment was held to include, *inter alia*, the right to rent premises, to tender, and to qualify for licences and concessions.

The Court went further in *Commission* v *Italy: re Housing Aid* (case 63/86). Here it held, in Article 169 proceedings, that a cheap mortgage facility, available under Italian law only to Italian nationals, was in breach of Article 7 EEC, even where such provision was an aspect of social law, and thus (it was implied) should be available on a basis of equality in Italy to EEC nationals providing services *as long as the nature of the services provided was such as to require a permanent dwelling there.*

Professional qualifications

Even though Directives have not been passed ensuring mutual recognition of diplomas, certificates and other evidence of formal qualifications in a particular trade or profession, it will be discriminatory, in breach of Articles 52 or 59 and 60 together with Article 7 to refuse permission to practise to a person whose qualifications have been recognised in some way as equivalent to those required in the State in which he seeks to practise.

In *Thieffry* v *Conseil de l'Ordre des Advocats à la Cour de Paris* (case 71/76), Article 177 proceedings, the Court held that the French Bar Council could not refuse to allow Thieffry, a Belgian national with a Belgian law degree, to undertake practical training for the French bar, since his Belgian degree had been recognised by the University of Paris and he had acquired a qualifying certificate in France for the profession of *avocat*. Similarly, in *Patrick* v *Ministre des Affaires Culturelles* (case 11/77), Article 177 proceedings, the Court held that Patrick, an Englishman, who had trained as an architect in England, was entitled to invoke Articles 52 and 7 in order to practise architecture in France, since, although no diplomatic convention ensuring recognition had been agreed, as was required by French law, and no EEC Directives relating to architects had at that time been passed, his English qualifications had been recognised as equivalent to the corresponding French degree under a Ministerial Decree of 1964.

Where a Directive has been issued for the mutual recognition or harmonization of qualifications in a particular profession that profession may no longer insist on compliance with its own requirements by persons who have qualified in another member State according to the terms of the Directive. Thus in *Broekmeulen* (case 246/80), Article 177 proceedings, the Dutch General Practitioners' Committee was unable to refuse Broekmeulen permission to practise as a GP in Holland even though he had qualified as a GP in Belgium, where it was not necessary to complete the three years' specialised training required for GPs in Holland. The EEC Directive 75/362 relating to training for GPs did not require GPs to undergo training additional to their original (three-year) qualification. Parties may not, however, claim freedom of establishment under Article 52 or freedom to provide services under Article 59 in reliance on a Directive issued under Article 57 until the period provided for its implementation has expired (*Auer* (case 136/78), Article 177 proceedings — re veterinary surgeons' Directive 78/1026).

Where a person is entitled to claim rights of establishment or freedom to provide services as a result of possessing recognised or equivalent qualifications (whether recognised by Directive or otherwise) he may do so even though he possesses the nationality, but not the qualifications, of the State in which he seeks to pursue his activities (*Knoors* (case 115/78), Article 177 proceedings; *Broekmeulen* (case 246/80); *Auer* (case 136/78)). In this case it is not regarded as a purely internal matter (cf. *Moser* v *Land Baden-Württemberg* (case 180/83), discussed in chapter 17).

Where qualifications obtained in a particular member State have *not* been subject to harmonisation or recognised in another State, it will not be discriminatory, in breach of EC law, for a State or a professional body to refuse a person possessing these qualifications permission to practise. As the Commission pointed out in 1985 in its White Paper on the completion of the internal market, this constituted a serious barrier to freedom of establishment and the freedom to provide services, as well as to the free movement of workers, in the single market.

A new approach

Because of the problems outlined above, and progress on harmonisation for the purpose of mutual recognition of qualifications had been so slow, the Community decided, following agreement by the Heads of State at Fontainebleau in June 1984, on a new approach. Instead of attempting to harmonise by profession, known as the sectoral or 'vertical' aproach, the Commission was henceforth to adopt a general or 'horizontal' approach, based not on harmonisation but on the mutual recognition of qualifications, and applicable not to individual professions but to all areas of activity for which a higher education diploma was required. Directive 89/48 ((1989) OJ No.L 19/16), based on these principles, was approved in December 1988.

The Directive applies only to regulated professional activities, although it is sufficient if they are regulated in only one State in the Community. It does not attempt to modify the rules applicable to particular professions in individual member States, nor does it apply to professions which were already subject to separate Directives providing for the mutual recognition of diplomas. Like the prior harmonisation Directives it will apply to workers as well as the self-employed.

The starting-point for the principle of mutual recognition is a higher education diploma awarded on completion of professional education and training of at least three years' duration, or the equivalent period part time. Where, in the host State, the taking up and pursuit of a regulated profession is subject to the possession of a diploma, the competent authority of that State may not refuse to authorise a national of a member State to take up and pursue that profession on the same conditions as apply to its own nationals, provided the applicant holds a diploma required in another State for the pursuit of the profession in question, *or* has pursued that profession for at least two years in a State which does not regulate that profession (Article 3).

Where the applicant's education and training is at least one year shorter than that which is required by the host State, or where there is a shortfall in the period of supervised practice required by the host State, the applicant may be required to provide *evidence of professional experience*. This may not exceed the shortfall in supervised practice, nor twice the shortfall in duration of education and training, required by the host State; in any event, it may not exceed four years (Article 4(1)(a)).

The host State may also require an *adaptation period* not exceeding three years:

(a)   where matters covered by the applicant's education and training differ substantially from those covered by that of the State; or

(b)   where the activities regulated in the host State are not regulated in the applicant's State of origin; or

(c)   where the profession regulated in the host State comprises activities which are not pursued in the State from which the applicant originates,

provided, in the latter two situations, the difference corresponds to *specific* education and training required in the host State and covers matters which differ *substantially* from those covered by the evidence of formal qualification (Article 4(1)(b)).

Instead of the adaptation period the applicant may opt for an aptitude test. However, for professions whose practice requires precise knowledge of national law and in which the giving of advice on national law is an essential and constant aspect of that activity, a State may stipulate either an adaptation period or an aptitude test (Article 4(1)(b)).

The requirements of periods of professional experience *and* adaptation cannot be applied cumulatively. Thus the total period cannot exceed four years.

In addition, the host State may allow an applicant to undertake in the host State, on a basis of equivalence, that part of his training which consists of supervised professional practice (Article 5).

Member States were required to implement the Directive by 4 January 1991. Thus provisions which are sufficiently clear, precise and unconditional, were directly effective from that date, at least against a 'public' body, an agency of the State (see chapter 2). Since professional bodies normally operate subject to statutory authorisation and control, it is submitted that this factor should constitute a sufficiently 'public' element for the purposes of the enforcement of the Directive. The Directive thus represents a significant breakthrough, removing many of the existing and substantial barriers to the free movement of the employed and the self-employed. Should there be problems over establishing direct effects, or in the case of claims arising before 4 January 1991, the Court has held 'that professional bodies of a member State, in deciding whether to allow persons who do not satisfy their own State's professional requirements, must take into account the applicant's qualification and compare them with the 'home' requirements, in order to assess whether they are in fact equivalent. Applicants are entitled to be given reasons for decisions, and must have an opportunity to challenge them in judicial proceedings (*Vlassopoulou* v *Ministerium für Justiz* (case C 340/89)).

Professional rules of conduct

As well as rules relating to qualifications and training, professional bodies lay down rules governing the conduct of the profession in question, relating both to access to the profession and practice within it. These rules are normally justified as in the public good. They do, however, constitute barriers to the free movement of persons, since, as in the case where national standards are applied to imported goods, compliance by persons who have qualified and practised according to the rules of another member State may be both difficult and expensive. Whilst persons who establish themselves in another member State either as workers or self-employed persons may be expected to comply in full with its rules, the burden on those who wish merely to provide services in that State may be excessive and unnecessary, since they will in all likelihood be subject to professional regulation, providing similar standards and safeguards, in the State in which they are established. In some cases, where national rules restrict the categories of persons entitled to practise certain professions the practice of a profession in which a person is fully qualified in his home State may be impossible (e.g. in Italy and France, certain forms of 'alternative' medicine may only be practised by medical doctors: *Nino* (cases C 54/88, C 91/88 & C 14/89) (biotherapy, pranotherapy); *Bouchoucha* (case C 61/89) (osteopathy)).

It is no doubt with these problems in mind that the Court of Justice has sought to impose some limits on a member State's powers to demand observance of its own professional rules by persons providing services on its territory.

In *Van Binsbergen* (case 33/74) it was acknowledged, in the context of a challenge to a residence requirement imposed by the Dutch Bar on those seeking to provide certain legal services in Holland, that specific requirements imposed on a person providing services would not infringe Articles 59 and 60 where they have as their purpose the application of professional rules justified by the general good — in particular, rules relating to organisation, ethics, qualifications, supervision and liability, which are binding on any person established in the territory of the State in which the service is provided. The person providing the service cannot take advantage of his right to provide services to avoid the professional rules of conduct which would be applied to him if he were established in that State.

The Court suggested that even a permanent residence requirement for persons engaged in certain activities (e.g., administration of justice) would be permissible where it was objectively justified by the need to ensure the observance of professional rules of conduct.

However, a residence requirement could not be imposed if the desired ends could be achieved by less restrictive means. Thus according to *Van Binsbergen* such rules are in principle permissible provided they are:

(a)   non-discriminatory,
(b)   objectively justified, and
(c)   not disproportionate.

These principles were subsequently applied in *Webb* (case 279/80) in the context of the provision of manpower services. The Court added in *Webb* that, in ascertaining whether its own rules are justified, the host State must take into account the justifications and safeguards already provided by the applicant in order to pursue the activity in question in his State of establishment (approved in *Commission* v *Germany; re Lawyers' Services* (case 427/85)).

The principles expressed in *Van Binsbergen* and *Webb* were refined and developed in 1986 in the 'insurance' cases (*Commission* v *Germany (Re Insurance Services)* (case 205/84), *Commission* v *Ireland (Re Co-insurance Services)* (case 206/84), *Commission* v *France* (case 220/83), *Commission* v *Denmark (Re Insurance Services)* (case 252/83), Article 169 proceedings). These actions were based on alleged infringements of Articles 59 and 60 and Directive 78/473 (insurance directive) by the defendant member States in their rules regulating the provision of insurance services. The rules and the breaches alleged in each state were similar. In *Commission* v *Germany,* the rules required, *inter alia*, that a person providing direct insurance must be established and authorised to practise in the State in which the service is provided.

In giving judgment the Court firstly distinguished between establishment, covered by Article 52, and the provision of services, covered by Articles 59 and 60, defining establishment broadly (as noted above, page 186). Also assimilated to establishment was the enterprise established abroad but whose activity is entirely or mainly directed towards the territory in which it is providing services and which is thereby intending to evade the rules of conduct which would be applicable if it were established in the target State.

With regard to the provision of services, the Court held that Articles 59 and 60 require the removal not only of all discrimination based on nationality but also *all restrictions on his freedom to provide services imposed by reason of the fact that he is established in a member State other than that in which the services are provided.*

Because of this, the Court held that not *all* the legislation applicable to nationals or those engaged in permanent activities could be applied to the *temporary* activities of enterprises established in another member State. It could only be applied if three criteria were satisfied:

(a)   it is justified by imperative reasons relating to the public interest;
(b)   the public interest is not already protected by the rules of the State of establishment; and
(c)   the same result cannot be obtained by less restrictive means.

Thus, in the field of services, the Court seems to be moving towards a test for professional rules not unlike the *Cassis de Dijon* (case 120/78) test applied to goods (see chapter 8). As with that test, it is likely that the criteria will be strictly applied to ensure that each rule is necessary and genuinely justified. If not, it will breach Articles 59 and 60. In *Commission* v *Germany* the Court found that the establishment requirement was not justified; indeed, it was the very negation of the freedom to provide services and would only be permissible if indispensable. The authorisation requirement, on the other hand, at least as related to the rules concerning technical reserves, might be justified for the protection of policyholders and insured persons. Thus the Commission's action failed in this respect.

The principles in the above cases were laid down in the context of the freedom to provide services. It is unclear whether, or to what extent, they may be applied in the area of establishment. They are certainly capable of being so extended, although in the case of establishment the justification for compliance with the rules of the host State may be more compelling. It is suggested that as with services, each case, indeed each rule, will have to be decided on its merits.

Where Directives have been passed harmonising or recognising professional rules the provisions of the Directive will be conclusive on the matter. However, in each case it will be necessary to decide whether the rule in question has been covered by the Directive. For example, the lawyer's Directive (Directive 77/249) gives limited rights to provide services: it does not give rights of establishment. In *Commission* v *Germany* (case 205/84) the insurance Directive was found to be designed to ensure that undertakings were solvent; it did not attempt to harmonise national rules concerning technical reserves. Thus the rules protecting this interest fell to be judged according to the three-fold criteria laid down by the Court.

In *Gulling* v *Conseils des Ordres des Barreaux de Colmar et de Saverne* (case 292/86) a requirement of registration with the professional body of the host State was held to be permissible in respect of a barrister seeking rights of establishment in Germany where such registration was required of its own nationals.

In both the field of education and training and professional rules, and whether or not the activity in question is subject to EEC Regulation, the Court has indicated that Community law may not be used (or abused) in order to undermine the legitimate rules and standards of member States. For example, in *Van de Bijl* v *Staatssecretaris van Economische Zaken* (case 130/88), the Court was asked to rule on a claim by a Dutch decorator, based on EEC Directive 64/427, which provides, inter alia, for the mutual recognition of qualifications for self-employed persons in small craft industries. Under the Directive States are required to accept a certification of competence and work experience provided by the appropriate authorities of another member State in respect of work performed in that State. It was suggested in Van de Bijl's case that the certificate issued by the UK authorities, which the Dutch authorities had refused to accept as a basis for registration in Holland, was based on questionable evidence. The Court held that the host (i.e. Dutch) State was entitled to take steps (e.g. verification of evidence) to prevent the relevant Community rules being used for the purpose of circumventing the rules relating to particular occupations applicable to its nationals (see also Advocate-General Darmon in *R* v *HM Treasury, ex parte Daily Mail and General Trust plc* (case 81/87)).

A new approach

As with the area of professional qualifications and training, the Commisson, in its White Paper of 1985, determined on a new approach to professional rules and standards with a view to the completion of the internal market in services by January 1992. In place of the 'endless fruitless search for common rules and standards', the Commission was to adopt an approach similar to that which it was to apply to goods (see chapter 8). This was to be based on:

(a)   the harmonisation of *essential* safeguards and standards applicable to activities as a whole; and
(b)   within that framework, acceptance of the standards of other member States on a basis of mutual trust and recognition, on the principle of home country control and supervision.

Essential to the effective functioning of these principles would be the concept of the single licence. This would allow an institution licensed in one member State to offer its services to another State, either by establishing a branch or agency in that State or by supplying its services there.

These principles have formed the basis for important legislation in the field of banking, insurance and financial services. It is intended that the market in these areas be fully freed by the end of 1992. For details see *Directory of Community Legislation in Force*, ch. 06.

Other barriers to freedom

In addition to rules governing qualifications and standards of practice there may be other measures taken by member states capable of hindering the freedom of establishment or the freedom to provide services. It might have been expected that the Court's approach in such cases would have followed the *Cassis de Dijon* (case 120/78) line of reasoning, as it did with professional rules in the insurance cases (cases 205/84, 206/84, 220/83 and 252/83). Once a hindrance has been established the measure may only be justified on the grounds of 'imperative reasons of public interest' and must be proportionate. This has not so far occurred.

The issue arose in *Society for the Protection of Unborn Children Ltd* v *Grogan* (case C 159/90). The plaintiff society had obtained an injunction from the Irish High Court to prevent the distribution in Ireland by student bodies of information concerning clinics in other member States where abortion services were available. The provision of such information was found contrary to Article 40.3.3 of the Irish constitution which had been amended in 1983, following a referendum and fierce debate, to include a 'right to life of the unborn'. The defendants, appealing against the injunction, argued that Irish law imposed a restriction on member States' freedom to provide abortion services, in breach of Article 59 of the EEC Treaty. Advocate-General Van Gerven suggested, arguing from the rule of reason of Article 30 and Article 36, that although the giving of advice was a restriction on the freedom to provide services it was justified for imperative reasons of public policy (the protection of the unborn) and it was not disproportionate.

The Court did not adopt his reasoning. It agreed that the provision of abortion services for remuneration was a service within Article 60. But the connection between an information service, independent of that economic service, and the abortion service itself was 'too tenuous' to be regarded as a restriction on the freedom to provide services within the meaning of Article 59. The distributor of information was not linked, commercially or otherwise, with the supplier of the service. There was therefore no breach of EEC law.

In *R* v *HM Treasury, ex parte Daily Mail & General Trust plc* (case 81/87), in the context of a claim based on the right of establishment, the Court was asked to rule on the compatibility with EC law of British rules requiring the Treasury's consent before a company can transfer its head office to another member State, designed, *inter alia*, to ensure that the company settles its tax position in the UK prior to transferring elsewhere. Again the *Cassis De Dijon* line of reasoning might have seemed appropriate, particularly since the rule was concerned with fiscal supervision. However, the Court did not take this approach. It held that whilst freedom of establishment was a fundamental right, in the absence of Community Directives governing the matter in question:

Articles 52 and 58 . . . conferred no right on a company incorporated under the legislation of a member State and having its registered office there to transfer its central management and control to another member State.

Since the purpose of Articles 52 and 59 is to permit freedom of establishment within the Community it may be asked on what principle and for what reason (apart from the absence of EEC legislation) was the Court prepared thus to undermine the very substance of these provisions?

It is likely that in *Grogan* the Court had no wish to become embroiled in sensitive issues of Irish constitutional law concerning abortion. At the same time it appears from the result in both *Grogan* and the *Daily Mail* case that the

Court felt that the restrictions imposed by domestic law were justified. It is therefore regrettable that it did not address the question of justification according to existing principles. The rulings in both cases were sufficient only to dispose of the case in hand; they provided little guidance on matters of principle. As a result it remains unclear what restrictions on the freedom of establishment may be permitted under the *Daily Mail* ruling, which appears excessively wide, and abortion law in Ireland continues to be challenged on the basis of Community law. Although a subsequent case involving a 14-year-old rape victim, who had been subject to an injunction preventing her from leaving Ireland in order to obtain an abortion, was resolved by the Irish Supreme Court in the victim's favour on the basis of an Irish constitutional obligation to pay 'due regard to the equal right to life of the mother', those who oppose Irish anti-abortion law will continue to look to EC law in order to achieve their ends. Whatever one's views on women's rights to abortion, and despite the fact that Irish law may prevent Irish women from exercising their fundamental Community right to move freely within the Community in order to receive abortion services , arguably, as Advocate-General Van Gerven suggested in *Grogan*, such fundamental matters concerning abortion should fall within the margin of discretion allowed to member states on public policy grounds under Community law (see Articles 56, 66 EEC). This seems to have been the view taken at Maastricht when a protocol was issued to the effect that:

> Nothing in the Treaty on European Union, or in the Treaties establishing the European communities, or in the Treaties or Acts modifying or supplementing those Treaties, shall affect the application in Ireland of Article 40.3.3 of the Constitution of Ireland.

The Irish government, which even in *Grogan* had declared that it did not wish to prevent a pregnant woman from exercising her right to travel abroad to receive an abortion, is currently seeking an amendment to the protocol ensuring 'freedom to travel between member States' [and] the right to obtain in Ireland information relating to services lawfully available in member States'. Thus the Irish government's stance is clear. The issue will, however, require a final determination by referendum by the Irish people.

Hopefully *Grogan* and the *Daily Mail* case will prove exceptional. Since the Court did not expressly reject the *Cassis* line of reasoning in these cases (it was not argued in the *Daily Mail* case) perhaps it can be persuaded to follow the principles laid down in *Van Binsbergen* (case 33/74) and the insurance cases to *all* obstacles to the freedom to provide or receive services.

Activities connected with the exercise of official authority

Article 55 provides that:

> The provisions of this Chapter [right of establishment] shall not apply, so far as any given member State is concerned, to activities which in that State are connected, even occasionally, with the exercise of official authority.

Article 55 also applies to the provision of services (Article 66). This derogation has been considered in some detail in chapter 18 in the context of Article 48(4) relating to workers. The principles applicable to workers will apply equally to the establishment and services provisions. As in the case of workers, the derogation has been given the narrowest scope.

It was invoked in *Reyners* v *Belgian State* (case 2/74). One of the arguments raised by the Belgian government in defending the Belgian Bar's rule restricting the profession of *avocat* to Belgian nationals was that the profession of *avocat* fell within Article 55; it was connected with official authority. The Court disagreed. Article 55 applied only to 'activities' connected with the exercise of official authority; it did not apply to professions or occupations as a whole. The derogation, the Court held, was aimed at the exercise of *prerogative power*. Whilst the exercise of judicial power would represent an exercise of official authority, the activities of an *avocat* would not.

Freedom to provide services and the exercise of industrial property rights

It was held in *Coditel* v *Ciné Vog* (case 62/79), Article 177 proceedings, that the freedom to provide services granted by Article 59 could not be invoked to prevent the legitimate exercise of industrial property rights. Here, SA Ciné Vog Films, a Belgian film distribution company owning performing rights in certain films in Belgium, including a film called *Le Boucher,* sought to prevent Coditel, which operated a cable television service in Belgium, from picking up *Le Boucher* from German television and transmitting it in Belgium, in breach of Ciné Vog's copyright. Coditel argued that to prevent it from so doing would constitute an interference with its freedom to provide services, in breach of Article 59. On a reference from the Tribunal de Première Instance, Brussels, the Court of Justice held that Article 59 does not encompass limits on the exercise of certain economic activities which have their origin in the application of national legislation for the protection of intellectual property, save where such application constitutes a means of arbitrary discrimination or a disguised restriction on trade between member States. Such would be the case if that application enabled parties to an assignment of copyright to create artificial barriers to trade between member States. This was not found to be the case with Ciné Vog.

Thus, as with the application of Article 36 in the context of goods (see chapter 9) the legitimate use of industrial property rights is protected; its misuse is not.

Freedom to receive services

The freedom provided by Articles 59 and 60 is expressed in terms of the freedom to *provide* services. It has now been extended by the Court of Justice to embrace the freedom to *receive* services.

The point was originally raised in *Watson and Belmann* (case 118/75), where the Commission suggested that the freedom to move within the Community to receive services was the necessary corollary to the freedom to provide services.

This was approved by the Court in *Luisi* v *Ministero del Tesoro* (case 286/82) in the context of criminal proceedings in Italy against Luisi and Carbone for breach of Italian currency regulations. They were accused of taking foreign currency out of the country in excess of the maximum permitted under Italian law. They had taken the money out for the purposes of tourism and medical treatment. The question referred to the Court of Justice was whether payment for such services represented movements of capital, within Articles 67-73 of the EEC Treaty, or payments for the provision of services; if the latter, was it governed by Articles 59-66?

Advocate-General Mancini, arguing from *Watson and Belmann* (case 118/75) suggested that Article 59 was concerned with the receipt of services as well as their provision. In support of this view he cited the general programme for the abolition of restrictions on the freedom to provide services (*Common Market Reporter*, para. 1545 JO 1962, 32), Directive 64/221, which expressly refers in Article 1(1) to 'freedom of movement for employed or self-employed persons or the *recipients* of services' and Directive 73/148, Article 1(1)(b), which requires member States to abolish restrictions on the movement and residence of 'nationals of member States wishing to go to another member State as *recipients* of services'.

The Court, following Advocate-General Mancini, found the money to be payment for services and held that freedom to provide services, as provided by Article 59, includes the freedom, for recipients of services, to go to another member State, without restriction, in order to receive a service there. Recipients of services were held to include tourists, persons receiving medical treatment and persons travelling for the purposes of education and business.

Thus the right to enter and remain in another member State for the purpose of receiving services is established. The right of residence exists during the period for which the service is provided (Directive 73/148, Article 4(2)). Any restrictions on these freedoms will prima facie breach Articles 59 and 60, subject to limitation on the grounds of public policy, public security and public health (Articles 56 and 66). The question remains whether the recipient of services, by reason of his status or his right of residence, can invoke these Articles, together with Article 7, to claim equality of treatment with nationals of the host State. A number of services, such as education and medicine, are publicly funded and provided not so much as a commercial activity but as a public service. Are these to be available to nationals of the member States on the same basis as to the States' own citizens?

Education: vocational training

This matter was considered in the context of educational services in *Gravier* v *City of Liège* (case 293/83), Article 177 proceedings. The applicant in this case was a young French woman who had applied to and been accepted by the Liège Académie des Beaux-Arts for a four-year course in the art of strip cartoons. As a foreign student she was charged a special fee, known as a *'minerval'*, for the course. This was not payable by Belgian citizens, whether or not they lived or paid taxes in Belgium, nor by EEC nationals working in Belgium, or members of their families. She brought an action before the Belgian Courts, claiming the fee was discriminatory. Her case rested on two arguments.

First, she suggested that the *minerval* constituted an obstacle to her freedom of movement to receive services as established in *Luisi* v *Ministero del Tesoro* (case 286/82) in breach of Article 59. Her second argument was based on the vocational nature of the course. Vocational education fell within the scope of the Treaty; as a matter covered by EEC law it was discriminatory, in breach of Article 7, to charge higher prices to EEC nationals who were not Belgian citizens or resident in Belgium. This argument was based primarily on *Forcheri's* case (case 152/82), see chapter 18. Here Mrs Forcheri, the wife of an Italian working in Brussels, had succeeded in challenging the higher fees demanded of her as a non-national, to attend a social work course in Brussels. Although her success was based primarily on her lawful residence in Belgium as the wife of an EEC worker, which brought her 'within the scope and application of this Treaty' and thus Article 7, it rested in part on the fact that the course for which she subscribed was vocational. Vocational training, the Court held, was one of the matters covered by Community law; covered in general terms by Article 128 ('The Council shall, acting on a proposal from the Commission and after consulting the Economic and Social Committee, lay down general principles for implementing a common vocational training policy'); and specifically, at least for workers and their children, in Regulation 1612/68 (Articles 7(3) and 12, see chapter 18). Therefore provision of vocational training was subject to Article 7 of the EEC Treaty.

The Court of Justice, following Advocate-General Sir Gordon Slynn, found in Ms Gravier's favour on this second ground. Access to vocational training was a matter covered by Community law; moreover, it was an essential element in promoting freedom of movement for persons throughout the Community. The Court expressly dissociated itself from the wider issues involved, discussed at length by Sir Gordon Slynn, concerning the organisation and financing of such courses, and confined its judgment merely to conditions of access to a course affecting foreign students alone, and relating to a particular kind of course, namely vocational education. However, its definition of vocational education was very wide. It was held to include all forms of teaching which prepares for and leads directly to a particular profession, trade or employment, or which provides the necessary skills for such profession, trade or employment, even if the programme of instruction includes an element of general education.

The decision in *Gravier* caused considerable concern amongst member States. This decision, with its wide definition of vocational training, meant that many courses, including perhaps university courses, often entailing substantial contributions from public funds (the Belgians pointed out that the *minerval* itself only covered 50% of the cost of the education provided), would have to be offered on equal terms to all EEC nationals. Moreover, the precise scope of the term 'vocational training' was unclear. Subsequent cases have provided some answers to these questions.

In *Blaizot* v *University of Liège* (case 24/86), Article 177 proceedings, in the context of a claim by university students of veterinary science for reimbursement of the *minerval*, based on *Gravier*, the Court applied the *Gravier* definition of vocational training and held that university education could constitute vocational training:

> not only where the final exam directly provides the required qualification but also insofar as the studies provide specific training (i.e. where the student needs the knowledge so acquired for the pursuit of his trade or profession), even if no legislative or administrative provisions make the acquisition of such knowledge a prerequisite.

In general university courses would meet these criteria. The only exception would be courses designed for persons seeking to 'improve their general knowledge rather than prepare themselves for an occupation'. Even where, as in veterinary or medical science, the training comprises two stages, the second representing the practical stage, the first, academic stage must be regarded as vocational. The two stages must be viewed as a single unit.

Similar reasoning informed the Court's decision in *Belgian State* v *Humbel* (case 236/86), Article 177 proceedings. This case concerned a claim by the Belgian authorities for the payment of the *minerval* in respect of *secondary* education received in Belgium by the son of a French national living in Luxembourg. Although the course as a whole appeared to be vocational, the fees giving rise to the dispute concerned one year within that course of general education. The Court held that such a course of general education must none the less be treated as 'vocational' if it forms an integral part of an overall programme of vocational education.

Finally, on the same day as the decision in *Humbel*, the Court, in a case brought by the Commission against Belgium (*Commission* v *Belgium* (case 42/87)) challenging its rules on access to higher education, revised in the light of *Gravier*, allowing access, inter alia, to only 2% of 'outsiders', held that inasmuch as the rules related to vocational training they were in breach of Article 7 EEC.

Thus, where educational courses are concerned, provided they are found *overall* to be vocational, according to the generous interpretation provided by the Court, EEC nationals who are neither migrant workers nor the children of migrant workers living in the State in which the education is provided, may claim equal access under equal conditions to nationals of the home State, even if the courses are financed or subsidised by the State as a matter of social policy.

Gravier was indeed a landmark case, an example of the Court in activist mood. The legal basis for the decision, resting on Article 128, is slender. Whilst Article 128 may provide a sufficient legal basis for the issuing of Directives in the field of vocational training (as the Court found in *UK* v *Commission* (case 56/88), Article 173 proceedings) it may be doubted that it was sufficiently clear, precise and unconditional to give rise to direct effects.

Scholarships and grants

The Court in *Gravier* (case 293/83) refrained from considering whether the right of EEC nationals to vocational training carried with it a right to grants and scholarships from the host State to enable them to take up these courses. Advocate-General Sir Gordon Slynn was clearly of the opinion that such a right was not included in the right to receive services. In this same context the Belgian, Danish and British governments regarded such a result as unthinkable in view of the differences which exist between the number of students moving, for educational purposes, into different member States. The matter was resolved in *Brown* and *Lair* (cases 197/86, 39/36: for detailed discussion of these cases see chapter 18). Both *Brown* and *Lair* involved claims for maintenance grants for university courses. In both cases their entitlement to the grants as 'workers', or the 'children of migrant workers', was doubtful. So they sought also to rely on *Gravier*, arguing that the course in question constituted vocational training, to which Article 7 applied. Thus they were entitled to be treated on a footing of equality with nationals.

The Court, no doubt anxious to quell the anxieties of member States on this issue, disagreed. Although university courses (following *Blaizot*) were capable of constituting vocational training, to which they were entitled to equal access in respect of fees, Article 7 did not apply to maintenance grants. Assistance in the form of maintenance grants, the Court held, fell outside the scope of the EEC Treaty. It was a matter of educational policy, and, as such, had not been entrusted to the Community institutions; it was also a matter of social policy, which fell within the competence of member States insofar as it was not covered by the provisions of the EEC Treaty.

Whilst there is little logic in the distinction between fees, which relate to conditions of access to vocational training, and maintenance grants, which do not, it is clear that the judgments in *Brown* and *Lair* reflected the Court's desire, on grounds of policy, to call a halt to the development of a Community educational policy by means of judicial decision. The judgments were greeted with relief by member States.

The specific right of students to residence lasting for the duration of their course of studies was enacted in Directive 90/366 (Article 2) (OJ L 180, 13.7.90, p. 30). Families' rights are confined to spouses and dependent children. The Directive expressly provides that it 'shall not establish any entitlement to the payment of maintenance grants by the host member State on the part of students benefiting from the right of residence (Article 3).

Scope of equality principle

One further question, raised but not answered in *Gravier* (case 293/83), was whether the equality principle could be applied as an adjunct to the right, established in *Luisi* (case 286/82) to move within the Community to *receive* services under Article 59. In considering the question in *Gravier*, Advocate-General Sir Gordon Slynn suggested that in the sphere of education a distinction should be drawn between education which was provided by private finance, with a view to profit, and education as a public service, financed wholly or partly by the State, as an aspect of social policy. Similar reasoning was adopted by the Court in *Humbel* (case 236/86). Here, the claimant, a French youth, living with his family in Luxembourg, sought to resist the payment of the *minerval* in respect of his secondary education in Belgium on the basis of his right to receive services under Article 59. (His claim under Article 7 and vocational training has been noted above.) The Court pointed out that Article 59 applies to 'services provided for remuneration' (Article 60(1)). The essential characteristic of remuneration is that it 'constitutes the countervailing financial advantage for the services in question and is normally fixed between the supplier and the recipient of the services' (para. 17). This characteristic is not present in the case of a course of study provided in the framework of a national educational system. In providing such a system the State is fulfilling its duty to its people in the social, cultural, or educational field.

Thus apart from the area of vocational training (access and fees) which is governed by *Gravier*, services such as health and education provided by the State for the benefit of its citizens, and not for commercial reasons, with a view to profit, cannot be claimed on a basis of equality by EEC nationals who have temporary residence as recipients of services but do not enjoy 'lawful residence' on a 'settled' or permanent basis as 'favoured Community citizens' in the State providing the services.

The equality principle was applied to benefit a recipient of services in rather different circumstances in *Cowan* v *French Treasury* (case 186/87). Here the plaintiff, an Englishman on holiday in Paris, was claiming compensation for personal injuries sustained as a result of a mugging in the Paris Metro. Under French law compensation in respect of such injuries was provided out of public funds and payable only to French nationals. Cowan claimed that since he was claiming as a tourist, exercising his freedom to receive services, this rule was in breach of Article 7. The Court of Justice, on a reference under Article 177 from the French Criminal Injuries Compensation Board, held that as a recipient of services he was entitled to equal protection against, and compensation for, the risks of assault. This right was a corollary of his right to receive services.

Since the judgment was expressed in narrow, specific terms, it remains to be seen what rights are to be regarded as a 'corollary' to the right to receive services. However, it is clear following *Humbel* that a recipient of services cannot claim a right to equal treatment in respect of *the provision of the service itself* where that service is in the social, cultural or educational field, and is financed, wholly or partly, out of public funds.

Harmonisation of company law

As an adjunct to the right of establishment for companies 'formed in accordance with the law of a member State and having their registered office, central administration or principal place of business within the Community' granted by Article 58, the Treaty provided, in Article 54(3)(g), for the coordination of safeguards 'for the protection of the interests of members and others . . . with a view to making such safeguards equivalent throughout the Community'. This was thought to be necessary to promote freedom of establishment for companies and to avoid possible distortion in the pattern of establishment resulting from the wide disparity in the rules and safeguards provided by company laws in the different member States.

Pursuant to this Article the Commission embarked on an extensive programme of harmonisation of company law. No less than 13 Directives have been proposed, of which nine have been passed (first, second, third, fourth, sixth, seventh, eighth, eleventh, twelfth), one has lapsed (ninth) and three await approval (fifth, tenth, thirteenth). In addition a number of other measures relevant to company law have been passed or proposed, of which the most important are Regulation 2173/85 (OJ No.L 100/1) on the European Economic Interest Grouping (EEIG), which provides a new framework to enable businesses, whatever their legal nature, to cooperate effectively when carrying on business activities across national frontiers, Directive 89/592 on insider dealing ((1989) OJ No.L 334/30), and the long proposed Regulation for a Statute for a European Company ((1989) OJ No.C 263/41). Details of the legislation adopted are contained in the *Encyclopaedia of European Community Law*, vol. C, part 3, *Directory of Community Legislation in Force*, ch. 19.

Directives affecting companies have also been passed in the field of employment law. Regretfully, apart from the area of sex discrimination, these lie outside the scope of this present edition. Details may be obtained from the above encyclopaedia (vol. C, part 13) or *Directory of Community Legislation in Force*, ch. 05..

Where the date for implementation of the above Directives has expired their provisions (provided they are sufficiently clear and precise) will be directly effective against any undertaking of a public nature (*Marshall* v *Southampton and South West Hampshire Area Health Authority (Teaching)* (case 152/84)); they may, and should, also be invoked as an aid to interpretation against private undertakings (*Von Colson* v *Land Nordrhein-Westfalen* (case 14/83); *Harz* v *Deutsche Tradax GmbH* (case 79/83), even if the domestic legislation predates the Directive (*Marleasing* (case C 106/89), see chapter 2). Where a national court is unwilling, or feels unable, to do so a remedy in damages against the State may be available in limited circumstances, as it was in *Francovich* (cases 6 and 9/90) see chapters 2 and 23).

Further reading

See reading for chapters 17 and 18 and

Dine, J., 'The Community Company Law Harmonisation Programme' (1989) 14 EL Rev 322.
Flynn, J., 'Vocational Training in Community Law and Practice (1988) 8 YEL 60.
Lonbay, J., 'Education and Law: the Community Context' (1989) 14 EL Rev 363.
Roth, W. H., 'The European Community's Law on Services: Harmonisation' (1988) 25 CML Rev 35.
Van der Woude, M., & Meade, P., 'Free Movement of the Tourist in Community Law' (1988) 25 CML Rev 117.

TWENTY

Free movement of persons: limitation on grounds of public policy, public security or public health (Directive 64/221)

The exception provided by Articles 48(3) and 56 was implemented in Directive 64/221, to give substance to the rather vague and potentially catch-all provisions of the Treaty. The scope of the Directive is twofold. First it lays down the principles on which a State may refuse entry or residence to those who would otherwise be eligible, on the grounds of public policy, public security or public health; and secondly it lays down stringent procedural safeguards which must be followed by the relevant authorities when they are seeking to exclude non-nationals on one of the permitted grounds. The Directive applies to all those who come within the freedom of movement provisions of the Treaty, both employed or self-employed, as well as to their families; it also extends to those who move within the Community as 'recipients of services' (first recital) and to those entitled to free movement under Directives 90/364 (persons of independent means); 90/365 (retired persons) and 90/366 (students) (Article 2). Since all the main provisions are directly effective the Directive provides a rich source of substantive and procedural rights.

The Directive seeks to lay down the circumstances in which measures taken by member States on the grounds of public policy, public security or public health, may, and may not, be permitted.

'Measures' taken on the grounds of public policy, public security or public health were defined in *R* v *Bouchereau* (case 30/77), Article 177 proceedings, as any action affecting the rights of persons coming within the field of application of Article 48 to enter and reside freely in a member State on the same conditions as apply to nationals of the host State.

Public policy, public security, public health

Whilst public security and public health are self-explanatory, the meaning and scope of the public policy derogation are less clear. In *Van Duyn* v *Home Office* (case 41/74), Article 177 proceedings, the Court held, on a reference from the English High Court, that the concept of public policy must be interpreted strictly; its scope cannot be determined unilaterally by member States without being subject to control by the institutions of the Community. However, the Court conceded that the concept of public policy must vary from State to State; States must have an area of discretion within the limits defined by the Treaty. The Court took a rather stricter view in *Rutili* v *Ministre de l'Intérieur* (case 36/75), in the context of an action by Rutili, an Italian, and a noted political agitator, to annul a decision from the Minister which restricted his activities to certain regions of France. The Court held that restrictions cannot be imposed on the right of a national of a member State to enter the territory of another member State, to stay there and to move within it, unless his presence constitutes a *genuine and sufficiently serious threat to public policy ('une menace réelle et suffisamment grave pour l'ordre public')*. This principle, the Court added, was an embodiment of the principles contained in the European Convention on Human Rights (1953) that no restrictions in the interests of national security or public safety shall be placed on the rights secured by Articles 8 to 11 of the convention other than such as are *necessary* for the protection of those interests in a democratic society. Restrictions are thus subject to the proportionality principle.

The concept was narrowed even further in *R* v *Bouchereau* (case 30/77) where the court added that the concept of public policy must always presuppose a genuine and sufficiently serious threat to the requirements of public policy *affecting one of the fundamental interests of society*.

Directive 64/221 lays down a number of circumstances in which measures taken on the grounds of public policy or public security will *not* be justified:

(a)   They 'shall not be invoked to service economic ends' (Article 2(2)). Here the Directive makes explicit what was found to be implicit in Article 36, in the context of goods. To allow an economic justification would clearly run counter to the fundamental aims of the Treaty.

(b)   'Previous criminal convictions shall not *in themselves* constitute grounds for the taking of such measures' (Article 3(2), emphasis added). Thus under certain circumstances past criminal convictions may constitute sufficient grounds, but they will not necessarily do so. (See *R* v *Bouchereau* (case 30/77) to be discussed below.)

(c)   'Expiry of the identity card or passport used by the person concerned to enter the host country and to obtain a residence permit shall not justify expulsion from the territory' (Article 3(3)). As was noted in *Procureur du Roi* v *Royer* (case 48/75), the right of residence does not depend on the possession of a residence permit, it merely provides proof of such a right, which derives from the Treaty itself. The same principle applies to identity cards and passports. As was established in *Watson and Belmann* (case 118/75), Article 177 proceedings, a State may impose penalties for failure to comply with administrative formalities, provided the penalties are not disproportionate, but a failure to comply with such formalities can never provide grounds for deportation.

Where public health is concerned, the only diseases or disabilities justifying refusal of entry or refusal to issue a first residence permit are those listed in the Annex to Directive 64/221 (highly infectious or contagious diseases, e.g., tuberculosis and syphilis; drug addiction; profound mental disturbance). Moreover, diseases or disabilities occurring *after* a first residence permit has been issued 'shall not justify refusal to renew the residence permit or expulsion from the territory' (Article 4(2)).

What kind of measures, then, will be justified on public policy or public security grounds?

Measures taken on the grounds of public policy or public security must be based *exclusively* on the *personal conduct* of the individual concerned (Article 3(1)).

Personal conduct

To justify exclusion, the personal conduct does not have to be illegal. In *Van Duyn* v *Home Office* (case 41/74) the plaintiff, Ms Van Duyn, a Dutch national, was refused entry into the UK on the grounds of public policy. She was seeking to enter the UK to take up employment with the Church of Scientology. The practice of scientology was not illegal in the UK but it was regarded as socially undesirable. The refusal was claimed to be on the basis of her personal conduct. Two questions were referred, *inter alia,* to the Court of Justice by the English High Court. First, can membersip of an organisation count as 'personal conduct' within the meaning of Article 3(1)? Secondly, if it can, must such conduct be illegal in order to provide grounds for exclusion on public policy grounds?

In reply to the first question, the Court distinguished between past and present association; past association cannot count as personal conduct; present association, being a voluntary act of the person concerned, can.

With regard to the second question, the Court held that the conduct does not have to be illegal to justify exclusion of non-nationals, as long as the State has made it clear that it considers the activities in question to be 'socially harmful', and has taken administrative measures to counteract the activities. *Van Duyn* must now be read in the light of the more restrictive test advanced in *R* v *Bouchereau* (case 30/77); the activities in question must be sufficiently socially harmful to pose a genuine and sufficiently serious threat to the requirements of public policy affecting one of the fundamental interests of society.

In *R* v *Escuriaza* [1989] 3 CMLR 281 the English Court of Appeal suggested that the principles enunciated in *Bouchereau* 'simply mirrored the law and practice in England', whereby an alien may be deported 'if his continued presence in the UK would be to its detriment'. Whilst a deportation order was no doubt justified under Community law on the facts of *Escuriaza*, the appellant having been convicted of a number of theft and burglary offences, including the theft of drugs, it is submitted that the weaker English test should not be applied in the context of the exercise of Community rights or, if it is applied, it must be *interpreted* in such a way as to comply with the stricter Community rule.

The kind of evidence needed to prove that a particular activity is considered by the State to be sufficiently harmful to justify exclusion on the grounds of public policy was considered by the Court of Justice, in the context of many questions referred by the Liège District Court, in the case of *Adoui and Cornuaille* v *Belgian State* (cases 115 & 116/81), Article 177 proceedings. Here two prostitutes were appealing against the Belgian authorities' refusal to grant them a residence permit in Belgium, where they were seeking to practise their arts. The Court held that member States could not deny residence to non-nationals by reason of conduct which, when attributable to a State's own nationals, did not give rise to repressive measures or other genuine and effective measures to combat such conduct. Thus, evidence of measures of this nature will have to be adduced to prove that the public policy justification is genuine.

Article 3(2) expressly provides that previous criminal convictions shall not in themselves constitute grounds for measures taken on public policy grounds. The same principle applies to current criminal convictions. In *Bonsignore* v *Oberstadtdirektor of the City of Cologne* (case 67/74), Article 177 proceedings, Bonsignore, an Italian worker living in Germany, bought a pistol in breach of German firearms law, and accidentally shot his brother. The action against his brother carried no punishment, but he was fined for unlawful possession of a firearm, and his deportation was ordered. On a reference on appeal from the Vervaltungsgericht, the German authorities argued that his deportation was necessary as a general preventive measure, to deter other immigrants from committing similar offences. The Court of Justice rejected this argument, holding that the concept of personal conduct expresses the requirement that a deportation order may only be made for breaches of the peace and public security which might be committed by the individual concerned. Thus deportation could not be based on reasons of a general preventive nature.

The conduct in *R* v *Bouchereau* (case 30/77) was more serious. Mr Bouchereau was a French national who took up employment in the UK in 1975. In June 1976 he was found guilty of unlawful possession of drugs. He had already pleaded guilty to a similar offence in January 1976, and had received a 12-month conditional discharge. In June 1976 the court (Marlborough Street Magistrates) wished to make a deportation order against him. He claimed this was contrary to Article 48 of the EEC Treaty and Directive 64/221. One of the questions referred to the Court of Justice concerned Article 3(2) of the Directive and 'previous criminal convictions'. If they could not 'in themselves' constitute grounds for exclusion, when could they be taken into account? Were they relevant only in so far as they manifested a propensity to act in such a manner, contrary to public policy or public security? The Court held that the existence of previous convictions could only be taken into account as evidence of personal conduct constituting a *present* threat to the requirements of public policy, as showing a propensity to act in the same way again. However, past conduct alone *could* constitute a threat to the requirements of public policy. Thus, it would depend on the gravity of the conduct, past or present, whether it would in fact constitute a present threat to the requirements of public policy.

Since a denial of residence must be based exclusively on personal conduct it follows that a worker who is entitled to residence cannot be refused entry or deported merely because he is involuntarily unemployed or unable to work through incapacity, even if he becomes a charge on public funds (see *Lubbersen* v *Secretary of State for the Home Department* [1984] 3 CMLR 77, Immigration Appeal Tribunal). The same applies to his family. This accords with Directive 68/360.

The Court of Justice held in *Rutili* (case 36/75) that derogation on the grounds of public policy, public security or public health can only apply to a *total* ban on residence in a member State; partial restrictions on the right of residence of non-nationals cannot be imposed unless such measures are also applied to nationals. This aspect of the decision has been criticised as an unnecessary restriction on Articles 48(3) and 56 of the EEC Treaty. The derogation exists precisely in order to enable member States to discriminate against non-nationals on limited and specific grounds. As the Court of Justice pointed out in *Van Duyn* (case 41/74), it is a principle of international law that States cannot deny rights of residence to their own nationals. To require a total ban where a partial ban would suffice is surely to impose on non-nationals greater restrictions than are necessary to protect the particular interest concerned.

Procedural rights

Directive 64/221 provides extensive procedural safeguards for parties seeking to assert rights of entry or residence in member States. Since these rights are directly effective, any decision issued in violation of these rights may be challenged as contrary to EEC law.

(a) *Temporary residence.* Where a person's identity card or passport has expired or the nationality of the holder is in dispute the State which issued that identity card or passport must allow its holder to re-enter its territory without formalities (Article 3(4)).

A person awaiting a decision to grant or refuse a first residence permit in a member State must be allowed to remain temporarily in that State pending that decision. The decision must be taken as soon as possible and not more than six months from the date of application (Article 5(1)).

In the event of a decision to refuse the issue of a residence permit or to expel a person from the territory of a member State that person shall be allowed, 'save in cases of urgency', not less than 15 days (if he has not yet been granted a residence permit), or one month (in all other cases), in which to leave the country (Article 7).

(b) *Reasons for decisions.* 'The person concerned shall be informed of the grounds of public policy, public security or public health upon which the decision taken in his case is based, unless this is contrary to the interests of the security of the State involved' (Article 6). The Court held in *Rutili* (case 36/75) that the authority making the decision must give the applicant a precise and comprehensive statement of the ground for his decision, to enable him to take effective steps to prepare his defence.

In *R* v *Secretary of State for the Home Department (ex parte Dannenberg)* [1984] 2 CMLR 456 the English Court of Appeal quashed a deportation recommendation made by the Mid-Sussex Magistrates' Court for failure to comply with Article 6. Thus magistrates will be required in this type of case to supply adequate reasons for their decisions.

(c)   *Remedies: rights of defence.* By Article 8:

The person concerned shall have the same legal remedies in respect of any decision concerning entry, or refusing the issue or renewal of a residence permit, or ordering expulsion from the territory, as are available to nationals of the State concerned in respect of acts of the administration.

Thus all domestic public law remedies must be made available to him. By Article 9(1):

Where there is no right of appeal to a court of law, or where such an appeal may be only in respect of the legal validity of the decision, or where the appeal cannot have suspensory effect, a decision refusing renewal of a residence permit or ordering the expulsion of the holder of a residence permit from the territory shall not be taken by the administrative authority, save in cases of urgency, until an opinion has been obtained from a competent authority of the host country before which the person concerned enjoys such rights of defence and of assistance or representation as the domestic law of that country provides for.

This authority shall not be the same as that empowered to take the decision refusing renewal of the residence permit or ordering expulsion.

Where the remedies under Article 8 are insufficient, Article 9 provides a safety net, incorporating the minimum requirements of natural justice. Under this Article, as the Court pointed out in *Rutili* (case 36/75), the person concerned must at the very least be able to exercise his rights of defence before a competent authority, which must not be the same as that which adopted the measure which restricted his freedom.

Questions concerning the scope of Article 9 were raised before the Court of Justice in *R* v *Secretary of State for the Home Department (ex parte Santillo)* (case 131/79), Article 177 proceedings. Santillo, an Italian, had been convicted in the UK of a number of crimes of violence including rape, buggery and indecent assault. He was sentenced to eight years in gaol, with a recommendation for deportation at the end of his sentence. Nearly five years later the Home Secretary made a deportation order against him. He applied for judicial review to quash this decision. Two issues were raised in the proceedings. First, whether the trial judge's recommendation was an 'opinion from a competent authority', as required by Article 9; and secondly, if so, whether a lapse of time between the issuing of this 'opinion' and the making of the order could deprive the judge's recommendation of its status as an 'opinion' under Article 9. The Court of Justice, on a reference for interpretation from the English High Court, held that the trial judge's recommendation did amount to an 'opinion' within Article 9; but that the safeguard provided by Article 9 could only be a real one if that opinion were sufficiently proximate in time to the decision recommending deportation, to ensure that the factors justifying deportation still existed at the time when the order was made. A change of heart or political climate could mean that the public policy justification had ceased to exist.

Following the ruling from the Court of Justice Donaldson LJ in the Queen's Bench Divisional Court ([1980] 1 CMLR 1) found that the trial judge's 'opinion' was still valid, since there was no evidence that the position had changed since the time when the original recommendation was made.

In *Monteil* v *Secretary of State for the Home Department* [1984] 1 CMLR 264, Immigration Appeal Tribunal, the applicant was more fortunate. M Monteil was a Frenchman, who had been convicted in the UK of a number of offences, including importuning and indecency, and sentenced to 12 months' imprisonment. At the end of his sentence the authorities sought to deport him. He appealed against the deportation order, claiming that he was a 'new man'. His crimes had been the result of alcoholism of which he now claimed he was cured. His arguments and his evidence succeeded before the Immigration Appeal Tribunal. Citing *Santillo* (case 131/79) and *Bouchereau* (case 30/77), the tribunal concluded the deportation would only be justified if he showed a propensity to commit the same crimes again. This would not be the case if he were cured.

Similar arguments succeeded, also before the Immigration Appeal Tribunal, in *Astrid Proll* v *Entry Clearance Officer, Dusseldorf* [1988] 2 CMLR 387. The appellant, Ms Proll, a German citizen, had been a member of a terrorist organisation, the Bader Meinhof gang, and had been convicted of a number of offences for her activities in the group. She had applied for permission to enter the UK in 1980, 1981, and 1985, on the latter occasion in order to carry out photographic work for a German magazine. Her application was rejected on each occasion. On appeal, the Immigration Appeal Tribunal found that, even in 1979 when she was convicted, the German court had found that she had undergone a 'change of heart' in respect of her political beliefs and activities, as a result of which it had imposed a minimum 12-month sentence. There was no evidence before the Immigration Appeal Tribunal that she had undergone further change since that time. Thus, since her conduct presented no present threat to the requirements of public policy or public security, UK rules (para. 83 of HC 169), which allowed deportation to be ordered in respect of *past* offences, could have had 'no application' to Ms Proll.

Further reading

Hall, S., 'The European Convention on Human Rights and the Public Policy Exception to the Free Movement of Workers under the EEC Treaty' (1991) EL Rev 466.

O'Keefe, D., 'Practical Difficulties in the Application of Article 48 of the EEC Treaty' (1982) 19 CML Rev 35.
Van Overbeek, P. M., 'Aids/HIV Infection and the Free Movement of Persons in the European Economic Community' (1990) 27 CML Rev 791.

TWENTY ONE
Social security

The freedom of movement granted by the Treaty to workers and the self-employed and their families would have been deprived of much of its effect if persons, in exercising these rights, risked losing out on social security benefits acquired in their home State. Under the laws of member States, both eligibility for benefit and the amount of benefit paid may depend on the number and extent of contributions made to the institution responsible for social security in the relevant state. Eligibility may also be conditional on the claimant's residence in the State responsible for payment and benefits.

It was to meet these problems that Article 51 of the EEC Treaty provided for measures to be adopted in the field of social security to secure for migrant workers and their dependants the implementation of two fundamental principles:

    (a)   aggregation, for the purpose of acquiring and retaining the right to benefit and of calculating the amount of benefit, of all periods taken into account under the laws of the several countries;

    (b)   payment of benefits to persons resident in the territories of member States.

To this end, Regulation 1408/71 was passed, replacing the earlier Regulation 3/58. Regulation 1408/71 was implemented and supplemented by Regulation 574/72. Initially applying only to workers and their families these Regulations were amended to include the self-employed by Regulations 1390/81 and 3795/81.

The aim of EEC legislation on social security is not to harmonise member States' social security legislation but to *coordinate* their provision in order to secure the objectives of Article 51; to ensure that claimants' contributions in different member States are *aggregated* for the purpose outlined in Article 51(a) of the EEC Treaty, and that persons entitled to benefits may *collect* them wherever they are resident in the Community. The system is designed to abolish as far as possible the territorial limitations on the application of the different social security schemes within the Community (*Hessische Knappschaft* v *Maison Singer et Fils* (case 44/65), Article 177 proceedings). However, in securing these objectives, clearly member States' social security laws will be modified. Where States have not amended their laws to comply with EEC law, EEC law, on the principle of the supremacy of EEC law, should prevail (see chapter 3, and *Costa* v *Enel* (case 6/64); *Simmenthal SpA* (case 106/77)).

Regulation 1408/71, as supplemented by Regulation 574/72, is long and complex. It is not possible in a book of this nature to examine each substantive provision in detail. Instead it is proposed to examine its general scope, both in terms of the *persons* and the *kind of benefits* covered, and the *principles* on which the detailed provisions are based. An understanding of these principles will often provide a better basis for the interpretation of specific provisions than a detailed study of those provisions themselves. As with other EEC secondary legislation, the preamble provides a vital key to interpretation.

The complexity of Regulations 1408/71 and 574/72, and the difficulty of reconciling the autonomous systems of member States with the demands of Community law, have inevitably resulted in loopholes and anomalies, beyond the power of the Court of Justice to resolve. Where this has occurred Regulations amending Regulations 1408/71 and 574/72 have been passed (Regulations 2001/83 (OJ No.L 230/6); 1305/89 (OJ No.L 131/1); 2332/89 (OJ No.L 224/1)) and proposed ((1989) OJ No.C 206/2), designed to remedy the more obvious deficiencies. (See also Regulations 1390/81, 3795/81 (self-employed).)

Personal scope

Regulation 1408/71 covers the same groups as are covered by the other legislation relating to free movement of persons: workers, the self-employed and their families and survivors. The workers and self-employed must be nationals of one of the member States. It also covers survivors who are EEC nationals irrespective of the nationality of the worker, and stateless persons and refugees (Article 2).

However, the definition of the employed and self-employed and of members of the family is different.

Employed and self-employed   The employed and self-employed to whom the Regulation applies are defined as '. . . any person who is *insured*, compulsorily or on an optional continued basis, for *one or more* of the contingencies covered by the branches of a social security scheme for employed or self-employed persons' (Article 1(a)(i) as amended by Regulation 1390/81, Article 1(2)(a)).

As the Court held in *Hoekstra (née Unger)* (case 75/63), Article 177 proceedings, the concepts of worker (and self-employed) in the context of social security have a Community meaning, referring to all those who, as such, and under whatever description, are covered by different national schemes of social security. The scheme may be compulsory or optional; contributory or non-contributory; it may cover different kinds of benefit. These factors are irrelevant. As long as the employed or self-employed person is covered by some national scheme for insured persons in one of the member States he will be covered by the Regulation, even, it seems, if he is or has been working outside the Community (see *Laborero* (cases 82 & 103/86) — claimants working in Belgian Congo). Nor need the worker be currently insured; provided he *has been* insured under such a scheme the Regulation will apply to him (Regulation 1408/71, Article 2(1); *Unger* (case 75/63)).

Also by contrast with other legislation relating to workers, EEC law on social security is not confined to those who move within the Community in the context of employment. In *Hessische Knappschaft* v *Maison Singer et Fils* (case 44/65) a German worker was killed in a road accident whilst on holiday in France. His dependants were paid by the German social security authorities who then sought to sue the driver of the vehicle responsible for the accident in France. To do so they needed to rely on their rights of subrogation under Regulation 3/58 (now Regulation 1408/71, Article 93(1)). It was argued that the rights arising under Article 51 of the EEC Treaty were such as to promote freedom of movement for workers as workers, not *qua* holidaymakers. The Court disagreed, holding that nothing in Article 51 required that the concept of worker be limited solely to migrant workers *sensu stricto*, or to workers required to move for the purpose of their employment.

Thus in the case of social security the economic nexus rests on the fact of insurance and not on the fact of employment. It follows that the part-time worker will only benefit from EEC legislation in this area if he is or has been insured under a national insurance scheme. However, inasmuch as a difference in treatment between part and full-time workers as regards access to social security schemes and levels of benefit may constitute indirect sex discrimination, part-time workers may acquire social security rights under Directive 79/7, which provides for the equal treatment of men and women in matters of social security (see chapter 22).

Members of the family   'Member of the family' is defined in Article 1(f) as 'any person defined or recognised as a member of the family or designated as a member of the household by the legislation under which benefits are provided', and 'where . . . the said legislations regard as a member of the family or a member of the household only a person living under the same roof as the worker, this condition shall be considered satisfied if the worker in question is mainly dependent on that worker'. Clearly the definition of member of the family will differ from State to State, as it may also differ, depending on the benefit claimed, even within a State. Given that national laws on social security continue to be applied (although in modified form), a definition by reference to the laws of member States was perhaps the only feasible solution. But it was bound to lead to anomalies. The Court of Justice has not hesitated, by reverting to the general principles expressed in the preamble to Regulation 1408/71, or by arguing from Regulation 1612/68, to extend a State's definition of family where it was necessary to promote freedom of movement for workers (e.g., *Mr & Mrs F* v *Belgian State* (case 7/75); *Piscitello* (case 139/82), both Article 177 proceedings).

Both families' and survivors' benefits under EEC social security legislation derive from the worker's insurance, unless they are or have been themselves insured under the appropriate scheme. The Court has not infrequently made exceptions to this principle (e.g., *Mr & Mrs F* v *Belgian State* to be discussed later in this chapter). However, it is submitted that any benefit which does not derive from the worker's insurance should now be claimed alternatively or additionally under Regulation 1612/68, Article 7(2), as a 'social advantage'. This seems to accord with more recent trends in the Court's jurisprudence (see chapter 18).

Principles

The general principles underlying Regulation 1408/71 are stated in the preamble; they are laid down in more detailed form in the Regulation itself. Most of these principles are designed to secure one further overriding goal, that the migrant worker and his family should suffer no disadvantage as a result of moving within the Community.

Non-discrimination on grounds of nationality This is perhaps the most important principle. It has certainly been the most frequently invoked. Article 3(1) of Regulation 1408/71 provides that:

> Subject to the special provisions of this Regulation, persons resident in the territory of one of the member States to whom this Regulation applies shall be subject to the same obligations and enjoy the same benefits under the legislation of any member State as the nationals of that State.

Article 3(1) is thus a specific application of the general principle of non-discrimination expressed in Article 7 of the EEC Treaty, and like that provision it applies to all forms of discrimination, direct and indirect. Discrimination will often take the form of a residence or length of residence requirement. A benefit covered by the Regulation cannot be refused in breach of Article 3. Unlike other areas of EEC law it appears that in its social security rules reverse discrimination is not permitted. The Court held in *Kenny* v *Insurance Officer* (case 1/78), Article 177 proceedings:

> . . . it is for the national legislation to lay down the conditions for the acquisition, retention, loss or suspension of the right to social security benefits so long as those conditions apply without discrimination to *the nationals of the member State concerned* and to those of other member States (para. 16, emphasis added).

Payment regardless of residence This principle derives from Article 51(b) of the EEC Treaty. Article 10(1) of Regulation 1408/71 provides that:

> Save as otherwise provided in this Regulation, invalidity, old-age or survivors' cash benefits, pensions for accidents at work or occupational

diseases and death grants acquired under the legislation of one or more member States shall not be subject to any reduction, modification, suspension, withdrawal or confiscation by reason of the fact that the recipient resides in the territory of a member State other than that in which the institution responsible for payment is situated.

It will be noted that this principle, known as the 'exportability' principle, is not expressed to apply to *all* social security benefits; sickness benefits and family benefits, for example, are subject to special provision in Regulation 1408/71 and Regulation 574/72. Article 10 is expressed to apply only 'save as otherwise provided'.

No overlapping of benefits Article 12(1) of Regulation 1408/71 provides that:

This Regulation can neither confer nor maintain the right to several benefits of the same kind for one and the same period of compulsory insurance.

Where a worker has contributed to social security schemes in two or more member States, he may have become entitled to benefit in respect of the same contingency from more than one State. Article 12 operates to prevent him receiving double benefit. However, since entitlement is subject to the single State principle (see below), and the 'competent' State is determined according to Community law, Article 12 could result in the claimant receiving a lesser sum from the competent State than that to which he would be entitled under the law of another State. Where this occurs the Court has held he is entitled to receive the difference between the smaller and the larger sum, the difference payable by the competent institution in the more 'generous' State. 'A worker cannot be deprived of more favourable allowances by substituting the benefits available from one member State for the benefits due from another member State' (see e.g. *Baldi* (case 1/88), family allowances; *De Felice* (case 128/88), retirement pension; *Georges* (case 24/88), family allowances).
   Article 12(1) does not apply to benefits in respect of invalidity, old age, death (pensions) or occupational disease, for which there is special provision for apportionment amongst member States (Article 12(1)).

Aggregation This principle, derived from Article 51(a) of the EEC Treaty, is spelt out specifically with regard to each type of benefit covered. Article 18(1) for example, relating to sickness and maternity benefit, provides (as amended by Regulation 2864/72, Article 1(3)) that:

The competent institution of a member State whose legislation makes the acquisition, retention or recovery of the right to benefits conditional upon the completion of insurance periods or periods of employment or residence shall, to the extent necessary, take account of insurance periods or periods of employment or residence completed under the legislation of any other member State as if they were periods completed under the legislation which it administers.

Other Articles provide in similar terms for each specific benefit, e.g., Article 38, invalidity benefit; Article 45, old age and death pensions; Article 64, death grants; Article 67, unemployment benefits; Article 72, family benefits.

Thus, *where necessary*, account must be taken of periods of *contribution*, *employment* and *residence* in all the member States in which the insured person has worked in order to ascertain:

(a)   his eligibility for benefit, and
(b)   the amount of benefit to which he may be entitled.

The single State principle   This is provided by Article 13, which states as a general rule that:

A worker to whom this Regulation applies shall be subject to the legislation of a single member State only.

The specific rules for determining which legislation is applicable are contained in Articles 14-17 which will be discussed later in this chapter.

No disadvantage   As noted above, the Court has held that a worker may not be allowed to suffer disadvantage as a result of the application of Community rules. EEC rules against overlapping cannot result in a loss of advantages for a migrant worker. Nor can he, as a result of moving from one State to another be put in a worse position than a worker who has not availed himself of his right of free movement (*Masgio* (case C 10/90)). There appear, however, to be certain exceptions to this principle. Where the disadvantage results from national rules concerning conditions of *affiliation* to a social security scheme, Community law cannot be applied to remedy this deficiency; such rules are regarded as a matter of national law alone (see *Schmitt* (case 29/88); *Coonan* (case 110/79)). Similarly, the Court has held that it is for member States to determine the *temporal effect* of its social security rules. Thus, where new rules are introduced without retrospective effects, Community law cannot be invoked to allow these rules to be applied to remedy inequalities suffered prior to their introduction (*Jordan* (case 141/88)).

Material scope

Article 4(1) of Regulation 1408/71 provides that:

This Regulation shall apply to all legislation concerning the following branches of social security, reflecting the nine official categories recognised by the ILO:

(a)   sickness and maternity benefits;
(b)   invalidity benefits, including those intended for the maintenance or improvement of working capacity;
(c)   old-age benefits;

(d)   survivors' benefits;
(e)   benefits in respect of accidents at work and occupational diseases;
(f)   death grants;
(g)   unemployment benefits;
(h)   family benefits.

Article 4(2) provides that the Regulation shall apply 'to all general and special social security schemes, whether contributory or non-contributory'.

However, the Regulation does *not* apply to 'social and medical assistance, to benefit schemes for victims of war or its consequences, or to special schemes for civil servants and persons treated as such', (Article 4(4)).

Thus, provided a person is or has been insured under a general scheme for the whole population covering 'one or more' (Article 2(1)) of the contingencies provided for under Article 4(1), he, or a person claiming through him, may invoke the principles and detailed rules of the Regulation (and Regulation 574/72 where appropriate) to support a claim for any of these benefits or to challenge a refusal to grant such benefits in breach of these Regulations. Only the benefits listed in Article 4(4) lie outside the scope of the Regulations, the most important exclusion being benefits in the form of 'social assistance'.

Social assistance

Since the term 'social assistance' is not a term of art, is not defined in Regulation 1408/71, and will be subject to different interpretations in different member States, interpretation has been left to the Court of Justice, largely on reference from national courts seised with the problem. Not surprisingly the Court has given the term the narrowest scope.

In a series of cases, starting with *Frilli* v *Belgium* (case 1/72), Article 177 proceedings, the Court, in assessing whether a particular benefit, which may look like social assistance, qualifies as social security, has applied a 'double function' test. Some kinds of benefit, the Court reasons, perform a double function; they are akin to social assistance, since need is the essential criterion, and eligibility is not dependent on employment; yet they are akin to social security since they confer on the beneficiary a legally defined position. Since such difficulties must not be allowed to prejudice the rights of workers, such benefits must be deemed to be social security benefits, and assimilated where possible to the social security benefits listed in Article 4(1). Applying this test in *Frilli*, a non-contributory guaranteed minimum income, unrelated to insurance, payable in Belgium to Belgian citizens or those resident for a minimum period of five years, was assimilated to the old age pension and deemed to be social security; as such it could not be denied to Frilli in breach of Regulation 1408/71, Article 3. Similarly in *Callemeyn* v *Belgian State* (case 187/73), Article 177 proceedings, a special payment to the handicapped, unrelated to either employment or contributions (the claimant being the wife of a migrant worker), refused by the Belgian authorities on the grounds of her nationality, was assimilated to invalidity benefit and held, applying the same test, to constitute social security.

In *Mr and Mrs F* v *Belgian State* (case 7/75) the claimant was the 14-year old handicapped son of an Italian worker in Belgium. He had been refused a special grant for handicapped persons, again because he could not fulfil the (Belgian) nationality or (15-year) residence requirement. Prima facie the benefit was social assistance; it was not a 'family' benefit, nor a workers' invalidity benefit; it was not related to contributions and was available to the whole (handicapped) population. Nevertheless, applying the double function test the Court found it to be social security within Regulation 1408/71. In a remarkable judgment, the Court, arguing from the general aims of the Treaty, as expressed in Articles 2, 7 and 51, from the preamble to Regulation 1408/71, and from Regulation 1251/70, concluded that a dependent person such as Mr and Mrs F's son was entitled to equality of treatment as long as his parents were resident in a member State. Even when he ceased to be a minor his right to equality of treatment would not cease. The migrant worker, as Advocate-General Trabucchi suggested, must be treated not just as a source of labour but as a human being.

These cases were followed by many others (e.g., *Inzirillo* (case 63/76); *Vigier* (case 70/80); *Piscitello* (case 139/82)) in which benefits of extremely dubious status as social security benefits were upheld as such, whether or not they were claimed as supplements to existing benefits (as was the case in *Frilli* (case 1/72) and *Callemeyn* (case 187/73)), and even when they could not be assimilated to any of the existing categories of social security benefits (e.g., *Palermo* (case 237/78), Article 177 proceedings — special non-contributory allowance to elderly mothers of large families designed to increase the birth rate in France). The only criterion by which a claim might still be excluded as constituting 'social assistance', applied by the Court in *Fossi* (case 79/76) and *Tinelli* (case 144/78), was if the benefit involved a discretionary assessment of need or personal circumstances. Needless to say this test did not serve to exclude many claims (*Fossi* and *Tinelli* were claiming as 'victims of war' and as such in any case within Regulation 1408/71, Article 4(4)).

The Court's desire to extend the principle of equality of treatment to *all* social benefits is understandable. To allow States to discriminate against migrant workers in the provision of social assistance would undoubtedly create barriers to the free movement of workers and to their and their families' integration into the host State. But if its aims were wholly legitimate, in interpreting the social assistance exclusion of Article 4(4) virtually out of existence, the same cannot be said of the means chosen to achieve its ends.

Perhaps sensing that it had gone too far, the Court switched its approach in the 1980s. Instead of stretching Regulation 1408/71 to encompass 'social assistance' type claims the Court chose an alternative route, treating the benefits as 'social advantages' under Article 7(2) of Regulation 1612/68, the scope of which was being expanded following the introduction of the 'lawful residence' test in *Even* (case 207/78) (the *Even* formula; see chapter 18 and cases such as *Reina* (case 65/81) and *Forcheri* (case 152/82)). In *Reina*, it will be recalled, the Court held that Article 7(2) of Regulation 1612/68 applied even to benefits granted on a discretionary basis, the one remaining acknowledged indicium of 'social assistance'.

As a result of its new approach, in *Castelli* (case 261/83), Article 177 proceedings, an Italian mother, legitimately resident with her son (who was also a pensioner, having worked and retired in Belgium), was found entitled to a guaranteed income (not a pension) paid in Belgium to all old people, and in *Hoeckx* (case 249/83) and *Scrivner* (case 122/84) the claimants were held entitled to the Belgian minimum income allowance, the 'minimex', not, as previously in *Frilli* (case 1/72), on the basis of Regulation 1408/71, but on the basis of Article 7(2) of Regulation 1612/68. Since in all cases the claimants were 'lawfully resident' in Belgium, they were entitled to be treated equally with Belgian nationals. The nationality and residence requirement required for eligibility for the benefits would not be enforced against them. On similar reasoning, in *Frascogna (No. 1)* (case 157/84) and *(No. 2)* (case 256/86), unreported, an Italian widow who went to live with her son, who was a worker in France, was held entitled under Article 7(2) of Regulation 1612/68 to a special old-age allowance granted by the French authorities. The 15-year residence qualification required of foreigners under French law could not be applied to Mrs Frascogna to deprive her of her rights. It is interesting to note that Mrs Frascogna's claim under Regulation 1408/71 was rejected.

Following these cases it seems that the doubtful claims, i.e., those which do not obviously qualify as social security, will now be more likely to succeed under Regulation 1612/68 than under Regulation 1408/71. *A fortiori* claims by those such as part-time workers, who are often not insured under a general social security scheme.

Regulation 1408/71 will, of course, continue to apply, and apply alone, to 'genuine' social security benefits, and, if a claimant wishes to 'export' a benefit this can only be achieved under the specific provisions of that Regulation. 'Social advantages' under Regulation 1612/68 cannot be exported unless the benefits are exportable as a matter of *national* law (e.g., *Carmina di Leo* (case 308/89)). In *Piscitello* (case 139/82), Article 177 proceedings, Mrs Piscitello's claim for an Italian 'social aid pension' to be exported and paid to her in Belgium, where she went to live with her daughter, was assimilated to the category of 'old-age pension' and export was permitted under Article 10 of Regulation 1408/71. It has been argued that it was legitimate to do so in this case since she was entitled to the pension in her own right as an Italian citizen; but as a general rule it is undesirable that benefits which are not strictly speaking social security benefits should be exported, since 'assistance'-type benefits usually require an on-the-spot assessment of need and are tied to national standards of living. Unlike the social security provision set up by Regulation 1408/71, there exists within member States no reciprocal machinery for the processing of such claims. As the law has now developed it is submitted that Mrs Piscitello's claim could now equally be brought against the Belgian authorities for the equivalent Belgian provision under Regulation 1612/68, on the same basis as *Frascogna*. On the principle of no overlapping of benefits she would clearly not be entitled to both.

A claimant who wishes to invoke the aggregation principle will likewise have to show that his claim falls within Regulation 1408/71. In *Campana* (case 11/85), unreported, Article 177 proceedings, the Court held that a special (contributory) benefit providing aid for vocational training for unemployed workers was included within the benefits covered by Regulation 1408/71, Article 4(1); therefore the claimant was entitled to invoke the aggregation principle in order to qualify for the benefit. It seems that the benefit was assimilated to unemployment benefit even though the claimant was employed at the time of applying for the aid; it was held to be justified as designed to prevent *future* unemployment. In *Newton* v *Chief Adjudication Officer* (case C 356/89) a mobility allowance, payable under British law, which as the Court acknowledged had 'much in common' with social assistance, was assimilated to an invalidity allowance and held to be claimable in France, where the plaintiff had gone to retire. However, in this case the claimant had been employed in France. The Court suggested that the allowance in question could not be claimed as a social security benefit outside national territory by persons who had been subject, as employed or self-employed persons, to the *exclusive* legislation of the State from which they were claiming.

From the above cases it is clear that the Court of Justice will use all the means at its disposal to ensure that migrant workers and their families are in no way disadvantaged as a result of moving within the Community. In order to achieve its ends the Court will not be deterred by apparent shortcomings in EEC legislation.

Operation of the system

The principles on which EEC law are based have already been considered. It remains to examine the operation of the system in practice, concluding with a brief reference, by way of example, to certain more detailed provisions relating to specific benefits.

If benefits are to be governed by the single State principle (Regulation 1408/71, Article 13(1)) and each State is to continue to apply its own rules as to:

    (a)   the kind of benefits to be provided, and
    (b)   the conditions for eligibility for these benefits,

the crucial question for the migrant worker, who may have lived and worked in a number of member States, or who may reside in one State and work in another, is which social security law will apply in his case?

Applicable law: *lex laboris*

The general rule is simple: the applicable law is the law of the State in which a person works — *lex laboris*. This is governed by Regulation 1408/71, Article 13(2)(a), as amended by Regulation 1390/81, which provides that:

> a person employed in the territory of one member State shall be subject to the legislation of that State even if he resides in the territory of another member State or if the registered office or place of business of the undertaking or individual employing him is situated in the territory of another member State.

Furthermore, Article 13(2)(b) provides that:

> a person who is self-employed in the territory of one member State shall be subject to the legislation of that State even if he resides in the territory of another member State.

If the applicable law is the law of the State in which a person works, then that is the State with which he is currently insured, and the institution responsible in that State for such insurance will be responsible for payment of benefits. The *lex laboris* principle applies from the moment when he takes up employment.

The institution with which the worker is insured at the time of application for benefits, and which is thus responsible for payment of benefits, is known as the 'competent institution' (Article 1(o)).

The State in whose territory the competent institution is situated is known as the 'competent State' (Article 1(q)).

There is special provision in Article 13 for civil servants (13(2)(d)), the armed forces (13(2)(e)), and seamen on board a vessel flying the flag of a member State (13(1)(c)).

Article 14 provides a number of exceptions to the *lex laboris* principle. These exceptions relate to:

(a)   the temporary worker;
(b)   the worker who is employed in two or more member States, and
(c)   the frontier worker.

(a)   *The temporary worker.* Article 14(1)(a) as amended by Regulation 1390/81 provides that:

> A person employed in the territory of a member State by an undertaking to which he is normally attached who is posted by that undertaking to the territory of another member State to perform work there for that undertaking shall continue to be subject to the legislation of the *first* member State, provided that the anticipated duration of that work does not exceed 12 months and that he is not sent to replace another person who has completed his term of posting.

Scope for extension of the 12-month period is provided by Article 14(1)(b).

In *Manpower Sàrl* (case 35/70), Article 177 proceedings, the Court held that a worker, provided on a temporary basis by a German company providing manpower services, would fall within these provisions as long as he remained paid by, and answerable to, the company providing the services. By contrast, in *Hakenberg* (case 13/73) a commercial traveller, paid by commission, representing an undertaking in one member State, and spending nine months of each year canvassing for orders in other member States, did not fall within Article 14(1)(a) (originally Article 13(1)(a) or Regulation 3).

(b)   *The worker employed in two or more member States* (Article 14(2)). This category embraces (i) the worker in international transport (Article 14(2)(a)) and (ii) 'others' (Article 14(2)(b)). In these cases the order of priority will be:

(1)   The law of his State of residence if he is employed there either principally (Article 14(2)(a)(ii), worker in international transport) or partly (Article 14(2)(b)(i), 'other').

(2)   The law of the State where he is employed by a permanent branch or agency.

(3)   The law of the State where the registered office or place of business of the undertaking with which he is employed is situated.

(c)   *The frontier worker* (Article 14(3)). The frontier worker is defined as a person 'employed in the territory of one member State by an undertaking which has its registered office or place of business in the territory of another member State and which straddles the common frontier of these States'. Here the applicable law is the law of the State in which the undertaking has its registered office or place of business.

Article 14 is enacted in similar terms for the self-employed in Article 14a, which was added by Regulation 1390/81.

Once the applicable law has been determined, depending on whether the normal (*lex laboris*) principle or one of the exceptions applies, the competent institution within that State must, on an application for benefit, apply the aggregation principle. In order to ascertain the question of the applicant's eligibility and the extent of his entitlement, insurance periods and periods of employment or residence *completed under the legislation of any other member State* must be taken into account to the extent that this is necessary under the law of the competent State. Once this has been ascertained, the person eligible for benefit is entitled (pursuant to Article 10(1) of Regulation 1408/71 and subject to the reservations contained therein) to *receive* these benefits wherever he may be resident in the Community on the following terms:

(a)   *benefits in cash* according to the law of the competent State, and
(b)   *benefits in kind* according to the law of the State of residence.

This principle is spelt out in general terms in Article 19 and in specific terms throughout the Regulation, e.g., Article 22 (sickness benefit), Article 25 (unemployment benefit), Article 55 (industrial injury benefit). Benefits in kind can include certain cash payments, for example, to cover medical expenses payable by way of reimbursement. The distinction between payments in cash and payment in kind is made purely for practical, administrative purposes. Although the host State provides the benefits through the appropriate national agencies, it is the competent institution which is ultimately responsible for payment, whether the benefit is in the form of cash or kind (Article 19). Thus claims will be processed and reimbursement provided on a reciprocal basis, under machinery provided by Regulations 1408/71 and 574/72. No such provision exists for benefits in the form of 'social advantages' claimed under Article 7(2) of Regulation 1612/68.

Principle of apportionment

Where certain social security benefits are concerned, one further principle may apply, the principle of apportionment. This principle, which applies to what may be called the substantial or long-term benefits, the invalidity, old-age and survivors' pensions, means that the financial burden may, if beneficial to the claimant, be divided between the competent institutions in member States in which a person has worked and contributed throughout his working life in proportion to the length of time he has worked in each State. In this way each institution will bear its own share of the burden and the worker will receive in benefit a share appropriate to his contributions in each State in which he has worked (for details see Article 46). In order that the worker should not lose out under this system, provision is made that a worker cannot receive as a total sum less than he would have been entitled to had he received his entire pension according to the law of his State of residence (Article 50).

There exists no similar provision for apportionment of liability for benefits received as 'social advantages' under Regulation 1612/68.

Payment of benefits to persons resident outside the competent State: special provisions

Unemployment benefits Since the right to unemployment benefit normally depends on the claimant being available for work in the competent State, specific provision was made in Regulation 1408/71 to enable unemployed persons to go to another member State in order to seek employment without losing their entitlement to benefit from the competent institution. Under Article 69, a person wishing to retain his entitlement must:

(a) register with the employment services of the competent State as a person seeking work, and remain available for at least four weeks after becoming unemployed. The competent institution may authorise his departure before such time has expired (Article 69(1)(a)). He must then

(b) register as a person seeking work with the employment services of each of the member States to which he goes within seven days of the day when he ceased to be available to the employment services of the State he left (Article 69(1)(b)).

If he complies with these requirements his entitlement to benefits from the competent State (which may be paid in his State of residence: Article 70) will continue for up to three months, provided he is eligible for benefits of this duration.

If he does not find work, and returns to the competent State before the expiry of the three-month limit, his entitlement to benefits from the competent State will continue; if he does not return within that period he will 'lose all entitlement to benefits under the legislation of the competent State' (Article 69(2)). In exceptional cases, the time-limit may be extended by the competent institution.

As a general rule, the competent State in the case of unemployment benefit is the State in which the claimant was last employed and insured. He must, however, remain available for work in that State, subject to the provisions of Article 69. Should he return to reside in his 'home' State, responsibility for unemployment benefit will transfer to that State provided he registers as available for work there.

Family benefits In accordance with the principle of payment regardless of residence Article 73(1) as amended by Regulation 1390/81 provides that:

An employed person subject to the legislation of a member State other than France shall be entitled to the family benefits provided for by the legislation of the first member State for members of his family residing in the territory of another member State, as though they were residing in the territory of the first State.

Where family benefit is claimed under this Article a worker cannot be refused benefit on the grounds that he only works part-time: nor can his rights depend on having been insured on particular calendar days (*Bestuur der Sociale Verzekeringsbank* v *Kits van Heijningen* (case C 2/89)).

Article 73(2) provided an exception to the rule in Article 73(1) in the case of France, to the effect that an employed person subject to French legislation shall be entitled:

in respect of members of his family residing in the territory of a member State other than France, to the family allowances provided by the legislation of the member State in whose territory those members of the family reside...

This exception, which was included on the insistence of the French, whose family benefits at the time were more substantial than those provided in other member States, was challenged, successfully, in *Pinna* (case 41/84). The Court held that since disparities already existed as a result of the application of the different national systems of social security law, Community law could not be allowed to add to these disparities. Although the exception applied to all EEC claimants, including the French, it was in breach of the general principle of non-discrimination since its *effects* would be more likely to fall on migrant workers. Thus the general principle of exportability, as provided by Article 73(1), applied.

Article 74 provides for unemployed persons on the same terms as Article 73. Where family benefits are payable under Article 74 for dependent children under 21 it is not permitted to require children who are unemployed to be available for employment in the competent State as a condition for the award of benefit. The condition of availability for work must be regarded as fulfilled where the child is at the disposal of the employment office of the member State in which he resides (*Bronzino* (case C 228/88); *Gatto* (case C 12/89)).

In order to avoid overlapping of benefits, Article 10(1) of Regulation 574/72 provides that where entitlement to family benefits in a particular member State is *not* subject to conditions of insurance of employment they shall be suspended where benefits are due in pursuance of Article 73. *However,* if the spouse of the worker or unemployed person referred to in Article 73(1) *exercises a trade or professional activity* in the territory of the said member State, the right to family benefits or family allowances due in pursuance of Article 73(1) 'shall be suspended; and only those family benefits or family allowances of the member State in whose territory the member of the family is residing shall be paid, the cost to be borne by that member State' (Article 10(1)(a)).

Thus, where the spouse looking after the family is herself economically active, responsibility shifts from the originally competent institution to the institution of the family's State of residence. However, in order that the family should not lose out by moving, where in the latter case the sum received is lower than that which would have been received as a result of the application of Article 73, entitlement under Article 73(1) is suspended only up to the amount received in respect of the same period and the same member of the family in the State of residence of the spouse pursuing a professional or trade activity in that State (*Beeck* (case 104/80), Article 177 proceedings; see also *Georges* (case 24/88), noted above, *Dammer* (case 168/88), parents working in State A and B, family residing in State C).

These cases demonstrate that the Court will always interpret against the literal meaning of a specific provision where a literal interpretation would conflict with the principles and purpose behind the legislation, particularly when to do otherwise would create a barrier to the free movement of workers.

A practical exercise

Consider the issues of EEC law raised by the following problem:

John Smith, a UK national employed in the UK in the construction industry, went to work in France in 1976 with his wife Wendy, also a UK national, and their two children. In 1980 he changed his job and went to work in Germany, together with his family. In 1986 he returned to work in France. Two months after his return he sustained an accident at work which left him permanently incapacitated.

To help the family finances Wendy has taken up employment in Germany where she is currently residing, together with the children. For the moment John has decided to remain in France. John's mother Mary, who is in receipt of a widow's pension in the UK, wishes to come to France to help look after John.

Further reading

Steiner, J., 'The Right to Welfare: Equality and Equity under Community Law' (1985) 10 EL Rev 21.
Watson, P., 'Minimum Income Benefits: Social Security or Social Assistance?' (1985) 10 EL Rev 335.

TWENTY TWO

Sex discrimination

Introduction

EEC law on sex discrimination comprises:

—

(a) Article 119 of the EEC Treaty, which lays down a general principle of *equal pay for equal work* for men and women.

(b) Directive 75/117, which implements the principle of equal pay in more specific terms, to include equal pay for work of equal value.

(c) Directive 76/207, which provides for *equal treatment* for men and women in the context of employment.

(d) Directive 79/7, which applies the equal treatment principle to matters of social security.

(e) Directive 86/378, which extends the equal treatment principle to occupational pension schemes.

(f) Directive 86/613, which provides for equal treatment in self-employment.

As part of its Social Action Programme the Commission introduced a number of draft Directives in 1990 (OJ No. C 254, 9.10.90, p. 4) with a view to abolishing existing inequalities between part-time and temporary workers and full-time workers which would clearly benefit women, who represent the vast majority of the part-time and temporary workforce. These proposals have not yet received the required unanimous approval of member States, the UK having been the most consistent opponent of such measures. The shift to qualified majority voting for those 11 States which signed the Agreement on Social Policy at Maastricht in December 1991 (see chapter 1) means that such measures may now be approved by those States by a qualified majority vote. Such legislation would not be binding in the UK unless expressly agreed. However, in the absence of the required legislative approval the Court of Justice has done a great deal via the concept of indirect discrimination to eliminate inequalities as between part and full-time workers (see, e.g., *Bilka Kaufhaus GmbH* (case 170/84) to be discussed later).

The equality principle, which applies to both men and women, applies, unlike our own Sex Discrimination Act 1975, only in the context of employment. It has been described as one of the 'foundations of the Community', designed, according to the Court of Justice in *Defrenne* v *Sabena (No. 2)* (case 43/75), apropos Article 119, to achieve a 'double objective', economic and social. It seeks as an economic goal to ensure that States which have implemented the equality principle do not suffer a competitive disadvantage *vis-à-vis* those which have not; and as a social goal to achieve 'social progress', the 'improvement of the living and working conditions of their peoples', as required by the Treaty (preamble, Article 117).

No doubt because of this double objective, EEC law on sex discrimination, unlike the fundamental Treaty provisions relating to goods and workers, is not limited in its application to migrant workers. Its application may be, and invariably is, 'wholly internal'. It is, however, confined strictly within the economic context; it is not designed to settle questions concerned with the organisation of the family or to alter the division of responsibility between parents (*Hofmann* v *Barmer Ersatzkasse* (case 184/83) — (failed) claim by father for paternity leave on birth of his child, based on Directive 76/207). Nor is the prohibition on discrimination absolute; a difference in treatment as between men and women may be permitted as long as it is 'objectively justified'.

Since Article 119 and, to a more limited extent, the Directives on sex discrimination have been declared directly effective (see chapter 2), EEC law has been invoked on a number of occasions by individuals seeking to challenge allegedly discriminatory practices which are nonetheless permissible under domestic law. Although member States have altered their laws to comply with EEC requirements, domestic implementation has frequently been found inadequate. Where it is patently so the Commission has brought proceedings under Article 169 to obtain compliance. Many such actions have been brought. No less than two actions have been brought against the UK. Moreover EEC sex discrimination law has been invoked more frequently before domestic courts and tribunals in the UK than in any other member State. The reason for our apparent deficiencies in this field lies not, it is submitted, in any greater reluctance, or even a greater failure on our part, to observe Community law, but rather in the different styles of drafting and interpretation prevailing under the two legal systems. The broad general principles of EEC law are enacted in our own Equal Pay Act 1970 and Sex Discrimination Act 1975 as precise and detailed rules. Such rules lend themselves to, and often receive, a literal interpretation by our courts. As a result, action which is plainly discriminatory may fail to fall within the specific wording of the Act. For example, in *Macarthys Ltd* v *Smith* [1979] ICR 785, Court of Appeal, the literal wording of our Equal Pay Act 1970 was found by a majority of the Court of Appeal to limit the right to equal pay to men and women engaged in 'like work' in *contemporaneous* employment ('where the woman *is* employed': s. 1(2)(a) and (b)). Thus a woman warehouse manager who wished to compare her pay with that of her male predecessor *in the same job* was unable to claim equal pay on the basis of English law alone. (For a similar approach in the Irish High Court see *Murphy* v *An Bord Telecom Eireann* [1987] 1 CMLR 559 — Keane J 'unable' to grant female applicant equal pay to her male comparator under Irish law even though her job had been found of *greater* value than his, since the right to equal pay under the Irish Anti-Discrimination (Pay) Act 1974 was expressed in terms of *equal* value; matter referred to the ECJ case 157/86; applicant held entitled to equal pay under the broad principles of Article 119.) Similarly, in *O'Brien* v *Sim Chem Ltd* [1980] ICR 429, Court of Appeal, although the plaintiff's job had been found in a job evaluation study to be of equal value to that of her more highly paid male comparators she was held by the Court of Appeal to be unable to claim equal pay because on a literal interpretation of the Equal Pay Act it was necessary for the job evaluation scheme to have been implemented for the equal pay principle to apply. The House of Lords ([1980] ICR 573) finally found for the applicant, but only after deciding to 'jettison the words of Parliament' to give effect to its 'manifest intention'.

It seems likely that *O'Brien* v *Sim Chem Ltd* precipitated the Commission's first action against the UK under Article 169 (case 61/81). The case resulted in the UK being found in breach of its obligation under Directive 75/117 to ensure equal pay for work of equal value, since English legislation provided no means whereby a worker who considers that his post is of equal value to another may pursue his claim if the employer refuses to introduce a job classification scheme. Arguably all that was necessary to comply with the Court's judgment was to ensure that, where it appears, as in *O'Brien* v *Sim Chem Ltd* that the jobs done by men and women *are* of equal value, the equal pay principle will be justiciable. The amendments to the Equal Pay Act 1970 introduced as a result of the judgment, setting up a detailed and elaborate system for the appraisal of equal value claims, probably go beyond what was necessary to fulfil our EC law obligations. Yet these precise provisions may still contain loopholes through which a deserving claim may fall.

A second reason for the disproportionate number of cases brought under EC law in the UK in the area of sex discrimination lies with our Equal Opportunities Commission, which has seen and seized on the potential of EC law to remedy the deficiencies in domestic legislation, challenging inequalities of pay or treatment as between men and women even when they do not appear to result from discrimination on the grounds of sex. In such a case, as the House of Lords found in *Rainey* v *Greater Glasgow Health Board* [1987] AC 224, in the context of a claim for equal pay brought by a female prosthetist employed by the Board, a claim under EC law must fail. Although the applicant in *Rainey,* who was recruited direct to the NHS, was paid less than the (male) prosthetists recruited from the private sector, the difference in treatment arose from the need to attract prosthetists from the private sector, where the rates of pay were higher. The discrimination, although blatant, and arguably unjustified on grounds of equity, was not based on sex at all. The fact that the applicant was a woman, and the more highly paid prosthetists were men, appeared to be fortuitous.

Equal pay for equal work: Article 119

Article 119 provides:

Each member State shall during the first stage ensure and subsequently
maintain the application of the principle that men and women should receive
equal pay for equal work.

For the purpose of this Article, 'pay' means the ordinary basic or
minimum wage or salary and any other consideration, whether in cash or in
kind, which the worker receives, directly or indirectly, in respect of his
employment from his employer.

Equal pay

If the concept of pay is generously defined in Article 119, it has been even more
generously construed. It was applied in *Garland* v *British Rail Engineering Ltd*
(case 12/81), Article 177 proceedings, to cover the grant of special travel
facilities to ex-employees after retirement, even though the benefit was
received following termination of employment and was not granted pursuant
to any contractual entitlement. The Court held that the argument that the
facilities are not related to a contractual obligation is immaterial. The legal
nature of the facilities is not important for the purposes of the application of
Article 119 provided that they are granted in respect of the applicant's
employment. On similar reasoning in *Worringham* v *Lloyds Bank Ltd* (case
69/80), Article 177 proceedings, a supplementary payment made by employers
to male employees under the age of 25, for the purpose of contribution to the
employees' occupational pension scheme was held to be pay. Sums which are
included in the calculation of the gross salary payable to the employee and
which directly determine the calculation of other advantages linked to the
salary, such as redundancy payments, unemployment benefits, family allowances and credit facilities, form part of the worker's pay. Since the payment
was not made to female employees under the age of 25 the scheme was in breach
of Article 119.

Worringham v *Lloyds Bank Ltd* was followed in *Bilka-Kaufhaus GmbH* v
Weber von Hartz (case 170/84), Article 177 proceedings, in the context of a
claim by a female part-time worker, Ms Weber, who was seeking to challenge
her employer's occupational pension scheme. The scheme was noncon-
tributory, financed solely by the employer. Under the scheme part-timers were
only entitled to benefit if they had worked with the firm for at least 15 out of a
total of 20 years. No such limitation was imposed on full-timers. Ms Weber
alleged that the scheme was indirectly discriminatory, in breach of Article 119,
since the majority of part-time workers were women. The Court agreed that it
was *capable* of falling within Article 119, since the scheme was contractual, not
statutory, in origin; it originated from an agreement made between Bilka and
the works council representing the employees, and the benefits were financed
solely by the employer as a supplement to existing social security schemes. The
benefit thus constituted consideration paid by the employer to the employee in
respect of his employment.

The reasoning in *Bilka-Kaufhaus GmbH* (case 170/84) seemed to imply that
benefits paid by an employer pursuant to or in lieu of a *statutory* scheme might
not constitute pay. In *Defrenne* v *Belgian State (No. 1)* (case 80/70), Article

177 proceedings, the Court had held that although payment in the nature of social security benefits was not excluded in principle from the concept of pay, it was not possible to include in this concept, as defined in Article 119, social security schemes and benefits, especially retirement pensions, which were directly settled by law without reference to any element of consultation within the undertaking or industry concerned, and which covered without exception all workers in general. Thus although Ms Defrenne (an air hostess) was entitled to invoke Article 119 against her employer to claim equal pay to that of her male counterparts (cabin stewards) (*Defrenne* v *Sabena (No. 2)* (case 43/75), Article 177 proceedings), she was unable to challenge a Belgian law requiring different contributions in respect of male and female employees, made by the employer, to a social security scheme directly imposed by law. Such benefits are, the Court held, 'no more emoluments paid directly by the employer than are roads, canals, or water drains'.

However, the ambit of statutory social security schemes excluded from Article 119 in *Defrenne* has been whittled down by subsequent decisions of the Court. In *Liefting* (case 23/83) a statutory pension scheme applicable to a *particular group* of workers, namely civil servants, was found to be within the scope of Article 119. The Court held that:

> sums which public authorities are required to pay, though not in themselves pay, become pay if they are included in calculating their employees' gross pay used in the calculation of other salary benefits. If as a result the salary-related benefits are not the same for men as for women Article 119 is infringed.

Liefting may be compared with *Newstead* v *Department of Transport* (case 192/85). Here, in a claim by a male employee, a deduction from the gross pay of male but not female civil servants, paid into their employer's occupational pension scheme, a contracted-out scheme, to provide for widows' pensions, was held not to constitute pay. The deduction, although resulting in a reduction in the *net* pay received by employees, in no way affected their *gross* pay, on the basis of which other salary-related benefits were calculated. Thus the factor giving rise to the disparity was neither a benefit paid to workers nor a contribution to a pension scheme paid by the employer on behalf of his employee. Moreover the scheme itself, which operated as a substitute for the statutory social security scheme, fell within Article 118, not Article 119.

Article 119 was, however, held applicable to a statutory social security benefit in *Rinner-Kuhn* v *FWW Spezial Gebaudereinigung GmbH & Co KG* (case 171/88). The case concerned a claim by a part-time worker, an office cleaner, against her employer, involving a challenge to German legislation permitting employers to exclude part-time workers (defined as persons working 10 hours or less a week) from entitlement to sick pay. Prima facie the claim appeared analogous to the statutory social security scheme held in *Defrenne* and *Newstead* to be outside the scope of Article 119. Nevertheless, the Court found that the continued payment of wages to a worker in the event of illness fell within the definition of pay provided in Article 119, para. 2;

therefore national legislation such as the legislation in question, which *allowed* employers to maintain a global difference between the two categories of workers (one of which was predominantly female) must be regarded as contrary to the objectives pursued in Article 119. It would only be acceptable if objectively justified. *Rinner-Kuhn* was followed, on similar facts, in *Kowalska* (case C 33/89).

Finally in *Barber* v *Guardian Royal Exchange Assurance Group* (case C 262/88), Article 177 proceedings, the Court found, in a claim by a group of male employees who were seeking to challenge their employer's contracted-out pension scheme, which operated as a substitute for the statutory social security scheme, and was payable at different ages for men and women, that such a scheme constituted 'pay' within Article 119, as did payments made under a statutory redundancy scheme, since the worker received these benefits from his employer *as a result of his employment*. The fact that the benefits were payable at different ages for men and women resulted overall in a difference of pay.

Thus, inasmuch as it concerned employers' contracted-out pension schemes *Newstead* can no longer be regarded as good law; the only statutory social security schemes which appear now to fall outside Article 119 are statutory social security pension schemes provided for workers in general as a matter of social policy.

This broad interpretation of pay to include benefits relating in the widest sense to retirement or even death (provided they are not social security benefits *sensu stricto*) is important, since the Equal Pay Act 1970 excludes from its scope 'any provision made in connection with death or retirement' (s. 6(1A)). This section was interpreted broadly by the Court of Appeal in *Garland* v *British Rail Engineering Ltd* [1979] ICR 558 and *Worringham* v *Lloyds Bank Ltd* [1982] ICR 299 as any provision about retirement, thereby excluding many claims which would qualify as 'pay' under Article 119. Although the House of Lords in *Garland* v *British Rail Engineering Ltd* [1983] 2 AC 751 declared that domestic law *must* be construed to conform with directly effective EEC law, and did construe the Equal Pay Act 1970, s. 6(1), to comply with Article 119, there is always a danger that entrenched interpretations of national law will prevail (see *Duke* v *GEC Reliance Ltd* [1988] AC 618, House of Lords). However, the House of Lords in *Pickstone* v *Freemans plc* [1989] AC 66 now provides clear authority that national courts must interpret domestic law to comply with directly effective Community law, even though this may 'involve a departure from a number of well established rules of interpretation' (per Lord Oliver; cf Court of Appeal's approach, which was to apply Article 119 directly, [1989] AC 66).

Because the ruling in *Barber* was likely seriously to affect the financial balance of contracted-out pension schemes, contributions and calculations for which had been based on different retirement ages for men and women, and because, as the Court conceded, both member States and the parties concerned were reasonably entitled to consider that Article 119 did not apply to pensions paid under contracted-out pension schemes, the Court held that its ruling as regards such schemes could not be applied retrospectively. Article 119 might not be relied on to claim entitlement to a pension with effect prior to the date of judgment, except in the case of workers, or those claiming under them, who had before that date initiated legal proceedings or raised an equivalent claim under the applicable national law (para. 45). Following dispute over the scope of this ruling, as to whether Article 119 applied to all claims for *pensions arising* after the date of judgment or only to claims based on *benefits earned* after this date, the matter was finally resolved by a protocol issued at Maastricht in favour of the latter more restrictive view. According to the Protocol:

> For the purposes of Article 119 of [the Treaty establishing the European Community], benefits under occupational social security schemes shall not be considered as remuneration if and insofar as they are attributable to periods of employment prior to 17 May 1990, except in the case of workers or those claiming under them who have before that date initiated legal proceedings or introduced an equivalent claim under the applicable national law.

In order to satisfy the equal pay principle, it is not enough that the overall package of remuneration received by men and women be equal. The Court held in *Barber* that each element of the consideration paid to both sexes must be equal. The system of pay must be 'transparent', in order that clear comparisons as between men and women may be made.

Equal work

Equal work has been defined in Directive 75/117 as the 'same work' or 'work to which equal value has been attributed'.

Same work   In *Macarthys Ltd* v *Smith* (case 129/79), Article 177 proceedings. Advocate-General Capotorti suggested that 'same work' is not confined to identical work; it should include jobs which display a high degree of similarity the one to the other, even if there is not total identity between them. It would thus correspond to work of a 'broadly similar nature' under the Equal Pay Act 1970, s. 4(4). Since 'similar' work will shade into work 'of equal value', which is also subject to the equality principle, a precise definition of 'same' work is unnecessary.

Work of equal value   This concept was introduced into EEC law by Directive 75/117. However, since the Court has held (*Jenkins* v *Kingsgate (Clothing Productions) Ltd* (case 96/80), Article 177 proceedings) that Directive 75/117 is merely confined to restating the principle of equal pay as set out in Article 119, and in no way alters the content and scope of Article 119, a claim for equal pay for work of equal value may be brought under Article 119 as well as under Directive 75/117. Indeed, a claim under Article 119 is advisable since it avoids possible problems over the direct effects of the Directive. The concept of work of equal value will be further discussed in the context of Directive 75/117.

Any comparisons made for the purpose of deciding whether a man and a woman are engaged on 'equal work' must be confined to parallels which may be drawn on the basis of concrete appraisals of the work actually performed by employees of different sex within the same establishment or service (*Macarthys Ltd* v *Smith* (case 129/79)). Thus comparisons cannot be made with the 'hypothetical male'. However, they are not necessarily limited to the same establishment or service. In *Defrenne* v *Sabena (No. 2)* (case 43/75), the Court of Justice held that Article 119 applied to discrimination which has its origin in legislative provisions ('general' social security provision excepted) or in collective labour agreements and which may be detected on a purely legal analysis of the situation. However, in the absence of job evaluation schemes affecting undertakings or industries at a national level, it is submitted that comparisons cannot be made *across* undertakings or industries.

As is clear from *Macarthys Ltd* v *Smith* comparisons are not limited to men and women engaged in contemporaneous employment. Nor is it necessary that the employment should be in the same State. Thus a limitation, as in the Equal Pay Act 1970, s. 1(1), and Sex Discrimination Act 1975, s. 6(1), to employment 'in Great Britain' (see also *Haughton* v *Olau Line (UK) Ltd* [1986] ICR 357) would appear to conflict with EEC law.

Discrimination

Discrimination, in breach of Article 119, can be direct or indirect. Where the discrimination is direct, on the basis of sex alone, a difference in pay can never be justified. However, where the difference in pay is indirectly discriminatory, being based on factors other than sex, different rules apply. In *Jenkins* v *Kingsgate (Clothing Productions) Ltd* the Court of Justice was asked, on reference from the Employment Appeal Tribunal, whether a difference in pay (in this case 10%) between part-time and full-time workers could constitute discrimination when the category of part-time workers was exclusively or predominantly female (only one, exceptional male was employed part-time). The Court held that such a difference would not infringe Article 119 provided that the difference in pay was 'objectively justified' and in no way related to discrimination based on sex. However, such inequality of pay would breach Article 119 where, having regard to the difficulties encountered by women in arranging to work the minimum (full-time) number of hours a week, the pay policy of the undertaking cannot be explained by factors other than discrimination based on sex.

In *Bilka-Kaufhaus GmbH* v *Weber von Harz* (case 170/84), Article 177 proceedings, the Court was faced again with a claim by a part-time worker, this time challenging her employer's occupational pension scheme, which discriminated overtly against part-time workers. Here both full and part-time work-forces comprised both men and women, but of the men employed (28% of the total work-force), only 10% worked part-time, as against 27.7% of the female work-force. Overall male part-time workers comprised only 2.8% of the total work-force. The disadvantage suffered by part-timers thus fell disproportionately on the women. The Court of Justice was asked whether such a scheme might breach Article 119. Citing para. 13 of the judgment in *Jenkins* v *Kingsgate (Clothing Productions) Ltd* almost verbatim, the Court held (at para.

29) that if it was found that a considerably smaller percentage of men than of
women worked part-time, and if the difference in treatment could not be
explained by any other factor than sex, the exclusion of part-time workers from
the occupational scheme would be contrary to Article 119. The difference in
treatment would, however, be permissible if it were explained by objectively
justified factors which were unrelated to discrimination based on sex. It would
be for the employer to prove, and for national courts to decide, on the facts,
whether the difference in treatment was in fact objectively justified.

Objective justification

Guidelines as to what might constitute objective justification were laid down
in *Bilka-Kaufhaus GmbH* v *Weber von Harz* (case 170/84). There the Court
held that in order to prove that a measure is objectively justified the employer
must prove that the measures giving rise to the difference in treatment:

(a)   correspond to a 'genuine need of the enterprise',
(b)   are suitable for obtaining the objective pursued by the enterprise, and
(c)   are necessary for that purpose.

These principles, reminiscent of *Cassis de Dijon* (see chapter 8), were
reiterated by the Court in *Rummler* v *Dato-Druck GmbH* (case 237/85). What
factors, then, will be regarded by the Court as providing 'objective justification' meeting a 'genuine need of the enterprise'? *Jenkins* v *Kingsgate (Clothing
Productions) Ltd* and *Bilka-Kaufhaus GmbH* suggest that the justification will
be primarily economic. In *Bilka-Kaufhaus GmbH* the defendants argued that
part-time workers were less economic; they were less ready to work on
Saturdays and in the evening; that it was necessary to pay more to attract
full-timers. Justification on these grounds was not disputed in principle.
Whether it would in fact be accepted would depend on whether the need for
the difference in pay could be proved, and if so whether the proportionality
principle were satisfied. In applying this ruling the German court found that
it was not.

In *Rinner-Kuhn* (case 171/88) the Court suggested that a justification based
on a 'genuine objective of social policy' might be acceptable, provided that the
means selected were appropriate and necessary to the attainment of that
objective. However, it firmly rejected an argument that the difference in
treatment as regards sick pay between part and full-time workers was justified
on the grounds that part-timers were not integrated into the business in the
same way as full-time workers. 'These considerations', the Court said, 'only
represent generalised statements concerning certain categories of workers and
do not admit the conclusion of objective justification unrelated to any
discrimination on the grounds of sex'. Since women form the majority of the
part-time workforce, it is they, as the Commission pointed out in *Rinner-Kuhn*,
who are most vulnerable and in need of protection; thus a social policy objective
resulting in discrimination against part-time workers is unlikely to be seen as

Sex discrimination   257

valid justification. A justification on the grounds of social policy has, however, been accepted in a number of social security cases not involving part-time workers (e.g., *Teuling* (case 30/85); *Commission* v *Belgium* (case C 229/89)).

It is clear from both *Jenkins* and *Bilka-Kaufhaus GmbH* that the fact that the group adversely affected by a particular measure comprises both sexes does not prevent it being discriminatory on the grounds of sex, as long as it affects one sex to *a disproportionate extent*. If this were not so, as Nicholls LJ pointed out in the Court of Appeal in *Pickstone* v *Freemans plc* [1989] AC 66, as long as there is a man there doing the same work, 'which in some cases might be wholly fortuitous or even, possibly, a situation contrived by an unscrupulous employer', the woman cannot make the comparison, even if the difference in pay is attributable solely to grounds of sex. According to the Court of Appeal in *Pickstone*, this could have occurred under the 'unambiguous words' of the Equal Pay Act 1970, s. 1(2). However, unless one sex is disproportionately affected, a claim under Article 119 of discrimination *based on sex* is unlikely to succeed.

Since national courts and tribunals are left themselves to assess this crucial question of objective justification, with little guidance as to what may constitute a 'genuine need', it is vital that the genuineness of the justification and its *necessity* be both probed and proved. In *R* v *Secretary of State for Employment, ex parte Equal Opportunities Commission* [1992] 1 All ER 585, the Divisional Court unanimously decided that certain provisions of the UK Employment Protection (Consolidation) Act 1978, which permitted discrimination as between part and full-time workers, whilst being indirectly discriminatory against women, were objectively justified. The court reached that conclusion on the basis of the Employment Secretary's suggestion that opportunities for part-time work would be reduced as a result of the additional burdens imposed on potential employers by the need to treat all workers equally. There was no enquiry into the question of proportionality.

Where our courts have applied the principle of proportionality it tends to be equated with the laxer standard of reasonableness, or 'reasonable necessity' (see Sir Nicholas Browne-Wilkinson in *Jenkins* v *Kingsgate (Clothing Productions) Ltd* [1981] ICR 715 at p. 716; *Clymo* v *Wandsworth London Borough Council* [1989] ICR 250). Thus, as Lord Dillon pointed out in *Bromley* v *Quick* [1988] 2 CMLR 468 (CA), subjective factors are at work in the 'objective' process; where a subjective element is involved, 'care must be taken to see that discrimination is not inadvertently let in'. Moreover, a finding that a particular practice is objectively justified is a primary finding of fact; as such it is unlikely to be disturbed on appeal, except in a case of manifest error (see *Clymo* v *Wandsworth BC*).

Equal pay for work of equal value (Directive 75/117)

As has been noted, Directive 75/117, which was based on Article 119, was introduced merely to implement and supplement Article 119. Article 1 provides:

The principle of equal pay for men and women outlined in Article 119 of the Treaty, hereinafter called 'principle of equal pay', means, for the same work or for work to which equal value is attributed, the elimination of all discrimination on grounds of sex with regard to all aspects and conditions of remuneration.

In particular, where a job classification system is used for determining pay, it must be based on the same criteria for both men and women and so drawn up as to exclude any discrimination on grounds of sex.

Article 2 requires member States to:

introduce into their national legal systems such measures as are necessary to enable all employees who consider themselves wronged by failure to apply the principle of equal pay to pursue their claims by judicial process after possible recourse to other competent authorities.

In addition, Article 6 requires member States, in accordance with their national circumstances and legal systems, to:

take the measures necessary to ensure that the principle of equal pay is applied. They shall see that effective means are available to take care that this principle is observed.

In *Commission* v *United Kingdom (Re Equal Pay for Equal Work)* (case 61/81) the UK was found to have failed, in breach of Directive 75/117 (Articles 1 and 6), to provide a means whereby claims of equal value might be assessed in the absence of a job evaluation scheme having been implemented by the employer.

Neither Articles 1 or 6 of Directive 75/117 nor *Commission* v *United Kingdom* (case 61/81) require that a claim to equal value must be assessed pursuant to a job evaluation study; indeed, the Court pointed out in *Commission* v *United Kingdom* that a system of job classification is only one of the several methods for determining pay for work to which equal value is attributed. All that seems to be required under EEC law is that where a prima facie claim to equal value exists, either as a result of a job evaluation study, as in *O'Brien* v *Sim-Chem Ltd* [1980] ICR 573, House of Lords, or otherwise, an assessment must be made, if necessary in adversary proceedings, by a body with the requisite power to decide whether work has the same value, after obtaining such information as may be needed. The UK was left to decide for itself how best this might be achieved. Extensive machinery has now been provided by an amendment (s. 2A(1)) made to the Equal Pay Act 1970 by SI 1983 No. 1791.

It is regrettable that the Court in *Commission* v *United Kingdom* did not spell out in greater detail the scope of member States' obligations in this field. Clearly some comparability must exist before a legitimate claim to equal value can arise. But how 'like' must two different jobs be for them to be deemed to be comparable? And if they are 'broadly' comparable, how, and in what detail, are they to be assessed in order to decide whether they are equal value? Must every benefit received by the man and woman be weighed and compared individually, as the House of Lords found in *Hayward* v *Cammell Laird Shipbuilders Ltd (No. 2)* [1988] AC 894, or is it sufficient, as the Court of Appeal had suggested ([1988] QB 12), that the overall package received by men and women be equal? Will a 'felt fair' order of jobs, depending on the general level of expectation as to the value of the job, be adequate, as the Employment Appeal Tribunal suggested in *Bromley* v *J & J Quick Ltd* [1987] IRLR 456, or should not, as the Court of Appeal decided, a full analytical study be made? If such a study is undertaken, what criteria are to be applied? Clearly the answers to all these questions, and the solutions adopted, will vary from State to State, as will their cost to the State. Moreover, a finding of equal value will have serious repercussions on costs, both for the individual concerned and possibly for an entire industry. This in turn will affect its competitiveness within the common market. Thus unless the rules relating to the application of the principle of equal value are determined and applied in a uniform manner throughout the Community they are likely to defeat the very 'economic objectives' which they were designed, in part, to achieve. Such uniformity is unlikely to come about without further clarification and harmonisation at Community level.

Where a job classification scheme is devised as a means of determining comparability, some general guidance as to its content was provided by the Court of Justice in *Rummler* v *Dato-Druck GmbH* (case 237/85), Article 177 proceedings. Here a woman packer, classified under wage group III under a job evaluation scheme implemented by her employers, and not, as she considered appropriate, under group IV, was seeking to challenge the criteria on which the scheme was based. These criteria included the muscular effort, fatigue and physical hardship attached to the job. She claimed this was discriminatory. On a reference to the Court of Justice that Court held that a job classification scheme based on the strength required to carry out the work or the degree of physical hardship which the work entailed was not in breach of Directive 75/117 as long as:

(a) the system as a whole precluded discrimination on grounds of sex and

(b) the criteria employed were objectively justified. To be objectively justified they must:

(i) be appropriate to the tasks to be carried out, and

(ii) correspond to a genuine need of the undertaking.

In addition, the classification scheme as a whole, if not to be discriminatory, must take into account the criteria for which each sex has a particular aptitude. Criteria based exclusively on the values of one sex contain, the Court suggested, 'a risk of discrimination'.

The principles of *Rummler* v *Dato-Druck* were extended significantly in *Handels- og Kontorfunktionærernes Forbund i Danmark* v *Dansk Arbejdsgiverforening for Danfoss* (case 109/88), Article 177 proceedings, in the context of a challenge by the Danish Employees' Union to the criteria agreed by the Danish

Employers Association and applied by the firm of Danfoss. These included, *inter alia*, the criteria of 'flexibility' and 'seniority'. Whilst the minimum pay for each grade was the same for men and women, it was found that the average pay *within* each grade was lower for women than for men. The applicants alleged that the criteria were indirectly discriminatory. The Court of Justice held that where the application of neutral criteria, such as the criterion of quality (one element of 'flexibility'), was shown to *result* in systematic discrimination against female workers, this could only be because the employer applied it in an abusive manner. The criteria applied must be 'of importance for the specific duties entrusted to the workers concerned'. Where a pay system is characterised by a 'total lack of "transparency"', that is, when the criteria for determining pay increments are not explicit, and where a female worker establishes, by comparison with a relatively large number of employees, that the average pay of female workers is lower than that of male workers, the onus is on the employer to prove that the criteria employed are justified. Moreover, in view of the greater difficulties faced by women in organising their time in a flexible manner, the criterion of adaptability (another element of 'flexibility'), which was prima facie capable of justification, would also require proof of justification from the employer. The criterion of seniority was found by the Court to be sufficiently transparent not to require justification by the employer. Thus, where the criteria employed are not transparent, or where they operate to the patent disadvantage of women, the employer must carry the burden of justification. It has been suggested that this case represents an enactment, by judicial means, at least in part, of a Directive concerning the burden of proof in equal treatment cases, proposed by the Commission in 1988 and vetoed by the British government in 1989.

Finally, under Article 4 of Directive 75/117, States are required to ensure that provisions of collective agreements, wage scales, wage agreements or individual contracts of employment contrary to the principle of equal value 'shall be, or may be declared, null and void or may be amended'.

States must also, under Article 5, ensure full protection for employees against dismissal as a reaction to a complaint or to legal proceedings 'aimed at enforcing compliance with the principle of equal pay'.

Since the provisions of Directive 75/117 merely define the scope and substance of Article 119 they may be invoked, vertically or horizontally, in the context of a claim under that Article. As *Defrenne* v *Sabena (No. 2)* (case 43/75) established, Article 119 is effective against *all* parties. Following *Marshall* v *Southampton and South West Hampshire Area Health Authority (Teaching)* (case 152/84), Directive 75/117, as a Directive, will not *in itself* be horizontally effective (see chapter 2).

Principle of equal treatment for men and women (Directive 76/207)

Directive 76/207, which is based not on Article 119 of the EEC Treaty but on the institutions' general powers under Article 235, lays down the principle of equal treatment for men and women in Article 1(1):

as regards access to employment, including promotion, and to vocational training and as regards working conditions and, on the conditions referred to in paragraph 2, social security.

'Working conditions' are defined to include 'conditions governing dismissal' (Article 5).

Article 1, paragraph 2, provides for further action to implement the principle of equal treatment in matters of social security. This has now been achieved with Directives 79/7 (statutory schemes) and 86/378 (occupational schemes).

The principle of equal treatment is defined in Article 2 as meaning that:

there shall be no discrimination whatsoever on grounds of sex either directly or indirectly by reference in particular to marital or family status.

Derogation from the equal treatment principle is provided under Article 2(2) for activities for which, 'by reason of their nature or the context in which they are carried out, the sex of the worker constitutes a determining factor', and by Article 2(3), which allows for exception for 'provisions concerning the protection of women, particularly as regards pregnancy and maternity'.

The principal context in which the equal treatment Directive has been invoked in the UK has been to challenge different retirement ages as between men and women, since like the Equal Pay Act 1970, the Sex Discrimination Act 1975, s. 6(4) excludes from its scope 'provision' in relation to death or retirement'. Directive 76/207 contains no such exclusion, but Directive 79/7, Article 7(1), governing equal treatment in matters of social security, allows member States to exclude from the scope of the equal treatment principle 'the determination of pensionable age for the purposes of granting old-age and retirement pensions and the possible consequences thereof for other benefits'. Directive 86/378 (Article 9) provides a parallel exclusion in respect of occupational pension schemes.

The scope of Directive 76/207 as modified by Directive 79/7 was considered in *Burton* v *British Railways Board* (case 19/81), Article 177 proceedings, in the context of a challenge by a railway worker, Mr Burton, to a voluntary redundancy scheme operated by British Rail. Under the scheme women were entitled to apply for voluntary redundancy at 55, and men at 60. Mr Burton, who, at 58, wished to take early retirement, alleged that the scheme was discriminatory. Since it fell within the exemption of the Sex Discrimination Act 1975, s. 6(4), as interpreted by the Court of Appeal in *Garland* v *British Rail Engineering Ltd* [1979] ICR 558 and *Worringham* v *Lloyds Bank Ltd* [1982] ICR 299, Directive 76/207 offered him his only chance of success. On reference from the Employment Appeal Tribunal for an interpretation on the scope and application of Directive 76/207 the Court of Justice held that the Directive applied in principle to conditions of access to voluntary redundancy schemes. Moreover, the word 'dismissal', brought within the equality principle by Article 5, must be widely construed to cover termination of the employment relationship, even as part of a redundancy scheme. However, since in this case the ages for voluntary retirement were calculated by reference to, and tied to, the statutory retirement age (60 for women, 65 for men), Article 7 of Directive

79/7, which permitted States to exclude from the equal treatment principle 'the determination of pensionable age' applied. Thus his claim under Directive 76/207 must fail.

Undeterred by *Burton* v *British Railways Board,* the applicant in *Marshall* v *Southampton and South West Hampshire Area Health Authority (Teaching)* (case 152/84) brought a similar claim under Directive 76/207. Ms Marshall, an employee of the AHA, was seeking to challenge its compulsory retirement policy, under which women employees were required to retire at 60, and men at 65. On a reference from the Employment Appeal Tribunal under Article 177 the Court of Justice, following *Burton* v *British Railways Board* interpreted the retirement scheme as a 'condition governing dismissal' within Article 5 of Directive 76/207. However, distinguishing *Burton,* on the slenderest grounds (benefits *tied to* a national scheme which lays down a different minimum pensionable age for men and women) the Court found that her case was *not* within the exclusion of Article 7 of Directive 79/7. This Article allowed member States to exclude from the equal treatment principle the determination of pensionable age *'for the purposes of granting old-age and retirement pensions and the possible consequences thereof for other benefits'.* Where pensionable age was being determined *for other purposes,* e.g., as in *Marshall,* for the purpose of *retirement* the equal treatment principle would apply.

The Court of Justice took the same line, on the same reasoning, in *Roberts* v *Tate & Lyle Industries Ltd* (case 151/84). This time the applicant failed in her challenge to her employer's compulsory early retirement scheme. Although the scheme entitled those retiring to an accelerated pension under the firm's occupational pension scheme, it was held to fall within the scope of Directive 76/207 as a condition governing dismissal, and not Directive 79/7. However, in this case it was not discriminatory, since the age for retirement was fixed at 55 for both men and women (see also *Beets-Proper* v *F. van Landschot Bankiers NV* (case 262/84)).

Thus member States' power under Article 7 of Directive 79/7 to exclude from the equal treatment principle 'the determination of pensionable age' in view of the fundamental importance of the principle of equal treatment, has been given the narrowest scope. It seems it will only apply where the difference in age is *for the purpose* of the granting of old-age and retirement *pensions* and the possible consequences thereof for other benefits 'falling within the statutory [or occupational] social security schemes' (*Marshall,* para. 35). Moreover, the exclusion from the equal treatment principle only applies to the determination of pensionable age for the purposes of granting *statutory* social security pensions. Despite the express exclusion in respect of the 'determination of pensionable age for the purposes of granting old-age or retirement pensions' as regards *occupational* pension schemes, contained in Directive 86/378, the Court held in *Barber* (case C 262/88) that the setting of different retirement ages for men and women for the granting of such pensions was in breach of Article 119, since the difference in age *resulted* in a difference in pay. On similar reasoning different ages of access to statutory redundancy benefit for men and women were also held in breach of Article 119. *Burton* v *British Railways Board* (case 19/81) appears to have been distinguished out of existence.

The troublesome exclusions of the Equal Pay Act and Sex Discrimination Act concerning provisions relating to death or retirement (Equal Pay Act 1970, s. 6(1A); Sex Discrimination Act 1975, s. 6(4)) have now been amended by the Sex Discrimination Act 1986, which rendered discriminatory retirement ages illegal, and the Employment Act 1989, which fixed a single retirement age of 65 for men and women for the purposes of redundancy benefit. However, these Acts do not have retrospective effect. Where discrimination has been suffered prior to the entry into force of the new provisions, it may be possible, subject to national limitation periods, to bring a claim based on Directive 76/207, at least against a 'State' employer against whom the Directive is directly effective. These periods may be extended following the decision in *Emmott v Minister for Social Services* (case C 208/90) (see chapter 2). However, following *Barber* it may no longer be necessary in such cases to resort to Directive 76/207. If the difference in age results in a difference in pay, unless the 'pay' in question is a statutory social security pension, the appropriate remedy will lie in Article 119.

Like Directive 75/117, Directive 76/207 requires States to 'take the necessary measures to ensure that any laws, regulations and administrative provisions contrary to the principle of equal treatment be abolished' (Article 3(2)(a)) and 'any provisions contrary to the principle of equal treatment . . . in collective agreements, individual contracts of employment, internal rules of undertakings or in rules governing the independendent occupations and professions shall be, or may be declared, null and void or may be amended' (Article 3(2)(b)). The UK was found in breach of these provisions in *Commission v United Kingdom (Re Equal Treatment for Men and Women* (case 165/82).

Derogation from the equal treatment principle (Article 2(2), 2(3) and 2(4)

Article 2(2) and (3) of Directive 76/207, which provides for exemption from the equal treatment principle for 'activities . . . for which . . . the sex of the worker constitutes a determining factor' (Article 2(2)), and for 'provisions concerning the protection of women, particularly as regards pregnancy and maternity' (Article 2(3)), may be seen as a specific implementation of the principle of 'objective justification' considered in the context of equal pay. In addition, Article 2(4) provides some scope for positive discrimination, by allowing for 'measures to promote equal opportunities for men and women, in particular by removing existing inequalities which affect women's opportunities in the areas referred to in Article 1(1)'. These Articles provide for derogation from the equal treatment principle in the case of *direct* discrimination, based on the sex of the worker. However, Articles 2(2) and 2(3), which could be invoked to the detriment of women, have been given the narrowest scope.

Article 2(2) was considered by the Court of Justice in the Commission's second action under Article 169 against the UK (*Commission v United Kingdom (Re Equal Treatment for Men and Women)* (case 165/82)) for failure to comply with the equal treatment Directive. One of the failures alleged was the exemption from the equal treatment principle, provided under the Sex Discrimination Act 1975, for employment in a private household (s. 6(3)(a)) and for firms employing less than six staff (s. 6(3)(b)). The UK argued that these provisions were justifiable under Article 2(2) of Directive 76/207. The Court disagreed. Whilst exemption under Article 2(2) might be available in the *individual* case under such circumstances, where the sex of the worker was a determining factor, Article 2(2) did not justify a blanket exclusion. It did, however, provide a valid defence to a charge against the UK in respect of its restriction, under the Sex Discrimination Act, s. 41, on male access to the profession of midwifery. The Court found that this was an activity for which the sex of the worker was a determining factor.

In *Stoeckel* (case C 245/89) a general ban on night work for women, provided for under German law, allegedly to protect women, was held by the Court not permissible under Article 2(2).

Article 2(2) was also raised as a defence in the case of *Johnston* v *Chief Constable of the Royal Ulster Constabulary* (case 222/84), Article 177 proceedings (see chapter 4). This action was brought by a female member of the Royal Ulster Constabulary (RUC) against a decision by the RUC refusing to renew her contract of employment. The RUC had decided as a matter of policy not to employ women as full-time members of the RUC reserve, since they were not trained in the use of firearms nor permitted to use them. In proceedings before the Court of Justice under Article 177 concerning the interpretation of Directive 76/207 and in particular the scope for derogation from the equal treatment principle available under EEC law the RUC argued, by analogy with Article 48(3) of the EEC Treaty (see chapter 20), that in view of the political situation in Northern Ireland derogation was justified on public safety or public security grounds; it was also justified under Article 2(2) of Directive 76/207. To allow women to carry and use firearms, the RUC claimed, increased the risk of their becoming targets for assassination. The Court held that there was no general public safety exception to the equal treatment principle available under the EEC Treaty. A claim for exemption could *only* be examined in the light of the provisions of Directive 76/207. With regard to Article 2(2), the Court held that:

(a)   The derogation provided under Article 2(2) could be applied only to specific *duties*, not to activities in general. Nonetheless, it was permissible to take into account the *context* in which the activity takes place.

(b)   Where derogation is justified in the light of (a) the situation must be reviewed periodically to ensure that the justification still exists.

(c)   Derogation must be subject to the principle of proportionality.

It was for national courts to decide whether these conditions are satisfied.

Similar principles were applied, if somewhat leniently, in *Commission* v *France* (case 318/86), Article 169 proceedings. The Commission's action was in respect of recruitment practices in the French civil service, in particular the prison service and the police. Under the system in force men and women were subject to different recruitment procedures, with a fixed percentage of posts being allocated according to sex. The complaint concerning the prison service centred on access to the post of head warder (in male prisons), which was not accessible to women. The complaint regarding the police concerned recruitment to certain police corps generally.

In the case of the prison service the Court found that it was justifiable to discriminate on the grounds of Article 2(2) in respect of the post of *warder*. Since professional experience acquired as a warder was desirable for the performance of the duties of a prison governor (a post for which head warders were eligible), and since it was desirable to provide promotion opportunities for those in the lower (warders') posts, it was acceptable to treat the *head* warder's post in the same way. The recruitment practices were justified under Article 2(2). The recruitment practices of the police, on the other hand, were not permissible under Article 2(2). The exclusion provided by Article 2(2), the Court held, allows exceptions to the non discrimination principle only in relation to specific *activities,* and these exceptions must be sufficiently transparent to permit effective scrutiny. The fact that certain police functions cannot be performed by men and women does not justify discriminatory treatment in admission to the police force in general. The application of Article 2(2) requires a *specific* assessment of the *specific* duties to be performed in individual cases.

In *Johnston* v *Chief Constable of the RUC* the RUC also sought to justify its action under Article 2(3), as 'concerning the protection of women, particularly as regards pregnancy and maternity'. The Court found that the risks to policewomen arising from the situation in Northern Ireland were not within the scope of Article 2(3). Article 2(3) was intended to protect women's biological condition.

This interpretation of Article 2(3) had been supplied in *Hofmann* v *Barmer Ersatzkasse* (case 184/83), Article 177 proceedings, in response to a claim by a father to six months' leave following the birth of his child to look after the child while the mother went back to work. German law, which granted such leave only to the mother, was, he claimed, discriminatory, in breach of Directive 76/207. The Court disagreed. Special provision for maternity leave was, the Court held, permissible under Article 2(3), which was concerned to protect two types of female need. It protected:

(a)   the biological condition of women during and after pregnancy; and
(b)   the relationship between mother and child during the period following pregnancy and birth.

Directive 76/207 was not intended to cover matters relating to the organisation of the family or to change the division of responsibility between parents.

A second case brought by the Commission against France (*Commission* v *France* (case 312/86)) related to special privileges in the form of, *inter alia,* extended maternity leave, lower retirement age, extra time off to allow for children's illness and holidays, and extra allowances to meet the cost of nursery schools and child minders, awarded under French law to married women. The French sought to justify these privileges under Article 2(3) and 2(4). The Court, citing *Hofmann*, found that such measures fell outside the limits of Article 2(3); nor was there any indication that the rights claimed corresponded to the situation envisaged under Article 2(4). Thus, if such privileges are to be justified, they can only be justified on objective grounds *unrelated to sex,* such as the need to assist persons who carry primary responsibility for the welfare of the family, and particularly of children. As the Court pointed out in *Commission* v *France,* such responsibility may be undertaken by men. (As an example of the application of 'neutral' criteria, see *Teuling* (case 30/85) *infra.*)

The above cases all concern direct discrimination. Where the discrimination is indirect the same principles apply as apply in the field of pay; a difference in treatment as between one group of workers and another which *affects* one sex disproportionately will require objective justification. Here the justification need not be brought within Article 2 of Directive 76/207, since the difference in treatment for which justification is required is not between men and women, but between one group of workers (e.g. part-timers) and another (e.g. full-timers). Following *Danfoss* (case 109/88) the onus of proving justification will fall on the employer.

Pregnancy

The precise extent to which, and circumstances in which, a dismissal or refusal to employ a woman for reasons connected with pregnancy and childbirth will breach Directive 76/207 remains unclear. In *Dekker* v *VJV-Centrum* (case C 177/88) the defendant employer had withdrawn his offer of employment to the plaintiff when he discovered she was pregnant. He argued that his action was justified; her absence during maternity leave would not on the facts be covered by insurance, and he could not afford to pay for a replacement worker. The Court of Justice held that a refusal to employ a woman on the grounds of pregnancy constituted direct discrimination on the grounds of sex; as such it could not be justified on the basis of financial detriment to the employer.

The effect of this ruling was mitigated in the Court's judgment in *Handels- og Kontorfunktionærernes Forbund i Danmark* v *Dansk Arbejdsgiverforening (Hertz)* (case C 179/88) delivered on the same day. This case concerned a claim by a female employee against dismissal on the grounds of her extended absence from work as a result of illness which, though connected with pregnancy and childbirth, was suffered some time *after* the end of her maternity leave. The Court held that in this case there was no need to distinguish between illness resulting from pregnancy and maternity and any other illness such as might be suffered by a man. The dismissal was thus not directly discriminatory and could be justified. The reason for the distinction between *Dekker* and *Hertz,* suggested in *Hertz,* lay in Article 2(3) of Directive 76/207 which provides for measures concerning the protection of women, particularly as regards pregnancy and maternity.

Hertz was seized upon by the English Court of Appeal in *Webb* v *EMO Air Cargo (UK) Ltd* [1992] 2 All ER 43, in the context of a claim at first sight closer to *Dekker,* for discrimination on the grounds of pregnancy. The plaintiff had been engaged to replace another employee who had become pregnant. Two weeks after accepting the post she discovered she too was pregnant. When she informed the employer of this fact she was dismissed. Glidewell LJ, following counsel for the employer's advice, chose to read *Dekker* and *Hertz* together. Dismissal on the grounds of pregnancy might under *some* circumstances constitute direct discrimination. But on these facts, where the plaintiff had been employed specifically to replace another pregnant worker, the situation should rather be compared with that of a man in a similar situation, for example, a man with an arthritic hip, who found, shortly after taking up employment, that he was soon to be called for a hip replacement operation necessitating a long absence from work. Since an employer would have been justified in dismissing a man under these circumstances, the plaintiff's dismissal was not discriminatory on the grounds of sex.

Whilst it may be possible to sympathise with Glidewell LJ's view that a finding of direct discrimination *under these circumstances* 'would be . . . lacking in fairness and in the proper balance to be struck in the relations between employer and employee' the decision is no doubt at odds with the Court's decision in *Dekker*. A 'fair balance between employer and employee' might have been better achieved had the Court, in *Dekker*, found, as it might legitimately have done, that the employer's action was indirectly discriminatory. If indirectly discriminatory, dismissal for reasons of pregnancy might under some circumstances (such as those obtaining in *Webb*?) be objectively justifiable, subject to the test of proportionality.

Direct effects of Directive 76/207

One of the central problems with the equal treatment Directive was, until recently, the extent to which it might be directly effective. Whilst a claim for equal pay under Directive 75/117 may be brought under Article 119 of the EEC Treaty, no such option exists for a claim to equal treatment, since it is based on the general law-making powers of Article 235. Whilst it has for some time been clear that a Directive may be vertically effective, i.e., effective against the State, there was some doubt whether it could be invoked against the State *in its capacity as employer*. Even more doubtful was the question of whether a Directive might be horizontally effective, i.e., could be invoked against a private person, in the case of Directive 76/207, a 'private' employer. These matters have been fully discussed in chapter 2.

The question was finally resolved in *Marshall* v *Southampton and South West Hampshire Area Health Authority (Teaching)* (case 152/84). Here the Court held that Ms Marshall could invoke Directive 76/207 against the hospital authority, since the authority, even acting in its capacity as employer, was an 'emanation of the State'. The Directive could not, on the other hand, be invoked *directly* against a private person, since as a Directive it was binding, under Article 189, only on its addressee, the State. This principle was affirmed in *Roberts* v *Tate & Lyle Industries Ltd* (case 151/84). In neither of these cases did it operate to the detriment of the applicant, since in *Roberts* the measure was found not to be discriminatory.

Where the Directive cannot be invoked directly, as against a 'private' employer, the Court has held that national courts must strive to interpret domestic law to comply with the Directive (the *Von Colson* principle of 'indirect effects', see chapter 2). However, our courts have been reluctant to apply this principle in the context of sex discrimination claims. In *Duke* v *GEC Reliance Ltd* [1988] AC 618, in a claim challenging different retirement ages for men and women, based on *Marshall*, the House of Lords held that s. 2(4) of the European Communities Act 1972 did not 'enable or constrain a British court to distort the meaning of a British statute in order to enforce against an individual a Community Directive which has no direct effect between individuals'. This statement by Lord Templeman was cited with approval in equal treatment claims in *Finnegan* v *Clowney Youth Training Programme Ltd* [1990] 2 AC 407 (HL), *Marshall* v *Southampton & South West Hampshire Health Authority (Teaching) (No. 2)* [1991] ICR 136 (CA), and *Webb* v *EMO Air Cargo (UK) Ltd* [1992] 2 All ER 43 (CA). This attitude on the part of our courts, like their rather restrictive approach to the question of whether a defendant undertaking is a 'public' body (see *Doughty* v *Rolls Royce plc* [1992] IRLR 126 (CA) noted chapter 2), may result from the Court of Justice's 'bold' interpretation of the equal treatment Directives, sometimes contrary to their natural or expected meaning (e.g., *Marshall, Barber*). In these circumstances our courts appear unwilling to presume that Parliament intended domestic legislation to have the meaning contended for by the Court, especially when an interpretation in conformity with the Directive would impose, retrospectively, onerous financial burdens on employers.

The Court of Justice, no doubt aware of the problems concerning the application of Directives, has been ingenious in its attempts to overcome them. It has enlarged the scope of Article 119, to the extent that it is no longer necessary in many cases to rely on the Equal Treatment Directives. And in *Francovich* v *Italian State* (cases C 6 and 9/90) it suggested a potential alternative. Where the plaintiff suffers loss as a result of the State's failure to implement the Directive, he may claim damages against the State, provided that:

(a) the Directive involves rights conferred on individuals, and
(b) the content of those rights can be identified on the basis of the provisions of the Directive.

The scope of application of *Francovich* in the context of sex discrimination law is uncertain. It clearly applies where the State has failed, or failed adequately, to implement a Directive, and the Court has given judgment under Article 169 to this effect, as in *Francovich* itself. But its application to situations such as in *Duke* v *GEC Reliance Ltd*, where the State's 'failure' to implement the Directive had not been made explicit, and was only revealed following a judgment from the Court in Article 177 proceedings (in *Marshall*), is less clear. It is arguable whether the State should under such circumstances be retrospectively liable; a national court might take the view that liability in damages should only arise when the State has failed knowingly to fulfil its obligations in respect of Directives. (See further chapter 23.)

Principle of equal treatment in matters of social security
(Directive 79/7)

Directive 79/7, which implements the principle of equal treatment for men and women in matters of social security, became directly effective once the date for its implementation by member States had expired, on 23 December 1984 (see *Netherlands State* v *Federatie Nederlandse Vakbeweging* (case 71/85); *McDermott* v *Minister for Social Welfare* (case 286/85); *Clark* v *Chief Adjudication Officer* (case 384/85), Article 177 proceedings). No extension of time will be permitted for transitional arrangements (*Dik* v *College van Burgemeester en Wethouders* (case 80/87)). Since Directive 79/7 applies only to *statutory* social security schemes its effects must inevitably be vertical. Also, since Directive 79/7 merely implements the principle of equal treatment in the field of social security expressed in Directive 76/207 (Article 1(1)) there is, as *Burton* v *British Railways Board* (case 19/81) illustrates, some overlap between the two Directives.

Personal and material scope Directive 79/7 applies to the working population, defined broadly to include 'self-employed persons, workers and self-employed persons whose activity is interrupted by illness, accident or involuntary unemployment and persons seeking employment', and to 'retired or invalided workers and self-employed persons' (Article 2). In *Drake* v *Chief Adjudication Officer* (case 150/85), Article 177 proceedings, the Court held that the term 'working population' must be defined broadly, to include persons who have been working but whose work has been interrupted. Thus Mrs Drake, who had given up work to look after her invalid mother, was entitled to claim a right to equal treatment under Directive 79/7. Directive 79/7 may also be invoked by the spouse of a person falling within Article 2, provided that the benefit claimed is within the scope of the Directive; 'others too may have an interest in seeing the principle of non-discrimination respected on behalf of the person protected' (*Verholen* (cases C 87, 88 and 89/90)). However, Article 2 cannot be invoked by persons who have not been employed and are not seeking work, or by those who have worked but whose work has not been interrupted by one of the risks referred to in Article 3(1) (*Achterberg-te Riele and Others* v *Sociale Verzekeringsbank* (cases 48, 106, 107/88), Article 177 proceedings).

The principle of equal treatment under Directive 79/7 applies to:

(a)   statutory schemes providing protection against sickness, invalidity, old age, accidents at work or occupational diseases and unemployment; and

(b)   social assistance, in so far as it is intended to supplement or replace these schemes (Article 3(1)).

In an uncharacteristically restrictive interpretation the Court, contrary to Advocate-General Tesauro's recommendations, in *R* v *Secretary of State for Social Security, ex parte Smithson* (case C 243/90), denied the claimant's right to equality of treatment in respect of housing benefit under Directive 79/7 on the grounds that it was not within the scope of the Directive. Although eligibility for the benefit, and the amount of benefit, was ascertained, *inter alia*, by reference to a (discriminatory) invalidity pension, the benefit was not 'directly and effectively' linked to the protection provided against one of the risks specified in Article 3(1). The Court's attitude may be contrasted with its past cavalier attitude to the 'social assistance' exemption in Social Security Regulation 1408/71 (see chapter 21).

Survivors' benefits, and family benefits not granted by way of increases to the benefits covered by the Directive, are excluded (Article 3(2)). In *Drake* the Court held that the benefits covered by the Directive must constitute whole or part of a statutory scheme providing protection against one of the specified risks or a form of social assistance having the same objective. It appears that the statutory scheme must be one for workers in general, and not one, as in *Leifting* (case 23/83), relating to persons employed by the State. A contracted-out scheme operating as a substitute for the statutory scheme will be treated as an occupational pension scheme, within Directive 86/378 (*Newstead* v *Department of Transport* case 192/85)).

Provided that the benefit in question is covered by Directive 79/7 the fact that it may be payable under national legislation to a third party does not take it outside the scope of the Directive. Otherwise, as the Court pointed out in *Drake*, it would be possible, by making formal changes to existing benefits covered by the Directive, to remove them from its scope. On this reasoning Mrs Drake was held entitled herself to invoke Directive 79/7 in respect of an invalidity allowance payable on behalf of her mother.

Scope of the equal treatment principle   The principle of equal treatment means, according to Directive 79/7, Article 4(1), that:

there shall be no discrimination whatsoever on grounds of sex either directly, or indirectly by reference in particular to marital or family status, in particular as concerns:

— the scope of [social security] schemes and the conditions of access thereto,
— the obligation to contribute and the calculation of contributions,
— the calculation of benefits including increases due in respect of a spouse and for dependants,
and
— the conditions governing the duration and retention of entitlement to benefits.

Thus in *Drake* an invalidity allowance payable to a married man but not to a married woman was found in breach of Article 4(1). By contrast in *Teuling* (case 30/85) an invalidity benefit, the amount of which was determined by marital status and either the (low) income derived from the spouse's occupation or the existence of a dependent child, designed to compensate for the 'greater burden' borne by persons in these categories, was held to be compatible with Article 4(1). Although indirectly discriminatory against women, it was objectively justified (case followed by the Court of Appeal in *Blaik* v *Department of Health and Social Security* [1991] 1 CMLR 539; see also *Commission* v *Belgium* (case C 229/89) (1991) IRLR 393).

Supplementary benefits payable in respect of a spouse or persons deemed to be dependent on the claimant are payable under Article 4(1) irrespective of the sex of the claimant. This applies even if it results in double payment, for example, payment to both spouses in respect of the same dependants. In response to the Irish government's argument in *Cotter* v *Minister for Social Welfare* (case C 377/89) that this would result in unjust enrichment the Court held that a defence based on this principle would enable the authorities to use their own unlawful conduct as a ground for depriving Article 4(1) of the Directive of its full effect.

In *Ruzius-Wilbrink* (case 102/88) Article 177 proceedings, in a judgment with far-reaching consequences, the ECJ held that the principle of equal treatment expressed in Article 4(1) was capable of being applied to part-time workers. The claim concerned invalidity benefits provided under the Dutch social security system. Under the scheme the amount payable to part-timers was linked to the claimant's previous income; full-time workers, regardless of the size of their previous income, were entitled to a guaranteed 'minimum subsistence income'. The claimant, who had been a part-time worker, claimed that the system was indirectly discriminatory against women, since the part-time work force in the Netherlands contained a much smaller percentage of men than women. The Court held that in these circumstances the difference in treatment would breach Article 4(1) of Directive 79/7 unless it could be justified by objective factors unrelated to sex. The fact that it would be unfair, as was argued by the Netherlands Social Insurance Board, to grant part-time workers an allowance higher than the wages they had previously received in employment was held not to amount to objective justification, since in a substantial number of cases the amount granted to those entitled to a minimum subsistence income also was higher than their previous income. Moreover, Article 4(1) was sufficiently precise to be relied upon by a party in proceedings before a national court for the purpose of persuading that court to invalidate any provision of national law which infringed the said article.

The principle of equal treatment is 'without prejudice to the provisions relating to the protection of women on the grounds of maternity' (Article 4(2)). These provisions are likely to be interpreted according to the same principles as apply to Article 2(3) of Directive 76/207.

Article 7 expressly allows member States to exclude certain matters from the scope of the equal treatment principle. These are:

(a) the determination of pensionable age for the purposes of old-age and retirement pensions and possible consequences thereof for other benefits;

(b) benefits or entitlements granted to persons who have brought up children;

(c) wives' derived old-age or invalidity benefits, and

(d) increases granted in respect of dependent wives related to long-term invalidity, old-age, accidents at work and occupational disease benefits.

Article 7 must now be read in the light of the Court's case law under Directive 76/207, and in particular *Marshall* (case 152/84), *Roberts* (case 151/84) and *Beets-Proper* (case 262/84). The exemption for the determination of pensionable age will apply *only* for the purposes of old-age and retirement pensions and possible consequences thereof for other social security benefits. (For a recent and exemplary application of Article 7(1), see *Re Invalid Care Allowance* [1989] 3 CMLR 205 (EAT).) It is likely that the other exceptions will be equally narrowly construed. States are required under Article 7(2) periodically to examine matters excluded under Article 7(1) to ascertain whether they are still justified.

Principle of equal treatment in occupational pension schemes (Directive 86/378)

Directive 86/378, which is complementary to Directive 79/7, implements the equal treatment principle in the field of occupational, as opposed to statutory, pension schemes. The Directive is subject to a three-year implementation period, which expired on 31 July 1989 (Article 12). However, under Article 8 States are given until 1 January 1993 to take 'all necessary steps to ensure that the provisions of occupational [pension] schemes contrary to the principle of equal treatment are revised'. This implies that whilst States may be liable for failure to implement the Directive from 1 August 1989, the Directive will not be *fully* effective until January 1993. However, where the difference in treatment arises from the employer's contribution, direct or indirect, to the pension scheme, by way of consideration paid by the employer to the employee in respect of his employment, as in *Worringham* v *Lloyds Bank Ltd* (case 69/80), *Bilka-Kaufhaus GmbH* v *Weber von Harz* (case 170/84) and *Barber* (case 262/88), it may fall to be treated under Article 119 as 'pay'. Following *Bilka-Kaufhaus* such benefits can even be claimed by part-time workers where the discriminatory effects fall disproportionately on one sex, provided that the difference in treatment is not objectively justified. Where the matter falls within Article 119 any problems concerning the direct effects of the Directive will be avoided. Moreover, since Directive 86/378, like Directive 79/7, merely gives substance to the equal treatment principle expressed in Directive 76/207 (Article 1(1)), it may be invoked, as Directive 79/7 was invoked in *Burton* v *British Railways Board* (case 19/81), together with Directive 76/207, to demonstrate the scope of the equal treatment principle in the area of occupational pensions even before it becomes directly effective. This seems to have occurred in *Newstead* v *Department of Transport* (case 192/85).

With a few important exceptions Directive 86/378 is enacted in near-identical terms to Directive 79/7. It applies to occupational schemes 'not governed by Directive 79/7 whose purpose is to provide workers . . . with benefits intended to supplement the benefits provided by statutory social security schemes or to replace them' (Article 2). It applies to the same categories of persons (Article 3) in respect of the same risks (Article 4). Directive 86/378, however, contains no exclusions for survivors' and family benefits parallel to that of Article 3(2) of Directive 79/7, *provided* these benefits form part of the consideration paid by the employer by reason of the employee's employment (Article 4).

Article 6 gives a list of examples of provisions contrary to the equal treatment principle. Article 6(f) prohibits the fixing of different retirement ages for men and women, and Article 6(j) the laying down of different standards or standards applicable only to a specified sex. Article 6(h) prohibits the setting of different levels of benefit 'except in so far as it may be necessary to take account of actuarial calculation factors which differ according to sex in the case of benefits designated as contribution-defined'. Similarly although different levels of employee contribution are prohibited in principle (Article 6(i)) they *may* be set 'to take account of the different actuarial calculation factors' (Article 9(c)). Thus differences in treatment may be objectively justified. Different levels of employer contribution may also be permitted if they are set 'with a view to making the amount of [contribution-defined] benefits more equal' (Article 6(i)).

Article 9, like Article 7 of Directive 79/7, enables member States to exempt from the equal treatment principle the 'determination of pensionable age for the purposes of granting old-age or retirement pensions, and the possible implications for other benefits'. This provision was construed seemingly out of existence in *Barber* (case C 262/88): hence the Court's decision that its ruling on this issue should not be retrospective.

Article 9(b) provides that 'survivors' pensions which do not constitute consideration paid by the employer are exempt from the equal treatment principle until the date on which equality is achieved in statutory schemes, or at the latest, until equality is required by a Directive'. Following *Barber* such benefits, being paid by the employer as a result of the employment relationship, are likely to be construed as consideration and thus will not be exempt under Article 9(b). *Newstead* (case 192/85), which had decided otherwise, thereby excluding the employer's provision for survivors from the equality principle under Article 9(b), is unlikely to be followed. Survivors' pensions which do *not* constitute consideration paid by the employer are also exempt from the equal treatment principle *either* until the date on which equality is achieved in statutory schemes, *or*, at the latest, until equality is required by a Directive (Article 9(b)).

In *Newstead* v *Department of Transport* (case 192/85) a compulsory deduction under a civil service pension scheme from male, but not from female, employees, towards a widows' pension scheme, repaid with interest in the event of the employee leaving the civil service unmarried, was held to be exempt from the equal treatment principle, as a 'survivor's' pension. Thus a claim of discrimination by a 'confirmed bachelor' brought under Directive 76/207 failed: the matter fell within the 'social security' exception of Directive 76/207, (Article 1(2)).

Where the difference in treatment cannot be dealt with under Article 119 as 'pay' or under Directive 76/207, a claim to equal treatment under Directive 86/378 alone will not be possible until the Directive is fully effective, i.e., until 1 January 1993. Even after that date, as a Directive, it will not be horizontally effective (*Marshall* (case 152/84)). Nevertheless, following *Von Colson* and

Harz (cases 14 & 79/83), from that date domestic courts will be under a duty to construe domestic law to comply with the Directive.

Equal treatment in self-employment (Directive 86/613)

Directive 86/613 is designed to ensure the application of the equal treatment principle 'as between men and women engaged in an activity in a self-employed capacity, or contributing to the pursuit of such an activity, as regards those aspects not covered by Directives 76/207 and 79/7 (Article 1). It is thus essentially complementary to Directive 76/207.

The Directive applies to 'all persons pursuing a gainful activity for their own account . . . including farmers and members of the liberal professions' and to 'their spouses, not being employees or partners, where they habitually . . . participate in the activities of the self-employed worker and perform the same tasks or ancillary tasks' (Article 2).

The principle of equal treatment implies 'the absence of discrimination on the grounds of sex, either directly or indirectly, by reference in particular to marital or family status' (Article 3). This is without prejudice to measures concerning the protection of women during pregnancy and motherhood (preamble, ninth recital).

Under Article 4 member States are required to take all necessary measures to ensure the elimination of all provisions which are contrary to the principle of equal treatment as defined in Directive 76/207, especially in respect of the establishment, equipment or extension of a business or the launching or extension of any other form of self-employed activity including financial facilities.

Member States are also required: 'Without prejudice to the specific conditions for access to certain activities which apply equally to both sexes' to take the measures necessary to ensure that the conditions for the formation of a company between spouses are not more restrictive than the conditions for the formation of a company between unmarried persons (Article 5).

Where a contributory social security scheme exists for self-employed workers in a member State, the States must take the necessary measures to enable those spouses who participate in the activities of the self-employed worker, and who are not protected under the self-employed worker's social security scheme, to join a contributory social security scheme voluntarily (Article 6).

States are required to introduce 'such measures as are necessary to enable all persons who consider themselves wronged by failure to apply the principle of equal treatment in self-employed activities to pursue their claims by judicial process, possibly after recourse to other competent authorities' (Article 9).

Member States are required to bring into force the measures necessary to comply with the Directives by 30 June 1989. The date for compliance is extended to 30 June 1991 for states which have to amend their legislation on matrimonial rights and obligations in order to secure the principle of equal treatment in the formation of companies (Article 12). The Directive will become directly effective as against the State on the expiry of the applicable time-limit. Once the date for implementation has passed it may, and should, be invoked as an aid to interpretation against private parties (*Von Colson* and *Harz* (cases 14 & 79/83)).

Remedies

Article 6 of Directive 76/207 requires States to 'introduce into their national legal systems such measures as are necessary to enable all persons who consider themselves wronged by failure to apply the principle of equal treatment . . . to pursue their claims by judicial process after possible recourse to other competent authorities'.

In *Von Colson* v *Land Nordrhein-Westfalen* (case 14/83) and *Harz* v *Deutsche Tradax GmbH* (case 79/83) the Court held that Article 6 imposes a duty on national courts to provide remedies which ensure 'real and effective' protection for individuals' community rights. Problems have arisen as to what constitutes effective protection in this sphere. Following the Court of Justice's ruling in *Marshall* (case 152/84), the Southampton Industrial Tribunal, relying on *Von Colson*, decided that the damages awarded under the Sex Discrimination Act 1975, which at the time were limited to £6,250, were ineffective to compensate for the losses suffered by Mrs Marshall as a result of her discriminatory treatment, and awarded a sum of £19,405. This sum included £7,710 in respect of interest. The employers made an *ex gratia* payment of the capital sum awarded above the statutory limit but challenged the award of interest. Their appeal succeeded before the Employment Appeal Tribunal (*Marshall* v *Southampton & South West Hampshire Health Authority (Teaching) (No. 2)* [1990] ICR 6). Mrs Marshall appealed to the Court of Appeal [1991] ICR 136). Although only concerned with the award of interest, that court considered the question of the statutory limits. Were those limits applicable, Mrs Marshall would already have received a capital sum far in excess of the limit. Thus the question of whether she was entitled to interest would be superfluous.

The Court of Appeal acknowledged its obligation under Article 6 of Directive 76/207 to secure an effective remedy. It even suggested that the damages to which she would be entitled under British law might not constitute an effective remedy. But it found, by a 2–1 majority, that the Directive did not include any unconditional and sufficiently precise obligations as regards sanctions for discrimination. In these circumstances the statutory limits must apply. Following an appeal to the House of Lords, a number of questions on the scope of Community law as regards damages in this context have now been referred to the Court of Justice.

It is submitted that the Court of Appeal was correct in its analysis. If a particular level of damages is to be provided, and applied uniformly throughout all member States, it must be determined precisely as a matter of EEC law. It is unlikely that this can be done by the Court in Article 177 proceedings. (For further discussion of remedies see chapter 23.)

Further reading

Arnull, A., 'Article 119 and the principle of Equal Pay for work of Equal Value' (1986) 11 RL Rev 200.

Curtin, D., 'Effective Sanctions and the Equal Treatment Directive; the *Von Colson* and *Harz* cases' (1985) 22 CML Rev 505.

Curtin, D., 'Scalping the Community Legislator: Occupational Pensions and *Barber*' (1990) 27 CML Rev 475.

Docksey, C., 'The Principle of Equality between Men and Women: a Fundamental Right under Community Law' (1991) 20 ILJ 258.

Docksey, C., and Fitzpatrick, B., 'The Duty of National Courts to Interpret Provisions of National Law in Accordance with Community Law' (1991) 20 ILJ 113.

Hepple, R., 'Enforcing EEC Social Rights' (1989) 18 ILJ 197.

Hervey, T., 'Justification for Indirect Sex Discrimination in Employment: European Community and United Kingdom Law Compared' (1991) 40 ICLQ 807.

Prechel, S., 'Remedies after *Marshall*' (1990) 21 CML Rev 451.

Shaw, J., 'European Community Judicial Method: its Application to Sex Discrimination Law' (1990) 19 ILJ 228.

Steiner, J., 'Sex Discrimination under UK and EEC law; Two plus four equals One' (1983) 32 ICLQ 399.

Szyszczak, E., 'Pay Inequalities and Equal Value Claims' (1985) 48 MLR 139.

Wyatt, D., 'Enforcing EEC Social Rights in the UK' (1989) ILJ 197.

PART THREE

Remedies and enforcement
of EEC law

TWENTY THREE
Introduction

The foregoing chapters, which by no means cover the whole range of Community law, should be sufficient to illustrate the extent to which EEC law now permeates our lives. In addition to the law stemming from the Treaty, a wealth of secondary legislation has been, and is in the constant process of being, enacted, covering a wide and ever-increasing range of activities. Much of this law is directly effective (see chapter 2), and will, under the principle of primacy of EEC law (see chapter 3), take precedence over any conflicting rules of national law. It thus forms an important source of *rights* and *obligations* for both States and individuals.

An effective system of enforcement requires that the rights arising under EEC law may be enforced against three groups of people:

(a)   *The institutions of the Community,* who in their law-making or administrative capacity may have acted or failed to act in breach of EEC law.

(b)   *Member States,* which in carrying out or failing to carry out their obligations under the Treaty or secondary legislation may have acted in breach of EEC law.

(c)   *Individuals,* who in failing to comply with their obligations under the Treaty or secondary legislation may have acted in breach of EEC law.

The EEC Treaty itself provides an extensive range of remedies. It provides, by way of *direct* action before the European Courts, for actions against the institutions of the Community and against member States.

Actions against the institutions of the Community comprise:

(a)   Actions for judicial review, in the form of actions to 'review the legality of acts of the Council and the Commission other than recommendations or opinions' (Article 173, the 'annulment action', and Article 184, the 'plea of illegality'), and an action for 'failure to act' (Article 175),

(b)   Actions for damages (Articles 178 and 215(2)), and

(c)   Actions in respect of disputes between the Community and its servants ('staff cases' (Article 179)).

Certain actions under (a) and (c) above (competition and staff cases), will now be dealt with by the Court of First Instance (CFI).

Actions against member States comprise:

(a)   Action by the Commission against a member State for failure 'to fulfil an obligation under this Treaty' (Article 169).
(b)   Action by a member State against another member State for failure 'to fulfil an obligation under this Treaty' (Article 170).
(c)   Action by the Commission against a member State, via accelerated procedures similar to those provided under Article 169, for breach of its obligation to notify the Commission under Article 93(2)(b) (State aids) and Article 100A(4) (unilateral restrictions on free movement of goods).
(d)   Similar accelerated proceedings brought by the Commission under Article 225 where emergency measures taken by member States under Articles 203 (to protect essential security interests) and 204 (in the event of serious internal disturbances) distort conditions of competition within the Community.

The Courts have power to order 'any necessary interim measures' in any of the above proceedings (Article 186 EEC, Articles 83, 84 Rules of Procedure). Interim measures may not be ordered 'unless there are circumstances giving rise to urgency and factual and legal grounds establishing a prima facie case for the measures applied for' (Article 83(2) Rules of Procedure). The urgency of the application will be assessed according to the necessity for such an order in order to prevent serious and irreparable damage. Moreover, the interim measures requested must be of such a nature as to prevent the alleged damage (*Commission* v *United Kingdom (Re Merchant Shipping Rules)* (case 246/89R)). In such proceedings relief can be very speedy. In *Commission* v *Ireland (Re Dundalk Water Scheme)* (case 45/87R) an interim injunction was granted *ex parte* within three days of application.

There is no provision in the EEC Treaty for direct action before the Court of Justice against individuals. Individuals may however be vulnerable to fines and penalties under EEC secondary legislation (e.g. Regulation 17/62, see chapter 15), which may be challenged before the CFI. Under Article 172 the Court of Justice has unlimited jurisdiction in regard to the penalties provided in such Regulations.

In addition to these direct remedies before the European Court(s) questions of infringement of EEC law by Community institutions and member States may also be raised before national courts. In describing Regulations as 'directly applicable' (Article 189) and in providing a means whereby national courts might refer questions of interpretation and validity of EEC law to the Court of Justice (Article 177) the Treaty clearly envisaged a role for national courts in the enforcement of EEC law. This role has been greatly enlarged by the development by the Court of Justice of the principle of direct effects.

This alternative route via national courts is of particular importance for individuals, since they have no *locus standi* to bring a direct action before the Court of Justice in respect of infringements of EEC law by member States, nor any power to compel the Commission to bring such an action (see *Alfons Lütticke GmbH* v *Commission* (case 48/65), Article 173, 175 proceedings; chapters 27 and 28), and their *locus standi* in direct actions against the institutions for judicial review is limited. Moreover, national courts remain the only fora in which action can be brought *by* individuals in respect of infringements of EEC law *against* individuals.

Although matters of EEC law may not be raised *directly* before national courts, they may, if directly effective, be raised *indirectly* before any national court or tribunal, in the context of any proceedings of national law, public or private, in which they are relevant, in pursuit of any remedy available under national law. The Court of Justice has held that 'every type of action provided for by national law must be available for the purpose of ensuring observance of Community provisions having direct effect' (*Rewe* v *Hauptzollampt Kiel* (case 158/80)), and that the remedies and sanctions provided for breach of Community law must be 'such as to guarantee full and effective protection' for individuals' Community rights (*Harz* v *Deutsche Tradax* (case 79/83)). Thus EEC law may be invoked as a defence to a criminal charge (e.g., *Ratti* (case 148/78)) or to resist payment of a charge exacted, or support a claim for the return of money withheld, in breach of EEC law (e.g., *Van Gend en Loos* (case 26/62)). It may provide a basis for an injunction, to prevent or put an end to action in breach of EEC law (e.g., *Garden Cottage Foods Ltd* v *Milk Marketing Board* [1982] QB 1114, Court of Appeal; [1984] AC 130, House of Lords) or a declaration, e.g., that a particular national measure is illegal, being based on an invalid EEC Regulation (e.g., *Royal Scholten-Honig* v *Intervention Board for Agricultural Produce* (cases 103 & 145/77). Damages may be obtained in lieu of an injunction (*Garden Cottage Foods Ltd* (H.L.)), and, if the breach of EEC law can be proved to constitute a tort, it may give rise to a claim for unliquidated damages (*Bourgoin SA* v *Ministry of Agriculture, Fisheries and Food* [1986] QB 716, Court of Appeal; cf. *An Bord Bainne Co-operative Ltd* v *Milk Marketing Board* (1987) *Independent,* 19 November 1987, Court of Appeal). In this way acts of member States or of Community institutions which are illegal under EEC law may be challenged, and remedies provided. Whilst the illegal acts are not set aside as a result of the action, they cannot be enforced.

In order to assist national courts in their task of enforcing EEC law, Article 177 gives the Court of Justice jurisdiction to give preliminary rulings concerning the interpretation of EEC law and the validity of acts of the institutions of the Community at the request of national courts. Although the Court of Justice has no power to *decide* the issue before the national court, an interpretation on the matter of Community law involved, or on the validity of the act in question, will normally be sufficient to establish whether an infringement of EEC law has occurred. On this basis the national court may then supply the appropriate remedy.

Although EEC law does not itself prescribe specific remedies and procedures to be adopted by national courts in respect of directly effective Community rights the need to ensure 'effective' protection for individuals seeking to enforce those rights has led the Court of Justice to require domestic courts to modify national law in these respects. In *R* v *Secretary of State for Transport, ex parte Factortame Ltd (No. 2)* (case C 213/89) the Court held that English courts were obliged to provide interim injunctions against the Crown where there was no other means of protecting individuals' Community rights, even though, as the House of Lords had found in that case ([1990] 2 AC 85) no such remedy was available as a matter of national law. In *Emmott* v *Minister for Social Welfare* (case C 208/90) the Court required national limitation rules to be modified in the context of directly effective Directives. It pointed out that where a Directive has not been fully transposed into domestic law an individual may not be aware of his right to invoke it directly, direct effects being available only in 'specific circumstances', as a 'minimum guarantee'. As long as the law is in a state of uncertainty individuals are unable to ascertain the full extent of their rights. Therefore, whilst the right to claim under a Directive may vest as soon as it becomes directly effective, that is, any time after the expiry of the implementation period, time for limitation purposes will not begin to run until the Directive has been fully transposed into domestic law.

In the absence of Community-wide provision it is likely that further modifications to the national laws of member States may be necessary to guarantee effective protection for individuals' Community rights. In exercising its discretion to grant interim relief under s. 37 of the Supreme Court Act 1981 in *R* v *Secretary of State for Transport, ex parte Factortame Ltd* [1991] 1 AC 603 the House of Lords had the benefit of an interim decision from the Court of Justice (*Commission* v *United Kingdom (Re Merchant Shipping Rules)* (case 246/89R)) and two decisions of that Court on the substance of some of the relevant provisions of the Merchant Shipping Act 1988 (*R* v *Ministry of Agriculture Fisheries & Food, ex parte Agegate Ltd* (case C 3/87); *R* v *Ministry of Agriculture, Fisheries & Food, ex parte Jaderow Ltd* (case C 216/87). Meanwhile, the relevant provisions of the Merchant Shipping Act 1988 had been amended (SI 1988 No. 2006). From these developments it appeared that the applicants' challenge appeared to be 'prima facie a strong one'. Since the House was of the view that no cross-undertaking in damages could be imposed on either party the matter fell to be decided on the balance of convenience. Their lordships concluded that the damage to the public interest in suspending the legislation was not sufficient to outweigh the damage which would be caused to the applicants if no interim relief were granted, and an interim order was made. The Court of Justice has since found that the relevant residence and domicile provisions of the Merchant Shipping Act 1988 were in fact in breach of EEC law (case C 221/89). Thus the plaintiffs' claim was vindicated.

It may be doubted whether the applicants' rights would have been effectively protected had their case appeared less strong, and the House of Lords refused to order interim relief, since it had taken for granted that no cross-undertaking in damages could be required of the Crown. Had this been the case the applicants would have suffered irreparable loss as a result of an infringement of their Community rights, without compensation.

It was this reasoning which persuaded the English Court of Appeal, in *Kirklees Metropolitan Borough Council* v *Wickes Building Supplies Ltd* [1991]

3 WLR 985, to require the local authority, which was seeking an interim injunction to restrain the defendant retailers from trading on Sunday, in breach of s. 47 of the Shops Act 1950, the provisions of which the defendants claimed were in breach of Article 30 of the EEC Treaty, to provide a cross-undertaking in damages as a condition for the award of the injunction. The decision has now been reversed by the House of Lords.

Another question, which arose in *Marshall* v *Southampton & South West Hampshire Health Authority (Teaching) (No. 2)* [1991] ICR 136 is whether the imposition of statutory limits on damages, as provided for example under the Sex Discrimination Act 1975 and other British employment protection legislation, is contrary to the requirement of 'effective' protection for individuals' Community rights. The Court of Appeal in *Marshall* [1991] ICR 136 considered that it might be so, but that Community law, in this case Directive 76/207 on the Equal Treatment of Men and Women, was not sufficiently clear and precise to give rise to a *specific* remedy. These questions have now been referred to the Court of Justice by the House of Lords (see chapter 22).

A significant, perhaps historic development in the area of remedies occurred in *Francovich* v *Italian State* (cases C 6 and 9/90). Here the Court held that even where EEC law is not directly effective an individual may claim damages *against the State* where he has suffered loss as a result of the non-implementation of a Directive, provided that the Directive involves identifiable rights conferred upon him. However, the scope of *Francovich* is uncertain. It clearly applies in cases of non-implementation, and where the State's failure has been established by the Court of Justice under Article 169 and the State has failed to comply with the Court's judgment. Whether it applies to faulty or inadequate implementation of Directives, particularly where the State's failure is inadvertent, is in doubt (see further, chapters 2 and 22). There are problems too over the question of damages. In *Francovich* the Court held that liability must be assessed on the basis of national law. But it is not clear, where damages are concerned, which English law principles are applicable. A claim, based on *Francovich*, for damages against the State is *sui generis*. If, as is submitted, the nearest English equivalent is the tort of misfeasance in public office, requiring a knowing or intentional failure on the part of the State (see *Bourgoin SA* v *Ministry of Agriculture, Fisheries & Food* [1986] QB 716 (CA)), would this be sufficient to protect an individual's Community rights? If it is an action for breach of statutory duty, might not this, as a rule of strict liability, impose too onerous a burden on the State, especially since the damage suffered will often be purely economic? Furthermore, the principles governing State liability, including those concerning causation and remoteness, vary significantly from State to State. Thus, if *Francovich* is to be fairly and uniformly applied throughout the Community, arguably its application should be subject to common Community rules.

Whatever the answer to these questions, *Francovich* has undoubtedly enhanced the useful effect of Directives: indeed it could be extended to provide damages for losses due to other 'failures' of the State where those failures result in a loss of rights conferred on individuals by Community law. Some EEC legislation already provides for the award of damages against public bodies (e.g., Public Procurement Remedies Directive 89/665). The House of Lords in *Kirklees BC* v *Wickes* (*Independent*, 26 June 1992) decided that in view of the State's interest in securing the enforcement of domestic law by local authorities, such authorities should not be required to give a cross undertaking in damages as a condition for the granting of an interim injunction; if national law ultimately proved to be inconsistent with Community law the appropriate remedy for those suffering loss as a result of the injunction would be against the State. The implications of this important decision, apparently based on *Francovich*, have yet to be explored.

All these developments, together with the Heads of States' agreement at Maastricht to permit the imposition of fines on States which fail to comply with the Court's judgments under Article 169, indicate that the question of *States'* liability for breach of Community law is likely to be a major area of judicial concern in the 1990s.

Further reading

Barav, A., 'The Enforcement of Community Rights in the National Courts: the Case for Jurisdiction to Grant Interim Relief' (1989) 26 CML Rev 369.
Bebr, G., Casenote on *Francovich* (1992) 29 CML Rev 557.
Bridge, D., 'Procedural Aspects of the Enforcement of EEC Law through the Legal Systems of the Member States' (1985) 10 EL Rev 28.
Gravells, N., 'Disapplying an Act of Parliament; Constitutional Enormity or Community Law Right?' [1989] PL 568.
Oliver, P., 'Enforcing Community Rights in English Courts' (1987) 50 MLR 881.
Steiner, J., 'How to make the Action fit the Case; domestic remedies for breach of EEC Law' (1987) 12 EL Rev 102.
Wyatt, D., 'Enforcing EEC Social Rights in the UK' (1989) 18 ILJ 191.

TWENTY FOUR

The preliminary rulings procedure (Article 177)

Introduction

A glance through the preceding chapters of this book will reveal that the majority of cases cited, and almost all the major principles established by the Court of Justice, were decided in the context of a reference to that court for a preliminary ruling under Article 177. Cases such as *Van Gend en Loos* (case 26/62), *Costa v ENEL* (case 6/64) and *Defrenne v Sabena (No. 2)* (case 43/75), concerned with questions of interpretation of EEC law, enabled the Court of Justice to develop the crucial concepts of direct effects and the supremacy of EEC law. *Internationale Handelsgesellschaft mbH* (case 11/70); *Stauder v City of Ulm* (case 29/69) and *Royal Scholten-Honig (Holdings) Ltd* (cases 103 & 145/77) (see chapters 4 and 26), which raised questions of the validity of EEC law, led the way to the incorporation of general principles of law into EEC law. In all areas of EEC law, the Article 177 procedure has played a major role in developing the substantive law. Staff cases apart (the Court of Justice has jurisdiction under Article 179 to decide disputes between the Community and its servants), the procedure accounts for 40% to 50% of all cases heard by the Court of Justice. It thus plays a central part in the development and enforcement of EEC law.

If the procedure has been valuable from the point of view of the Community, as a means of developing and clarifying the law, it has been equally valuable to the individual, since it has provided him with a means of access to the Court of Justice when other, direct avenues have been closed. In this way he has been able indirectly to challenge action by member States (e.g., *Van Gend en Loos* — import charge levied in breach of Article 12) or by Community institutions (e.g., *Royal Scholten-Honig* — EEC Regulation invalid for breach of principle of equality) before the Court of Justice and obtain an appropriate remedy from his national court.

The importance of the Article 177 procedure, both in absolute terms and relative to other remedies, has been greatly increased by the development by the Court of Justice of the concept of direct effects. Where originally only 'directly applicable' Regulations might have been expected to be invoked before national courts, these courts may now be required to apply Treaty Articles, Decisions and even Directives. As a result, national courts now play a major role in the enforcement of EEC law.

Although the Article 177 procedure has assumed such an importance in the ways outlined above, its primary and original purpose was to ensure, by means of authoritative rulings on the interpretation and validity of EEC law, the correct and uniform application of EEC law by the courts of member States. In assessing its effectiveness, and the attitudes of national courts and the Court of Justice towards its use, this function, as well as its importance both for individuals and for the Community, should be borne in mind.

The procedure

Article 177 provides that:

The Court of Justice shall have jurisdiction to give preliminary rulings concerning:

(a) the interpretation of this Treaty;
(b) the validity and interpretation of acts of the institutions of the Community;
(c) the interpretation of the statutes of bodies established by an act of the Council, where those statutes so provide.

Where such a question is raised before any court or tribunal of a member State, that court or tribunal may, if it considers that a decision on the question is necessary to enable it to give judgment, request the Court of Justice to give a ruling thereon.

Where any such question is raised in a case pending before a court or tribunal of a member State, against whose decisions there is no judicial remedy under national law, that court or tribunal shall bring the matter before the Court of Justice.

The Article 177 procedure is not an appeals procedure. It merely provides a means whereby national courts, when questions of EEC law arise, may apply to the Court of Justice for a preliminary ruling on matters of interpretation or validity prior to themselves applying the law. It is an example of shared jurisdiction, depending for its success on mutual cooperation. As Advocate-

General Lagrange said in *De Geus en Uitdenbogerd* v *Robert Bosch GmbH* (case 13/61), the first case to reach the Court on an application under Article 177:

> Applied judiciously — one is tempted to say loyally — the provisions of Article 177 must lead to a real and fruitful collaboration between the municipal courts and the Court of Justice of the Communities with mutual regard for their respective jurisdiction.

In order to assess how this collaboration operates, in principle and in practice, it is necessary to examine the procedure from the point of view of: (a) the Court of Justice, and (b) national courts.

Jurisdiction of the Court of Justice

The jurisdiction of the Court of Justice is twofold. It has jurisdiction to give preliminary rulings concerning:

(a) interpretation, and
(b) validity.

Interpretation   In its interpretative role, the Court may rule on the interpretation of the Treaty, of acts of the institutions, and of statutes of bodies established by an act of the Council, where those statutes so provide. Its jurisdiction with regard to interpretation is thus very wide. 'Interpretation of the Treaty' includes the EEC Treaty and all treaties amending or supplementing it. 'Acts of the institutions' covers not only binding acts in the form of Regulations, Directives and Decisions, but even non-binding acts such as Recommendations and Opinions, since they may be relevant to the interpretation of domestic implementing measures. On the same reasoning the Court has held that an act need not be directly effective to be subject to interpretation under Article 177 (*Mazzalai* (case 111/75)). The Court has also given rulings on the interpretation of international treaties entered into by the Community, on the basis that these constitute 'acts of the institutions' (see *R. & V. Haegeman Sprl* v *Belgian State* (case 181/73)). However, it has held in the context of a claim based on the Statute of the European School that it has no jurisdiction to rule on agreements which, although linked with the Community and to the functioning of its institutions, have been set up by agreement *between member States* and not on the basis of the Treaty or EEC secondary legislation (*Hurd* v *Jones* (case 44/84), Article 177 proceedings — headmaster of European School unable to invoke Statute against HM Tax Inspectorate).

Validity   Here the Court's jurisdiction is confined to acts of the institutions. It has been suggested, by extension of the reasoning in *R. & V. Haegeman Sprl* v *Belgian State,* that 'acts of the institutions' would include international agreements entered into by the Community. Here, however, the ruling would be binding only on the Community members; it would be ineffective against third-party signatories.

Limitations on the Court's jurisdiction

Matters of Community law   The Court is only empowered to give rulings on matters of Community law. It has no jurisdiction to interpret domestic law nor to pass judgment on the compatibility of domestic law with EEC law. The Court has frequently been asked such questions (e.g., *Van Gend en Loos* (case 26/62); *Costa* v *ENEL* (case 6/64)), since it is often the central problem before the national court. But as the Court said in *Costa* v *ENEL:* '. . . a decision should be given by the Court not upon the validity of an Italian law in relation to the Treaty, but only upon the interpretation of the above-mentioned [Treaty] Articles in the context of the points of law stated by the Giudice Conciliatore'. Where the Court is asked to rule on such a matter it will merely reformulate the question and return an abstract interpretation on the point of EEC law involved.

Interpretation, not application   The Court maintains a similarly strict dividing line between interpretation and application. It will not advise national courts on the application of EEC law. Again, if asked a question relating to application (and this too is often a problem for national courts) it will rephrase the question and return an abstract ruling in the form which it considers will best assist the national judge.

Non-interference   The Court maintains a strict policy of non-interference over matters of what to refer, when to refer and how to refer. Such matters are left entirely to the discretion of the national judge. As the Court said in *De Geus en Uitdenbogerd* v *Robert Bosch GmbH* (case 13/61), its jurisdiction depends 'solely on the existence of a request from the national court'. However, the Court has held that it has no jurisdiction to give a ruling when, at the time when it is made, the procedure before the court making it has already been terminated (*Pardini* (case 338/85); *Grogan* (case C 159/90)).

No formal requirements are imposed on the framing of the questions. Where the questions are inappropriately phrased the Court will merely reformulate the questions, answering what it sees as the relevant issues. Nor will it question the timing of a reference. However, since 'it is necessary for the national court to define the legal context in which the interpretation requested should be placed, the Court has suggested that it might be convenient for the facts of the case to be established and for questions of purely national law to be settled at the time when the reference is made, in order to enable the Court to take cognisance of all the features of fact and law which may be relevant to the interpretation of Community law which it is called upon to give (*Irish Creamery Milk Suppliers Association* v *Ireland* (cases 36 & 71/80), Article 177 proceedings; approved in *Pretore di Salo* (case 14/86), Article 177 proceedings). The Court will not, however, reject a request for failure to supply such details.

The above limitations of the Court's jurisdiction are more apparent than real. The line between matters of Community law and matters of national law, between interpretation and application are more easily drawn in theory than in practice. An interpretation of EEC law may leave little room for doubt as to the legality of a national law and little choice to the national judge in matters of application if he is to comply with his duty to give priority to EEC law. Similarly in rephrasing and regrouping the questions the Court is able to select the issues which it regards as significant, without apparently interfering with the discretion of the national judge. Sometimes, where an important point of principle is concerned the Court may come close to overstepping the line (e.g., *Johnston* v *Chief Constable of the Royal Ulster Constabulary* (case 222/84) — Certificate from Secretary of State deemed inadequate judicial control, see chapter 4). Thus beneath its guise of passive cooperation the Court is highly activist.

This activism, no doubt necessary in the early years of the Community, has not gone without criticism, as inviting 'rebellion' and even 'defiance' on the part of national courts (see Rasmussen, noted chapter 1). Whether in response to such criticism, or merely as a result of the more dynamic role played by the Commission and the Council since the passing of the Single European Act, recent decisions of the Court, particularly in Article 177 proceedings, have been decidely 'low-key', tending merely to confirm established principles whilst stressing national courts' role in *applying* Community law. There are, however, some notable exceptions, particularly in the field of sex discrimination (e.g., *Rinner-Kühn* (case 171/88); *Barber* v *Guardian Royal Exchange Assurance Group* (case C 262/88), chapter 22).

With few exceptions, the Court has striven to maintain an open door. One exception to this policy occurred in the cases of *Foglia* v *Novello (No. 1)* (case 104/79) and *Foglia* v *Novello (No. 2)* (case 244/80). Here for the first time the Court refused its jurisdiction to give a ruling in both a first and a second application in the same case. The questions, which were referred by an Italian judge, concerned the legality under EEC law of an import duty imposed by the French on the import of wine from Italy. It arose in the context of litigation between two Italian parties. Foglia, a wine producer, had agreed to sell wine to Mrs Novello, an exporter. In making their contract the parties agreed that Foglia should not bear the cost of any duties levied by the French in breach of EEC law. When duties were charged and eventually paid by Foglia, he sought to recover the money from Mrs Novello. In his action before the Italian court for recovery of the money that court sought a preliminary ruling on the legality under EEC law of the duties imposed by the French. The Court of Justice refused its jurisdiction. The proceedings, it claimed, had been artificially created in order to question the legality of the French law; they were not 'genuine'.

The parties were no more successful the second time. In a somewhat peremptory judgment the Court declared that the function of Article 177 was to contribute to the administration of justice in the member States; not to give advisory opinions on general or hypothetical questions.

The Court of Justice's decision has been criticised. Although the proceedings were to some extent artificial, in that the duty should ideally have been challenged at source, by the party from whom it was levied, the Italian judge called upon to decide the case was faced with a genuine problem, central to which was the issue of EEC law. If, in his discretion, he sought guidance from the Court of Justice in this matter, surely it was not for that Court to deny it.

It has been suggested that the importance of this decision should not be exaggerated. No doubt political considerations and national (wine) rivalries played their part (the Court 'must display special vigilance when . . . a question is referred to it with a view to permitting the national court to decide whether the legislation of another member State is in accordance with Community law': *Foglia* v *Novello (No. 2)*). Perhaps too, conscious of its increasing workload, the Court opted for this decision *'pour décourager les autres'*. If so, it would appear to have been successful, since a similar situation has not so far recurred. In *Dzodzi* v *Belgium* (cases C 297/88 and C 197/89) the Court was prepared to provide a ruling on the interpretation of EEC social security law in a purely 'internal' matter, for the purpose of clarifying provisions of Belgian law invoked by a *Togolese national*. The Court held that it was 'exclusively for national courts which were dealing with a case to assess, with regard to the specific features of each case, both the need for a preliminary ruling in order to enable it to give judgment, and the relevance of the question'.

Jurisdiction of national courts

Jurisdiction to refer to the Court of Justice under Article 177 is conferred on 'any court or tribunal'. With one exception (*Nordsee Deutsche Hochseefischerei GmbH* (case 102/81) to be discussed below), this has been interpreted in the widest sense. In *Pretore di Salo* v *X* (case 14/86), the Court of Justice held that this applied to any court acting in the general context of a duty to act, independently and in accordance with the law, upon cases in which the law has conferred jurisdiction upon it.

Thus the name of the body is irrelevant. Provided it performs a judicial function, i.e., has power to give binding determinations of the legal rights and obligations of individuals, it will be a court or tribunal within Article 177. Whether a particular body qualifies as a court or tribunal within Article 177 is a matter of *Community* law.

In *Broekmeulen* (case 246/80), Article 177 proceedings, the Court was faced with a reference from the appeal committee of the Dutch professional medical body. The plaintiff in the case, Mr Broekmeulen, was appealing against the Dutch GP's registration committee's refusal to register him as a GP. His appeal was based on EEC law. One of the questions referred was whether the appeal committee was a 'court or tribunal' within Article 177. The Court held that it was

. . . in the practical absence of an effective means of redress before the ordinary courts, in a matter concerning the application of Community law, the appeal committee, which performs its duties with the approval of the public authorities and operates with their assistance, and whose decisions are accepted following contentious proceedings and are in fact recognised as final, must be deemed to be a court of a member State for the purpose of Article 177.

It was imperative to ensure the proper functioning of Community law that the Court of Justice should have the opportunity of ruling on issues of interpretation and validity.

The Court did not take such a generous view in *Nordsee Deutsche Hochseefischerei GmbH* (case 102/81), Article 177 proceedings. The case arose from a joint shipbuilding project which involved the pooling of EC aid. The parties agreed that in the event of a dispute they would refer their differences to an independent arbitrator. Their agreement excluded the possibility of recourse to the ordinary courts. They fell into disagreement and a number of questions involving the interpretation of certain EC Regulations were raised before the arbitrator. He sought a ruling from the Court of Justice as to, *inter alia,* whether he was a 'court or tribunal' within the meaning of Article 177. The Court held that he was not. The question, the Court held, depends on the nature of the arbitration. Here the public authorities of member States were not involved in the decision to opt for arbitration, nor were they called upon to intervene automatically before the arbitrator. If questions of Community law were raised before such a body, the ordinary courts might be called upon to give them assistance, or to review the decision; it would be for *them* to refer questions of interpretation or validity of Community law to the Court of Justice.

The Court's decision ignored the fact that in this case recourse to the courts was excluded, and the arbitrator was thus required to interpret a difficult point of Community law, of central importance in the proceedings, unaided.

Since in *Nordsee Deutsche Hochseefischerei GmbH* there was no effective means of redress before the ordinary courts and the decisions of the arbitrator were accepted following contentious proceedings and recognised as final it seems that the only factor distinguishing it from *Broekmeulen* was the element of *public* participation or control. This, it seems, will be essential.

It is likely that the decision in *Nordsee Deutsche Hochseefischerei GmbH* (as in *Foglia* v *Novello (No. 1)* (case 104/79)), was dictated to some extent by a fear of the floodgates. Whilst the Court of Justice was anxious in the early days of the Community to encourage referrals under Article 177, its very success in this respect has led to an ever-increasing work-load (delays in obtaining preliminary rulings have tripled, and now take an average of 18 months to two years) resulting in some attempts by the Court to shift some of the load on to national courts. Whilst there is much to be said for encouraging national courts, now more experienced in the application of EEC law, to decide matters for themselves, there is no justification for a position whereby access to the Court of Justice is totally excluded. It is regrettable that the arbitrator in *Nordsee Deutsche Hochseefischerei GmbH* did not ask the Court whether the position would be the same if recourse to the ordinary courts had been excluded.

Whilst any court or tribunal may refer questions to the Court of Justice under Article 177, a distinction must be drawn between those courts or tribunals which have a discretion to refer ('permissive' jurisdiction) and those for which referral is mandatory ('mandatory' jurisdiction). Under Article 177(3), where a question concerning interpretation is raised 'in a case pending before a court or tribunal of a member State, *against whose decisions there is no judicial remedy under national law*, that court or tribunal *shall* bring the matter before the Court of Justice' (emphasis added). For all courts other than those within Article 177(3) referral is discretionary.

The purpose of Article 177(3) must be seen in the light of the function of Article 177 as a whole, which is to prevent a body of national case law not in accordance with the rules of Community law from coming into existence in any member State (*Hoffman-La Roche AG* v *Centrafarm Vertiebsgesellschaft Pharmazeutischer Erzeugnisse mbH* (case 107/76)). To this end Article 177(3) seeks to ensure that, when matters of EEC law arise, there is an obligation to refer to the Court of Justice at some stage in the proceedings. This purpose should be kept in mind when questions of interpretation of Article 177(3) arise.

The scope of Article 177(3) is not entirely clear. Whilst it clearly applies to courts or tribunals whose decisions are *never* subject to appeal (the 'abstract theory'), such as the House of Lords in England, or the Conseil d'Etat in France, it is less clear whether it applies also to courts whose decisions *in the case in question* are not subject to appeal (the 'concrete theory'), such as the Italian magistrates' court (*guidice conciliatore*) in *Costa* v *ENEL* (case 6/64) (no right of appeal because sum of money involved too small). And when leave to appeal from the Court of Appeal (or, in certain criminal matters, from the High Court) to the House of Lords is refused, or when the High Court refuses leave for judicial review from a tribunal decision, do these courts become courts 'against whose decisions there is no judicial remedy under national law'?

Lord Denning MR in *H. P. Bulmer Ltd* v *J. Bollinger SA* [1974] Ch 401, Court of Appeal, appeared to espouse the narrower 'abstract' theory when he said '. . . short of the House of Lords, no other English court is bound to refer a question to the European Court at Luxembourg'. Stephenson and Stamp LJJ expressly withheld comment on this point. In *Re a Holiday in Italy* [1975] 1 CMLR 184 the National Insurance Commissioner followed Lord Denning and refused to refer in the context of an application for judicial review.

The judgment of the Court of Justice in *Costa* v *ENEL* appears, albeit *obiter*, to support the wider, 'concrete' theory. In that case, in the context of a reference from the Italian magistrates' court, from which there was no appeal due to the small amount of money involved, the Court said, with reference to Article 177(3): 'By the terms of this Article . . . national courts against whose decisions, *as in the present case*, there is no judicial remedy, *must* refer the matter to the Court of Justice' (emphasis added). Taking into account the function of Article 177(3) and particularly its importance for the individual, this would seem to be the better view.

It has been suggested that where the right of appeal or judicial review depends on the granting of leave, a lower court or tribunal from which a reference under Article 177 is sought must *either* grant leave or refer to the Court of Justice. Where this is not done, and leave depends on permission from a superior 'final' court, that latter court should be obliged to grant the requested leave. Any other course would frustrate the purpose of Article 177 and amount to a denial of the individual's Community rights.

This point was raised, but unfortunately not referred to the Court of Justice, in *SA Magnavision NV* v *General Optical Council (No. 1)* [1987] 2 CMLR 262, Queen's Bench Division. In this case the appellant company manufactured reading glasses in Belgium and had been prosecuted for selling its spectacles through concessionary outlets within shops in the UK, in breach of the rules of the General Optical Council. Under these rules the selling of spectacles in the UK was prohibited except under the supervision of a doctor or optician. The company was found guilty by Cardiff Magistrates and its appeal before Macpherson J in the High Court (*Magnavision (No. 1)* [1987] 1 CMLR 887) failed. That court refused to grant the appellant leave to appeal to the House of Lords. The company subsequently applied to the Divisional Court for leave to appeal to the House of Lords on a point of general public importance; namely, if the Divisional Court refuses leave to appeal in such a case does it become a court of last resort within Article 177(3)? Since judgment had already been given (although the order had not been drawn up) in the original case Watkins JL clearly thought it a 'most daring application'. Although he admitted that the refusal of leave to appeal from *Magnavision (No. 1)* had turned the Divisional Court into a 'final' court, representing 'the end of the road' for the plaintiff, he refused to grant the leave requested. There was no longer any point in referring, he said, 'We are *functus* in every sense'. Thus the matter still awaits an authoritative ruling from the Court of Justice.

Whilst Watkins LJ's decision was no doubt correct, and consistent with the ECJ's view in *Pardini* (case 338/85) and *Grogan* (case C 159/90), it is submitted that a reference to the Court of Justice at some stage on the substantive issue in *Magnavision (No. 1)* would have been highly desirable, since the point of law was not a simple one and was of considerable importance to the appellant.

Discretionary or 'permissive' jurisdiction: the effect of national precedent

Courts or tribunals which do not fall within Article 177(3) enjoy, according to the Court of Justice, an unfettered discretion in the matter of referrals. A court or tribunal at any level is free, 'if it considers that a decision on the question is necessary to enable it to give judgment', to refer to the Court of Justice in any kind of proceedings, including interlocutory proceedings (*Hoffman-La Roche AG* v *Centrafarm Vertriebsgesellschaft Pharmazeutischer Erzeugnisse mbH* (case 107/76), at any stage in the proceedings. As the Court held in *De Geus en Uitdenbogerd* v *Robert Bosch GmbH* (case 13/61), national courts have jurisdiction to refer whether or not an appeal is pending; the Court of Justice is not even concerned to discover whether the decision of the national judge has acquired the force of *res iudicata*, although following *Pardini* (case 338/85) and *Grogan* (case C 159/90), if proceedings have been terminated and it is aware of this fact it may refuse jurisdiction on the grounds that its ruling is not necessary to enable the national court to give judgment.

Even if the Court of Justice has already ruled on a similar question, national courts are not precluded from requesting a further ruling. This point was made in *Da Costa en Schaake NV* (cases 28-30/62). There the Court held, in the context of a reference for interpretation of a question substantially the same as that referred in *Van Gend en Loos,* that the Court should retain a legal right to depart from its previous judgments. It may recognise its errors in the light of new facts. It ruled in similar terms in the context of a request concerning the effect of a prior ruling of validity in *International Chemical Corporation Spa* v *Amministrazione delle Finanze dello Stato* (case 66/80). Here it held that whilst national courts could assume from a prior declaration of invalidity that the Regulation was invalid, they should not be deprived of an opportunity to refer the same issue if they have a 'real interest' in making a further reference.

This discretion to refer is in no way affected by national rules of precedent. This important principle was established in the case of *Rheinmühlen-Düsseldorf* (case 166/73); (case 146/73), Article 177 proceedings. In this case, which concerned an attempt by a German cereal exporter to obtain an export rebate under Community law, the German federal tax court (the Bundesfinanzhof), hearing the case on appeal from the Hessian tax court (Hessische Finanzgericht), had quashed the Hessian court's judgment and remitted the case to that court for a decision on certain issues of fact. The Hessian court was not satisfied with the Finanzgericht's ruling since questions of Community law were involved. It sought a ruling from the Court of Justice on the interpretation of the Community law, and also on the question of whether it was permissible for a lower court to refer in this way when its own superior court had already set aside its earlier judgment on appeal. On an appeal by Rheinmühlen-Düsseldorf to the Bundesfinanzhof challenging the Hessian court's right to refer to the Court of Justice the Bundesfinanzhof itself referred certain questions to the Court of Justice. The principal question, raised in both cases, was whether Article 177 gave national courts an unfettered right to refer or whether that right is subject to national provisions whereby lower courts are bound by the judgments of superior courts.

The Court's reply was in the strongest terms. The object of the Article 177 procedure, the Court held, was to ensure that in all circumstances the law was the same in all member States. A provision of domestic law cannot take away the power provided by Article 177. The lower court must be free to make a reference if it considers that the superior court's ruling could lead it to give judgment contrary to Community law. It would only be otherwise if the question put by the lower court were substantially the same. The Court of Justice's view may be compared with that of Wood J in the Employment Appeal Tribunal in *Enderby* v *Frenchay Health Authority* [1991] ICR 382. Here he suggested that lower English Courts were bound even in matters of Community law by decisions of their superior courts; thus they should not make references to the Court of Justice but should leave it to the House of Lords, *a fortiori* when the House has decided on a particular issue that British law does not conflict with EEC law. Whilst the decision not to refer may have been right on the facts, Wood J's general observations are clearly at odds with Community law. It appears that *Rheinmühlen-Düsseldorf* was not cited before the tribunal. A reference to the Court of Justice has now been made in this case by the Court of Appeal ([1992] IRLR 15).

If national courts have the widest discretion in matters of referral, when, and on what basis, should they exercise this discretion? Two aspects of this problem may be considered.

First the national judge must consider that a decision on a question of community law is *'necessary* to enable it to give judgment'; then, if it is necessary, he must decide whether, in his discretion, he should refer.

Guidelines on both these matters have been supplied by the Court of Justice and by national courts. It is submitted that as the ultimate arbiter on matters of Community law only the Court of Justice's rulings are fully authoritative on this point.

When will a decision be necessary?

The Court of Justice was asked to consider this matter in *CILFIT Srl* (case 283/81), Article 177 proceedings. Although the reference was from the Italian Supreme Court, the Cassazione, and concerned national courts' mandatory jurisdiction under Article 177(3), the guidelines supplied as to when a decision on a question of Community law is *necessary* will apply a *fortiori* to their discretionary jurisdiction. The Court held that it would not be 'necessary' if:

(a) the question of EEC law is irrelevant; or
(b) the provision has already been interpreted by the Court of Justice; or
(c) the correct application is so obvious as to leave no room for doubt. This matter must be assessed in the light of the special nature of EEC law, its particular difficulties, and the risk of divergence in judicial interpretation.

These guidelines may be compared with Lord Denning's in *H. P. Bulmer Ltd* v *J. Bollinger SA* [1974] Ch 40, Court of Appeal. He suggested that a decision would only be 'necessary' if it was 'conclusive' to the judgment. Even then it would not be necessary if:

(a) the Court of Justice had already given judgment on the question, or
(b) the matter was reasonably clear and free from doubt.

Although the criteria in both cases are similar, the first and third *CILFIT Srl* criteria are clearly stricter; it would be easier under Lord Denning's guidelines to decide that a decision was not 'necessary'. Lord Denning's guidelines were applied by Taylor J in *R* v *Inner London Education Authority (ex parte Hinde)* [1985] 1 CMLR 716 and he decided not to refer. The issues at stake in that case have proved to be both important and difficult, and were only finally resolved by the Court of Justice in the cases of *Brown* (case 197/86) and *Lair* (case 39/86) (for full discussion of the issues see chapter 18).

Acte clair

Criteria (b) and (c) of *CILFIT Srl* (case 238/81) and (a) and (b) of *H. P. Bulmer Ltd* v *J. Bollinger SA* [1974] Ch 40 could be described as versions of *acte clair*.

Acte clair is a doctrine originating in French administrative law, whereby if the meaning of a provision is clear no 'question' of interpretation arises. The doctrine was introduced in the context of interpretation of treaties, in order to strengthen the powers of the Conseil d'État *vis-à-vis* the executive. If doubts existed concerning the interpretation of a treaty, the courts were obliged to refer to the government. If the provision was found to be *acte clair*, there was no need to refer. The utility of the doctrine, in that context, is clear.

The doctrine was first invoked in the sphere of EEC law by Advocate-General Lagrange in *Da Costa en Schaake NV* (cases 28-30/62), in the context of a reference on a question of interpretation almost identical to a matter already decided by the Court in *Van Gend en Loos* (case 26/62). Like *CILFIT Srl*, it arose in a case concerning the court's mandatory jurisdiction under Article 177(3). Whilst asserting that Article 177(3) 'unqualifiedly' required national courts to submit to the Court of Justice 'every question of interpretation raised before the court' the Court added that this would not be necessary if the question was materially identical with a question which had already been the subject of a preliminary ruling in a similar case.

This case has been taken as an endorsement by the Court of *acte clair*, albeit interpreted in a very narrow sense. The principle was approved in *CILFIT Srl*.

Acte clair was applied in a much wider sense, in very different circumstances, in the French case of *Re Société des Pétroles Shell-Berre* [1964] CMLR 462. This case involved a number of difficult questions of French and EC competition law. These questions had not been subject to prior rulings under Article 177. Nevertheless the Conseil d'État, led by the Commissaire du Gouvernement, Madame Questiaux, took the view that only if the judge is not competent to determine the meaning of an act is he faced with a 'question of interpretation' and decided that there was no doubt as to the meaning and so there was no need to refer.

The dangers of *acte clair* were revealed in the Court of Appeal in the case of *R* v *Henn* [1978] 1 WLR 1031. There Lord Widgery suggested that it was clear from the case law of the Court of Justice that a ban on the import of pornographic books was not a quantitative restriction within Article 30 of the EEC Treaty. A subsequent referral on this matter by the House of Lords revealed that it undoubtedly was. Lord Diplock, giving judgment in the House of Lords ([1981] AC 850), warned English judges not to be too ready to hold that because the meaning of an English text seemed plain to them no question of interpretation was involved. He did, however, approve a version of *acte clair* consistent with that of the Court of Justice in *Da Costa en Schaake NV* and *CILFIT Srl* in *Garland* v *British Rail Engineering Ltd* [1983] 2 AC 751 when he suggested that where there was a 'considerable and consistent line of case law' from the European court the answer would be 'too obvious and inevitable' to be capable of giving rise to what could properly be called a question within the meaning of Article 177.

Although most of the above cases arose in the context of Article 177(3) they have been discussed at this stage because they may equally be invoked in the context of national courts' discretionary jurisdiction, and they demonstrate that *acte clair* can be applied both in a narrow sense, as in *Da Costa en Schaake NV* ('provision materially identical') and *CILFIT Srl* ('so clear as to leave no room for doubt, taking into account' etc.) and in a looser, more subjective sense, as in *H. P. Bulmer Ltd* v *J. Bollinger SA* ('reasonably clear and free from doubt') and *Shell-Berre* ('no doubt'). Although a loose interpretation does not have such serious consequences in the context of a court's discretionary jurisdiction as in its mandatory jurisdiction, a narrow interpretation is preferable if the pitfalls of *R* v *Inner London Education Authority (ex parte Hinde)* [1985] 1 CMLR 716 and *R* v *Henn* are to be avoided. Where a disappointed party does not have the means or the stamina to appeal it may result in a misapplication of EEC law.

Exercise of discretion

If courts within the area of discretionary jurisdiction consider, applying the *CILFIT* criteria, that a decision from the Court of Justice is necessary, how should they exercise their discretion?

On the question of timing, the Court of Justice has suggested that the facts of the case should be established and questions of purely national law settled before a reference is made (*Irish Creamery Milk Suppliers Association* v *Ireland* (cases 36 & 71/80)). This would avoid precipitate referrals, and enable the Court of Justice to take cognisance of all the features of fact and law which may be relevant to the issue of Community law on which it is asked to rule. A similar point was made by Lord Denning MR in *H. P. Bulmer Ltd* v *J. Bollinger SA* [1974] Ch 401 ('Decide the facts first') and approved by the House of Lords in *R* v *Henn*. However, Lord Diplock did concede in *R* v *Henn* that in an urgent, e.g., interlocutory, matter, where important financial interests are concerned, it might be necessary to refer *before* all the facts were found.

With regard to other factors, Lord Denning suggested in *H. P. Bulmer Ltd* v *J. Bollinger SA* that time, cost, work-load of the Court of Justice and the wishes of the parties should be taken into account by national courts in the exercise of their discretion.

Factors such as time and cost need to be treated with care, weighing the fact, as did Bingham J in *Commissioners of Customs and Excise* v *Samex ApS* [1983] 3 CMLR 194 that deferring a referral may in the end increase the time and cost to the parties: there may be cases where it is appropriate to refer at an early stage. The more difficult and uncertain the issue of EEC law, the greater the likelihood of appeal, requiring, in the end, a referral to the Court of Justice under Article 177(3).

The work-load of the Court of Justice is an increasing problem and no doubt a reason for some modification in recent years of its open-door policy. However, whilst it may justify non-referral in a straightforward case it should not prevent referral where the point of EEC law is difficult or novel. The *CILFIT* criteria should operate to prevent unnecessary referrals.

The wishes of the parties also need to be treated with caution. If the point of EEC law is relevant (which under *CILFIT* it must be) and difficult or uncertain, clearly *one* of the parties' interests will be better served by a referral.

As Templeman LJ said in the Court of Appeal in *Polydor Ltd* v *Harlequin Record Shops Ltd* [1980] 2 CMLR 413 when he chose to refer a difficult point of EEC law in proceedings for an interlocutory injunction, '. . . it is the right of the plaintiff to go to the European Court'.

Another factor which might point to an early referral, advanced by Ormrod LJ in *Polydor Ltd* v *Harlequin Record Shops Ltd* is the wider implications of the ruling. In *Polydor Ltd* v *Harlequin Record Shops Ltd* there were a number of similar cases pending. The issue, which was a difficult one, concerned the protection of British copyright law in the context of an international agreement between the EEC and Portugal, and affected not merely the parties to the case but the record industry as a whole.

Finally, in *R* v *Henn* Lord Diplock suggested that in a criminal trial on indictment it might be better for the question to be decided by the national judge and reviewed if necessary through the hierarchy of the national courts. Although this statement could be invoked to counter spurious defences based on EEC law, and unnecessary referrals, it is submitted that where a claim is genuinely based on EEC law, and a ruling from the Court of Justice would be conclusive of the case, delay would serve no purpose. The time and cost of the proceedings would only be increased.

Where matters of validity are concerned special considerations apply. Whilst a national court may find a Community act to be valid, it has no power to make a finding of invalidity. Thus, despite the apparent permissive words of Article 177(2), where a court has serious doubts as to the validity of the act in question, provided that a decision on the question of EEC law is 'necessary', a referral to the Court of Justice should be made. A national court may, however, grant an interim injunction based on the (alleged) invalidity of Community law. These matters, hinted at in *Foto-Frost* v *Hauptzollamt Lübeck-Ost* (case 314/85), have now been confirmed in *Zuckerfabrik Süderdithmarschen AG* v *Hauptzollamt Itzehoe* (cases C 143/88 and C 92/89), Article 177 proceedings.

Mandatory jurisdiction (Article 177(3))

Which courts and tribunals fall within the mandatory jurisdiction of Article 177(3) has already been discussed. It is submitted that the wider interpretation of Article 177(3), the 'concrete theory' is more in accordance with the functions and purposes of Article 177 than the stricter 'abstract theory'. *Costa* v *ENEL* (case 6/64) may be invoked to support this view.

Where a court or tribunal falls within Article 177(3), this creates, as the Court pointed out in *Da Costa en Schaake* (cases 28-30/62) an absolute obligation to refer. However, this obligation only arises if the court 'considers that a decision on the question is necessary to enable it to give judgment' (Article 177).

Whilst it is clearly not necessary for 'final' courts to refer questions of Community law in every case, a lax approach by such courts towards their need to refer, resulting in non-referral, may lead to an incorrect application of Community law and, for the individual concerned, a denial of justice. For him, this is the end of the road.

It is here that the doctrine of *acte clair* is of crucial significance. Under this doctrine, if the court is satisfied that the answer to the question of Community law, whether concerning interpretation or validity, is clear, then no decision on the question is 'necessary'. The judge is thus relieved of his obligation to refer.

As has been noted, the application of *acte clair* prevented the French Conseil d'État in *Shell-Berre* from referring to the Court of Justice when the matter of EEC law seemed, to many eyes, far from clear. What seemed clear to Lord Widgery in *R* v *Henn* turned out to be incorrect. Moreover, the doctrine, depending as it does on a subjective assessment as to what is clear, can all too easily be used as a means of avoiding referral. This appears to have occurred in *Minister of the Interior* v *Cohn-Bendit* [1980] 1 CMLR 543. In this case, heard by the French Conseil d'État, the supreme administrative court, Cohn-Bendit sought to invoke an EEC Directive (Directive 64/221, see chapter 20) to challenge a deportation order made by the French authorities. Certain provisions of the Directive had already been declared by the Court of Justice to be directly effective (*Van Duyn* v *Home Office* (case 41/74); see chapter 2). Despite urgings from the Commissaire du Gouvernement, M. Genevois, that in such a situation the Conseil d'État must either follow *Van Duyn* and apply the Directive, or seek a ruling from the Court under Article 177(3), the Conseil d'État declined to do either. In its opinion, the law was clear. The Directive was not directly effective.

The role of *acte clair* in EEC law was clarified by the Court of Justice in *CILFIT Srl* (case 283/81) in the context of a question from the Italian Cassazione (supreme court) concerning its obligation under Article 177(3), namely, did Article 177(3) create an absolute obligation to refer, or was referral conditional on a prior finding of a reasonable interpretative doubt? From the Court's response, that there was no need to refer if the matter was (a) irrelevant, (b) materially identical to a question already the subject of a preliminary ruling, or (c) so obvious as to leave no room for doubt, the second and third criteria may be taken as endorsing a version, albeit a narrow one, of *acte clair*. On the second criterion, which was a reiteration of its position in *Da Costa en Schaake*, the Court held that the questions at issue need not be identical, as long as the Court has already dealt with the point in question. Of particular importance to its third criterion is the Court's rider that, in deciding whether a matter was free from doubt, account must be taken of the special nature of EEC law, its particular difficulties, and the risk of divergence in judicial interpretation. Similar points were made by Lord Diplock in *R* v *Henn* and Lord Denning MR in *H. P. Bulmer Ltd* v *J. Bollinger SA*. Henceforth, if *acte clair* is to be invoked in the context of EEC law, it must be on the basis of the criteria supplied by *CILFIT Srl*.

However, the *CILFIT* criteria are not foolproof. In *R* v *Secretary of State for the Home Department (ex parte Sandhu)* (1985) *The Times*, 10 May 1985, the House of Lords was faced with a request for a ruling on the interpretation of certain provisions of Regulation 1612/68 (concerning rights of residence of members of the family of workers), in the context of a claim by an Indian, the divorced husband of an EEC national, threatened with deportation from the UK as a result of his divorce. The *CILFIT* criteria were cited, as was *Diatta* v *Land Berlin* (case 267/83), Article 177 proceedings, a case dealing with the rights of residence of a *separated* wife living apart from her husband, which was decided in the wife's favour. The House of Lords applied the second *CILFIT* criterion, found that the matter had already been interpreted in *Diatta*, and, on the basis of certain statements delivered *obiter* in *Diatta*, decided not to refer. On their lordships' interpretation Mr Sandhu was not entitled to remain in the UK. Thus a loophole in the *CILFIT* criteria was exploited with disastrous results for Mr Sandhu. (For further discussion of the case see chapter 18.)

A Court may avoid its obligations under Article 177(3) by deciding the case before it without considering the possibility of referral (see e.g. *Andre Mees* v *Association Générale de l'Industrie du Medicament Asbl* v *State* [1988] 3 CMLR 137, Belgian *Conseil d'État*). In *R* v *Secretary of State for Social Services, ex parte Wellcome* [1988] 3 CMLR 85 the House of Lords, in considering the factors to be taken into account by a licensing authority in issuing a licence to parallel import a trade-mark medicine, thought it 'highly undesirable to embark on considerations of Community law which might have necessitated a referral to the Court of Justice under Article 177'.

By contrast, the German Federal Constitutional Court has emphasised national courts' duty to refer under Article 177(3), according to the *CILFIT* criteria, in the strongest terms. In quashing the German Bundesfinanzhof's decision on the direct effects of Directives in *Re VAT Directive* [1982] 1 CMLR 527, [1989] 1 CMLR 873 (see chapter 2), it held that a court subject to Article 177(3) which deliberately departs from the case law of the Court of Justice and fails to make a reference under Article 177(3) is acting in breach of Article 101 of the German constitution. The principle of *acte clair* could not operate where there existed a ruling from the Court of Justice to the contrary (*Re VAT exemption* [1989] 1 CMLR 113). In *Re Patented Feedingstuffs* [1989] 2 CMLR 902 the same court declared that it would review an 'arbitrary' refusal by a court subject to Article 177(3) to refer to the European Court. A refusal would be arbitrary:

(a)   where the national court gave no consideration at all to a reference in spite of the accepted relevance of Community law to the judgment and the court's doubt as to the correct answer;

(b)   where the law consciously departs in its judgment from the case law of the European Court on the relevant questions, and nevertheless does not make a reference or a fresh reference; and

(c)   where there is not yet a decisive judgment of the European Court on point, or such judgments may not have provided an exhaustive answer to the relevant questions or there is a more than remote possibility of the European Court developing its case law further, and the national court exceeds to an indefensible extent the scope of its necessary judicial discretion, as where there may be contrary views of the relevant question of Community law which should obviously be given preference over the view of the national court.

These principles, applied in good faith, should ensure that a reference to the Court of Justice will be made, at least by the German courts, in the appropriate case. Perhaps other courts will be persuaded to follow the German Constitutional Court's example.

Effect of a ruling

Clearly a ruling from the Court of Justice under Article 177 is binding in the individual case. Given member States' obligation under Article 5 to 'take all appropriate measures . . . to ensure fulfilment of the obligations arising out of this Treaty or resulting from action taken by the institutions of the Community' and, in the UK, under the European Communities Act 1972, s. 3(2), to take judicial notice of any decision of the European Court, it should also be applied in all subsequent cases. This does not preclude national courts from seeking a further ruling on the same issue should they have a 'real interest' in making a reference (*Da Costa en Schaake* (cases 28-30/62) — interpretation; *International Chemical Corporation SpA* (case 66/80) — validity).

The question of the temporal effect of a ruling, whether it should take effect retroactively (*'ex tunc'*, i.e., from the moment of entry into force of the provision subject to the ruling) or only from the date of judgment (*'ex nunc'*) is less clear. In *Defrenne* v *Sabena (No. 2)* (case 43/75) the Court was prepared to limit the effect of Article 119 (see chapters 2, 22) to future cases (including *Defrenne* itself) and claims lodged prior to the date of judgment. 'Important considerations of legal certainty' the Court held, 'affecting all the interests involved, both public and private, make it impossible to reopen the question as regards the past'. The Court was clearly swayed by the arguments of the British and Irish governments that a retrospective application of the equal pay principle would have serious economic repercussions on parties (i.e., employers) who had been led to believe they were acting within the law.

However, in *Ariete SpA* (case 811/79) and *Salumi Srl* (cases 66, 127 & 128/79) the Court made it clear that *Defrenne* was to be an exceptional case. As a general rule an interpretation under Article 177 of a rule of community law 'clarifies and defines where necessary the meaning and scope of that rule as it must be or ought to be understood and applied *from the time of its coming into force'* (emphasis added). A ruling under Article 177 must therefore be applied to legal relationships arising prior to the date of the judgment provided that the conditions for its application by the national court are satisfied. 'It is only exceptionally', the Court said 'that the Court may, in the application of the principle of legal certainty inherent in the community legal order and in taking into account the serious effects which its judgments might have as regards the past, on legal relationships established in good faith, be moved to restrict for any person concerned the opportunity of relying on the provision as thus interpreted with a view to calling into question those legal relationships . . . '.

Moreover, 'such a restriction may be allowed *only* in the actual judgment ruling upon the interpretation sought' and 'it is for the Court of Justice *alone* to decide on the temporal restrictions as regards the effects of the interpretation which it gives'.

These principles were applied in *Blaizot* (case 24/86) and *Barra* (case 309/85). Both cases involved a claim for reimbursement of the Belgian minerval, based on *Gravier* (case 293/83, see chapter 19). In both cases the claims were in respect of periods prior to the Court of Justice's ruling in *Gravier*. In *Barra* it was not disputed that the course for which the minerval had been charged was vocational; but *Blaizot's* course, a university course in veterinary medicine, was, the defendant university argued, not vocational, thus not within the scope of the *Gravier* ruling.

Since *Barra's* case fell squarely within *Gravier* and the Court had imposed no temporal limits on the effect of its judgment in *Gravier* itself, that ruling was held to apply retrospectively in *Barra's* favour. *Blaizot* on the other hand raised new issues. In deciding that university education could, and a course in veterinary science did, constitute vocational training the Court, clearly conscious of the impact of such a ruling on Belgian universities if applied retroactively, decided that 'important considerations of legal certainty' required that the effects of its ruling should be limited on the same lines as *Defrenne*, that is, to future cases and those lodged prior to judgment.

Thus unless the Court can be persuaded to change its mind and reconsider the question of the temporal effect of a prior ruling in a subsequent case when *no* new issues are raised, the question of the temporal effect will need to be considered in every case in which a retrospective application may give rise to serious repercussions as regards the past. Yet it is in the nature of this kind of ruling that it, and therefore its consequences, are unpredictable. Should a party wish, subsequently, to limit the effects of an earlier ruling, it will be necessary to ensure, as in *Blaizot,* that some new issue of EC law is raised.

In *Barber* v *Guardian Royal Exchange Assurance Group* (case C 262/88) the court was again persuaded by 'overriding considerations of legal certainty' to limit the effects of its ruling that employers' contracted-out pension schemes fell within Article 119 of the EEC Treaty (see chapter 22). Unfortunately the precise scope of the non-retroactivity principle that 'Article 119 may not be relied upon in order to *claim entitlement* to a pension with effect prior to that of this judgment (except in the case of workers . . . who have initiated proceedings before this date or raised an equivalent claim under the applicable national law)' was disputed as being unclear. The more likely view is that the ruling was intended to apply to all those like Mrs Barber who became eligible to *claim a pension* after the date of judgment. This lack of specificity, a characteristic of the Court's style of judgment, can create problems in the context of rulings on interpretation under Article 177. In its reluctance not to overstep the boundaries of its jurisdiction the Court's judgment can on occasions be too Delphic, leaving too much to be decided by national courts. The ruling has since been 'clarified' by a protocol to the Maastricht Treaty in favour of a broad principle of non-retroactivity (see chapter 22).

The above cases relate to rulings on interpretation. Where matters of validity are concerned, the Court's approach is more flexible. It has assimilated the effects of a ruling of invalidity to those of a successful annulment action, as a result of which the illegal act is declared void. However, arguing from Article 174(2), which enables the Court, in a successful annulment action, to limit the effects of a Regulation which it has declared void (see chapter 27) the Court has limited the effects of a finding of invalidity in a number of cases, sometimes holding the ruling to be purely prospective (i.e., for the future only, *excluding* the present case, e.g., *Roquette Frères* v *French State* (case 145/79)), sometimes limiting its effects on the principles of *Defrenne* (e.g., *Pinna* (case 41/84)). The Court has not so far insisted that the effect of a ruling of invalidity can only be limited in the case in which the ruling itself is given.

The Court is more likely to be prepared to limit the effects of a ruling on validity than one on interpretation. Where matters of validity are concerned parties will have relied legitimately on the provision in question. A retrospective application of a ruling of invalidity may produce serious economic repercussions: thus it may not be desirable to reopen matters as regards the past. On the other hand too free a use of prospective rulings in matters of interpretation would seriously threaten the objectivity of the law, its application to all persons and all situations. Moreover, as the Court no doubt appreciates, a knowledge on the part of member States and individuals that the law as interpreted may not be applied retrospectively could foster a dangerous spirit of non-compliance.

Interim measures

As has been noted, a national court may be requested to order interim measures pending a ruling from the Court of Justice under Article 177. In *Foto-Frost* (case 314/85) the ECJ suggested that a national court might grant such relief even pending a ruling on validity. In *Portsmouth City Council* v *Richards* [1989] 1 CMLR 673 the English Court of Appeal was willing to grant a civil injunction to restrain the defendants from carrying on their sex shop business in breach of the criminal law, having been refused a licence to do so, pending a ruling from the Court of Justice on whether the Council's refusal to grant such a licence was in breach of Article 30. The Court of Appeal was not prepared to contemplate the 'virtual paralysis of the criminal process' in relation to the defendants' activities.

A claim for interim relief caused some difficulty in *Factortame* v *Secretary of State for Transport* [1989] 3 CMLR 1, particularly since relief in the form of an interim injunction was being sought against the Crown to prevent the application of the Merchant Shipping Act 1988. Following the Court of Justice's ruling (case C 213/89) that national courts must 'set aside' a rule which prevents the granting of such relief where this is necessary to ensure the full effectiveness of Community law, the House of Lords granted an interim injunction, applying the principles of *American Cynamid Co.* v *Ethicon Ltd* [1975] AC 396. However, it stressed that the importance of upholding the law of the land in the public interest was an important factor to be weighed in deciding whether to grant interim relief against the Crown. 'The Court should not restrain a public authority by interim injunction from enforcing an apparently authentic law unless it is satisfied . . . that the challenge to the validity of the law is so firmly based as to justify so exceptional a course being taken'. The strictness of this rule could undermine the effectiveness of Community law if, as the House suggested, a public authority is not required to give a cross-undertaking in damages as a condition for the granting of interim relief (but see now the House of Lords' decision in *Kirklees BC* v *Wickes*, noted, chapter 23).

Conclusions

The success of the Article 177 procedure depends on a fruitful collaboration between the Court of Justice and the courts of member States. Generally speaking both sides have played their part in this collaboration. The Court of Justice has rarely refused its jurisdiction or attempted to interfere with national courts' discretion in matters of referral and application of EEC law. National courts have generally been ready to refer; cases in which they have unreasonably refused to do so are rare.

However, this very separation of powers, the principal strength of Article 177, is responsible for some of its weaknesses. The decision whether to refer and what to refer rests entirely with the national judge. No matter how important referral may be to the individual concerned (e.g., *Sandhu*) he cannot compel referral; he can only seek to persuade. And although the Court of Justice will extract the essential matters of EEC law from the questions referred it can only give judgment *in the context of the questions referred* (see *Hessische Knappschaft* v *Maison Singer et Fils* (case 44/65), Article 184 proceedings). Thus it is essential for national courts to ask the right questions. In addition, since the relevance of the questions can only be assessed in the light of the factual and legal circumstances of the case in hand, these details too must be supplied. A failure to fulfil both these requirements may result in a wasted referral or a misapplication of EEC law.

As the body of case law from the Court of Justice develops and national courts acquire greater confidence and expertise in applying EEC law and ascertaining its relevance to the case before them, there will be less need to resort to Article 177. Thus the initial question, whether a decision on a question of EEC law is 'necessary', will be crucial. *CILFIT Srl* (case 283/81) has supplied guidelines to enable national courts to answer this question; these guidelines, applied in the light of the rider added by the court, should ensure that references are made in the appropriate case and unnecessary referrals avoided. Where a lower court is in doubt as to whether a referral is necessary the matter may be left to be decided on appeal. On the other hand where a final court has the slightest doubt as to whether a decision is necessary it should always refer, bearing in mind the purpose of Article 177(3) and its particular importance for the individual litigant. These courts would do well to follow the lead provided by the German Constitutional Court.

Further reading

Alexander, W., 'The Temporal Effects of Preliminary Rulings' (1988) 8 YEL 11.
Bebr, G., 'Preliminary rulings of the Court of Justice – their authority and temporal effect' (1981) 18 CML Rev 475.
Bebr, G., 'Arbitration Tribunals and Article 177' (1985) 22 CML Rev 498.

Bebr, G., 'The Reinforcement of the Constitutional Review of Community Acts under Article 177 EEC' (1988) 25 CML Rev 684.

Dashwood, A. and Arnull, A., 'English Courts and Article 177 of the EEC Treaty' (1984) 4 YEL 255.

Gray, C., 'Advisory Opinions and the European Court of Justice' (1983) 8 EL Rev 24.

Harding, C., 'The Impact of Article 177 on the Review of Community action' (1981) YEL 93.

O'Keefe, D., 'Appeals against an Order to Refer under Article 177 of the EEC Treaty' (1984) 9 EL Rev 87.

Pescatore, J., 'Interpretation of Community Law and the doctrine of the *Acte Clair*', Eds. Bathurst and Simmonds.

Rasmussen, H., 'The European Court's *Acte Clair* Strategy in CILFIT (1984) 9 CML Rev 242.

Rasmussen, H., 'Between Self-Restraint and Activism; a Judicial Policy for the European Court' (1988) 13 EL Rev 28.

Toth, A., 'The Authority of Judgments of the European Court of Justice; Binding Force and Legal Effects' (1984) 4 YEL 1.

Waelbroeck, M., 'May the Court of Justice limit the Retrospective Operation of its Judgments?' (1981) YEL 115.

Watson, J., 'Experience and Problems in applying Article 177 EEC' (1986) 23 CML Rev 207.

TWENTY FIVE

Enforcement actions (Articles 169 and 170, 93(2), 100A(4) and 225)

The principal remedy provided by the Treaty for infringements of EEC law by member States is the direct action before the Court of Justice under Article 169, which provides:

> If the Commission considers that a member State has failed to fulfil an obligation under this Treaty, it shall deliver a reasoned opinion on the matter after giving the State concerned the opportunity to submit its observations.
> If the State concerned does not comply with the opinion within the period laid down by the Commission the latter may bring the matter before the Court of Justice.

A similar procedure is provided for action by member States under Article 170.
Also, 'in derogation from the provisions of Articles 169 and 170', the Commission is empowered to bring a member State before the Court under Article 93(2) (infringement of Community rules on State aid provision, see chapter 11), Article 100A(4), para. 3 (improper use of derogation procedure provided by Article 100A(4), para. 1, see chapter 9) and Article 225 (measures taken to protect essential security interests or to prevent serious internal disturbances, see chapter 9).

Action by the Commission (Article 169)

Article 169, which gives the Commission power to bring member States before the Court of Justice when they have failed to fulfil their obligations under

Community law, is a specific example of the supranational nature of EEC law. Because of the danger of non-compliance by member States with their Community obligations, particularly in times of national or local difficulties, and because the success of the Community depends above all on solidarity and the uniform observance of its laws by all member States, it was thought necessary to provide in the Treaty for a procedure whereby States suspected of infringing EEC law might be called to account before the Court of Justice. The Commission, whose duty it is under Article 155 to 'ensure that the provisions of this Treaty and the measures taken by the institutions pursuant thereto are applied', was given the task of initiating and controlling this procedure.

The purpose of Article 169 is threefold. First, and primarily, it seeks to *ensure compliance* by member States with their Community obligations. Secondly, it provides a valuable non-contentious *procedure for the resolution of disputes* between the Commission and member States over matters of Community law: in 1989, out of 664 proceedings instituted by letters of formal notice, less than one sixth (96) went all the way to the Court of Justice. And finally, where cases do reach the Court of Justice the Court's decision serves to *clarify* the law for the benefit of all member States.

It is no doubt on account of the latter function that the Court has held that even if a State has complied with its obligations prior to the hearing before the Court the Commission is entitled to judgment; it is not necessary for the Commission to show the existence of a 'legal interest' (*Commission* v *Italy (Re Ban on Pork Imports)* (case 7/61)).

In keeping with its aims, Article 169 was not designed as a punitive measure. No sanctions were provided for States found by the Court in breach of their obligations; they are merely required 'to take the necessary measures to comply with the judgment of the Court of Justice' (Article 171). Nor is there a time-limit prescribed for member States' compliance. However, the Court has held (*Commission* v *Italy* (case 69/86)) that implementation of a judgment must be undertaken immediately and must be completed within the shortest possible time. Where a State fails to comply with these obligations the Commission can only seek to enforce the judgment by further Article 169 proceedings for breach of Article 171. Whilst few such actions were taken in the early days of the Community, their number has increased alarmingly in recent years. In 1989 the Commission instituted 26 'repeat' Article 169 proceedings.

Failure to fulfil an obligation

Although national governments appear before the Court as defendants in an Article 169 action, proceedings are brought against the *State*. Thus they may be brought in respect of a failure on the part of *any* agency of that State, executive, legislative or judicial. So far no action has been taken in response to a judicial failure. Although national courts have on occasions clearly acted in breach of their obligations (e.g., *Minister of the Interior* v *Cohn-Bendit* [1980] 1 CMLR 543 — French Conseil d'État failed to comply with its obligation under Article 177(3), see chapter 24) and action in respect of such infringements could have been undertaken in theory (per Advocate-General Warner in

Meyer-Burckhardt v *Commission* (case 9/75)), the Commission has so far preferred to operate through diplomatic channels in these cases, no doubt agreeing with Advocate-General Warner that such action should not be lightly undertaken. However, in its sixth annual report on the monitoring and application of Community law the Commission criticised both the Italian Consiglio di Stato and the French Conseil d'État for a number of failures, including their refusal to recognise the direct effect of Directives. Perhaps significantly, in its seventh Report it noted with approval a 'major reversal' in the French Conseil d'État's attitude to the application of EEC law in the case of *Nicolo* [1990] 1 CMLR 17 (see chapter 3).

The 'failure' may be in respect of any binding obligation arising from Community law. This would cover obligations arising from the EEC Treaty and its amending and supplementing Treaties; from international agreements entered into by the Community and third countries where the obligation lies within the sphere of Community competence; from EEC Regulations, Directives and Decisions; and even from general principles of law recognised as part of Community law where the breach of these principles occurs within the context of an obligation of EEC law. 'Failure' can include any wrongful act or omission, ranging from non-implementation to partial implementation to faulty implementation of Community law, or simple maintaining in force national laws or practices incompatible with EEC law. Notices of States' failures may come as a result of the Commission's own enquiries, from (increasing) complaints from the public, or from the European Parliament.

Procedure

The sensitive nature of an action under Article 169 is reflected in its procedure. It follows two stages. The first stage, between the Commission and the State, is administrative in nature, and is designed to achieve compliance by persuasion. Only if this fails is it necessary to proceed to the second, judicial stage before the Court of Justice. As has been noted, the success rate at the first stage is high.

First stage   The Commission opens proceedings by letters of formal notice, inviting the State concerned to submit its observations. In order that the State has a full opportunity to put its case the Commission must first inform the State of its grounds of complaint. The complaint need not at this stage be fully reasoned, but the State must be informed of *all* the charges which may be raised in an action before the Court. In *Commission* v *Italy (Re Payment of Export Rebates)* (case 31/69) the Commission alleged that Italy was in breach of its EEC obligations in failing to pay certain export rebates to its farmers, required under EEC Regulations; in opening the proceedings the Commission charged Italy with breaches up to 1967, but failed to mention a number of breaches committed after that date. When the matter came before the Court, the Court refused to consider the later breaches. The Court said that the member States must be given an adequate and realistic opportunity to make observations on the alleged breach of Treaty obligations.

Following the submission of the State's observations to the Commission the Commission issues a 'reasoned opinion'. This opinion will record the infringement and require the State to take action to end it, normally within a specified time-limit. Although the opinion must be 'reasoned' it need not set out the Commission's case in full. In the case of *Commisson* v *Italy (Re Ban on Pork Imports)* (case 7/61) the Court held, in response to the Italian government's claim that the Commission's reasoned opinion was inadequate, that the reasoned opinion need only contain a coherent statement of the reasons which had convinced the Commission that the Italian government had failed to fulfil its obligations. No formalism was required. The only purpose of the reasoned opinion was to specify the point of view of the Commission in order to inform the government concerned, and, possibly, the Court. The reasoning behind the decision is clear. If the State refuses to accept the Commission's opinion, it may proceed to the second stage before the Court. It will then be for the Court to weigh in detail the merits of the case on both sides.

The court has held (*Alfons Lütticke GmbH* v *Commission* (case 48/65)) that the reasoned opinion is merely a step in the proceedings; it is not a binding act capable of annulment under Article 173. Thus whilst the defendant State may choose to impugn the Commission's opinion in proceedings under Article 169 before the Court, where the State complies with the opinion, a third party, possibly adversely affected by the Commission's opinion, has no equivalent right. However, in *Essevi SpA* (cases 142 & 143/80) the Court held, in Article 177 proceedings, that the Commission has no power in Article 169 proceedings to determine conclusively the rights and duties of a member State. These may only be determined, and their conduct appraised, by a judgment of the Court. The Commission may not, in the opinion which it is obliged to deliver under Article 169, exempt a member State from compliance with its obligations under the Treaty or prevent individuals from relying, in legal proceedings, on the rights conferred on them by the Treaty to contest any legislative or administrative measure of a member State which may be incompatible with Community law. Thus a third party, dissatisfied with the Commission's opinion, could raise the issue of the legality of the State's action indirectly before his national court and seek a referral on the relevant questions of interpretation to the Court of Justice under Article 177. This was done in *Essevi SpA* in a domestic action for the recovery of taxes levied allegedly in breach of Article 95.

The same principle would apply where the Commission has decided in its discretion not to institute or pursue Article 169 proceedings. In *Alfons Lütticke GmbH* v *Commission* (case 48/65), Alfons Lütticke GmbH had complained to the Commission that its own (German) government was acting in breach of EEC law by introducing a levy on imported powdered milk in breach of EEC law. As an importer of powdered milk the levy affected it adversely. It asked the Commission to take action under Article 169 against Germany. The Commission refused. Germany had since withdrawn the levy and the Commission decided in its discretion not to take action. It was a political compromise. Lütticke, on the other hand, wished to establish the infringement in order to recover for losses suffered whilst the German law was in force. Since

Article 169 gave the Commission a discretion in the matter there was no way in which its refusal to bring Article 169 proceedings could be challenged either under Article 173 (annulment action) or Article 175 (failure to act) (see chapters 27 and 28). However, in a parallel action before its national courts in *Alfons Lütticke GmbH* v *Hauptzollamt Saarlouis* (case 57/65), it succeeded in obtaining a ruling under Article 177 from the Court of Justice on the direct effects of Article 95, the Article which it alleged the German government had breached. Since the Article was found directly effective, it could be applied in the company's favour.

Whilst there are no time-limits in respect of the stages leading up to the reasoned opinion, thereby giving both parties time for negotiation, the Commission will normally impose in its reasoned opinion a time-limit for compliance. A member State will not be deemed in breach of its obligations until that time-limit has expired. Where the Commission does not impose a time-limit the Court has held that a reasonable time must be allowed. A State cannot be relieved of its obligations merely because no time-limit has been imposed (*Commission* v *Italy (Re Premiums for Reducing Dairy Production)* (case 39/72)). The Commission has a complete discretion in the matter of time-limits, subject to the possibility of review by the Court. The Court may dismiss an action under Article 169 on the grounds of inadequate time-limits. An action by the Commission against Belgium for its failure adequately to implement the *Gravier* Decision (case 293/83) was dismissed on the grounds that the Commission had not given Belgium sufficient time to respond to its complaints, either before or after the issuing of its reasoned opinion (*Commission* v *Belgium (Re University Fees)* (case 293/85)). However, the Court has no power to alter the Commission's time-limits (*Commission* v *Italy* (case 28/81)).

Second stage   If a member State fails to comply with the Commission's reasoned opinion within the specified time-limit, proceedings move to the second, judicial stage before the Court. Again, the initiative rests with the Commission, which '*may* bring the matter before the Court of Justice' (Article 169). No time-limits are imposed; the Commission is free to choose the most appropriate means of bringing the infringement to an end (*Commission* v *France (Re the Euratom Supply Agency)* (case 7/71), proceedings brought under Euratom Treaty).

The judicial stage is not a review procedure, although at this stage the legality of the Commission's reasoned opinion may be reviewed (*Commission* v *Belgium* (case 293/85)). Here the Court, exercising plenary jurisdiction in contentious proceedings, conducts a full enquiry into the merits of the case and decides the matter *de novo*. Interested member States (but not individuals: *Commission* v *Italy (Re Import of Foreign Motor Vehicles)* (case 154/85R)) are entitled to intervene in the proceedings. The Commission is entitled to request, and the Court to order, interim measures (e.g. *Commission* v *UK (Re Merchant Shipping Rules)* (case 246/89R); *Commission* v *Ireland (Re Dundalk Water Scheme)* (case 45/87R), see chapter 23).

Defences

Many defences to an action under Article 169 have been attempted; few have succeeded. The best defence is clearly to deny the obligation. It may be conditional, for example, on a time-limit which has not expired. Where a breach of secondary legislation is alleged, the legislation may be attacked for illegality. Otherwise, the traditional defences of international law offer little hope of success.

The defence of *reciprocity,* an accepted principle of international law, even entrenched in some States' constitutions (e.g., France, Article 55), whereby in the event of a breach of his obligations by one party the other party is likewise relieved of his, was rejected by the Court in *Commission v Luxembourg and Belgium (Re Import of Powdered Milk Products)* (cases 90 & 91/63). Here the governments argued that their alleged breach of Article 12 of the EEC Treaty would have been legal but for the Commission's failure to introduce certain measures which they were authorised to enact. This argument, based on reciprocity, the Court held, was not applicable in the context of Community law. The Community was a new legal order; it was not limited to creating reciprocal obligations. Community law governed not only the powers, rights and obligations of member States, but also the *procedures* necessary for finding and sanctioning all violations that might occur.

The defence of reciprocity was also rejected in the context of a failure by another member State to comply with a similar obligation; it made no difference that Article 169 proceedings had not been instituted against that State in respect of a similar breach (*Commission v France (Re Restrictions on Imports of Lamb)* (case 232/78); *Steinike und Weinlig* (case 78/76), Article 177 proceedings).

Similar reasoning to that advanced in *Commission v Belgium and Luxembourg* led to the rejection of a defence of *necessity* in *Commission v Italy (Re Ban on Pork Imports)* (case 7/61). The Treaty provided, in Article 226, for procedures to be followed in cases of emergency. This precluded unilateral action on the part of member States.

A defence based on *force majeure* was rejected in *Commission v Italy (Re Transport Statistics)* (case 101/84). Here Italy was charged with non-implementation of a Community Directive; the reason for its non-implementation was that the data-processing centre involved in the implementation of the Directive had been bombed. The Court held that whilst this might amount to *force majeure,* which could provide an excuse for non-implementation, a delay of four and a half years, as in this case, was inexcusable. As the Court said, 'time will erode the validity of the excuse'.

The concept of *force majeure* was considered in the case of *McNicholl v Ministry of Agriculture* (case 296/86), not in Article 169 proceedings, but in order to challenge via Article 177 the forfeiture of a deposit for failing to comply with an export undertaking as required by Community law. The Court held that:

whilst the concept of *force majeure* does not presuppose an absolute impossibility of performance, it nevertheless requires that non-performance of the act in question be due to circumstances beyond the control of persons pleading *force majeure*, that the circumstances be abnormal and unforeseeable and that the consequences could not have been avoided through the exercise of all due care.

This definition should be equally applicable in Article 169 proceedings.

Another defence, frequently raised and consistently rejected by the Court, is based on *constitutional, institutional or administrative difficulties* within a member State. As the Court held in *Commission* v *Italy* (case 28/81), a member State cannot plead the provisions, practices or circumstances existing in its own legal system in order to justify a failure to comply with obligations resulting from Community Directives.

The same reasoning would apply to a failure to comply with any other Community obligations (e.g., *Commission* v *Italy (Re Premiums for Reducing Dairy Production)* (case 39/72 — Regulation).

Similarly in *Commission* v *United Kingdom (Re Tachographs)* (case 128/78) the Court refused to accept an argument based on political (i.e., trade union) difficulties, submitted as justification for a failure to implement a Community Regulation on the installation of tachographs.

Another popular but equally unsuccessful defence rests on the argument that whilst Community law may not be applied *de iure, administrative practices ensure that EEC law is in fact applied.* This argument was advanced in *Commission* v *France (Re French Merchant Seamen)* (case 167/73), in an action based on the French Code Maritime. The code was clearly discriminatory, since it required a ratio of three Frenchmen to one foreigner in certain jobs. The French government's argument that the code was not enforced in practice was unsuccessful. Enforcement by administrative practices, the Court held, is not enough. The maintenance of national laws contrary to EEC law gives rise to an ambiguous state of affairs, and leaves citizens of a member State in a state of uncertainty.

Similar reasons led to the rejection of another argument in the same case based on the *direct effects* of Community law. If the Community law in question, in this case Article 7 of the EEC Treaty, were directly effective, argued the French, this would be enough to ensure that the State fulfilled its obligations. The Court did not agree (see also *Commission* v *Belgium (Re Type Approval Directives)* (case 102/79)).

The Court took a (seemingly) more moderate line in *Commission* v *Germany (Re Nursing Directives)* (case 29/84). Here it conceded that a defence based on direct effects might succeed if the State's administrative practices guaranteed that the Directives would be applied fully and ensured that the legal position was clear and that all persons concerned were fully aware of their rights. These requirements were not, however, found to be satisfied in this case. It is submitted that they will rarely be satisfied. This seems to be borne out in the recent case of *Commission* v *Italy* (case 168/85) judgment of 15 October 1986, unreported, in which the Court held that the right of citizens to plead directly applicable provisions of the Treaty before national courts is only a minimum guarantee and insufficient in itself to ensure full and complete application of the Treaty.

The number of cases brought before the Court of Justice under Article 169 has risen steadily during the last decade. Between 1982 and 1988 it more than doubled, from 42 to 96. This increased activity is no doubt due to a change in policy on the part of the Commission as well as to an increase in the number of violations of Community law by member States. Whilst the Commission could rely on the enforcement of Treaty obligations and Regulations via the principle of direct effects, problems over the direct effects of Directives (see chapter 2) have necessitated direct action by the Commission as the only means of ensuring their full implementation.

Following the Single European Act 1986 and the Commission's new approach to harmonisation (see chapters 9 and 19), the Commission stepped up its action under Article 169 against unilateral measures in breach of Community law taken by member States in those areas subject to Community harmonisation, its top priority being action to protect and promote the single market. In its seventh annual report on the application of Community law (1990), it announced its intention to monitor the implementation of Directives by member States on a systematic basis, and to take prompt action against States which had failed to implement Directives on time.

However, the lack of adequate sanctions to secure enforcement of the Court's judgments under Article 169 has been a serious problem. In certain circumstances, where Community instruments or programmes authorise the suspension of payment to a member State if that State has been found in breach of its Community obligations, the Commission has been able to exert financial pressure in order to secure compliance. But it has had no general power to impose financial penalties on recalcitrant States. The Court's decisions in *Emmott* v *Minister for Social Welfare* (case C 208/90) and *Francovich* v *Italian State* (cases C 6 and 9/90) have gone some way to remedy this deficiency. Following *Emmott* it will not be possible for public bodies to invoke national limitation rules to prevent individuals from enforcing their directly effective rights under Directives before they have been fully implemented into national law. And, even more significantly, States which have failed to implement Directives will, under certain circumstances, risk facing an action for damages under *Francovich*. Whilst much uncertainty surrounds both of these remedies these cases will provide a powerful and much-needed spur to action to States which have failed to fulfil their obligations in respect of Directives. There seems no reason in principle why *Francovich* could not be applied to other failures on the part of member States provided the criteria for its application are fulfilled (see further chapters 22 and 23).

Finally, in December 1991, at Maastricht, member States agreed to provide for the payment of penalties by member States which fail to comply with the Court's judgment under Article 169. Under an amended Article 171 the Commission will be able to deliver a reasoned opinion on that failure and impose a time limit for compliance. If the State fails to comply within the time-limit the Commission may bring the case before the Court of Justice, specifying the appropriate penalty. If the Court finds non-compliance it can impose a penalty on the State concerned. The amount of the penalty, and the principles on which it is to be calculated, have yet to be decided.

Action by member States (Article 170)

Article 170 provides:

> A member State which considers that another member State has failed to fulfil an obligation under this Treaty may bring the matter before the Court of Justice.
> Before a member State brings an action against another member State for an alleged infringement of an obligation under this Treaty, it shall bring the matter before the Commission.
> The Commission shall deliver a reasoned opinion after each of the States concerned has been given the opportunity to submit its own case and its observations on the other party's case both orally and in writing.

> If the Commission has not delivered an opinion within three months of the date on which the matter was brought before it, the absence of such opinion shall not prevent the matter from being brought before the Court of Justice.

The procedure is thus similar to that of Article 169 save that it is initiated by a member State which, if the Commission fails to deliver a reasoned opinion within three months, is entitled to bring the matter before the Court of Justice. In addition, both parties are entitled to state their case and comment on the other's case both orally and in writing.

It has been suggested that since Article 170(1) gives States a general right to bring proceedings, the issuing of a reasoned opinion cannot preclude the complainant State from bringing proceedings before the Court if it is dissatisfied with the opinion or if it wishes to obtain a final judgment from the Court. This latter occurred in *France* v *United Kingdom (Re Fishing Net Mesh Sizes* (case 141/78).

In case of dispute between member States the Treaty also provides a further, voluntary procedure. Under Article 182 States may agree to submit to the Court of Justice any dispute relating to the subject-matter of the Treaty.

Special enforcement procedures: State aids (Article 93(2)), breach of Article 100A(4) procedures (Article 100A(4), para. 3) and measures to prevent serious internal disturbances (Article 225)

These procedures, which apply only within the areas specified, operate 'in derogation from the provisions of Articles 169 and 170'. There are certain essential differences between these procedures and Articles 169 and 170. In the case of Article 93(2) the Commission, after giving the parties concerned an opportunity to submit their comments, issues a *Decision* requiring the State concerned to alter or abolish the disputed aid within a specified time-limit. If the State concerned does not comply with the Decision within the prescribed time, the Commission or any other interested State may bring the matter to the Court of Justice. Since a *Decision*, unlike a reasoned opinion, is a binding act it will be subject to challenge under Article 173 (*Commission* v *Belgium* (case 156/77), Article 184 proceedings; see chapter 29).

Article 225 provides an accelerated procedure whereby the Commission can, without preliminaries, bring a member State directly before the Court of Justice if it considers that that State is making improper use of its powers provided under Articles 223 and 224. Under these provisions States are empowered to take emergency measures to protect essential security interests (Article 223) or in the event of serious internal disturbances, war or threat of war, or for the purposes of maintaining peace and international security (Article 224). A ruling of the Court under Article 225 is given in camera.

Article 100A(4), para. 3, introduced by the Single European Act 1986, provides for the same accelerated procedure, whereby the Commission *or a member State* may bring a State before the Court of Justice if it considers that the State is making improper use of the powers provided for in Article 100A(4), para. 1 to 'apply national provisions on grounds of major needs referred to in Article 36 or relating to protection of the environment or the working environment' (see chapter 9).

Further reading

Barav, A., 'Failure of Member States to Fulfil their Obligations' (1975) 12 CML Rev 369.

Commission's Sixth Report on the Monitoring and Application of Community Law (1989) OJ C 330, 30 December.

Commission's Seventh Report on the Monitoring and Application of Community Law (1990) OJ C 232, p. 1.

Dashwood A. and White R., 'Enforcement Actions and Articles 169 & 170' (1989) 14 EL Rev 388.

Evans, A., 'The Enforcement Procedure of Article 169 EEC; Commission Discretion' (1970) 4 EL Rev 442.

Everling, U., 'The Member States of the European Community before their Court of Justice' (1984) 9 EL Rev 215.

Gray, C., 'Interim measures of Protection in the European Court' (1979) 4 EL Rev 80.

TWENTY SIX
Judicial review: introduction

The institutions of the Community, in particular the Commission and the Council, have been given power under the Treaty to make laws binding on States and individuals. Their area of competence has been signficantly extended by the Single European Act, and now, the Maastricht Treaty. As well as creating rights and obligations for States and individuals, secondary legislation may empower the Commission to impose substantial fines and penalties (e.g., Regulation 17/62 in the area of competition law, see chapter 15). It is therefore essential that the exercise of such powers be subject to review by the Court of Justice (or now the Court of First Instance), whose responsibility it is to see that 'the law is observed' (Article 164).

As has already been noted (chapters 23 and 24), Community secondary legislation may be challenged *indirectly* before the courts of member States, and questions of validity referred to the Court of Justice under Article 177. Chapters 26-30 are concerned primarily with the means whereby States, and sometimes individuals, may challenge the institutions *directly* before the European Courts.

There are two ways in which control over the institutions needs to be exercised. First it is necessary to ensure that the legislation issued by the institutions is valid; i.e., that the institution has the power to issue the act concerned, that it has been passed according to the correct procedures, and exercised for the right purposes. This constitutes a check on the institutions' *activities*. This is provided under Article 173, and, as an adjunct to Article 173, Article 184. Secondly there is a need to check on the institutions' *inactivity;* to ensure that the institutions do not fail to act when they are under a legal duty to do so. This is provided by Article 175.

Judicial review under Articles 173 and 175 requires an examination of three separate questions. First there is the question of *locus standi:* does this applicant have the right, personally, to bring proceedings? Secondly, if the action is under Article 173, has he brought his action in time? These two questions relate to admissibility. And thirdly, if the first questions are answered in the affirmative, is he entitled to succeed on the merits?

Although the system of judicial review provided by the Treaty is modelled on French administrative law, many of the concepts will be familiar to English lawyers.

TWENTY SEVEN
Direct action for annulment (Article 173)

Article 173 provides:

> The Court of Justice shall review the legality of acts of the Council and the Commission other than recommendations or opinions. It shall for this purpose have jurisdiction in actions brought by a member State, the Council or the Commission on grounds of lack of competence, infringement of an essential procedural requirement, infringement of this Treaty or of any rule of law relating to its application, or misuse of powers.
>
> Any natural or legal person may, under the same conditions, institute proceedings against a decision addressed to that person or against a decision which, although in the form of a Regulation or a Decision addressed to another person, is of direct and individual concern to the former.
>
> The proceedings provided for in this Article shall be instituted within two months of the publication of the measure, or of its notification to the plaintiff, or, in the absence thereof, of the day on which it came to the knowledge of the latter, as the case may be.

Reviewable acts

Reviewable acts, defined as acts 'other than recommendations and opinions', are not confined, as they might appear to be, to Regulations, Directives or Decisions. The Court has held that they include all measures taken by the institutions designed to have legal effect, whatever their nature or form (*Commission* v *Council (Re European Road Transport Agreement)* (case 22/70)). The measures in this case were minuted 'discussions' in which the Council had participated prior to the signing of the road transport agreement. The Commission sought to challenge these 'discussions' since it considered that the matter lay outside the Council's sphere of competence. Applying the above test, the action was declared admissible.

Similarly in *Re Noordwijk's Cement Accord* (cases 8 - 11/66), the act challenged was a registered letter sent by the Commission to the applicant in the context of EEC competition policy, to the effect that the companies' immunity from fines was at an end. The letter was not called a 'decision'. Nevertheless it was held that since it produced legal effects for the companies concerned and brought about a change in their legal position it was an act capable of annulment under Article 173.

This principle, that it is the true nature and effect of a measure rather than its label which determines whether it may be reviewed under Article 173, is very important, since Article 173 is subject to a strict two-month time-limit. If the measure is not recognised as a binding act and challenged in time, the action will be declared inadmissible, whatever its merits (e.g., *Commission* v *Belgium*, (case 156/77) — no success under Article 184 because the original act (a letter) was not attacked in time; see chapter 29).

Although Article 173 refers only to 'acts of the Council and the Commission' the Court has held that Parliament's acts too may be challenged, and was prepared to entertain such actions in *Luxembourg* v *European Parliament* (case 230/81) and *Partie Écologiste 'Les Verts'* v *European Parliament* (case 294/83). The reason for extending the scope of Article 173, advanced by the Court in these cases, was that Parliament's powers had grown. Whilst the EEC Treaty in its original form conferred on Parliament only powers of consultation and political control, Parliament now had power to take actions which had legal force with regard to third parties (see chapter 1). In *Luxembourg* v *European Parliament*, Luxembourg was seeking to challenge Parliament's resolution to move its seat from Luxembourg to Strasbourg and Brussels. In *'Les Verts'* v *European Parliament* the Green party sought to challenge a decision of the Bureau of Parliament on the allocation of campaign funds for the 1984 European elections. Clearly Parliament's acts in these cases produced significant legal effects for both applicants. However, a further action brought by the Green party (*Les Verts* v *Parliament* (case 190/84)), in which the Greens sought to challenge Parliament's action in authorising and implementing expenditure agreed by the Bureau under the same item (No. 3708) of the 1984 Budget, parts of which had already been successfully challenged in case 294/83, was held to be inadmissible, on the grounds that the acts in question had only internal legal effect. They were, the Court held:

> the result of individual decisions calculating the share of appropriation to be allocated to each political grouping, which are now final and irrevocable, since they were never challenged before the Court and indeed *could not have been challenged* insofar as they were addressed to political groupings other than the applicant.

The distinction between the Bureau's decision on the allocation of funds in case 294/83 and its measures authorising and implementing that decision in case 190/84 is not immediately apparent, since both types of measure resulted, for the applicants, in an (allegedly) unfair share of the Budget. The Maastricht Treaty has now amended Article 173 to include as reviewable acts 'acts adopted jointly by the Council and Parliament' and Acts of Parliament 'intended to produce legal effects *vis-à-vis* third parties'. Acts of the European Central Bank are also to be reviewable under Article 173 (Article G(53) of the TEU).

Locus standi; who may bring an action?

Member States, the Council and the Commission are entitled to challenge *any* binding act under Article 173. Such a right is not conferred expressly on Parliament. Clearly as a body whose task it is to supervise the Council and the Commission it may have an interest in challenging the acts of those bodies. Its interest was patent in *Roquette Frères SA* v *Council* (case 138/79) and *Maizena GmbH* v *Council* (case 139/79) when it was permitted (on the basis of Article 37 of the Statute of the Court) to intervene before the Court in annulment proceedings brought by Roquette Frères SA under Article 173, and thereby help to establish a failure on the part of the Council to consult Parliament.

Since Parliament has *locus standi* under Article 175 to bring an action against the institutions for failure to act it had been suggested that it should have a parallel right under Article 173, especially since, as will be seen, an action under Article 175 may be blocked, leaving the applicant only to his remedy under Article 173. However, in *Parliament* v *Council* (*Comitology*) (case 302/87), a case in which Parliament was seeking to annul a Decision of the Council laying down procedures to be followed by the Commission in determining, *inter alia*, the composition of the Committee of Representatives of member States, the Court held that this was not the case. It held, somewhat surprisingly, that there was 'no necessary link' between an action for failure to act and an action for annulment.

The Court modified its position in *Parliament* v *Council* (*Chernobyl*) (case C 70/88). Here it held, in the context of a challenge to a Decision taken by the Council, allegedly in breach of its obligation to consult Parliament, that Parliament did have *locus standi* to challenge acts of the Council or the Commission under Article 173 where this was necessary to protect its prerogative powers. This position has now been confirmed in the amendment to Article 173 contained in the Maastricht Treaty. Regrettably the Heads of State at Maastricht chose not to grant Parliament a general right to challenge acts of the Council and the Commission. Arguably, as the only democratically elected EEC institution, with an express role in *supervising* Community activities, it should have been given this power.

Compared with member States and Community institutions the *locus standi* of individuals under Article 173 is much more limited. A 'natural or legal person' is entitled only to challenge:

(a)   a decision addressed to *himself*, or
(b)   a decision, in the form of a regulation or a decision addressed to another person, which is of direct and individual concern to himself.

No problem exists where the decision is addressed to the applicant; provided he brings his action within the two-month time-limit his claim will be admissible. Many such decisions have been successfully challenged (e.g., in competition law; see chapters 13-15). However, where the decision is addressed to another person (which has been held to include a member State: *Plaumann & Co.* v *Commission* (case 25/62)) problems arise. Despite dicta by the Court in *Plaumann*, that the provisions of the Treaty concerning the right to seek a legal remedy ought not to be interpreted strictly, the Court has adopted a very restrictive approach towards the individual seeking to challenge acts addressed to another person. For his claim to be admissible he must satisfy three criteria:

(a)   the measure must be equivalent to a decision;
(b)   it must be of direct concern to himself, and
(c)   it must be of individual concern to himself.

Since *all* of these criteria must be fulfilled the question of admissibility may be decided, and the application rejected, on the basis of any one of them. In the order in which it examines the above requirements, and in its approach to all three criteria, the Court has not been consistent.

The measure must be, as far as the applicant is concerned, a Decision   Since many of the Commission's policies, particularly in the highly regulated field of agriculture, are implemented by directly applicable Regulations, often with wide-ranging and adverse effects on individuals (e.g., withdrawal of subsidies, imposition of levies), many cases have arisen in which individual applicants have sought to challenge Regulations. Although it would have been open to the Court to interpret Article 173(2) to enable them to do so provided that the applicant could prove 'direct and individual concern', it has insisted that an individual cannot challenge a true Regulation. Thus in *Koninklijke Scholten-Honig NV* v *Council and Commission* (case 101/76) the applicant glucose producers' attempt to challenge certain Regulations requiring glucose producers to pay levies on the production of glucose, for the benefit of sugar producers, was held, despite the merits of the case, to be inadmissible. (See also *Calpak SpA* v *Commission* (cases 789 & 790/79) — attempt (failed) by Italian pear processors to challenge a Regulation fixing production aids for pear processors.)

However, whether a measure is, as far as the applicant is concerned, a 'true' Regulation or not involves a very subtle enquiry. In *Confédération Nationale des Producteurs de Fruits et Légumes* v *Council* (cases 16 & 17/62) the Court held that in order to determine the legal nature of an act it is necessary to consider the nature and content of an act rather than its form. It is the substance, not the label, which is crucial. A true Regulation is a measure of general application, i.e., normative; it applies to objectively determined situations and produces legal effects on categories of persons viewed abstractly and in their entirety. On the other hand the essential feature of a Decision, which is defined as 'binding upon those to whom it is addressed' (Article 189) arises from the limitation of the persons to whom it is addressed; a Decision concerns designated persons individually.

In *International Fruit NV* v *Commission (No. 1)* (cases 41-4/70) the applicants, a group of fruit importers, were held entitled to challenge a Community 'Regulation' laying down the quantity of import licences to be issued for a certain period. The quantity of licences was calculated on the basis of applications from, *inter alia,* the applicants, received during the preceding week; thus it applied to a finite number of people and was issued in response to their applications. Although it appeared to be a general measure it was found in fact to be a disguised bundle of decisions addressed to each applicant (see also *Roquette Frères SA* v *Council* case 138/79).

A 'Regulation' may also be deemed to be 'hybrid' in nature, i.e., it may be a measure of general application which is, nonetheless, in the nature of a decision for certain 'designated individuals'. In the *Japanese ball-bearings cases* (cases 113 & 118 - 21/77) four major Japanese producers of ball-bearings were held entitled to challenge an EEC anti-dumping Regulation. Although the measure was of general application some of its Articles specifically referred to the applicants. Similarly in *Allied Corporation* v *Commission* (cases 239 & 275/82) some of the applicant companies seeking to annul an anti-dumping Regulation were charged with illegal dumping in the Regulation itself. Thus for them it was in the nature of a Decision, and, as such, challengeable. Yet at the same time, *vis-à-vis* importers of the products concerned (chemical fertilisers), who, although adversely affected by the measure, were not singled out in any way by the Regulation, it was a Regulation, and their challenge was held inadmissible. (See also *Alusuisse Italia SpA* v *Council and Commission* (case 307/81) — anti-dumping Regulation not challengeable by importers.)

It is not necessary, for a claim by an individual to be admissible, that the Regulation, or part of the Regulation, be addressed *expressly* to the applicant. Provided its applicability to his particular situation is *implicit,* as in the *International Fruit Co. NV* case, it will be deemed to be in the nature of a Decision to him.

In *Timex Corporation* v *Council and Commission* (case 264/82) the applicant company, which succeeded in establishing *locus standi* to challenge another anti-dumping Regulation, was this time a complainant which, through its national trade association, had brought certain illegal dumping practices (concerning Russian watches and watch movements) to the Commission's attention. The Regulation had been issued as a result of enquiries following Timex's complaints. The court held that although the measure was legislative (i.e., normative) in nature, it was a decision of direct and individual concern to Timex since it had been issued in response to Timex's complaint and the company had given evidence to the Commission during the anti-dumping proceedings.

As will be seen the enquiry needed to establish whether a Regulation is in fact in the nature of a Decision to the individual applicant is much the same as that required to establish whether he is 'individually' concerned.

It should be noted that where the measure in question is described as a Decision, provided it has a specific addressee, the Court presumes it to be a Decision, even though, as in the case of a Decision addressed to a member State, it may lay down normative rules.

The measure must be of direct concern to the applicant   A measure will be of direct concern to the applicant if it leaves the State no real discretion in implementation. Often the Commission will issue a Decision to a State requiring, or authorising, the State to act in a particular manner. Whether the individual affected by such action may challenge the Community Decision will depend on whether the action affecting the applicant was within the area of the member State's discretion or not. In *Eridania* v *Commission* (cases 10 & 18/68) an Italian sugar-refining company sought to challenge three Commission Decisions granting aid to its competitors. Its action under Article 173 was declared inadmissible. Although the Commission's Decisions had authorised the granting of aid, and indeed named the companies concerned, those Decisions were not of direct concern to the applicants, since the decision regarding the *allocation* of the aid had been made by the Italian government. This was a matter within the government's discretion. Where the matter of which the applicant complains lies within the discretion of the State the appropriate challenge is to the national authority responsible for the relevant decision.

The question of whether a particular Community Decision leaves room for discretion on the part of a member State is susceptible of different interpretations. Interpreted broadly, as in *Plaumann & Co.* v *Commission* (case 25/62) and *SA Alcan Aluminium Raeren* v *Commission* (case 69/69), it could mean that where the Commission merely *permits* or *authorises* a State to act the State still retains a discretion as to whether to act or not. In *Alcan* the Court agreed with Advocate-General Roemer's suggestion in *Plaumann* that even where the Commission *refuses* permission to act, the State, in its discretion, may choose to act in disregard of this refusal and face the consequences of an action under Article 169. On the other hand, interpreting the question of discretion narrowly, as in the *Japanese ball-bearings* case (cases 113 & 118–21/77), it could be said that where implementation of a Community Decision is *automatic* or a *foregone conclusion,* as can be presumed where permission or authorisation is sought, no real discretion exists on the part of the State, and the measure will be of direct concern to the applicant.

A number of cases in which the applicant has succeeded in establishing *locus standi,* such as *Alfred Toepfer KG* v *Commission* (cases 106 & 107/63) and *Werner A. Bock KG* v *Commission* (case 62/70) have involved Decisions of confirmation (*Toepfer*) or authorisation (*Bock*). In these cases it seems to have been presumed that the measures were of direct concern to the applicants. In the more recent case of *AE Piraiki-Patraiki* v *Commission* (case 11/82), in the context of a Commission Decision authorising the French to impose a quota system on imports of Greek yarn, Advocate-General VerLoren van Themaat suggested that a Community measure would be of direct concern if its legal effects on interested parties and their identity could 'with certainty or with a high degree of probability be inferred'. The Court considered that the possibility that the French government would not take advantage of the Commission's Decision was 'purely theoretical'. Thus the more recent dicta and the practice of the Court indicate that the more generous attitude to questions of direct concern will be preferred to the restrictive approach of *Plaumann* and *Alcan.* Nonetheless on the question of direct concern *Plaumann* and *Alcan* still remain a trap for the unwary (see Commission's view in *Spijker Kwasten BV* v *Commission* (case 231/82)).

The measure must be of individual concern to the applicant   The concept of individual concern has been construed very restrictively by the Court. Because it operates to exclude so many cases it is often the first criterion to be examined, as it was in *Plaumann & Co.* v *Commission* (case 25/62). Plaumann & Co. were importers of clementines who sought to annul a Commission Decision, addressed to the German government, refusing the government permission to reduce its customs duties on clementines imported from outside the EEC. Plaumann & Co. claimed that as a large-scale importer of such clementines they were 'individually concerned'. The Court disagreed. The importing of clementines, the Court held, was an activity which could be carried out by anyone at any time. There was nothing in the Decision to distinguish Plaumann & Co. from any other importer of clementines. In order to establish individual concern, the applicant must prove that the Decision affects him because of certain characteristics which are peculiarly relevant to him, or by reason of circumstances in which he is differentiated from all other persons, and not by the mere fact that he belongs to a class of persons who are affected.

The *'Plaumann'* test has become the classic test for individual concern. It is, however, more easily stated than applied, since it does not specify *what* characteristics 'peculiarly relevant to him' the applicant must prove to establish individual concern.

It will *not* be sufficient to prove that his business interests have been adversely affected, as was clearly the case in *Plaumann & Co.* v *Commission*. *Nor* that they were affected in a different way, or more seriously, than other similar traders. These arguments were rejected in *Eridania* (cases 10 & 18/68), and in *Calpak* (cases 789 & 790/79), in which the applicant pear processors claimed that the Commission's mode of calculation of pear processing aids operated particularly unfairly on itself as a private company as compared with other pear producers such as public companies and cooperatives.

Nor is it sufficient that the applicant's identity is known to, or ascertainable by, the Commission when the measure is passed. In *UNICME* v *Council* (case 123/77) an association of Italian motorcycle importers was seeking to annul a Commission Regulation, authorising the Italian government to impose temporary quotas on motorcycles imported from Japan. The measure was in retaliation for the imposition by the Japanese of a quota on the import of Italian ski boots. Members of the association were the only persons concerned and they were all concerned. They were ascertainable and many had already applied for import licences. Their application was held inadmissable. The Court found it unnecessary to consider whether the contested measure was a true Regulation, since it was not of direct or individual concern to the applicants. It 'would only affect the interests of the applicants when their request for a licence was refused'. 'The possibility of determining more or less precisely the number or even the identity of the persons to whom the measure applies by no means implies that it must be regarded as being of individual concern to them.' Whilst the former statement may be open to question as a ground for denying direct and individual concern, since it could be applied to *any* act addressed to a third party, such as the Decisions in *Bock* and

International Fruit Co. NV, which were found to be of individual concern, the latter recurs consistently in the Court's case law on individual concern.

Will a measure be deemed of individual concern if a causal connection can be proved between a particular measure and the applicant's own case? This was not found to be the case in *Spijker Kwasten BV* v *Commission* (case 231/82). Here the Commission issued a Decision, at the request of the Dutch government, enabling the government to ban the import of Chinese brushes for a six-month period, from July to 31 December 1982. Prior to the above request being made the applicant had applied for a licence to import such brushes. There was no doubt a causal link between its application and the Dutch government's request. The request and the Commission's Decision were prompted by its application. Moreover the company was the only importer of these brushes in Holland, and the only one likely to want to import them during the six-month period in question. Yet it was held not to be individually concerned. The measure, the Court held, was of general application. There was nothing to stop others applying for licences during that same period.

This case also confirmed a point established earlier in *Glucoseries Réunies* v *Commission* (case 1/64), that the fact that the applicant (in this case the sole producer of glucose in Belgium and the principal exporter of glucose in France) is the *only* person likely to be affected by the measure is not a characteristic peculiarly relevant to him such as to give rise to individual concern, as long as there is a theoretical possibility that others can enter the field and be affected by the same measure.

What characteristic peculiarly relevant to him must the applicant then prove in order to establish individual concern?

Although there is no single satisfactory test a common thread runs through all the cases in which individual concern has been held to exist. In every case the measure which the applicant seeks to challenge, although addressed to another person, is referable specifically to his situation. Moreover, not only does it affect him as though he were the person addressed, but it affects him either *alone* or as a member of a fixed and *closed* class; no one else is capable of entering the field and being affected by the same measure.

For example, the measure may have been issued in response to a licence or tender application. In *Alfred Toepfer KG* v *Commission* (cases 106 & 107/63) Toepfer had, amongst others, requested a licence from the German government to import cereals from France. The Commission's Decision, made at the request of the German government, was a confirmation of the government's measure refusing to grant the import certificate. The only persons affected by the Decision were those who had already applied for licences. Thus they were individually concerned.

Similarly in *Werner A. Bock KG* v *Commission* (case 62/70), the firm of Bock had applied for a permit to import a consignment of Chinese mushrooms, for which it already had a firm offer. Since Chinese mushrooms at the time were in free circulation in the EEC, the German government, if it wished to prohibit their import into Germany, needed authority from the Commission to do so.

Following Bock's application, the German government, on 11 September, applied to the Commission for that authority, which the Commission granted by a Decision on 15 September. The Court held that Bock was individually concerned; the Decision was passed in response to its application. (See also *Simmenthal SpA* v *Commission* (case 92/78) — Decision issued in response to plaintiff's tender.)

A similar connection existed in *Philip Morris Holland BV* v *Commission* (case 730/79). Here the Decision in question, which was addressed to the Dutch government, requested the government to refrain from granting State aid to the applicant tobacco company, Philip Morris. The Court assumed without argument that the company was individually concerned.

International Fruit Co. NV v *Commission (No. 1)* (cases 41 - 4/70) concerned a Commission 'Regulation', controlling the issue of import licences for apples from non-member States. The Regulation was issued by the Commission on the basis of applications received during the preceding week, following an assessment of the overall situation. It applied *only* to those who had applied for licences during that week. It was held to be of individual concern to the applicants. On the same reasoning the measure was found not to be a true Regulation at all, but a bundle of Decisions.

However, even a 'true' Regulation can be of individual concern to *some* individuals, as it can be in the nature of a Decision to some individuals, if it is referable expressly or impliedly to their particular situation, either alone or as a member of a known and *closed* class (*Japanese ball-bearing case* (cases 113 & 118 - 21/77); *Allied Corporation* v *Commission* (cases 239 & 275/82); *CAM SA* v *Commission* (case 100/74), overruling *Compagnie Française Commerciale et Financière SA* v *Commission* (case 64/69)). *Sofrimport SARL* v *Commission* (case C 152/88) concerned a successful challenge of this nature. The applicants, who were fruit importers, were seeking to annul a number of Commission Regulations suspending the issue of import licences for apples from Chile and fixing quantities of such imports from third countries. Under one of the Regulations (2702/72) the Commission was required under Article 3 to take into account, when exercising its powers under the Regulations, the 'special position of products in transit' when the Regulations come into force. The applicants had goods in transit when the contested Regulations came into force. The Court held that they were individually concerned. 'Such persons constituted a restricted group *which could not be extended* after the contested measure took effect.'

The reason why the applicant in *Spijker Kwasten* (case 231/82) failed to establish individual concern was that, although there was a causal link between its licence application and the Commission's Decision, the latter measure allowing the Dutch authorities to introduce a quota was deliberately designed to take effect for the period *subsequent* to that for which the applicant had applied for licences. The applications it had already lodged were not affected by the measure: it applied only to future transactions: thus there was a theoretical possibility that other traders could be equally affected.

A rather different situation in which the necessary link has been held to exist between the applicant and the challenged act to constitute individual concern, is when the act is not 'directed at' him but issued as a result of proceedings in which the applicant has played a legitimate part. In *Metro-SB-Grossmärkte GmbH & Co. KG* v *Commission* (case 26/76) the applicant was seeking to challenge a Decision issued to another firm, SABA, in the context of EEC competition policy. The Decision was issued following a complaint by Metro under Article 3 of Regulation 17/62 (see chapter 15) that SABA was acting in breach of Article 85. The Court held, on the question of admissibility, that since persons with a legitimate interest were entitled, under Article 3 of Regulation 17/62, to request the Commission to investigate the infringement they should be allowed to institute Article 173 proceedings in order to protect that interest. Thus Metro was individually concerned.

On similar reasoning, in *Timex Corporation* v *Council and Commission* (case 264/82), Timex was deemed to be individually concerned and permitted to challenge an anti-dumping Regulation; the company had initiated the complaint (as it was entitled to do under a further anti-dumping Regulation) and had given evidence in the proceedings. (See also *COFAZ* v *Commission* (case 169/84) — applicants individually concerned in Commission Decision concerning State aids; they had initiated the complaint and taken part in the proceedings; see also *FEDIOL* v *Commission* (case 191/82).)

Apart from these two general categories of cases in which individual concern may be found, two exceptional cases must be mentioned. In *Partie Écologiste 'Les Verts'* v *European Parliament* (case 294/83) the Court found that the Green party was individually concerned in Parliament's Decision, taken in 1983, allocating funds for the European election campaign of 1984, even though the Decision affected all the political parties, actual and potential, seeking election in 1984. The Green party was thus only affected as a member of an indeterminate class. However, the Court's decision on this matter was clearly (and expressly) based on policy. It reasoned that the political parties represented on the Bureau making the Decision on the allocation of funds had themselves benefited from the allocation, and there was no way in which rival groupings might challenge this allocation in advance of the elections. The case was thus admissible and the applicants succeeded in their claim for annulment. As has been noted, the Court took a more restrictive view in the subsequent case of *Les Verts* v *Parliament* (case 190/84).

AE Piraiki-Patraiki v *Commission* (case 11/82) concerned rather different facts. The applicants were a group of Greek manufacturers and exporters of cotton yarn, who sought to challenge a Commission Decision addressed to the French government authorising the latter to impose a quota system on the import of Greek cotton yarn. Since the Decision applied generally and there were no factors linking it directly with the applicants' particular situation one might have imagined that individual concern would be lacking. This was not found to be the case. The Court found that for those who, prior to the Decision, had entered into contracts to be performed subsequently, the Decision was of individual concern. The Court's Decision was firmly based on Article 13(3) of the Act of Accession 1979, which imposes a duty on the Commission to consider those whose contracts may be affected by their measures. The Commission's Decision was held not to be of individual concern to manufacturers and exporters whose existing contracts were not affected by the measure.

In that the Act of Accession expressly required the Commission to take into account those manufacturers and exporters whose contracts might be affected by its measures the decision is consistent with *Sofrimport* (case C 150/88). Nevertheless whilst such a class is closed it is potentially very wide. Thus *AE Paraiki-Patraiki* must be seen as a case resting on its own special facts, and not as giving rise to a general claim for individual concern based on interference with the applicants' existing contracts. EC legislation will frequently interfere with existing business contracts: this will not of itself be sufficient to constitute individual concern.

It is no doubt this fear of opening floodgates, together with a desire not unduly to hamper the institutions in their task of implementing Community policies, problems common to all administrative law systems, which has led the court to interpret Article 173, particularly Article 173(2) concerning the *locus standi* of individuals, restrictively. In closing the door to an application under Article 173 the Court has often adverted to the possibility of alternative action before the applicant's national courts (e.g., *Spijker Kwasten BV* v *Commission* (case 231/82); *UNICME* (case 133/77)). It has been suggested that this roundabout approach to matters of validity (which can only be decided authoritatively by the Court of Justice) is prompted by a desire to filter out unnecessary claims and ensure that only the claims of genuine merit reach the Court of Justice. One such claim was *Royal Scholten-Honig (Holdings) Ltd* v *Intervention Board for Agricultural Produce* (cases 103 & 145/77) (decision of 7 October 1978, see chapters 4 and 24) in which the plaintiff finally succeeded in obtaining a declaration of invalidity on a reference under Article 177, having failed to establish *locus standi* in an action under Article 173 (*Koninklijke Scholten-Honig NV* v *Council and Commission* (case 143/77); decision of 5 May 1977) on the grounds that the disputed measure was a true Regulation. Thus where the merits of the case are clear and his *locus standi* under Article 173 doubtful, *a fortiori* where the measure appears to be a true Regulation, the better course for the individual would be to raise the issue of invalidity before his national court and press for an early reference to the Court of Justice under Article 177. This does, however, depend on there being an appropriate issue of national law in which the question of the validity of the Community measure may be raised. Where no such issue exists the individual has no option but to seek a direct remedy before the Court of Justice.

Time-limits

An applicant, whether an individual, a member State or a Community institution, must bring his claim for annulment within two months of:

   (a)   the publication of the measure, or
   (b)   its notification to the plaintiff, or, in the absence thereof,
   (c)   the day on which it came to the knowledge of the latter, as the case may be (Article 173(3)).

The Rules of Procedure of the Court of Justice 1985 provide that time runs from receipt by the person concerned of notification of the measure or, where the measure is published, from the 15th day after its publication in the *Official Journal* (Article 83(1)).

Since Regulations are required to be published (Article 191 of the EEC Treaty) time will run for them from the date of publication, subject to the 1985 Rules of Procedure. Although Directives and Decisions are normally published it seems that since they are addressed to member States or individuals the date of notification will be decisive.

The 'date of knowledge' is the date on which the applicant became aware of the measure. It is not the date on which he realised it was challengeable. Hence the importance of recognising an act as a measure capable of annulment.

The limitation period may be extended to take into account the distance between the Court of Justice at Luxembourg and the applicant's place of residence (Rules of Procedure, Article 81(2)). In the UK 10 days are allowed.

Once the two-month time-limit has expired a plaintiff cannot seek to challenge a measure by the back door, either by invoking Article 184 (*exception d'illégalité*, see *Commission* v *Belgium* (case 156/77)) or by alleging a failure to act (under Article 175) when the institution concerned refuses by Decision to amend or withdraw the disputed measure (see *Eridania* v *Commission* (cases 10 & 18/68)) or take the requested action (*Irish Cement* v *Commission* (cases 166/86, 220/86), see chapter 28).

An indirect challenge before the applicant's national court will, on the other hand, not be subject to the two-month limit. In actions before national courts national rules of limitation apply.

The merits

Once the Court has decided that the claim is admissible, the case will be decided on the merits. Article 173 provides four grounds for annulment, drawn directly from French administrative law. These are:

(a) Lack of competence.
(b) Infringement of an essential procedural requirement.
(c) Infringement of the Treaty or any rule of law relating to its application.
(d) Misuse of powers.

Lack of competence This is the equivalent to the English doctrine of substantive *ultra vires*. The institution responsible for adopting the measure in question must have the legal authority to do so. This may derive from the EEC Treaty or from secondary legislation. In the *ERTA* case (case 22/70) the Commission challenged the Council's power to participate in the shaping of the road transport agreement, since under the Treaty (Article 228) it is the Commission which is empowered to negotiate international agreements and the Council whose duty it is to conclude them. On the facts the Court found that the Council had not exceeded is powers.

Infringement of an essential procedural requirement This is equivalent to procedural *ultra vires*. Institutions, when enacting binding measures, must follow the correct procedures. These procedures may be laid down in the EEC Treaty or secondary legislation (e.g., Regulation 17/62 on competition law, see chapter 15). For example, Article 190 of the EEC Treaty requires that all secondary legislation must state the reasons on which it is based, and must refer to proposals and opinions which were required to be obtained. The Court has held that reasons must not be too vague or inconsistent; they must be coherent; they must mention figures and essential facts on which they rely. They must be adequate to indicate the conscientiousness of the Decision, and detailed enough to be scrutinised by the Court (*Germany* v *Commission (Re Tariff Quotas on Wine)* (case 24/62) — Commission Decision annulled; too vague, no facts and figures). The purpose of the requirement to give reasons is to enable those concerned to defend their rights and to enable the Court to exercise its supervisory jurisdiction. However, the Court will not annul an act for an insignificant defect. Nor will it annul an act on this ground unless the plaintiff can prove that, but for this defect, the result would have been different (*Distillers Co. Ltd* v *Commission* (case 30/78)).

In *Roquette Frères SA* v *Council* (case 138/79) and *Maizena GmbH* v *Council* (case 139/79) a Council Regulation was annulled on the grounds of the Council's failure to consult Parliament, as it was required to do under Article 43(2) of the EEC Treaty. Although the Council had consulted Parliament, it was held not to have given Parliament sufficient time to express an opinion on the measure in question. Where no time-limit is imposed it is presumed that Parliament must be given a reasonable time in which to express its opinion.

Infringement of the Treaty or any rule of law relating to its application Clearly when an act is invalid for lack of competence or for an infringement of an essential procedural requirement, this may involve an infringement of the Treaty, but this ground of annulment is wider since it extends to *any* Treaty provision. In *Adams* v *Commission (No. 1)* (case 145/83) action under Article 215(2) (see chapter 30), the Commission was found to have acted in breach of its duty of confidentiality under Article 214.

Infringement of any rule of law relating to the Treaty's application is wider again and certainly wider than any comparable rule of English law. This is where general principles of law, discussed at length in chapter 4, are relevant. A measure can be annulled if it is in breach not only of any general principle of law approved by the Court (e.g., equality, proportionality) but of any principle common to the constitutions of member States (*Internationale Handelsgesellschaft mbH* (case 11/70)) and even principles of international treaties in the field of human rights on which member States have collaborated (*J. Nold KG* v *Commission* (case 4/73)). In *Royal Scholten-Honig (Holdings) Ltd* v *Intervention Board for Agricultural Produce* (cases 103 & 145/77) a Community Regulation was held invalid for breach of the principle of equality. In *Transocean Marine Paint Association* v *Commission* (case 17/74) (see chapter 4) part of a Decision was annulled for breach of the principle of natural justice. In *August Topfer & Co. GmbH* v *Commission* (case 112/77) a Decision was annulled for breach of the principle of legal certainty. Thus this ground is one of considerable potential. Although it has not yet been done legislation could in principle be challenged for breach of the principle of subsidiarity, arguably even before the TEU is ratified (see chapter 1).

Misuse of power This concept stems from the French '*détournement de pouvoir*'. It means, broadly, the use of a power for purposes other than those for which it was granted, for example, where powers granted to help one group (e.g., producers) are used to benefit another (e.g., distributors) (see *Simmenthal SpA* v *Commission* case 92/78)). The concept is not confined to abuses of power, nor is an ulterior or improper motive essential; an improper or illegitimate use of power is all that is required. However, this provision has been narrowly interpreted. In *Fédération Charbonnière de Belgique* v *High Authority* (case 8/55), in interpreting the comparable provision (Article 33) of the ECSC Treaty, the Court held that a measure will not be annulled for misuse of power if the improper use had no effect on its substance; nor will it be annulled if the authority had acted from mixed motives, proper and improper, as long as the proper purpose was dominant. It is thus a difficult ground to establish.

The case of *Werner A. Bock KG* v *Commission* (case 62/70) was considered, but not decided, on this ground. Although there was no clear collusion between the German government and the Commission over the issuing of the Decision, there were definite signs of collaboration. The case was eventually decided, and the Decision annulled, for breach of the principle of proportionality. The Commission's action was more than was necessary in the circumstances, since the quantities of mushrooms at stake were so small as to be insignificant.

There is much overlap between the above grounds. The Court rarely examines each one precisely and is often vague as to which ground forms the basis of its decision. It is wise to plead as many grounds as seem applicable.

The grounds apply equally to an examination of the validity of a measure on reference from national courts under Article 177. They also apply to an enquiry into the validity of Regulations under Article 184 (chapter 29) and to an application for damages under Article 215(2) (chapter 30) where the action is based on an illegal act of the institutions.

If an annulment action under Article 173 is successful the act will be declared void under Article 174. Under Article 174(2), however, the Court may, following a successful action for annulment, 'state which of the effects of the Regulation which it has declared void shall be considered as definitive'. Thus, in the interests of legal certainty, the retroactive effects of a declaration under Article 174 may be limited where Regulations are concerned. A measure may be declared void in part only, provided that the offending part can be effectively severed.

Further reading

Bradley & St. Clair, K., 'The variable evolution of the standing of the European Parliament in proceedings before the Court of Justice' (1988) 8 YEL 27.

Bradley St Clair, K., 'Sense and Sensibility: *Parliament* v *Council* Continuing' (1991) 16 EL Rev 245.

Greaves, R., 'Locus Standi under Article 173 EEC when seeking annulment of a Regulation' (1986) 11 EL Rev 119.

Harding, C., 'The Private Interest in Challenging Community Action' (1980) 5 EL Rev 345.

Hartley, T.C., *The Foundations of European Community Law*, 2nd ed. (Oxford: Clarendon Press, 1988).

Rasmussen, H., 'Why is Article 173 interpreted against Private Plaintiffs?' (1980) 5 EL Rev 112.

Schermers, H.G., *Judicial Protection in the European Communities*, 4th ed. (London: Kluwer Law & Taxation Publishers, 1987).

de Wilmars, M., and Mertens, J., 'The Case Law of the ECJ in Relation to the Review of the Legality of Economic Policy in Mixed Economy Systems' (1982) 1 LIEI 1.

TWENTY EIGHT
Action for failure to act (Article 175)

If the institutions of the Community are to operate according to the rule of law, as they are obliged to do under Article 4 of the EEC Treaty, they must be answerable not only for their actions but for their failure to act in breach of EEC law. This is provided for by Article 175, as follows:

> Should the Council or the Commission, in infringement of this Treaty, fail to act, the member States and the other institutions of the Community may bring an action before the Court of Justice to have the infringement established.
>
> The action shall be admissible only if the institution concerned has first been called upon to act. If, within two months of being so called upon, the institution concerned has not defined its position, the action may be brought within a further period of two months.
>
> Any natural or legal person may, under the conditions laid down in the preceding paragraphs, complain to the Court of Justice that an institution of the Community has failed to address to that person any act other than a recommendation or an opinion.

Article 175 and Article 173 are essentially complementary remedies. As the Court of Justice held in *Chevalley* v *Commission* (case 15/70) when confronted with the applicant's uncertainty as to whether Article 175 or Article 173 was the appropriate form of action, it is not necessary to characterise the proceedings as being under one or the other Article, since both Articles merely prescribe one and the same method of recourse. They represent two aspects of the same legal remedy. For this reason it has been suggested that any inconsistency between the two provisions should be resolved by applying the same principles to both. This is known as the 'unity principle'. This is all the more important in the light of the Court's interpretation of Article 175, which may result in an action, begun under Article 175, being concluded under Article 173. However, the unity principle appears to have been denied in *Parliament* v *Council* (*Comitology*) (case 302/87), at least in the context of *locus standi*, when, contrary to Advocate-General Darmon's Submissions, the Court refused to admit an action by Parliament under Article 173, seeking to annul a Decision of the Council relating to the composition and role of Committees of Representatives of member States, on the grounds that there was 'no necessary link' between an action for failure to act and an action for annulment. Whilst the Court modified its position in *Parliament* v *Council (Chernobyl)* (case C 70/88) by allowing Parliament *locus standi* under Article 173 in order to protect its own prerogative powers, the Heads of State at Maastricht were content to reflect this position and, in amending Article 173, chose not to extend the unity principle to its logical conclusion.

Reviewable omissions

The institution's failure to act must, first and foremost, be 'in infringement of this Treaty'. Since this would include legislation enacted under the Treaty it would apply to any failure on the part of the institution to act when it was under a legal duty to do so. In *European Parliament* v *Council* (case 13/83), in an action by Parliament under Article 175 alleging the Council's failure to implement a Community transport policy, the Court held that 'failure' can cover a failure to take a number of decisions; the nature of the acts which may be requested need not be clearly circumscribed as long as they are sufficiently identified. The failures alleged by Parliament in this case were:

(a)   failure to introduce a common transport policy, as required by Article 74, and
(b)   failure to introduce measures to secure freedom to provide transport services, as required by Articles 75, 59, 60 and 61.

The Court held that Parliament was entitled to succeed on the second allegation but not on the first. Whilst the second obligation was complete and legally perfect, and should have been implemented by the Council within the transitional period, the former obligation was insufficiently precise to constitute an enforceable obligation. This case, together with the Single European Act, provided the momentum for the development of a Community transport policy during the past few years.

Although only non-binding acts in the form of recommendations and opinions are expressly excluded in the context of individual action under Article 175(3), the unity principle would suggest that a failure under Article 175 would only cover a failure to issue a binding act.

In conformity with Article 173, Article 175 is expressed to apply to a failure to act on the part of the Council and the Commission. However, since the Court has now declared that Parliament may be subject to Article 173 proceedings (*Luxembourg* v *European Parliament* (case 230/81); *Partie Écologiste 'Les Verts'* v *European Parliament* (case 294/83); see chapter 27) this provides a strong argument that Parliament should also be answerable to the Court under Article 175. Not only does it have power to take actions which have legal force with regard to third parties, it also has a duty to act in certain circumstances (e.g., increased consultative and budgetary role, see chapter 1). In the light of its new powers of co-decision granted under the Maastricht Treaty Parliament's omissions will be subject to review under an amended Article 175 as soon as the Treaty takes effect. Omissions of the European Central Bank will also be subject to review (see Article G(54) of the TEU).

Locus standi

Unlike the position under Article 173, Parliament, as one of the 'institutions' of the Community is, along with member States and the other institutions, a 'privileged applicant' under Article 175. Privileged applicants enjoy a right to challenge *any* failure on the part of the Council and the Commission, i.e., an omission to adopt *any* binding act which these institutions have a duty to adopt. Parliament's (partial) success in *European Parliament* v *Council* (case 13/83) illustrates the potential, as yet largely untapped, of Article 175 as a means of control of the two principal law-making institutions by a directly elected and determined Parliament. The European Central Bank will also have a general *locus standi* 'in the areas falling within [its] field of competence' (Article G(54) of the TEU).

By comparison with member States and Community institutions, individuals, as under Article 173, have a limited *locus standi* under Article 175(3). Natural or legal persons may only bring proceedings where the institution complained of has failed to address to that person any act other than a recommendation or an opinion. Since an act which is addressed to a designated person is in substance a Decision, this seems to mean that an individual's *locus standi* is limited to a failure on the part of the Council or Commission to adopt what is in essence a *Decision* addressed to *himself*. He has no express *locus standi* to challenge an omission to address to *another person* a Decision of direct and individual concern to himself.

This apparent deficiency has been remedied by the Court. In *Nordgetreide GmbH & Co. KG* v *Commission* (case 42/71) Advocate-General Roemer, invoking the unity principle, suggested that since Articles 173 and 175 constituted part of a coherent system, an individual should have a right to demand a Decision *vis-à-vis* a third party in which he was directly and individually concerned. In *Bethell* v *Commission* (case 246/81) this right was implied when the Court, in rejecting Lord Bethell's claim as inadmissible, held that he had failed to show that the Commission had failed to adopt, in relation to him, a measure *which he was legally entitled to claim*. Thus, in the context of Article 175, the equivalent to a Decision of direct and individual concern under Article 173, is a Decision which the applicant is *legally entitled to claim*. Many of the failed claims under Article 175 have failed because the applicant was seeking the adoption of an act which he was not entitled to claim (e.g., *Bethell; Firma C. Mackprang Jr* v *Commission* (case 15/71) — plaintiff seeking amendment of a Decision addressed to the German government; *Star Fruit Company SA* v *Commission* (case 247/87) — individual not entitled to demand action by Commission under Article 169)). On rather different reasoning in *Eridania* v *Commission* (cases 10 & 18/68) the Court held that the applicants could not invoke Article 175 in order to obtain a revocation by the Commission of a Decision addressed to third parties, since other methods of recourse, namely, Article 173, were provided by the Treaty; to allow parallel recourse via Article 175 would enable applicants to avoid the conditions (i.e. time-limits) laid down by the Treaty.

It is clear that the act demanded must be in substance a Decision. In *Nordgetreide GmbH & Co. KG* v *Commission* (case 42/71) the applicant company was seeking the amendment by the Commission of a Regulation. When the Commission rejected its request the company instituted two actions, one for failure to act, under Article 175, and one under Article 173 for annulment of the Commission's Decision refusing to act. The action under Article 175 would in any case have failed because, as Advocate-General Roemer pointed out, the company was seeking from the Commission what would have amounted to a normative act; in fact the Court found its claim inadmissible on different grounds (to be discussed below). The claim under Article 173 was also held inadmissible. Although the contested Decision was addressed to the company, the Court held that a Decision refusing to act (a 'negative' Decision) would only be open to attack under Article 173 if the *positive* measure being sought were open to attack (see also Advocate-General Gand in *Alfons Lütticke GmbH* v *Commission* (case 48/65)). Since the company was seeking to amend a Regulation, this would not be the case. This same reasoning would apply to a refusal by the Commission to issue a Decision to another person which the applicants were not entitled to claim. Thus, even though a Decision may have been addressed to the applicant, Article 173 cannot be invoked as an adjunct to Article 175 to annul a decision not to act, in order to compel an institution to act *when it has no duty to do so at the behest of the applicant*. Although this has been attempted on a number of occasions (e.g., *Alfons Lütticke GmbH* v *Commission* (case 48/65); *Star Fruit Company SA* v *Commission* — applicants demanding action by the Commission under Article 169 against a member State; *Bethell* v *Commission* (case 246/81) — applicant seeking to force Commission to take action under Article 89 against member States' airlines), it has always failed.

A case in which the applicant was entitled to demand action from the Commission, but in which its claim was surprisingly held inadmissible, was *Deutscher Komponistenverbande* v *Commission* (case 8/71). Here the applicant alleged that the Commission had failed in its obligation under EEC competition law (Regulation 17/62) to grant it, as a complainant under Article 3 of that Regulation, a hearing. Advocate-General Roemer suggested that acts susceptible of action under Article 175 should cover any measures which give rise to legal effects for the applicant; they should then include measures of a procedural nature. The Court disagreed, holding that Article 175(3) only applied to a failure to adopt a Decision; it did not cover the promulgation of a formal act. Nevertheless the Court did examine the merits and concluded that since the applicant had had an opportunity to make its submissions in writing there had been no failure on the part of the Commission.

It is submitted that Advocate-General Roemer's view is to be preferred to that of the Court. Since there was no doubt that the applicant was entitled to a hearing any failure to grant it that hearing should have been actionable under

Article 175. And if it was refused such a hearing, as it was, it should have been entitled to challenge that refusal under Article 173, since the positive measure requested was one which it was entitled to demand. No such challenge was made in *Deutscher Komponisternerbande* v *Commission*.

This view seems to have been taken by the Court in *FEDIOL* v *Commission* (case 191/82). In this case an EEC federation of seed crushers and oil processors was seeking to compel the Commission to take action against alleged dumping practices on the part of Brazil. As undertakings which considered themselves injured or threatened by subsidised imports, the applicants were entitled under Regulation 3017/79 (the principal anti-dumping Regulation) to lodge a complaint (Article 5), to be consulted (Article 6), and to receive information (Article 9). In April 1980 they lodged a complaint with the Commission. Following enquiries and negotiations with the Brazilian government the Commission decided to take no further action. In September 1981 FEDIOL instituted Article 175 proceedings. Following further correspondence between FEDIOL and the Commission the Commission informed FEDIOL by letter in May 1982 that it intended to take no further action against Brazil. FEDIOL then brought Article 173 proceedings to annul that letter. The Court held that since the Regulation under which they complained recognised specific rights on the applicants' part they were entitled to a review by the Court of any exercise of power by the Community institutions which might affect these rights. Thus the action was held admissible. Although the applicants could not compel the Commission to take action against Brazil, that being a matter within the Commission's discretion, they were entitled to a review by the Court of the Commission's letter of May 1982 to ensure that their procedural rights were respected.

It is submitted that this case can be reconciled with the earlier case of *GEMA* v *Commission* (case 125/78). Here GEMA initiated a complaint to the Commission under Article 3 of Regulation 17/62, alleging a breach by Radio Luxembourg of Articles 85 and 86. In March 1978 the Commission wrote to GEMA saying that it had decided not to pursue the matter. In May 1978 GEMA instituted Article 175 proceedings against this refusal to act. Subsequently, in March 1979 GEMA brought proceedings under Article 173 to annul the letter of March 1978. The action under Article 175 failed because the Commission was held to have defined its position in the letter of March 1978. The action under Article 173 failed on the grounds that, assuming that the letter could be contested, this did not entitle the applicants to a *final Decision* on the existence of an infringement under Article 86. In any case the letter had not been challenged in time and the parties' attempts to extend the limit on the grounds of fresh issues based on matters of fact and law (Rules of Procedure, Article 42(2)) failed.

Thus in *FEDIOL* and *GEMA* the parties were only entitled in law to protection by way of review under Articles 175 and 173 in order to protect their procedural rights. They had no right to compel the Commission to institute proceedings against third parties; that was a matter within the Commission's discretion.

By comparison with these cases, the plaintiff in *Bethell* v *Commission* (case 246/81), was found to have no rights at all. In this case Lord Bethell, member

of the House of Lords, Euro MP and veteran campaigner for the 'freedom of
the skies', was attempting to force the Commission to take action against a
number of European airlines for allegedly anti-competitive practices. Although air transport is subject in principle to EEC competition rules it was
excluded from the application of Regulation 17/62, being subject to enforcement under Article 89 of the EEC Treaty by the Commission. Under Article
89, unlike Regulation 17/62, no right is granted to persons with a 'legitimate
interest' to request the Commission to act in respect of suspected infringements. Lord Bethell complained to the Commission and requested action. The
Commission wrote back to Lord Bethell, explaining in detail why it had
decided not to take action in this matter. Lord Bethell then instituted Article
175 proceedings against the Commission for its failure to act, and Article 173
proceedings for the annulment of its letter of refusal to act. Both actions were
declared inadmissible. In order for his claim to be admissible under Article 175
it was necessary to prove that the Commission, having been called upon to act,
had failed to adopt in relation to him a measure *which he was legally entitled to
claim*. This he had clearly failed to prove. Nor was he entitled to challenge the
Commission's negative refusal under Article 173 since he was not in the
position of actual or potential addressee of a Decision which the Commission
had a duty to adopt with regard to him.

Where an individual does have a right to complain and to request action, as
in *FEDIOL* and *GEMA,* should the Commission take action and issue a
Decision to a third party, the complainant will be deemed to be directly and
individually concerned, and will be entitled to a full review of the Decision
under Article 173 (*Metro-SB-Grossmärkte GmbH & Co. KG v Commission*
(case 26/76); *Timex Corporation v Council and Commission* (case 264/82), see
chapter 27; *COFAZ* (case 169/84); *British-American Tobacco Co. Ltd v
Commission* (cases 142 & 156/84)).

Procedure

Where the applicant has a right to require an institution to act, and the
institution is thus under a corresponding duty, the applicant must first call
upon the institution to act. No time-limit is imposed in respect of the
institution's alleged failure, but the Court has held that proceedings must be
brought within a reasonable time of the institution's having demonstrated its
intention not to act (*Netherlands v Commission* (case 59/70) case brought under
Article 35 of the ECSC Treaty).

The institution then has two months within which it may either act in
accordance with the request, or 'define its position'.

If the institution fails to act or to define its position the plaintiff has two
months within which to bring his case before the Court of Justice, running
from the date on which the institution should have defined its position. Article
175 is silent as to what happens if the institution concerned defines its position.
Although it was not necessary so to construe Article 175 the Court held in
Alfons Lütticke GmbH v Commission (case 48/65) that a definition of position
brought proceedings under Article 175 to an end. The plaintiff in this case, it

will be remembered, was attempting to persuade the Commission to bring an action under Article 169 against the German government for its alleged infringement of Article 95. When the Commission refused to act Alfons Lütticke GmbH brought proceedings under Article 175 for failure to act. The Commission defined its position in a letter to Lütticke, again refusing to act, and Lütticke brought proceedings under Article 173 to annul that refusal.

There were a number of reasons, submitted by Advocate-General Gand, why both claims should fail. With regard to the action under Article 175:

(a) The Commission's refusal to take action under Article 169 was not an infringement of the Treaty; the decision as to whether or not to act was a matter within the Commission's discretion.

(b) The act requested by Lütticke was not a decision addressed to itself, but one addressed to a third party (the German government) which it was not entitled to demand.

(c) The Commission's refusal to act was a 'definition of position' within Article 175; this definition of position ended the Commission's failure to act.

The Court, in the briefest of judgments, chose to rely on the third ground. Since the Commission had defined its position the action under Article 175 was inadmissible.

With regard to the action under Article 173, Advocate-General Gand's submissions were again convincing. The applicant would only be entitled to challenge the Commission's refusal to act (the 'negative decision'), he suggested, if it would have been entitled to challenge the positive act requested. This it would not, since it had no right to demand action from the Commission *vis-à-vis* the German government. The Court, on the other hand, chose to treat the Commission's refusal not as a definition of position but as a 'reasoned opinion' under Article 169, which, as a purely preliminary act, was not, the Court held, capable of annulment.

The Court did adopt reasoning similar to that of Advocate-General Gand in *Lütticke* in *Star Fruit Company SA* v *Commission* (case 247/87). Here, as in *Lütticke,* the applicants, a firm of banana importers, were seeking to compel the Commission to institute Article 169 proceedings, this time against France in respect of the French regime regulating banana imports, which they considered was in breach of Article 30 EEC. They had complained to the Commission and the Commission had acknowledged their request. The applicants subsequently brought Article 175 proceedings against the Commission for their failure to take action against France, and Article 173 proceedings for the annulment of the Commission's letter of acknowledgment. On the claim under Article 175 the Court held that since the Commission was not required to instigate proceedings under Article 169, but on the contrary had a discretionary power, 'individuals were not entitled to require that the institution adopt a particular position'.

On the claim under Article 173, the Court pointed out that by requesting the Commission to set in motion a procedure under Article 169 the applicant was 'in reality requesting the adoption of acts which were not of direct and individual concern to it within the meaning of Article 173, and which in any event it could not challenge by means of an action for annulment'.

The Court has, however, consistently followed its position in *Lütticke* and held that, in Article 175 proceedings, a definition of position by the defendant institution ends its failure to act. Thus it is not surprising that so few cases have reached the Court of Justice under Article 175. However, this is not necessarily the end of the road for the applicant. In a *legitimate* case, *where he is entitled to demand action* from the institution concerned, he may challenge the definition of position, as a Decision addressed to himself, under Article 173, and provided that he does so in time, his application should be admissible. It is submitted that *Lütticke,* with its special facts (applicant not entitled to demand action), and its judgment cast in terms of Article 169, cannot be invoked to prevent such a challenge. *FEDIOL* (case 191/82) now exists to support this view. Although not described as such, the Commission's letter of May 1982, in which the Commission informed FEDIOL of its decision not to act, and which FEDIOL were held entitled to challenge under Article 173, was undoubtedly a 'definition of position' within Article 175 (see *GEMA* (case 125/78)). Such an interpretation may also be implied from *Irish Cement Co.* v *Commission* (case 220/86). Here the applicants, who had complained to the Commission of certain State aids granted by the Irish government to rival companies, which they alleged were in breach of Article 92, had failed to challenge the Commission's definition of position in time. As a result it was not necessary for the Court to pursue the question of whether the applicants were 'directly and individually concerned' in (i.e. entitled to demand) the Commission's decision in respect of action under Article 93(2).

Thus where an institution defines its position and refuses to act, an applicant who is not entitled to demand that action cannot challenge that refusal under Article 173; and even a legitimate claim under Article 175 is likely to result in an action to review that refusal under Article 173. In the latter case it is therefore essential that a definition of position be recognised as a Decision capable of challenge under Article 173, and that it be challenged in time (cf. *GEMA, Irish Cement Co.*). The extent of the review conducted by the Court under Article 173 will depend on the extent of the applicant's rights. Since the institutions have wide discretionary powers in the pursuit of economic policy objectives, individuals' rights, at last where action *vis-à-vis* third parties are concerned, are likely to be limited, and mainly of a procedural nature. However, as has been demonstrated in *European Parliament* v *Council* (case 13/83), Article 175 offers considerable scope for privileged applicants.

In *European Parliament* v *Council* (case 13/83) Parliament's case was heard before the Court of Justice under Article 175, since the Council's 'definition of position' was found to be inadequate. Since it neither confirmed nor denied the alleged failure (implementation of transport policy), and failed to reveal the Council's position with regard to the measure which the Council intended to adopt, it was held not to amount to a definition of position at all. Thus the Court was able to entertain a case of important constitutional significance without having to decide whether Parliament would have had *locus standi* to challenge the Council's definition of position under Article 173. Since, following this case, the institutions are likely to be more careful in defining their position, it is only a matter of time before this question arises before the Court. It was thought that the Court would then take the opportunity to 'square the circle' and extend *locus standi* under Article 173 to Parliament. This opportunity was offered and denied in general terms in *Parliament* v *Council (Comitology)* (case 302/87). Although inroads were made in *Parliament* v *Council (Chernobyl)* (case C 70/88), Parliament has not yet been given a *general* right of challenge under Article 173. However, the claim under Article 173 in *Parliament* v *Council* (case 13/83) was an *independent* action; it was not an attempt to annul a definition of position arising under Article 175. Indeed, the Court held in that case that 'a refusal to act under Article 175 could be brought before the Court on the basis of Article 175 where it did not put an end to the failure to act'. It is to be hoped that these principles will be followed, since in the absence of *locus standi* under Article 173 an action before the Court in respect of an alleged failure to act is the only way in which Parliament's rights under Article 175 may be adequately protected.

Consequences of a successful action

Whether the action is admitted before the Court under Article 175, as a failure to act, or under Article 173, as a claim for annulment of a decision not to act, the consequences of a successful action are the same. Under Article 176:

The institution whose act has been declared void or whose failure to act has been declared contrary to this Treaty shall be required to take the necessary measures to comply with the judgment of the Court of Justice.

Thus the institution will be required by the Court to take action to remedy its failure. It will not necessarily be the action required by the applicant. Should he wish to challenge the institution's implementation of the judgment he could do so under Article 173.

No sanctions beyond the possibility of further action under Article 175 are provided for non-compliance with the Court's judgment.

Further reading

Bradley & St. Clair, K., 'The variable evolution of the standing of the European Parliament in proceedings before the Court of Justice' (1988) 8 YEL 27.
Bradley St Clair, K., 'Sense and Sensibility: *Parliament* v *Council* Continuing' (1991) 16 EL Rev 245.
Hartley, T. C., *The Foundations of European Community Law*, 2nd ed. (Oxford: Clarendon Press, 1988).
Schermers, H. G., *Judicial Protection in the European Communities*, 4th ed. (London: Kluwer Law & Taxation Publishers, 1987).

TWENTY NINE

Indirect review before the Court of Justice (Article 184)

Article 184 provides:

> Notwithstanding the expiry of the period laid down in the third paragraph of Article 173, any party may, in proceedings in which a Regulation of the Council or of the Commission is in issue, plead the grounds specified in the first paragraph of Article 173, in order to invoke before the Court of Justice the inapplicability of that Regulation.

Although Article 184 entitles 'any party' to attack a Regulation 'notwithstanding the expiry' of the time-limit laid down in Article 173, it is not designed to provide a means of escaping the restrictions either of time or *locus standi* laid down in Article 173. No action can be brought *directly* against a Regulation under Article 184. As the Court held in *Milchwerke Heinz Wöhrmann & Sohn KG* v *Commission* (cases 31 & 33/62), in the context of an action brought under Article 184 to annul three Commission Decisions, a plea under Article 184 can be raised as an *incidental* matter *only* in the course of legal proceedings based on other provisions of the Treaty. In *Wöhrmann* the action was brought *solely* under Article 184, since the time-limits within which the Decisions should have been challenged under Article 173 had elapsed. Thus the application was rejected. (See also *Commission* v *Belgium* (case 156/77).)

The purpose of Article 184, the 'plea of illegality', or *'exception d'illégalité'*, as it is called in French law, from which it is taken, is to allow a party to question the legality of a general act on which a subsequent act (e.g., a Decision), or failure to act, is based. A Decision is often, indeed normally, based on some general authorising act. Although the Decision may be challengeable under Article 173, it may in itself be unimpeachable. But it may be based on a general act that is not. A non-privileged applicant has no *locus standi* to challenge a general act under Article 173. And even a privileged applicant, a member State or an institution, may not be aware of the illegality of the general act until affected by some subsequent act issuing from that 'tainted' source. By this time the two months within which the original act should have been challenged may have elapsed. Article 184 thus provides a means whereby this underlying act may be challenged *indirectly*, free of time-limits, before the Court of Justice in proceedings in which it is 'in issue', in much the same way as questions of EEC law may be raised indirectly in the context of domestic proceedings before national courts.

Proceedings in which Article 184 may be invoked

In theory Article 184 may be invoked in the context of any proceedings brought directly before the Court of Justice in which it is relevant. In *Hessische Knappschaft v Maison Singer et Fils* (case 44/65) the Court was not prepared to consider a claim under Article 184 in the context of a reference from a national court under Article 177. However, in that case the parties had attempted to raise the plea of illegality as a new issue; it had not been raised in the reference by the national court. Their attempt to raise it before the Court of Justice was thus seen by the Court as an interference with the national court's discretion, and, as such, unacceptable. Nevertheless, it would not be necessary to invoke Article 184 before a national court since these courts are free to refer to the Court of Justice under Article 177 questions of validity of *any* Community act, and are not constrained by the time-limits applicable to a direct challenge under Article 173 (see chapter 24).

The main context in which Article 184 is likely to be invoked is to support a challenge under Article 173 to the validity of a measure based on the original, allegedly invalid, act. If the underlying act, challenged under Article 184, is found invalid, it will be declared 'inapplicable' and the subsequent act, affecting the plaintiff, will be void. Thus the principal object of the exercise will be achieved. Article 184 may also be relevant to an action under Article 175 for failure to act, where the failure (e.g., to issue a Decision to the plaintiff) is based on an invalid general act (see *SNUPAT v High Authority* (cases 32 & 33/58), action under the equivalent provision of the ECSC Treaty, Article 35). It may also, in theory, be invoked to support an action for damages under Articles 178 and 215(2), or arising out of contract under Article 181 (which gives the Court of Justice 'jurisdiction to give judgment pursuant to any arbitration clause contained in a contract concluded by or on behalf of the Community') or in appeals against penalties under Article 172. It is submitted that Article 184 may also be invoked as a defence to an action against a member State under Article 169 (but see *Commission v Belgium* (case 156/77)). A legitimate challenge under Article 184 may be brought by the applicant or the defendant. There must, however, always be a 'direct judicial link' between the act (or failure to act) affecting the applicant and the general underlying measure subject to challenge (*Italy v Council and Commission* (case 32/65)).

Since Article 184 is only a complementary remedy it is essential to its success that the time-limits and *locus standi* requirements imposed in the principal action before the Court are observed. Article 184 does not provide a means of evading these limits (see *Wöhrmann* (cases 31 & 33/62); *Commission v Belgium* (case 156/77)).

Reviewable acts

Although Article 184 is expressed to apply only to Regulations, the Court, in keeping with its approach in Article 173 (it is the substance and effect of a measure, not its form, which determines its true nature), has held that Article 184 applies to any general act having binding force. In *Simmenthal SpA* v *Commission* (case 92/78) the plaintiff, a meat processing company, was seeking to annul, under Article 173, a Decision addressed to the Italian government, in which the company was directly and individually concerned. The basis of its claim for annulment was that the 'parent' measure, a general notice of invitation to tender, on which the Decision was based, was invalid. The Court held that since the notice was a general act, which, although not in the form of a Regulation, produced similar effects, it could be challenged under Article 184. The challenge was successful and resulted in the annulment of the Decision affecting the plaintiff.

Is the scope for challenge under Article 184 limited to general measures?

The principal reason for making an 'exception' for Regulations would appear to be to enable individuals, who are unable to challenge general acts under Article 173, to do so when they seek, legitimately, to rely on their invalidity in the context of other proceedings before the Court. A secondary reason would be that, since a Regulation is 'of general application' and is not addressed to anyone, its invalidity may not be apparent to the plaintiff until a subsequent individual measure, based on the general measure, brings it to his attention. Both reasons, i.e., lack of opportunity to challenge and absence of notification, would justify extending the scope of Article 184 to enable an individual to challenge, indirectly, any 'parent' act which was not addressed to him or in which he was not directly and individually concerned. The second reason would provide grounds for allowing a privileged applicant to challenge indirectly any 'parent' act which was not addressed to the applicant. This matter has yet to be decided by the Court.

Locus standi

Although *locus standi* under Article 184 appears to apply to 'any party', doubts have been expressed as to whether it extends to privileged applicants. It is argued that since member States and institutions (but not Parliament) are entitled to seek annulment of any act under Article 173, to allow them to invoke Article 184 would be to enable them to challenge acts which they should have challenged, within the time-limits, under Article 173. However, Advocate-General Roemer in *Italy* v *Council and Commission* (case 32/65) took the view that a member State *should* have *locus standi* under Article 184, since the wording of the provision was in no way restrictive, and the illegality of the general provision might not become apparent until it was applied subsequently in a particular case. The Court did not comment on the matter, since it found that the Regulations in issue were not relevant to the case, but its silence could be read as consent. Advocate-General Roemer's reasoning is persuasive. Moreover, Article 184 can never be used *merely* to circumvent time-limits; it can only be invoked as an incidental issue, when the plaintiff is affected by some subsequent act (or failure) arising from the original general act. This provides ample safeguard against abuse.

This is illustrated by *Commission* v *Belgium* (case 156/77). Here Article 184 was raised as a defence to an enforcement action against Belgium under Article 95(2) for infringement of Community law relating to State aids. The Belgians had failed to comply with a Commission Decision of May 1976, addressed to the Belgian government, requiring the Belgians to abolish certain State aids within a three-month period; nor had they attempted to challenge that Decision. In proceedings brought by the Commission in December 1977 for non-compliance with the Decision the Belgian government argued, invoking Article 184, that the Decision was invalid. The claim was held inadmissible. The Court found that the Belgians' claim was in essence a claim for the annulment of the Decision of May 1976. They had been free to contest this Decision under Article 173, but had failed to do so within the time-limit. They could not allow this limit to elapse and then challenge the Decision's legality under Article 184.

This case, it is submitted, does not decide that Article 184 can never be raised in enforcement proceedings against member States. The Belgians' claim under Article 184 was rejected on different and wholly legitimate grounds. They were not invoking Article 184 as a collateral issue; their defence was based *solely* on the legality of a Decision addressed to them which they had failed to challenge in time.

Grounds of review

The grounds on which Regulations may be challenged under Article 184 are the same as those provided under Article 173 (see chapter 27).

Simmenthal SpA v *Commission* (case 92/78) provides an interesting and rare example of a successful challenge based on Article 184. The general act challenged under Article 184 — the general notice of invitation to tender — was found to have been used for purposes other than those for which it had been granted. The power under which the notice was passed (contained in a prior Regulation) to set minimum purchase prices for beef, was *granted* in order to help processors; it was being *used* to help importers in general.

Consequences of a successful challenge

Where an action under Article 184 is successful, the Regulation is declared 'inapplicable'. Since there is no time-limit within which acts may be challenged under Article 184, it is not, for reasons of legal certainty, void, but voidable. However, a declaration of inapplicability will render a subsequent act, based on that act, void. Thus, although action under Article 184 is an 'incidental matter', it will be conclusive of the principal action before the Court. A declaration of inapplicability under Article 184 may also be invoked to prevent the application of the invalid act in a subsequent case.

Further reading

Hartley, T. C., *The Foundations of European Community Law,* 2nd ed. (Oxford: Clarendon Press, 1988).
Schermers, H. G., *Judicial Protection in the European Communities,* 4th ed. (London: Kluwer Law & Taxation Publishers, 1987).

THIRTY

Community liability in tort, action for damages (Articles 178 and 215(2))

Community liability in tort, described as 'non-contractual liability', is governed by Article 178 and Article 215(2). According to Article 178:

> The Court of Justice shall have jurisdiction in disputes relating to the compensation for damage provided for in the second paragraph of Article 215.

Article 215(2) provides that:

> In the case of non-contractual liability, the Community shall, in accordance with the general principles common to the laws of the member States, make good any damage caused by its institutions or by its servants in the performance of their duties.

Thus, the Community may be liable for both *'fautes de service'*, i.e., wrongful acts on the part of one of its institutions, and *'fautes personelles'*, wrongful acts on the part of its servants. Provided in both cases that the wrongful acts are committed in the performance of the perpetrator's Community functions the responsible institution may be sued. Where more than one institution is concerned, or where there is doubt as to which institution is responsible, both (or all) may be sued. In the case of *faute personelle*, the Community is liable on the principle of vicarious liability, albeit interpreted in a slightly narrower sense than that in which it is understood under English law (see *Sayag* v *Leduc* (case 9/69), proceedings under Article 188(2) of the Euratom Treaty, in which it was held that the Community is only liable for those acts of its servants which, by virtue of an internal relationship, are the *necessary* extension of the tasks entrusted to the institutions).

In determining liability 'in accordance with the general principles common to the laws of the member States', the Court has drawn on the common elements governing tortious liability in the member States in order to develop its own specific principles of Community law.

Locus standi

Unlike the position in the area of judicial review, there are no personal limitations on the right to bring an action under Article 215(2). Moreover, a specific, and generous limitation period of five years is provided (Article 43 of the Protocol on the Statute of the Court of Justice), running from the occurrence of the event giving rise to liability. However, the Court has held that the limitation period cannot begin until all the requirements for liability, particularly damage, have materialised (*Birra Wührer SpA* v *Council and Commission* (cases 256, 257, 265 & 267/80 & 5/81)). Thus, where the damage results from a legislative measure, time runs not necessarily from the date of enactment but from the date on which the injury occurs. These *locus standi* provisions are important, since, as will be seen, it may be possible to obtain a declaration of invalidity in the context of a claim for damages, thereby circumventing the *locus standi* limitations of Article 173 (see *Aktien-Zuckerfabrik Schöppenstedt* v *Council* (case 5/71)).

Elements of non-contractual liability

The basic elements of non-contractual liability are familiar. They embrace:

(a) a wrongful act (or omission) on the part of the institution (*faute de service*) or its servants (*faute personelle*),
(b) damage to the plaintiff, and
(c) a causative link between the two.

For liability to arise, all three elements must be proved. Although under certain Continental systems (e.g., France), a public body may be strictly liable where a plaintiff suffers exceptional or abnormal damage as a result of a public measure taken in the general interest, on the principle of *'égalité devant les charges publiques'* (equal apportionment of public burdens), the Court of Justice has not yet accepted a principle of liability without fault in EEC law.

Wrongful acts or omissions

Although, following Continental traditions, non-contractual liability is not divided up into specific 'torts', wrongful acts and omissions may be grouped under three broad categories:

(a) Failures of administration. Community institutions are under a duty of good administration. Failures of administration would include, for example, a failure to adopt satisfactory procedures, a failure to obtain the relevant facts before making the decision, the giving of misleading information or a failure to give the necessary information. Liability here thus approximates, loosely, to liability for 'operational' failures in negligence (see *Anns* v *Merton London Borough Council* [1978] AC 728, House of Lords). As with negligence, the decision taken or advice offered need not be right as long as it is adopted according to the correct procedures and the conclusions reached are reasonable in the light of the information to hand.

(b)   Negligent acts by a servant in the performance of his duties (e.g., in English law, *Ministry of Housing and Local Government* v *Sharp* [1970] 2 QB 223).

(c)   The adoption of wrongful (i.e., illegal or invalid) acts having legal effect, or the wrongful failure to adopt a binding act when under a duty to do so.

Since this latter is the most important area of non-contractual liability and is closely linked with the remedies considered so far relating to judicial review, the present chapter will focus principally on this issue.

Liability for wrongful acts having legal effect

There is some indication in the EEC Treaty that damages may be recoverable as a result of a wrongful failure to act. Article 176(2) provides that the obligation to remedy a failure to act under Article 175 'shall not affect any obligation which may result from the application of the second paragraph of Article 215'. From this it may be deduced, applying the 'unity' principle, that liability in damages for unlawful legislative acts exists and that liability under Article 215(2) exists as a *separate* remedy from the remedies under Articles 173 and 175 for judicial review.

This was not the view taken originally by the Court of Justice in *Plaumann & Co.* v *Commission* (case 25/62), Articles 173 and 215(2) proceedings). Here, it held that, since Plaumann & Co. lacked *locus standi* to challenge the contested Decision under Article 173 (see chapter 27), their claim for compensation, based on the illegality of that same decision, must fail. The Court cannot, by way of an action for compensation, take steps that would nullify the legal effects of a Decision which has not been annulled.

The Court changed its mind in *Alfons Lütticke GmbH* v *Commission* (case 4/69). In this case, Lütticke, having failed to establish the Commission's failure to act under Article 175 (see chapter 28), sought damages from the Commission in a separate action under Article 215(2). The action was held admissible. The Court said that the action for damages provided for under Article 178 and Article 215(2) was established as *an independent form of action with a particular purpose to fulfil*. It would be contrary to the independent nature of this action, as well as to the efficacy of the general system of forms of action created by the Treaty, to regard as a ground of inadmissibility the fact that, in certain circumstances, an action for damages might lead to a result similar to that of an action for failure to act under Article 175.

Although Lütticke failed on the merits (there being no wrongful failure), an important principle was established.

It was confirmed in *Aktien-Zuckerfabrik Schöppenstedt* v *Council* (case 5/71). On the reasoning cited above the Court held that the plaintiff company could sue the Council for damages on the basis of an allegedly illegal Regulation even though as a 'natural or legal person' they would have no *locus standi* to seek its annulment under Article 173. *Schöppenstedt* was subsequently approved and applied in *Krohn & Co. Import-Export GmbH & Co. KG* v *Commission* (case 175/84), Article 215(2) proceedings. Here the Court held that since an action under Article 215(2) was an autonomous form of action, the expiry of the time-limit for challenge under Article 173 did not render an action for damages inadmissible.

Thus the principle expressed initially in *Lütticke* (case 4/69) that action under Article 215(2) is an independent form of action now seems firmly established, and it will not be necessary in a claim for damages based on an illegal act (or failure to act) to bring a prior action for annulment or failure to act, nor even to establish *locus standi* to bring such action.

However, the problem with Article 215(2) lies not in establishing admissibility but in succeeding on the merits of the case. The Court of Justice has adopted a very restrictive approach towards Community liability in tort, particularly towards liability resulting from the adoption of wrongful acts (or the wrongful failure to adopt an act). Such an approach is common to most legal systems. And indeed there are strong policy reasons for limiting the non-contractual liability of public authorities. These bodies are charged by law to take decisions in the general interest over a wide range of activities. These decisions often involve the exercise of discretion and affect a substantial section of the public. Sometimes the decisions are unlawful. Whilst it is right that such decisions be subject to strict judicial review, it may be argued that to expose public bodies to liability in damages for unlawful acts in the absence of bad faith or an improper motive or (*quaere*) 'gross' negligence would unduly hamper the administrative process and impose an excessive burden on the public purse (see the 'policy' arguments expressed in *Rowling* v *Takaro Properties Ltd* [1988] AC 473, Privy Council), *a fortiori* in a community as large as the EEC.

Thus it is not sufficient for Community liability to arise that the measure in question is unlawful, nor that the institution has unlawfully failed to act. Where the action concerns a legislative measure which involves choices of economic policy the Community incurs no liability unless a sufficiently serious breach of a superior rule of law for the protection of the individual has occurred. This formula, known as the 'Schöppenstedt' formula (from *Aktien-Zuckerfabrik Schöppenstedt* v *Council* (case 5/71), Article 215(2) proceedings) must be satisfied.

The *Schöppenstedt* formula

This contains three essential elements. It requires:

(a) *A legislative measure involving choices of economic policy.* Although the term 'legislative act' relates primarily to Regulations it will apply to any binding act which purports to lay down general rules. The Decision in *Firma E. Kampffmeyer* v *Commission* (cases 5, 7 & 13-24/66), addressed to the German government and authorising it to withhold import licences for maize during a certain period would, it is submitted, constitute a legislative measure. The majority of legislative measures will involve choices of economic policy, since the institutions enjoy wide discretionary powers in all areas of activity, and even measures of a social nature can be construed as economic in the context of the EEC Treaty.

(b) *A breach of a superior rule of law for the protection of individuals.* Any general principle, such as equality or proportionality, accepted as part of Community law (see chapter 4) would constitute a superior law for the protection of individuals. A breach of the principle of legitimate expectations was argued successfully in a claim for damages in *Sofrimport SARL v Commission* (case C 152/88 see Chapter 27). Here the Commission, in issuing Regulations suspending import licences for imported apples from Chile, and imposing quotas on fruits from third countries, had failed to take account of the applicants' interest as undertakings with 'goods in transit' when the Regulations were issued, as required under Community law (Regulation 2702/72, Article 3). Most general principles of *Community* law (e.g., freedom of movement for workers; non-discrimination between producers and consumers (Article 40(3), agriculture) whether expressed in the EEC Treaty or in secondary legislation could likewise form the basis of a claim for damages. In *Société Commerciale Antoine Vloeberghs SA v High Authority* (cases 9 & 12/60), (action under ECSC Treaty) the Court held, in the context of a claim for damages based on the High Authority's alleged infringement of the principle of free movement of goods (in this case coal), that this principle was not intended for the benefit of coal importers. However in *Firma E. Kampffmeyer v Commission* (cases 5, 7 & 13-24/66) a provision in an EEC Regulation directed at ensuring 'appropriate support for agricultural markets' was construed as intending to benefit, *inter alia,* the interests of individual undertakings such as importers. The plaintiffs, as importers, were thus entitled to claim damages as a result of the Commission's action in breach of these provisions. It seems therefore that as long as the rule of law can be construed as designed in part to benefit a particular class of people it may be deemed to be 'for the protection of individuals'.

(c) *The breach must be 'sufficiently serious'.* A breach of a superior rule of law, even a fundamental rule such as the principle of equality, is not in itself sufficient to give rise to a claim in damages. The plaintiff must prove that the breach is 'sufficiently serious'. This principle has been very narrowly construed. In *Bayerische HNL Vermehrungsbetriebe GmbH & Co. KG v Council and Commission* (cases 83 & 94/76, 4 15 & 40/77), the Court suggested that in a legislative field in which one of the chief features is the exercise of a wide discretion, the Community does not incur liability unless the institution concerned has *manifestly and gravely disregarded the limits on the exercise of its power.*

In interpreting this requirement two approaches may be noted. Sometimes the Court looks at the *effect* of the measure to see who has been harmed, and how serious is the harm. Sometimes it looks at the nature of the breach; in what way, and to what extent, is the institution *culpable?* It seems from the developing case law (*Sofrimport SARL v Commission* (case C 152/88), Advocate-General Van Gerven's opinion in *Mulder v Council and Commission* (January 1992) (cases C 104/89 and C 37/90) that both enquiries are relevant. The breach must be both serious *and* inexcusable.

The effect of the measure   In *HNL* v *Council and Commission* the Court adopted an approach based on the effect of the measure. The action, brought by a number of animal feed producers, was for damages for loss suffered as a result of an EEC Regulation requiring animal feed producers to purchase skimmed milk powder instead of the cheaper and equally effective soya, as a means of disposing of surplus stocks of milk. This Regulation had been found by the Court in a prior ruling under Article 177 (*Bela-Mühle Josef Bergmann KG* v *Grows-Farm GmbH & Co. KG* (case 114/76); *Granaria BV* v *Hoofdproduktschap voor Akkerbouwprodukten (No. 1)* [1977] ECR 1247, [1979] 2 CMLR 83) (case 116/76)) to be in breach of the principles of non-discrimination and proportionality. In deciding whether the breach was sufficiently serious, whether the Commission had manifestly and gravely disregarded the limits on the exercise of its powers, the Court looked at the effect of the breach. It had affected a wide group of persons (all buyers of protein for the production of animal feed); the difference in price between the skimmed milk and soya had only a limited effect on production costs, insignificant beside other factors such as world prices; and the effect of the Regulation on their profits did not exceed the normal level of risk inherent in such activities. Thus the breach was not sufficiently serious.

The same approach proved more successful for the applicants in the 'gritz' and 'quellmehl' cases (e.g., *P. Dumortier Frères SA* v *Council* (cases 64 & 113/76, 167 & 239/78, 27, 28 & 45/79)). Here the plaintiffs, a group of gritz and quellmehl producers were seeking compensation for damage resulting from an EEC Regulation, withdrawing subsidies for gritz and quellmehl whilst retaining them for starch. All these products had previously benefited from subsidies, and all were to a certain extent in competition. As in *HNL* the Regulation had been held unlawful, in breach of the principle of equality, in Article 177 proceedings (see *Firma Albert Ruckdeschel & Co.* (case 117/76)). Following these proceedings the Commission restored the subsidies, but only from the date of the Court's judgment. The plaintiffs claimed damages for losses suffered during the period prior to that judgment. And they succeeded. In this case they were a small, clearly defined group, and their loss went beyond the risks normally inherent in their business.

Not only must the group affected be small and clearly defined but it seems from *Sofrimport SARL* v *Commission* (case C 152/88) that it must also be closed. In *Sofrimport* the Court pointed out that undertakings such as the plaintiffs, with goods in transit at the time when the Regulations were made, constituted a 'restricted group *which could not be extended* after the contested measures took effect'. *Mulder* (cases C 104/89 and C 37/90) involved a claim for damages by a number of milk producers based on an EEC Regulation which had been held invalid in an earlier judgment under Article 173 (cases 120/86 and 170/86) for breach of the principle of legitimate expectations. The Regulation, extending production levies on dairy products, had provided for exemption from the levies for quotas calculated by reference to undertakings in production during a particular year (the 'reference year'). Because of the choice of year the plaintiffs, who had made no milk deliveries during the reference year, received no levy-free quota. In order to decide whether the plaintiffs constituted a 'clearly defined and limited group' for the Community to be liable in damages, Advocate-General Van Gerven suggested that the number of persons (adversely) affected must be capable of being determined at the time when the ruling on compensation is given. Liability did not depend on the absolute number of persons adversely affected, but on 'whether certain groups, in comparison with other categories of undertaking, suffered specific adverse effects which others did not have to suffer'. As to whether the damage went beyond the bounds of the economic risks inherent in activities in the sector in question, this requirement would be met if the undertakings concerned suffered damage which was unforeseeable. Since both requirements were satisfied, the plaintiffs were entitled to damages. It remains to be seen whether the Court follows the Advocate-General's opinion on these matters. It is submitted that a test of unforeseeability lacks authority and is too imprecise to be used as a *general* test in this area.

The nature of the breach   In the 'Isoglucose' cases (*Koninklijke Scholten-Honig NV* v *Council and Commission* (case 143/77); *G.R. Amylum NV* v *Council and Commission* (cases 116 & 124/77)) the plaintiff glucose producers were seeking damages for losses suffered as a result of a Community Regulation which imposed levies on the production of glucose in order to increase consumption of Community sugar. Clearly there was some competition between glucose and sugar. The Regulation had been found invalid, in breach of the principle of equality, in a prior reference under Article 177 in *Royal Scholten-Honig (Holdings) Ltd* v *Intervention Board for Agricultural Produce* (cases 103 & 145/77), (see chapter 24). The plaintiffs were a small and closed group, and the damage which they suffered as a result of the Regulation was described as 'catastrophic'. One firm, the Dutch firm Koninklijke Scholten-Honig NV had been forced into liquidation. Yet they failed to obtain damages. Although the treatment of the glucose producers as compared with that of the sugar producers was 'manifestly unequal', the Court held that the defendants' errors were not of such gravity that their conduct could be regarded as 'verging on the arbitrary'.

Similarly, in *Roquette Frères SA* v *Commission* (case 20/88) Roquette failed in their claim for damages suffered as a result of a Regulation setting the level of monetary compensatory amounts (MCAs) which had been declared invalid in Article 177 proceedings in *Roquette Frères* v *France* (case 145/79) (see chapter 24). Since the ruling had been declared prospective only, Roquette had suffered loss by way of MCAs paid and profits lost prior to the date of judgment. The Court held that the Commission's fault in calculating MCAs was a purely 'technical error' which 'could not be regarded as amounting to a serious infringement of a superior rule of law or manifest and grave disregard by the Commission of the limits on the exercise of its powers'.

The plaintiffs in *Sofrimport SARL* v *Commission* (case C 152/88) on the other hand were successful. In *Sofrimport* the Court found that the Commission had 'failed completely' to take the plaintiffs' interests into account, as it was required to do under the Regulations concerned. Similarly in *Mulder*, Advocate-General Van Gerven, arguing in favour of imposing liability, stressed that the Council had 'failed completely to take account of the particular situation of traders without invoking any overriding public interest'.

Thus to succeed in a claim for damages resulting from a wrongful act in a field in which the Community institutions exercise a wide discretion, it will probably be necessary to prove that:

(a)   the measure has adversely affected a clearly defined group which is closed when the act is issued (*Sofrimport*) (cf. *Mulder* per Advocate-General Van Gerven: 'when the compensation order is made');
(b)   its effect goes beyond the normal level of risk inherent in the plaintiff's business; and
(c)   the institution's breach was a serious one, and was *without justification*.

A breach of an obligation designed to protect persons such as the plaintiff, as in *Sofrimport*, is likely to be regarded as sufficiently serious to ground a claim under Article 215(2) in the absence of strong justification. It may also be argued that the institution has no discretion in such a matter; such a failure does not involve 'choices of economic policy'. But even where the institution is clearly acting within the limits of its discretion, Advocate-General Van Gerven suggests that it cannot 'completely' ignore the interests of traders. Where choices are made which are likely to cause serious harm to certain groups they must be justified on the grounds of some overriding public or Community interest.

Where the Court rejects a claim for damages, as in the isoglucose cases, it often points out that applicants are not without a remedy. The action must be assessed having regard to the whole system of legal protection of individuals set up by the Treaty. Where a person suffers damage as a result of an unlawful act he may challenge that measure before his national courts and seek a ruling under Article 177 on its validity. The Court said that the existence of such an action is by itself of such a nature as to ensure the efficient protection of the individuals concerned. Not all would agree with this view. There may be no issue of national law in which to raise questions of EEC law. And as is borne out in *Koninklijke Scholten-Honig NV v Council and Commission*, heavy, even irreparable losses may be incurred while proceedings before the national courts are pending. An action before a national court may result in a declaration of invalidity, but a national court has no jurisdiction to award damages for wrongs attributable to the Community. Yet, as the Court pointed out in *Krohn* (case 175/84), national rights of action should provide an *effective* means of protection for the individual concerned and be capable of resulting in compensation for the damage alleged. Since the Court is understandably reluctant to expose the Community to unlimited claims, and, where the exercise of discretion by a Community institution is concerned, to apportion blame (for a similar approach towards matters of 'policy' see Lord Wilberforce in *Anns v Merton London Borough Council* [1978] AC 728, House of Lords), perhaps it could be persuaded, in exceptional cases, to accept some form of strict liability on the principle of '*égalité devant les charges publiques*'. It cannot be right that a few should bear a disproportionate burden as a result of measures enacted in the interest of the many.

Individual acts

It should be noted that the 'Schöppenstedt' formula only applies to legislative acts involving choices of economic policy; it does not apply to individual acts which do not involve the exercise of discretion. Since such acts affect only their addressees they do not raise the same floodgates problems, thus it is not necessary to subject them to such stringent criteria. Where an individual act threatens to cause damage to its addressee, it may be challenged under Article 173. Where he fails to challenge the measure in time he may still bring an independent action under Article 215(2) where damage has occurred as a result of its application (*Krohn* (case 175/84)).

Damage

The Court of Justice is as restrictive in its approach to damages as it is to fault. Although it will in principle award damages for economic loss, such losses must be specific, not speculative. Thus in *Firma E. Kampffmeyer* v *Commission* (cases 5, 7 & 13-24/66) the Court was prepared to award damages for lost profits on contracts which had already been concluded, which applicants had had to cancel as a result of the illegal Decision, although these damages were reduced to only 10% of the profits they might have expected to make, on account of the risks involved in the transactions in question. Applicants who had not concluded contracts prior to applying for import permits were awarded no damages at all. In *CNTA SA* v *Commission* (case 74/74) the Court found that the Commission had breached the principle of legitimate expectations when it introduced a Regulation, suddenly and without warning, which deprived the plaintiff of export refunds at a particular rate, fixed in advance. Although the Regulation was not in itself invalid, the Commission's mode of introduction of the measure was wrongful. Thus the Commission was liable in principle. However, although CNTA had entered into export contracts on the basis of its legitimate expectations, the Court held that it was only entitled to recover for losses actually suffered, not anticipated profits, and, since currency fluctuations at the time of import had resulted in its suffering no loss on the refunds themselves, it recovered no damages ([1976] ECR 797) (see also *Firma Gebrüder Dietz* v *Commission* (case 126/76)).

Where the loss has been passed on to third parties, or could have been passed on in higher prices, no damages will be recoverable (*Interquell Stärke-Chemie GmbH & Co. KG* v *Council and Commission* (cases 261 & 262/78), 'quellmehl' case). In *P. Dumortier Frères SA* v *Council* (cases 64 & 113/76, 167 & 239/78, 27, 28 & 45/79) the plaintiffs satisfied the Court that the losses could not have been passed on without risk of losing valuable markets.

Damages are payable in the applicant's national currency at the exchange rate applicable on the date of the judgment under Article 215(2). Interest on that sum is payable from the date of judgment (*Dumortier*).

Causation

The Court is similarly restrictive in its approach to matters of causation. In *Dumortier* it said that the principles common to the laws of member States cannot be relied on to deduce an obligation to make good every harmful consequence, even a remote one, of unlawful legislation. The damage must be a *sufficiently direct* consequence of the unlawful conduct of the institution concerned.

Thus in *Dumortier* the parties were entitled to recover the refunds which had been unlawfully withheld as a result of the invalid Regulation, but not for further alleged losses in the form of reduced sales or for general financial difficulties resulting in the closing of some factories. Even though these difficulties might have been exacerbated by the illegal Regulation they were not a sufficiently direct consequence of the unlawful act to render the Community liable. Other factors such as obsolescence and financial stringency were responsible.

Traders are expected to act as prudent business people. For example, in a claim based on misleading information the required causal link will be established only if the information would have caused an error in the mind of a reasonable person (*Compagnie Continentale France* v *Council* (case 169/73)).

Thus where other factors can be seen as contributing to the plaintiff's loss the damage is normally seen as too remote. The Court does not as a general rule attempt to apportion blame on the basis of contributory negligence. It appears that apportionment is reserved for claims of particular merit.

In *Adams* v *Commission (No. 1)* (case 145/83) Adams's damages for the Commission's breach of confidence, which had caused him irreparable financial and emotional damage, were reduced by 50% to take into account Adams's contribution in failing to protect his own interests (see chapter 15).

If a claim for damages for non-contractual liability, particularly a claim based on an unlawful legislative act, is unlikely to succeed for the many reasons outlined above, its value in the overall scheme of remedies available against the Community should not be underrated. Since an action under Article 215(2) is an independent form of action (*Lütticke* (case 4/69); *Schöppenstedt* (case 5/71); *Krohn* (case 175/84)), an action for damages based on invalidity or wrongful failure may be effective in obtaining a declaration of invalidity or failure to act notwithstanding that the applicant has no *locus standi*, either personal or temporal, to challenge that same act (or inaction) in proceedings under Article 173 or Article 175. Moreover, the Court has held (*Kurt Kampffmeyer Mühlenvereinigung KG* v *Council* (cases 56-60/74)) that where the damage to the plaintiff is imminent, or likely with a high degree of certainty to occur, the plaintiff may bring proceedings under Article 215(2) *before* the damage has occurred. Although he may not be found entitled in principle to damages, he may obtain a declaration of invalidity or unlawful failure to act in time to prevent the damage occurring.

It is submitted that the Court will only admit such actions under Article 215(2) where a claim for damages is genuine; it will not allow Article 215(2) to be used solely as a means of evading the *locus standi* limitations of Articles 173 and 175.

Concurrent liability

Since Community law is to a large extent implemented by national authorities, there may be cases in which it is unclear whether the cause of action, for example, for the return of money paid under an invalid Regulation, or for a wrongful failure on the part of a national body to pay a subsidy to which the applicant feels he is entitled, lies against the national authority, in national courts, according to national law, or against a Community institution, before the Court of Justice, or against both. Motivated no doubt by a desire to reduce its work-load and/or its potential liability, the Court, as illustrated by *Koninklijke Scholten-Honig NV* (case 143/77) (and countless other cases), prefers to direct applicants to seek a remedy before their national courts, leaving questions of validity to be referred to the Court of Justice, if necessary, under Article 177.

Largely as a result, it is submitted, of this preference the case law on what might loosely be termed concurrent liability is both confusing the contradictory.

Initially, in cases such as *Firma E. Kampffmeyer* v *Commission* (cases 5, 7 & 13-24/66) Article 215(2) proceedings, and *R. & V. Haegeman Sprl* v *Commission* (case 96/71), Article 173 proceedings, the Court of Justice espoused a doctrine of 'exhaustion of national law remedies'. In *Kampffmeyer* the applicant grain dealers were seeking, before the Court of Justice:

(a)   the return of levies paid to the German authorities, and
(b)   compensation for contracts cancelled

as a result of an invalid EEC Regulation. They had already begun parallel proceedings before the German courts, but those proceedings had been stayed pending the outcome of the Community proceedings.

The Court of Justice held that the German court should first be given the opportunity to decide whether the German authorities were liable. The proceedings were stayed accordingly.

In *Haegeman* the applicant was seeking the annulment of a Commission Decision refusing to return levies paid to the German authorities by the applicant as a result of an allegedly invalid Regulation. This time, unlike *Kampffmeyer,* the levies had been paid into Community funds, and Haegeman had not instituted parallel proceedings before its national courts. Again the Court refused to admit the action. Haegeman's claim should have been made against the national authorities to whom the refunds were originally paid.

There followed a series of cases in which claims before the Court of Justice

(a)   for the return of *sums unlawfully levied* (e.g., *Société Roquette Frères* v *Commission* (case 26/74), Article 215(2) proceedings), and
(b)   seeking payment of *sums unlawfully withheld* (*IBC* v *Commission* (case 46/75); *Lesieur Costelle et Associés SA* v *Commission* (cases 67-85/75); both Article 215(2) proceedings),

were held inadmissible on the grounds that the applicants should have brought their actions before their national courts.

On the other hand in *Compagnie d'Approvisionnement de Transport et de Crédit SA* v *Commission* (cases 9 & 11/71); *Merkur-Aussenhandels GmbH* v *Commission* (case 43/72); *Holtz & Willemsen GmbH* v *Council and Commission* (case 153/73); *CNTA SA* v *Commission* (case 74/74) the Court of Justice was prepared to admit claims seeking payment of *sums unlawfully withheld* without requiring claimants to proceed first before their national courts.

In *Firma Gebrüder Dietz* v *Commission* (case 126/76), and *CNTA* (case 74/74) the applicants were seeking damages for losses suffered as a result of the sudden introduction by the Commission of MCAs; they had not brought actions before their national courts. Their claims under Article 215(2) were held admissible.

In the second gritz and quellmehl cases, and the isoglucose cases, admitted under Article 215(2), proceedings had already been brought and the invalidity of the measures in question decided, before the applicants' national courts.

From the above cases the following tentative conclusions may be drawn:

(a)   A claim for the return of sums unlawfully paid to the relevant national authorities should always be brought before a national court, even though those sums may have been paid into Community funds (*Kampffmeyer, Haegeman, Roquette*).

(b)   A claim for sums unlawfully withheld, even when withheld by a national authority, may be brought *either* before national courts or the Court of Justice. The weight of authority (*Compagnie d'Approvisionnement, Merkur, Holtz & Willemsen, CNTA*) leans towards this view. However, the existence of *IBC* and *Costelle* render it advisable to bring such a claim before a national court, *provided* that no further damages are required from the Community *and* payment of the sums involved was required to be channelled through the national authority.

(c)   A claim for unliquidated damages for losses suffered as a result of illegal Community action (e.g., financial losses in *Dietz, CNTA, Dumortier*) can *only* be brought before the Court of Justice under Article 215(2). In this respect it is submitted that *Kampffmeyer* was wrong. Therefore, if these losses result from sums unlawfully withheld, the appropriate forum for recovery of *both* sums will be the Court of Justice.

Further support for principles (b) and (c) above may now be derived from *Krohn & Co. Import-Export GmbH & Co. KG* v *Commission* (case 175/84). Krohn & Co. was seeking compensation for financial losses suffered as a result of its national (German) authority's refusal to grant it licences to import manioc from Thailand. In rejecting its application the authorities were acting on mandatory instructions from the Commission. Krohn brought an action before the German courts seeking an annulment of the national authority's decision and an injunction requiring it to issue the licences, and a parallel action before the Court of Justice for compensation for losses suffered as a result of its action in denying him the licences. The Commission argued that the action under Article 215(2) was inadmissible, since:

(a)   the refusal of the licence came from the national authority;

(b)   the applicant should have exhausted its remedies before its national court; and

(c)   to admit liability would be equivalent to nullifying the Commission's Decision, which the applicant had failed to challenge in time.

All three arguments were rejected by the Court. With regard to (a) the Court found that although the refusal emanated from the national authority the unlawful conduct was to be attributed not to the German authorities but to the Community itself. The Commission was the 'true author' of the Decision.

With regard to (b) the Court held that whilst admissibility may be dependent on national rights available to obtain the annulment of a national authority's decision, that would only be the case where national rights of action provide an *effective means of protection* for the individual concerned and are capable of resulting in compensation for the damage alleged.

Clearly, since the alleged 'tort' had been committed by the Community, only the Community would be liable to pay compensation.

The Court's response to (c) has already been noted. An action under Article 215(2) was an autonomous form of action with a particular purpose to fulfil (*Lütticke* (case 4/69)).

Thus, in deciding whether action should be brought before a national court or before the Court of Justice, the appropriate question is whether action before a national court can provide an *effective means of protection* for the plaintiff's interests. Where he merely seeks the return of money paid, or payment of money unlawfully withheld, or a declaration of invalidity or an injunction to prevent the application of the unlawful act, a *fortiori* when the wrongful act can be laid at the door of the national authorities (see *Société des Grands Moulins des Antilles* v *Commission* (case 99/74); *Krohn*, in which it was held that national courts retain sole jurisdiction to order compensation for damage caused by national institutions), he should proceed before his national courts. Where he seeks damage from the Community for injury suffered as a result of wrongful acts attributable to the Community, his action must be before the Court of Justice. This is a right which cannot be 'exhausted' before a national court. Where remedies are required of both national authorities and the Community, it will be necessary to proceed against both. Clearly he cannot recover twice in respect of the same loss.

Further reading

Hartley, T. C., *The Foundations of European Community Law*, 2nd ed. (Oxford: Clarendon Press, 1988).
Schermers, H. G., *Judicial Protection in the European Communities*, 4th ed. (London: Kluwer Law & Taxation Publishers, 1987).

BIBLIOGRAPHY

Principal sources of EEC law

K. R. Simmonds (general ed.), *Encyclopedia of European Community Law* (London: Sweet & Maxwell, looseleaf). Constitutional Treaties, together with annexes and protocols. Secondary legislation.

Official Journal (L series): Community secondary legislation.

Official Journal (C series): non-binding community instruments; proposals, notices, opinions, resolutions, reports of proceedings in Parliament and the Court of Justice.

European Court Reports: reports of cases from the Court of Justice.

Common Market Law Reports: reports of cases from the Court of Justice and national courts.

Bulletin of the European Communities: reports on day-to-day activities of the Communities; supplements on specific topics.

Annual *General Report on the Activities of the European Communities*.

Annual *Report on Competition Policy*.

Halsbury's Laws of England, 4th ed., vols 51 and 52 (D. Vaughan, coordinating ed.) (London: Butterworths, 1986).

Databases:

CELEX – Official EEC database; full text of all primary and secondary legislation; ECJ and CFI case reports, legislative proposals and national measures implementing EEC Directives.

JUSTIS – provides access to CELEX (not full text).

LEXIS – commercial database containing European Court reports, European commercial cases, Commission competition decisions and access to CELEX (not full text) (Butterworths).

Further reading

Selected textbooks in specialised areas

(a) *Introductory*

Collins, L., *European Community law in the United Kingdom,* 4th ed. (London: Butterworths, 1990).

Edwards, D., *European Community Law – an Introduction* (London: Butterworths, 1991).

Mathijsen, P., *A Guide to European Law*, 4th ed. (London: Sweet & Maxwell, 1990).

(b) *Constitutional, institutional and administrative law*

Brown, N. & Jacobs, F., *The Court of Justice of the European Communities* (London: Sweet & Maxwell, 1983).

Hartley, T. C., *The Foundations of European Community Law*, 2nd ed. (Oxford: Clarendon Press, 1988.

Lasok, D. & Bridge, J., *Law and Institutions of the European Communities* (London: Butterworths, 1987).

Schermers, H. G., *Judicial Protection in the European Communities*, 4th ed. (London: Kluwer Law & Taxation Publishers, 1987).

(c) *Substantive law*

(i) *Agriculture*

Snyder, F. G., *Law of the Common Agricultural Policy* (London: Sweet & Maxwell, 1985).

Usher, J., *Legal Aspects of Agriculture in the European Community* (Oxford: Clarendon Press, 1988).

(ii) *Civil jurisdiction and enforcement of judgments*

Collins, L., *The Civil Jurisdiction and Judgments Act 1982.* (London: Butterworths, 1983).

Dashwood, Hacon & White, R., *A Guide to the Civil Jurisdiction and Judgments Convention* (London: Kluwer Law and Taxation Publishers, 1987).

Hartley, T. C., *Civil Jurisdiction and Judgments* (London: Sweet & Maxwell, 1984).

Kaye, P., *Civil Jurisdiction and Enforcement of Foreign Judgments* (Abingdon: Professional Books, 1987).

(iii) *Company law*

Drury, R., and Zuereb, P., *Company Laws: a Comparative Approach* (Dartmouth, 1991).

Gleichman, K., *Perspectives on European Company Law* (European Edition, 1991).

Pennington, R., & Wooldridge, F., *Company Law in the European Communities*, 3rd ed. (London: Oyez Longman, 1982).

(iv) *Competition law*

Bael, I. van, & Bellis, J. F., *Competition Law of the EEC* (Bicester: CCH Editions, 1987).

Bellamy, C. W., & Child, G. D., *Common Market Law of Competition*, 3rd ed. (London: Sweet & Maxwell, 1987).

Green, N., *Commercial Agreements and Competition Law* (London: Graham & Trotman, 1986).

Goyder, D., *EEC Competition Law*, 2nd ed. (Oxford, Clarendon Press, 1992).

Kerse, C., *EEC Antitrust Procedure* (London: European Law Centre, 1991).

Korah, V., *Competition Law of Britain and the Common Market*, 3rd ed. (The Hague, London: Nijhoff, 1982).

Korah, V., *An Introductory Guide to EEC Competition Law and Practice*, 3rd ed. (Oxford: ESC Publishing, 1986).
Merkin, R. & Williams, K., *Anti Trust Policy in the UK and the EEC* (London: Sweet & Maxwell, 1988).
Whish, R., *Competition Law* 2nd ed. (London: Butterworths, 1989).

    (v) *Environment*
Haigh, N., *EEC Environmental Policy and Britain* (London: Longmans, 1987).
Johnson, S. & Corcelle, G., *Environmental Policy of the EEC* (London: Graham & Trotman, 1989).

    (vi) *Free movement of goods*
Gormley, L., *Prohibiting Restriction on Trade within the EEC* (1985).
Oliver, P., *Free Movement of Goods in the EEC*, 2nd ed. (London: European Law Centre, 1988).
Beseler, H. F., & Williams, A. N., *Anti-dumping and Anti-subsidy Law* (London: Sweet & Maxwell, 1986).

    (vii) *Intellectual property*
Guy, D., & Leigh, G. I. F., *The EEC and Intellectual Property* (London: Sweet & Maxwell, 1981).

    (viii) *Tax*
Easson, A. J., *Tax Law and Policy in the EEC* (London: Sweet & Maxwell, 1980.)

    (ix) *The social dimension*
Nielsen, R. & Szyszczak, E., *The Social Dimension of the European Community* (Handelshøjskolens Forlag, 1991).
Prechal, S. & Burrows, N., *Gender Discrimination Law of the European Society* (Dartmouth: Gower, 1990).
Verwilghen, M., *Equality in Law between Men and Women in the European Community* (Louvain-la-Neuve: Presses Universitaires de Louvain 1987).
Watson, P., *Social Security Law of the European Communities* (London: Mansell Information Publishing, 1980).

Articles, casenotes and reviews

Cahiers de Droit Européen.
Common Market Law Review.
European Business Law Review.
European Competition Law Review.
European Intellectual Property Review.
European Law Review.
International and Comparative Law Quarterly.
Journal of Common Market Studies.
Journal of World Trade Law.
Legal Issues of European Integration.
Yearbook of European Law.

Information

Information Office of the European Commission, Jean Monnet House, 8 Storey's Gate, London SW1P 3AT. Tel: 071-222-8122.
European Business Information (Small Firms' Service), 11, Belgrave Road, London SW1V 1RB. Tel: 071-828-6201.
European Documentation Centres (in most major cities).
European Information Centres (in most major regional centres).

INDEX